COP 1

FEB 2 '79   REF. SERV.

A11703 964259

D0045209

A Title Guide
to the Talkies,
1964 through 1974

by

ANDREW A. AROS

(As conceived by Richard B. Dimmitt)

The Scarecrow Press, Inc.

Metuchen, N.J.   1977

Library of Congress Cataloging in Publication Data

Aros, Andrew A   1944-
   A title guide to the talkies, 1964 through 1974.

   Includes index.
   1. Moving-pictures--Catalogs. I. Dimmitt,
Richard Bertrand. A title guide to the talkies.
II. Title.
PN1998.A6695   791.43 ~~01 6~~ 8   76-40451
ISBN 0-8108-0976-1

Copyright © 1977 by Andrew A. Aros

Manufactured in the United States of America

FOR MY MOTHER AND FATHER

INTRODUCTION

Since their initial appearances (in 1965 and in 1967), both A Title Guide to the Talkies and An Actor Guide to the Talkies have proven themselves to be valuable reference tools. Students, film historians, and the general public have frequently referred to these volumes when needing information.

The original reason for the existence of these volumes was to provide the librarian with a bibliographic reference to which he could direct a reader who had seen a particular film, and was now interested in reading the book. This volume continues to list a source to which readers can go to read a novel, play, or non-fiction work that served as the source material of a motion picture.

But like everything else, the format has needed change. Therefore, the information available in the present volume has been expanded. While American films are still the standard of the industry, this volume also lists the numerous foreign films that are exhibited in this country.

The Title Guide now lists the distribution company, the year of the film's general release, and the source material from which the film was created. The producer credit has been dropped, and a director entry has been substituted.

This has been done for several reasons, the prime one being that in the past decade, the director has often proved to be just as important a box office draw as the stars themselves. With the rise of the auteur theory, and the ever growing "cult" of the director, I felt that such a listing would be more helpful.

Another change, although minor by comparison, should be noted. In many of the individual entries, the text may say something like "an original novelization based on the screenplay." This is the result of the many movie tie-ins published yearly, mainly by paperback companies. While often not very effective as literature, the film company may feel that it could possibly be an inexpensive publicity gimmick as well as a profitable side enterprise to offer movie audiences a chance to "read the book." It should be

v

remarked that movie tie-in titles continue to grow in number.

In all of the individual entries showing a novel or story to be the source of a film, the title of the novel or story is understood to be the same as the film unless specified otherwise.

Film literature has increased at an astounding rate, but this has also been coupled with a decrease in quality. Nearly every publisher of note has a film book in his catalog of current offerings. Many are pictorial works, often accompanied by a mediocre text, while others are the film scripts of the individual motion picture. There are still not enough published film scripts to suit many film historians and motion-picture buffs, but hopefully we shall witness a rise in the number of in-print scripts by the next volume of this series.

ACKNOWLEDGMENTS

So many people have had a part in the writing and preparation of this and the planned companion volume, An Actor Guide to the Talkies (i. e. , a continuation volume covering 1965 through 1974), it would indeed be impossible to thank every one of them individually. Yet to avoid giving credit to those who made substantial contributions to this project would be an unforgivable oversight. Therefore, I would like to thank the following people:

Mr. Richard B. Dimmitt, the creator of the series, who so kindly permitted me the honor of continuing his work.

The outstanding faculty of the Library School at California State University at Fullerton, who prepared me for this project through the many excellent courses I took while a student there.

Mrs. Jeanne Higashi, Mrs. Sandra Duncan, Mrs. Beverly Harada, Mrs. Kathryn Swank Long, Mrs. Clairene Almond, Ms. Karen Earl, and Mr. Eugene Drayton, of the Rio Hondo Regional Library of the Los Angeles County Public Library System, are also thanked for the variety of encouragement and aid they contributed during the long period this work was in preparation. Special thanks to Mrs. Marge Rodarte and Mrs. Elizabeth Martinez Smith.

Mr. Michael J. Venegas, Jr. , president and founder of Zero to Success, Inc. , for his unflagging moral support.

Mr. John C. Pearson, media specialist for the Orange County (California) Public Library, who made numerous useful suggestions and was always available and willing to help.

One of the most cohesive and unifying forces in my life has been my family, who have always been supportive in all of my endeavors.

Finally, the people of the motion picture industry are gratefully recognized, since without them, this book would never have materialized.

Andrew A. Aros
Diamond Bar, California
January, 1976

ABBREVIATIONS USED IN THE BOOK

AMPAS   Who Wrote the Movie and What Else Did He Write? Academy of Motion Picture Arts and Sciences, and Writers Guild of America, West: 1970. 491p.

FF   Filmfacts; American Film Institute, Washington, D. C.

FM   Limbacher, James L., comp. Film Music: From Violins to Video. Metuchen, N. J. : Scarecrow Press, 1974. 835p.

HR   Hollywood Reporter (daily).

LACOPL   Los Angeles County Public Library Book Catalog.

LC   Catalog of Copyright Entries, Motion Pictures 1960-1969. Washington, D. C. : Library of Congress, Copyright Office, 1971. 744p.

MCC   McCarty, Clifford. Published Screenplays: A Checklist. Kent, Ohio: Kent State University Press, 1971. 127p.

MFB   Monthly Film Bulletin. British Film Institute, London.

NYT   The New York Times (daily).

NYTFR   The New York Times Film Review. New York: New York Times & Arno Press, 1970. 6 Vols.

Q   International Motion Picture Almanac (annual). New York: Quigley Publishing Co.

SCH   Schoolcraft, Ralph Newman. Performing Arts/Books in Print: An Annotated Bibliography. New York: Drama Book Specialists/Publishers, 1973. 761p.

V   Variety (New York and Hollywood editions).

W   Willis, John, ed. Screen World (annual). New York: Crown Publishers.

A TITLE GUIDE TO THE TALKIES, 1964-1974

1 THE ABDICATION. (Warner Bros. -1974-Anthony Harvey). Screenplay by Ruth Wolff, based on her play. A novelization based on her screenplay was published. The Abdication by Ruth Wolff, Warner Paperback Library, 1974; 190p. (V, LACOPL).

2 THE ABDUCTORS. (Joseph Brenner-1972-Don Schain). Original screenplay by Liz Evans. (W).

3 THE ABOMINABLE DR. PHIBES. (American International-1971-Robert Fuest). Original screenplay by James Whiton and William Goldstein. (W, Q).

4 ACCATTONE! (Brandon-1968-Pier Paolo Pasolini). Screenplay by Pier Paolo Pasolini, based on his novel Una Vita Violenta (A Violent Life). (FF, NYTFR, W).

5 ACCIDENT. (Cinema V and London Independent Producers-1967-Joseph Losey). Harold Pinter wrote the screenplay, based on the novel Accident by Nicholas Mosley, Coward-McCann, Inc., 1965. (FF, NYTFR, FM, W, LACOPL, Q).

6 ACE ELI AND RODGER OF THE SKIES. (20th Century-Fox-1973-Bill Sampson). Screenplay written by Chips Rosen, based on a story by Steven Spielberg. (W, Q).

7 ACE HIGH. (Paramount-1969-Giuseppe Colizzi). Original screenplay written by Giuseppe Colizzi served as the basis for this film. (FF, W, Q).

8 ACROSS 110TH STREET. (United Artists-1972-Barry Shear). Luther Davis wrote the screenplay, based on the novel by Wally Ferris, Across 110th, Harper & Row, 1970; 262p. (W, LACOPL, FF, Q).

9 ACT OF THE HEART. (Universal-1970). No screenplay credit. (W, Q).

10 ACT OF VENGEANCE. (American International-1974-Robert Kelljchian). Original motion picture screenplay by Betty Conklin and H. R. Christian. (V).

11 THE ACTIVIST. (Regional-1969-Art Napoleon). Art and Jo Napoleon wrote the original screenplay. (W, Q).

12 ADALEN 31. (Paramount-1969-Bo Widerberg). An original screenplay by Bo Widerberg. (W, Q, V).

13 ADAM AT 6 A. M. (National General-1970-Robert Scheerer). Stephen and Elinor Karpf wrote the screenplay. (W, Q).

14 ADAM'S WOMAN. (Warner Bros. -1972-Philip Leacock). The screenplay by Richard Fielder, was taken from a story by Lowell Barrington. (W).

15 THE ADDING MACHINE₀ (Regional-1969-Jerome Epstein). Jerome Epstein wrote the screenplay, based on the play by Elmer Rice which may be found in John Gassner's Best American Plays, Supplementary Volume, 1918-1958, Crown, 1961. (FF, W, LACOPL, Q).

16 ADELAIDE. (Sigma III-1969-Jean Daniel Simon). The screenplay by Jean-Pierre Petrolacci and Jean-Daniel Simon, was based on a short story by Arthur Gobineau. (FF, W, Q).

17 ADIEU PHILLIPPINE. (New Yorker-1973-Jacques Rozier). The original screenplay is written by Jacques Rozier and Michel O'Glor. (W).

18 ADIOS GRINGO. (Trans-Lux-1968-George Finley). Jose Luis Jerez, Michele Villerot, and Giorgio Stegani, based their screenplay on the novel Adios by Harry Whittington. (FF, W).

19 ADIOS SABATA. (United Artists-1971-Frank Kramer). Renato Izzo and Gianfranco Parolini were responsible for the original screenplay. (W).

20 THE ADOLESCENTS. (1967-Gian Vittorio Baldi, Michel Brault, Jean Rouch). An episodic film: "Fiametta" written by Gian Vittorio Baldi; "Genevieve" written by Alex Pelletier; and "Marie-France" written by Jean Rouch. (NYTFR).

20a ADORABLE JULIA. (See-Art-1964-Alfred Weidenmann). A screenplay by Guy Bolton, Marc-Gilbert Savajon and Pascal Jardin, based on the story "Theatre" by Somerset Maugham. (FF, Q, NYTFR).

21 ADRIFT. (MPO-1971-Jan Kadar). The screenplay by Imre Byongyossy and Jan Kadar and Elmar Klos, was based on the novel Something Is Adrift in the Water by Lajos Zilahy. (W, Q).

21a ADVANCE TO THE REAR. (MGM-1964-George Marshall)₀ A screenplay by Samuel A. Peeples and William Bowers, from a story by Jack Schaefer, suggested by "The Company of Cowards" by William Chamberlain. (FF, Q, NYTFR, W).

22 THE ADVENTURERS. (Paramount-1970-Lewis Gilbert). Michael

Hastings and Lewis Gilbert wrote the screenplay, based on the Harold Robbins best-selling novel. Trident Press, 1966; 781p. (LACOPL, W, Q, V).

23 THE ADVENTURES OF BULLWHIP GRIFFIN. (Buena Vista-1967-James Neilson). Screenplay by Lowell S. Hawley, based on the novel By the Great Horn Spoon by Albert Sidney Fleischman; Little, Brown & Co., 1963, 204p. (FF, NYTFR, FM, W, LACOPL, Q).

23a ADVENTURES OF SCARAMOUCHE. (Embassy-1964-Antonio Isasi-Isamendi). Jorge Illa, Luis Cameron, Arturo Rigel and Antonio Isasi-Isasmendi wrote this screenplay, from a screen story by Guido Malatesta, based on the novel by Rafael Sabatini, Scaramouche, Houghton, 1931. (FF, LACOPL, NYTFR, W).

24 THE ADVERSARY. (Belle-Kay-1970-Larry Klein). Original screenplay written by Larry Klein. (W).

25 THE ADVERSARY. (Audio Brandon-1973-Satyajit Ray). The screenplay by Satyajit Ray, was taken from a story by Sunil Ganguly. (W).

THE AFFAIR see THERE'S ALWAYS VANILLA

26 AN AFFAIR OF THE HEART. (1967-Dusan Makavelev). Dusan Makavelev wrote the original screenplay. (NYTFR).

27 AFRICA--TEXAS STYLE! (Paramount-1967-Andrew Marton). The screenplay is credited to Andy White. (FF, NYTFR, FM, W, Q).

28 AFRICAN SAFARI. (Crown International-1969-Ron Shanin). Ron Shanin is responsible for the original screenplay. (W, Q).

29 AFTER THE FOX. (United Artists-1966-Vittorio De Sica). Neil Simon and Cesare Zavattini wrote this original screenplay. (FF, NYTFR, W).

30 AFTER YOU, COMRADE. (Continental-1967-Jamie Uys). An original screenplay by Jamie Uys. (NYTFR, W, Q).

31 AGE OF CONSENT. (Columbia-1970-Michael Powell). The screenplay by Peter Yeldham was taken from a novel by Norman Lindsay. (W, Q).

32 AGENT 008 3/4. (Continental-1965-Ralph Thomas). Lukas Heller wrote the original screenplay. (NYTFR, W, Q).

33 AGENT FOR H. A. R. M. (Universal-1966-Gerd Oswald). The screenplay is attributed to Blair Robertson. (FF, W, Q).

34 THE AGONY AND THE ECSTASY. (20th Century-Fox-1965-

Carol Reed). Screen story and screen play written by Philip
Dunne, based on the novel by Irving Stone; Doubleday, 1961.
(W, LC, Q).

35   THE AGONY OF LOVE. (Boxoffice International-1966-William
Rotsler). An original screenplay written by William Rotsler.
(FF).

36   AIRPORT. (Universal-1970-George Seaton). Screenplay by
George Seaton, from the novel Airport by Arthur Hailey; Doubleday, 1968. (W, Q).

37   AIRPORT 1975. (Universal-1974-Jack Smight). Screenplay written by Don Ingalls, inspired by the film Airport and based on
the novel by Arthur Hailey, Doubleday, 1968. (HR, V).

38   ALABAMA'S GHOST. (Ellman Enterprises-1973-Fredric Hobbs).
Fredric Hobbs wrote the original screenplay. (W).

39   ALEX IN WONDERLAND. (MGM-1970-Paul Mazursky). Larry
Tucker and Paul Mazursky were the authors of this original
screenplay. (W, Q).

40   ALEXANDER. (Cinema V-1969-Yves Robert). The screenplay
was written by Yves Robert and Pierre Levy-Corti, based on the
original short story by Yves Robert. (FF, W, Q).

41   ALF 'N' FAMILY. (Sherpix-1972-Norman Cohen). Johnny
Speight authored this screenplay which was based on his original
story and television series. (FF, Q).

42   ALFIE. (Paramount-1966-Lewis Gilbert). The screenplay was
written by Bill Naughton, and was based on his novel, Alfie,
published by Ballantine Books, 1966. (FF, NYTFR, W, Q).

43   ALFRED THE GREAT. (MGM-1969-Clive Donner). Screenplay
by Ken Taylor & James R. Webb, based on a story by James
R. Webb and the book Alfred the Great by Eleanor Shipley Duck-
ett, Macmillan, 1951; 337p. (W, Q, LACOPL).

44   ALFREDO, ALFREDO. (Paramount-1973-Pietro Germi). An
original story and screenplay by Leo Benvenuti, Piero de Bernardi, Tullio Pinelli, Pietro Germi, served as the basis for this
film. (W).

45   ALI. (New Yorker-1974-Rainer Werner Fassbinder). Rainer
Werner Fassbinder wrote the original screenplay. (HR).

46   ALICE DOESN'T LIVE HERE ANYMORE. (Warner Bros-1974-
Martin Scorsese). Robert Getchell authored the screenplay. An
original paperback novel based on the film of the same title was
written by Robert Getchell and published by Warner Paperback
Library, 1975; 142p. (V, LACOPL).

47   ALICE IN THE CITIES.   (1974-Wim Wenders).   Original screen-
      play by Wim Wenders & Veith von Furstenberg.   (V).

48   ALICE'S ADVENTURES IN WONDERLAND.   (American National-
      1972-William Sterling).   The screenplay by William Sterling was
      based on the novel by Lewis Carroll; Norton, 1971 434p.   (W,
      Q).

49   ALICE'S RESTAURANT.   (United Artists-1969-Arthur Penn).
      Venable Herndon and Arthur Penn wrote the screenplay, based
      on the song "The Alice's Restaurant Massacree" by Arlo Guth-
      rie.   The screenplay of Alice's Restaurant by Venable Herndon
      and Arthur Penn was published by Doubleday, 1970; 141p.   (FF,
      W, Q, SCH, LACOPL).

50   THE ALL-AMERICAN BOY.   (Warner Bros.-1973-Charles East-
      man).   The original screenplay written by Charles Eastman was
      published by Farrar, Straus and Giroux; 1973, 184p.   (W,
      LACOPL).

51   ALL MEN ARE APES.   (Adelphia-1965-J. P. Mawra).   Charles
      E. Mazin and Barnard L. Sackett wrote the original screenplay.

52   ALL NEAT IN BLACK STOCKINGS.   (National General-1969-
      Christopher Morahan).   This film was based on a screenplay by
      Jane Gaskell and Hugh Whitemore, based on the novel by Jane
      Gaskell.   (FF, W, Q).

53   ALL THE LOVING COUPLES.   (U-M-1969-Mack Bing).   Leo V.
      Golden authored the original screenplay.   (W, Q).

54   ALL THE OTHER GIRLS DO!   (Harlequin International-1967-
      Silvio Amadio).   An original screenplay by Silvio Amadio and
      Carlo Romano.   (NYTFR).

55   ALL THE RIGHT NOISES.   (20th Century-Fox-1973-Gerry O'-
      Hara).   Screenplay by Gerry O'Hara, based on his novel of the
      same name.   (W, FF).

56   ALL THE WAY BOYS.   (AVCO Embassy-1973-Giuseppe Colizzi).
      An original screenplay by Giuseppe Colizzi.   (W).

56a   ALL THESE WOMEN.   (Janus-1964-Ingmar Bergman).   Film
      was based on an original screenplay by Erland Josephson and
      Ingmar Bergman.   (Q, FF, NYTFR, W).

57   THE ALPHABET MURDERS.   (MGM-1966-Frank Tashlin).   The
      screenplay by David Pursall and Jack Seddon, was based on the
      novel The ABC Murders by Agatha Christie; Dodd, 1936.   (FF,
      NYTFR, W, Q, LACOPL).

58   ALPHAVILLE.   (Pathe Contemporary-1965-Jean-Luc Godard).
      The screenplay by Jean-Luc Godard was published by Simon &

Schuster; 1966, 100p. (NYTFR, LACOPL, W, Q, V).

59   ALVAREZ KELLY. (Columbia-1966-Edward Dmytryk). Franklin Coen and Elliott Arnold wrote the screenplay based on a
story by Franklin Coen. (FF, NYTFR, W, Q).

60   ALVIN PURPLE. (Bi-Jay-1974-Tim Burstall). An original
screenplay by Alan Hopgood. (HR).

61   AMARCORD. (New World-1974-Federico Fellini). Screenplay
by Federico Fellini and Tonino Guerra. A book, Amarcord:
Portrait of a Town, based on the film, was written by Federico
Fellini with Tonino Guerra; Berkley Publishing Co., 1973, 142p.
(V, NYT, LACOPL).

62   AMAZING GRACE. (United Artists-1974-Stan Lathan). An original screenplay by Matt Robinson. (V).

63   AMBUSH BAY. (United Artists-1966-Ron Winston). Marve Fein-
berg and Ib Melchior wrote the screenplay. (FF, NYTFR, W,
Q).

64   THE AMBUSHERS. (Columbia-1967-Henry Levin). Screenplay
by Herbert Baker is based on the novel by Donald Hamilton.
(FF, NYTFR, FM, W, Q).

64a AN AMERICAN DREAM. (Warner Bros.-1966-Robert Gist).
Mann Rubin's screenplay was based on the novel by Norman
Mailer, An American Dream; Dial Press, 1965. (FF, NYTFR,
LACOPL, W).

65   THE AMERICAN DREAMER. (EYR-1971-Lawrence Schiller).
A documentary film authored by Dennis Hopper, L. M. Kit Carson, and Lawrence Schiller. (W).

66   AMERICAN GRAFFITI. (Universal-1973-George Lucas). The
original screenplay by George Lucas, Gloria Katz, and Willard
Huyck was published by Ballantine Books, 1973; 189p. (W, V,
LACOPL).

67   THE AMERICANIZATION OF EMILY. (MGM-1964-Arthur Hiller).
Paddy Cheyevsky wrote the screenplay based on the novel by
William Bradford Huie; Dutton, 1959. (FF, W, LACOPL, Q,
NYTFR).

68   THE AMOROUS ADVENTURES OF MOLL FLANDERS. (Para-
mount-1965-Terrence Young). Dennis Cannan and Roland Kibbee's screenplay was based on the novel by Daniel Defoe, Moll
Flanders, Norton; 1973, 444p. (NYTFR, LACOPL, W).

69   THE AMOROUS MR. PRAWN. (Medallion-1965-Anthony Kimmins). Original screenplay by Anthony Kimmins and Nicholas
Phipps. (W).

70 L'AMOUR. (Altura-1973-Andy Warhol & Paul Morrissey). An original screenplay by Andy Warhol & Paul Morrissey. (W).

71 L'AMOUR FOU. (New Yorker-1972-Jacques Rivette). An original screenplay by Jacques Rivette and Marilu Parolini served as the basis for this motion picture. (FF).

72 AND HOPE TO DIE. (20th Century-Fox-1972-Rene Clement). This film was based on an original screenplay by Sebastien Japrisot. (W, FF, Q).

73 AND NOW FOR SOMETHING COMPLETELY DIFFERENT. (Columbia-1972-Ian MacNaughton). A screenplay by Graham Chapman, John Cleese, Terry Jones, Eric Idle, Terry Gilliam, and Michael Palin served as the basis for this film as well as the BBC television series, "Monty Python's Flying Circus." (FF, Q).

74 AND NOW MIGUEL. (Universal-1966-James B. Clark). Ted Sherdeman and Jane Klove wrote the screenplay which was based on the novel by Joseph Krumgold; Crowell, 1953, 245p. (FF, NYTFR, W, LACOPL, Q, AMPAS).

75 AND NOW THE SCREAMING STARTS. (Cinerama-1973-Roy Ward Baker). The original screenplay was authored by Roger Marshall. (W, Q).

76 AND SO TO BED. (Medallion-1965-Alfred Weidermann). No screenplay credits available. (W, Q).

77 AND SOON THE DARKNESS. (Levitt-Pickman-1971-Robert Fuest). Original story and screenplay by Brian Clemens and Terry Nation. (W, Q).

77a ...AND SUDDENLY IT'S MURDER! (Royal-1964-Mario Camerini). Rodolfo Sonego, Giorgio Arlorio, Stefano Strucchi, Luciano Vincenzoni, and Oreste Biancoli are credited with this original screenplay. (NYTFR, FF, Q).

78 AND THERE CAME A MAN. (Brandon-1968-Ermanno Olmi). An original screenplay by Ermanno Olmi and Vincenzo Labella, which was based on the life of Pope John XXIII. (FF, W, NYTFR, Q).

79 THE ANDERSON TAPES. (Columbia-1971-Sidney Lumet). Frank R. Pierson wrote the screenplay which he based on the novel of the same name by Lawrence Sanders; Putnam, 1970, 254p. (W, LACOPL, Q).

80 ANDREI RUBLEV. (Columbia-1973-Andree Tarkovsky). Original screenplay credited to Andrei Mikhalkov-Kontchalovsky, and Andrei Tarkovsky. (W).

81 THE ANDROMEDA STRAIN. (Universal-1971-Robert Wise).
Screenplay by Nelson Gidding, from the novel by Michael Crichton; Knopf, 1969, 295p. (W, LACOPL, Q).

82 ANDY. (Universal-1965-Richard C. Sarafian). Story and
screenplay written by Richard C. Sarafian. (FF, W, AMPAS).

ANGEL, ANGEL, DOWN WE GO see CULT OF THE DAMNED

83 ANGEL IN MY POCKET. (Universal-1969-Alan Rafkin). Screen
story and screenplay by Jim Fritzell and Everett Greenbaum.
(AMPAS, FF, W, Q).

84 THE ANGEL LEVINE. (United Artists-1970-Jan Kadar). Screenplay by Bill Gunn and Ronald Ribman, based on a story by Bernard Malamud. (W, Q).

85 ANGEL UNCHAINED. (American International-1970-Lee Madden). A story by Lee Madden and Jeffrey Alladin Fiskin served
as the basis for the screenplay by Jeffrey Alladin Fiskin. (W).

86 ANGELS DIE HARD. (New World-1970-Richard Compton).
Richard Compton authored the screenplay. (W).

87 ANGELS FROM HELL. (American International-1968-Bruce
Kessler). An original screenplay by Jerome Wish. (FF, FM,
NYTFR, W, Q).

88 ANGELS HARD AS THEY COME. (New World-1971-Joe Viola).
Jonathan Demme and Jo Viola wrote the original screenplay.
(FF, W).

89 THE ANGRY BREED. (Commonwealth United-1969-David Commons). This screenplay written by David Commons was based
on a story by Rex Carlton. (FF).

90 THE ANIMALS. (Levitt-Pickman-1971-Ron Joy). An original
screenplay by Hy Mizrahi. (W, FF).

91 ANN AND EVE. (Chevron-1970-Arne Mattsson). Ernest Hotch
is credited with this original screenplay. (W, Q).

92 ANNE OF THE THOUSAND DAYS. (Universal-1969-Charles
Jarrott). Bridget Boland and John Hale based their screenplay
on the stage play by Maxwell Anderson of the same name;
Sloane, 1948, 123p. (W, LACOPL, Q, AMPAS).

93 THE ANNIVERSARY. (20th Century-Fox-1968-Roy Ward Baker).
A screenplay by Jimmy Sangster based on the play by Bill Mac-
Ilwraith. (FF, NYTFR, FM, W, Q, AMPAS).

94 THE ANONYMOUS VENETIAN. (Allied Artists-1971-Enrico
Maria Salerno). An original screenplay by Enrico Maria

Salerno and Giuseppe Berto served as the basis for the film.
(W).

95   ANTONIO DAS MORTES. (Grove-1970-Glauber Rocha).   Origi-
     nal screenplay written by Glauber Rocha.   (W).

96   ANTONY AND CLEOPATRA.   (Rank-1973-Charlton Heston).
     This screenplay was written by Charlton Heston, which he
     adapted from the play by William Shakespeare; Bantam Books,
     1966, 274p.   (W, LACOPL, V).

97   ANY GUN CAN PLAY.   (Golden Eagle-1968-Enzo G. Castel-
     lari).   An original screenplay by Romolo Guerrieri, George
     Simonelli, Enzo G. Castellari, Fabio Carpi, and Scavolini.
     (FF, Q, NYTFR).

98   ANY WEDNESDAY.   (Warner Bros.-1966-Robert Ellis Miller).
     Julius J. Epstein wrote the screenplay based on the play by
     Muriel Resnik; Stein and Day, 1964, 124p.   (FF, NYTFR, W,
     Q, LACOPL, AMPAS).

99   ANYONE CAN PLAY.   (Paramount-1968-Luigi Zampa).   Ettore
     Scola and Ruggero Maccari authored this original screenplay.
     (FF, Q).

100 ANZIO.   (Columbia-1968-Edward Dmytryk).   Screenplay by
     Harry A. L. Craig, based on the book Anzio by Wynford
     Vaughan-Thomas; Holt, 1961, 243p.   (FF, NYTFR, W,
     LACOPL, Q, AMPAS).

100a APACHE RIFLES.   (20th Century-Fox-1964-William H. Witney).
     An original screenplay by Charles B. Smith.   (Q, FF, W).

101 APACHE UPRISING.   (Paramount-1966-R. G. Springsteen).
     Harry Sanford and Max Lamb wrote this original screenplay
     based on the novel Way Station by Harry Sanford and Max
     Steeber.   (FF, W, Q, AMPAS).

102 APARTMENT ON THE 13TH FLOOR.   (Hallmark-1973-Eloy
     De La Iglesia).   No screenplay credit available.   (W).

102a THE APE WOMAN.   (Embassy-1964-Marco Ferreri).   An origi-
     nal screenplay written by Marco Ferreri and Rafael Azcona.
     (FF, NYTFR, Q).

103 THE APPALOOSA.   (Universal-2966-Sidney J. Furie).   James
     Bridges and Roland Kibee based their screenplay on the novel
     by Robert MacLeod.   (AMPAS, FF, NYTFR, Q, W).

104 APPASSIONATA.   (PAC-1974-Gian Luigi Calderone).   Screen-
     play by Gian Luigi Calderone, Alessandro Parenzo, and Com-
     enico Rafele.   (V).

105 THE APPRENTICESHIP OF DUDDY KRAVITZ. (Paramount-1974-Ted Kotcheff). Screenplay written by Mordecai Richler, based on his novel; adapted by Lionel Chetwynd. Little, Brown & Co., 1959. (V, HR, LACOPL).

106 The APRIL FOOLS. (National General-1969-Stuart Rosenberg). Screenplay and original story by Hal Dresner. (AMPAS, FF, Q, W).

107 ARABELLA. (Universal-1969-Mauro Bolognini). An original screenplay by Adriano Barocco. (W, Q).

108 ARABESQUE. (Universal-1966-Stanley Donen). Screenplay by Julian Mitchell, Stanley Price and Pierre Marton, based on the novel The Cipher by Gordon Cotler. (AMPAS, FF, NYTFR, Q, W).

109 THE ARCH. (Cinema V-1972-Shu Shuen). An original screenplay written by Shu Shuen. (FF).

110 ARIZONA BUSHWHACKERS. (Paramount-1968-Lesley Selander). The screenplay by Steve Fisher was based on a story by Steve Fisher and Andrew Craddock. (AMPAS, FF, Q, W).

111 ARIZONA RAIDERS. (Columbia-1966-William Witney). Screenplay by Alex Gottlieb and Mary and Willard Willingham, based on a story by Frank Gruber and Richard Schayer, and the 1951 Columbia release,"The Texas Rangers. " (AMPAS LC, Q, W).

112 ARNOLD. (Cinerama-1973-Georg Fenady). An original screenplay by Jameson Brewer and John Fenton Murray. (W).

113 ARNOLD'S WRECKING CO. (Cine Globe-1973-Steve De Souza). Steve De Souza wrote the original screenplay. (W).

114 AROUND THE WORLD UNDER THE SEA. (MGM-1966-Andrew Marton). A screenplay by Arthur Weiss and Art Arthur, from a story by Elmer Parsons. (FF NYTFR, W, Q, AMPAS).

115 AROUSED. (Cambist-1968-Anton Holden). Credit for this original screenplay goes to Anton Holden and Ray Jacobs. (FF, W).

116 THE AROUSERS. (New World-1972-Curtis Hanson). An original screenplay attributed to Curtis Hanson. (FF, W).

117 THE ARRANGEMENT. (Warner Bros.-7 Arts-1969-Elia Kazan). The screenplay by Elia Kazan was based on his novel; Stein & Day, 1967, 544p. (W, LACOPL, Q, AMPAS).

118 ARRIVEDERCI, BABY! (Paramount-1966-Ken Hughes). Screenplay by Ken Hughes and Ronald Harwood, suggested by the

story "The Careful Man" by Richard Deming. (AMPAS, FF, NYTFR, Q, W).

119   ARRUZA. (AVCO Embassy-1972-Budd Boetticher). Screenplay by Budd Boetticher. (FF).

120   THE ART OF LOVE. (Universal-1965-Norman Jewison). Screenplay by Carl Reiner, from a story by Richard Alan Simmons and William Sackheim. (AMPAS, NYTFR, Q, W).

121   ASH WEDNESDAY. (Paramount-1973-Larry Peerce). Original screenplay by Jean-Claude Tramont. (W).

122   THE ASPHYX. (Paragon-1973-Peter Newbrook). An original screeplay by Brian Comfort. (W, FF).

123   THE ASSASSIN. (Toho-1973-Masahiro Shinoda). No screenplay credit available. (W).

124   THE ASSASSINATION BUREAU. (Paramount-1969-Basil Dearden). Michael Relph's screenplay was based on an idea in The Assassination Bureau Ltd., a novel by Jack London and Robert Fish; McGraw-Hill, 1963. (FF, W, LACOPL, Q, AMPAS).

125   THE ASSASSINATION OF TROTSKY. (Cinerama-1972-Joseph Losey). An original screenplay by Nicholas Mosley and Masolino D'Amico. (W, FF, Q).

126   ASSAULT ON A QUEEN. (Paramount-1966-Jack Donohue). Rod Serling wrote the screenplay based on the novel by Jack Finney; Simon & Schuster, 1959, 244p. (FF, NYTFR, W, Q, LACOPL, AMPAS).

127   ASSIGNMENT K. (Columbia-1968-Val Guest). A screenplay by Val Guest, Bill Strutton, and Maurice Foster which was based on the novel Department K by Hartley Howard. (FF, NYTFR, FM, W, Q, AMPAS).

128   ASSIGNMENT TO KILL. (Warner Bros.-7 Arts-1969-Sheldon Reynolds). An original screenplay by Sheldon Reynolds. (FF, W, Q, AMPAS).

129   THE ASTRO-ZOMBIES. (Gemini-1969-Ted V. Mikels). An original screenplay by Ted V. Mikels and Wayne M. Rogers. (FF, W).

130   ASYLUM. (Cinerama-1972-Roy Ward Baker). An original screenplay written by Robert Bloch. (W, FF, Q).

131   ATRAGON. (American International-1965-Inoshiro Honda). This motion picture was based on a screenplay by Shinichi Sekizawa. (FF, W).

132   ATTACK ON THE IRON COAST. (United Artists-1968-Paul
      Wendkos). An original screenplay by Herman Hoffman, based
      on a story by John C. Champion. (FF, FM, NYTFR, W,
      AMPAS).

133   AU HASARD, BALTHAZAR. (Cinema Ventures-1970-Robert
      Bresson). The screenplay was written directly for the screen
      by Robert Bresson. (W).

134   AU PAIR GIRLS. (Cannon-1973-Val Guest). Val Guest and
      David Adnopoz authored this original screenplay. (W).

135   AN AUTUMN AFTERNOON. (New Yorker-1973-Yasujiro Ozu).
      Kogo Noda and Yasujiro Ozu wrote this original screenplay.
      (W).

136   AVANTI! (United Artists-1972-Billy Wilder). This screenplay
      was written by Billy Wilder and I. A. L. Diamond, based on
      a play by Samuel Taylor. (W, FF, Q).

137   THE AVENGER. (Medallion-1965-Albert Band). No screen-
      play credits available. (W, Q).

137a THE AWFUL DR. ORLOF. (Sigma III-1964-Jesus Franco).
      Jesus Franco wrote the screenplay based on a novel by David
      Kuhne. (FF, NYTFR).

138   AWOL. (BFB-1973-Herb Freed). This original work for the
      screen was authored by Richard Z. Chesnoff and Herb Freed.
      (W).

139   B. J. PRESENTS. (Maron-1971-Yabo Yablonsky). Yabo Ya-
      blonsky wrote the screenplay from a story by John Durin.
      (W).

140   B. S. I LOVE YOU. (20th Century-Fox-1971-Steven Hillard
      Stern). An original work for the screen by Steven Hillard
      Stern. (W, Q).

141   THE BABY. (Scotia International-1973-Ted Post). This origi-
      nal screenplay is attributed to Abe Polsky. (W).

142   BABY LOVE. (AVCO Embassy-1969-Alastair Reid). Alastair
      Reid, Guido Coen and Michael Klinger wrote the screenplay
      which was based on the novel by Tina Chad Christian. (FF,
      W, Q).

143   THE BABY MAKER. (National General-1970-James Bridges).
      The author of this original screenplay is James Bridges. (W,
      Q).

144 BABY THE RAIN MUST FALL. (Columbia-1965-Robert Mulligan). Horton Foote wrote the screenplay, based on his play,
The Traveling Lady. (FF, LC, W, Q, AMPAS).

145 THE BABYSITTER. (Crown International-1969-Don Henderson).
An original screenplay by James E. McLarty, based on a story
by George E. Carey and Don Henderson. (W, Q).

146 BACCHANALE. (Amaro-1970-John and Lem Amaro). Written
for the screen by John and Lem Amaro. (W).

147 BACK DOOR TO HELL. (20th Century-Fox-1965-Monte Hellman). Richard A. Guttman and John Hackett wrote the screenplay which was based on a story by Richard A. Guttman. (W,
LC, AMPAS; Q & FF give 1964 as date).

148 THE BACK ROW. (Cedarlane-1973-Doug Richards). No
screenplay credit could be ascertained. (W).

149 BACKFIRE. (Royal Films-1965-Jean Becker). The screenplay
by Didier Goulard, Maurice Fabre, Daniel Boulanger, and Jean
Becker, was based on a novel by Clet Coroner. (FF, W,
Q).

150 BACKTRACK. (Universal-1969-Earl Bellamy). Borden Chase
wrote this original screenplay. (FF, W).

151 BAD CHARLESTON CHARLIE. (International Cinema-1973-
Ivan Nagy). This screenplay was authored directly for the
screen by Ross Hagen, Ivan Nagy, and Stan Kamber.
(W).

152 BAD COMPANY. (New Yorker-1969-Jean Eustache). An original screenplay by Jean Eustache. (FF, W, Q).

153 BAD GIRLS DON'T CRY. (Medallion-1965-Mauro Bolognini).
This original story and screenplay was conceived by Pier Paolo
Pasolini. (W).

154 BADGE 373. (Paramount-1973-Howard W. Koch). Pete Ham-
ill wrote the original screenplay for this film. (W).

155 THE BALLAD OF CABLE HOGUE. (Warner Bros.-1970-Sam
Peckinpah). John Crawford and Edmund Penney wrote this
original screenplay from their own screen story. (W, AMPAS,
Q).

156 THE BALLAD OF JOSIE. (Universal-1968-Andrew V. McLaglen). The film was taken from an original screenplay by

Harold Swanton. (FF, FM, NYTFR, W, AMPAS, Q).

157 A BALLAD OF LOVE. (Artkino-1966-Mikhail Bogin). An original screenplay by Mikhail Bogin and Yuri Chulyukin. (FF, NYTFR, W, Q).

158 BAMBOLE! (Royal-1965-Dino Risi, Luigi Comencini, Franco Rossi and Mauro Bolognini). An episodic film with screen credits to Gianni Polidori ("The Telephone Call"), Rodolfo Sonego and Luigi Magni ("The Soup"), and Leo Benvenuti and Piero de Bernardi ("Monsignor Cupid"). These were freely adapted from the Decameron of Boccaccio; Stravon, 1946. (NYTFR, W, LACOPL, Q).

159 BAMBOO GODS AND IRON MEN. (American International-1974-Cesar Gallardo). An original screenplay by Kenneth Metcalfe and Joseph Zucherro. (HR).

160 BAMBOO SAUCER. (World Entertainment-1968-Frank Telford). The screenplay by Frank Telford, was based on an original story by Rip Von Ronkel and John Fulton. (FF, W, LC).

161 BAMSE. (Chevron-1970-Arne Matsson). An original screenplay by Arne Matsson and Elsa Prawitz. (W).

162 BANANA PEEL. (Pathe Contemporary Films-1965-Marcel Ophuls). An original screenplay written by Marcel Ophuls and Claude Sautet. (FF, W, Q).

163 BANANAS. (United Artists-1971-Woody Allen). An original screenplay attributed to Woody Allen. (W, Q).

164 BAND OF ASSASSINS. (Toho-1971-Tadashi Sawashima). An original screenplay by Kenro Matsura. (W).

165 BAND OF OUTSIDERS. (Royal-1966-Jean-Luc Godard). A screenplay by Jean-Luc Godard, based on the novel Fool's Gold by Dolores and B. Hitchens, 1958. (FF, NYTFR, W, LACOPL, Q).

165a BANDITS ON THE WIND. (Toho-1964-Hiroshi Inagaki). This original screenplay was written by Masato Ide. (FF, NYTFR).

166 BANDOLERO! (20th Century-Fox-1968-Andrew V. McLaglen). A screenplay by James Lee Barrett, based on an unpublished story, "Mace," by Stanley L. Hough. (FF, NYTFR, FM, W, LC, AMPAS, Q).

167 THE BANG BANG GANG. (Eden-1970-Van Guylder). An original screenplay by Van Guylder. (W).

168 THE BANG BANG KID. (Ajay-1968-Stanley Praeger). Howard Berk is the author of this original screenplay. (FF).

169   BANG! BANG! YOU'RE DEAD! (American International-
      1967-Don Sharp). This film was based on a screenplay by
      Peter Yeldham and a story by Peter Welbeck. (FF, NYTFR,
      AMPAS, W, Q).

170   BANG THE DRUM SLOWLY. (Paramount-1973-John Hancock).
      Mark Harris wrote the screenplay based on his novel published
      in 1956. (W, LACOPL).

171   BANK SHOT. (United Artists-1974-Gower Champion). A film
      based on a screenplay by Wendell Mayes, taken from the novel
      by Donald E. Westlake; Simon & Schuster, 1972, 224p. (V,
      HR LACOPL).

172   BANNING. (Universal-1967-Ron Winston). James Lee wrote
      the screenplay which he based on a story by Hamilton Maule.
      (FF, W, AMPAS, Q).

173   BARBARA. (Olympia-1970-Walter Burns). The screenplay by
      Josef Bush was based on a novel by Frank Newman. (W).

174   BARBARELLA. (Paramount-1968-Roger Vadim). Terry South-
      ern authored the screenplay in collaboration with Roger Vadim,
      Brian Degas, Claude Brule, Jean-Claude Forest, Tudor Gates,
      Clement Biddle Wood, and Vittorio Bonicelli, which was based
      on the book by Jean-Claude Forest. (FF, NYTFR, FM, W,
      LC, AMPAS, Q).

175   THE BAREFOOT EXECUTIVE. (Buena Vista-1971-Robert But-
      ler). The screenplay by Joseph L. McEveety was based on a
      story by Lila Garrett, Bernie Kahn, Stewart C. Billet. (W,
      Q).

176   BAREFOOT IN THE PARK. (Paramount-1967-Gene Saks).
      Neil Simon's screenplay was based on his play of the same
      name, published by Random House, 1964, 143p. (FF, NYTFR,
      FM, W, LC, AMPAS, Q).

177   BARON BLOOD. (American International-1972-Mario Bava).
      An original screenplay by Vincent Fotre, adapted by William A.
      Bairn. (W, Q).

178   BARQUERO. (United Artists-1970-Gordon Douglas). George
      Schenck and William Marks are credited with this original mo-
      tion picture screenplay. (W, Q).

179   BARREN LIVES. (Pathe Contemporary-1969-Nelson Pereira
      Dos Santos). The screenplay by Nelson Pereira Dos Santos was
      based on the novel by Graciliano Ramos; University of Texas
      Press, 1965. (FF, W, LACOPL).

180   BARRIER. (1967-Jerzy Skolimowski). An original screenplay
      by Jerzy Skolimowski served as the inspiration for the film.
      (NYTFR).

181   BARTLEBY. (Maron-1972-Anthony Friedmann). Anthony
      Friedmann and Rodney Carr-Smith based their screenplay on
      the short story "Bartleby, the Scrivener" by Herman Melville,
      which may be found in Selected Writings of Herman Melville:
      Complete Short Stories, "Typee" and "Billy Budd, Foretop-
      man, " Modern Library, 1952.   (W, LACOPL, Q).

182   BATMAN. (20th Century-Fox-1966-Leslie H. Martinson). The
      screenplay by Lorenzo Semple, Jr. , was based on the charac-
      ters created by Bob Kane in a comic strip as well as a tele-
      vision series. (FF, NYTFR, LC, AMPAS, W, Q).

183   BATTLE BENEATH THE EARTH. (MGM-1968-Montgomery
      Tully). L. Z. Hargreaves wrote the original story and screen-
      play (FF, W, LC AMPAS, Q).

      THE BATTLE FOR ANZIO see ANZIO

184   BATTLE FOR THE PLANET OF THE APES. (20th Century-
      Fox-1973-J. Lee Thompson). Credited with the screenplay are
      John William Corrington and Joyce Hooper Corrington, from a
      story by Paul Dehn, and based on characters created by Pierre
      Boulle. A novelization based on the screenplay was written by
      David Gerrold and published by Award Books; 1973, 158p. (W,
      LACOPL, Q).

185   THE BATTLE OF ALGIERS. (Allied Artists-1967-Gillo Ponte-
      corvo). Franco Solinas wrote the screenplay based on a story
      by Gillo Pontecorvo and Franco Solinas. (FF, NYTFR, W,
      AMPAS, Q).

186   THE BATTLE OF BRITAIN. (United Artists-1969-Guy Hamil-
      ton). The film was based on a screenplay by James Kennaway
      and Wilfred Greatorex. Excerpts from the screenplay are con-
      tained in Leonard Oswald Mosley's, The Battle of Britain:
      The Making of a Film; Ballantine Books, 1969, 249p. (W, LC,
      AMPAS, LACOPL, Q).

187   THE BATTLE OF LOVE'S RETURN. (Standard-1971-Lloyd
      Kaufman). An original screenplay by Lloyd Kaufman. (W).

188   BATTLE OF NERETVA. (American International-1972-Veljko
      Bulajic). Ratko Djurovic, Steve Bulajic, Veljko Bulajic, Ugo
      Pirro and Alfred Weidenmann authored this original screen-
      play. (FF, W, AMPAS, Q).

189   BATTLE OF THE AMAZONS. (American International-1973-
      Al Bradley). Mario Amendola, Bruno Corbucci, and Fernando
      Izcaino Casas wrote this original screenplay. (W).

190   BATTLE OF THE BULGE. (Warner Bros. -1965-Ken Annakin).
      Credited with the original screenplay are Philip Yordan, Mil-
      ton Sperling and John Melson. NYTFR, LC AMPAS, W, Q).

191   THE BATTLE OF THE VILLA FIORITA. (Warner Bros. -1965-
      Delmer Daves). Delmer Daves based his screenplay on the
      novel by Rumer Godden; Viking, 1963, 312p. (NYTFR, LC,
      AMPAS, W, LACOPL, Q).

192   BAXTER. (National General-1973-Lionel Jeffries). An origi-
      nal screenplay by Reginald Rose. (W, Q).

192a BAY OF THE ANGELS. (Pathe Contemporary-1964-Jacques
      Demy). Jacques Demy was the author of this original screen-
      play (FF, NYTFR, W, Q).

193   BEACH BALL. (Paramount-1965-Lennie Weinrib). David Mal-
      colm authored this original screenplay. (W, LC, AMPAS, Q).

194   BEACH BLANKET BINGO. (American International-1965-Willi-
      am Asher). This motion picture was based on an original
      screenplay by William Asher and Leo Townsend. (W, LC,
      AMPAS, Q).

195   BEACH GIRLS AND THE MONSTERS. (U.S. Films-1965-Jon
      Hall). Joan Gardner wrote this original screenplay. (W,
      AMPAS).

196   BEACH RED. (United Artists-1967-Cornel Wilde). Clint John-
      ston, Donald A. Peters, and Jefferson Pascal based their
      screenplay on the novel, Red Beach; Random House, 1945. (Q,
      FF, NYTFR, W, LC, AMPAS, LACOPL).

197   THE BEAR AND THE DOLL. (Paramount-1971-Michel Deville).
      The original screenplay was written by Nina Companeez and
      Michel Deville. (W, Q).

198   THE BEARS AND I. (Buena Vista-1974-Bernard McEveety).
      John Whedon authored the screenplay which was based on the
      book by Robert Franklin Leslie; Dutton, 1968, 224p. (HR,
      LACOPL).

199   THE BEAST MUST DIE. (Cinerama-1974-Paul Annett). Mi-
      chael Winder wrote this original screenplay. (V).

200   BEAST OF BLOOD. (Marvin-1971-Eddie Romero). This film
      was based on a screenplay written by Eddie Romero, and based
      on a story by Beverly Miller. (W).

201   BEAU GESTE. (Universal-1966-Douglas Heyes). The screen-
      play is attributed to Douglas Heyes, which is based on the nov-
      el by Percival Christopher Wren; Stokes, 1925. (FF, NYTFR,
      LC, AMPAS, W, LACOPL, Q).

202   THE BEAUTIFUL SWINDLERS. (Continental-1968-Roman Pol-
      anski, Ugo Gregoretti, Claude Chabrol, & Hiromichi Horikawa).

An episodic film with segments authored by Roman Polanski and Gerard Brach ("Amsterdam"), and others who did not receive credit. (FF, W).

202a BEBO'S GIRL. (Continental-1964-Luigi Comencini). Marcello Fondato wrote this screenplay which was based on the novel of the same name by Carlo Cassola; Pantheon, 1964. (FF, LACOPL, NYTFR, W, Q).

203 BECKET. (Paramount-1964-Peter Glenville). Edward Anhalt's screenplay was based on the play by Jean Anouilh; Coward, 1960, 128p. (FF, LACOPL, AMPAS, W, NYTFR, Q).

203a BED AND BOARD. (Columbia-1971-François Truffaut). The original screenplay by François Truffaut, Claude De Givray, and Bernard Revon is included in the book, The Adventures of Antoine Doinel by François Truffaut; Simon & Schuster, 1971, 320p. (W, Q, LACOPL).

204 THE BED SITTING ROOM. (United Artists-1969-Richard Lester). This film was based on a screenplay by John Antrobus, adapted by Charles Wood, from a play by Spike Milligan and John Antrobus. (W, Q).

205 BEDAZZLED. (20th Century-Fox-1967-Stanley Donen). An original screenplay by Peter Cook which was based on an idea by Peter Cook and Dudley Moore. (FF, NYTFR, FM, W, LC, AMPAS, Q).

206 THE BEDFORD INCIDENT. (Columbia-1965-James B. Harris). James Poe wrote the screenplay on which this film was based, from the book by Mark Rascovich; Atheneum, 1963. (NYTFR, LC, AMPAS, W, LACOPL, Q).

207 BEDKNOBS AND BROOMSTICKS. Buena Vista-1971-Robert Stevenson). This screenplay by Bill Walsh and Don DaGradi is based on the book by Mary Norton; Harcourt, Brace, & World, 1957, 189p. (W, LACOPL, Q).

207a BEDTIME STORY. (Universal-1964-Ralph Levy). An original screenplay by Stanley Shapiro and Paul Henning. (AMPAS, FF, NYTFR, Q, W).

208 BEEN DOWN SO LONG IT LOOKS LIKE UP TO ME. (Paramount-1971-Jeffrey Young). Robert Schlitt wrote his screenplay from the novel by Richard Fariña; Random House, 1966. (W, LACOPL, Q).

209 BEFORE THE REVOLUTION. (New Yorker-1965-Bernardo Bertolucci). An original screenplay by Bernardo Bertolucci. (W, Q).

210 BEFORE WINTER COMES. (Columbia-1969-J. Lee Thompson).

Andrew Sinclair based his screenplay on the short story by
Frederick L. Keefe, "The Interpreter." (FF W, LC, AMPAS,
Q).

211 THE BEGUILED. (Universal-1971-Donald Siegel). The screenplay by John B. Sherry and Grimes Grice was based on the
novel by Thomas Cullinan; Horizon Press, 1966. (W, Q,
LACOPL).

211a BEHOLD A PALE HORSE. (Columbia-1964-Fred Zinnemann).
J. P. Miller's screenplay was based on the novel Killing a
Mouse on Sunday by Emeric Pressburger; Harcourt, Brace &
World, 1961, 180p. (FF, LACOPL, AMPAS, NYTFR, Q, W).

212 BELATED FLOWERS. (Artkino-1972-Abram Room). Abram
Room's screenplay was based on the novella by Chekhov, Late
Blooming Flowers and Other Stories; McGraw-Hill, 1964. (W,
LACOPL).

213 BELIEVE IN ME. (MGM-1971-Stuart Hagmann). Israel Horovitz is credited with this original screenplay. (W, Q).

214 BELLE DE JOUR. (Allied Artists-1968-Luis Buñuel). The
screenplay by Luis Buñuel and Jean-Claude Carrière was based
on the novel by Joseph Kessel; St. Martin's Press, 1962. The
screenplay was also published by Simon & Schuster, 1971, 168p.
(FF, NYTFR, W, LC, AMPAS, LACOPL, Q).

215 BEN. (Cinerama-1972-Phil Karlson). Gilbert A. Ralston authored this original screenplay, which was based on characters
created by Stephen Gilbert. (See WILLARD). (FF, Q).

216 BENEATH THE PLANET OF THE APES. (20th Century-Fox-
1970-Ted Post). The screenplay by Paul Dehn was taken from
a story by Paul Dehn and Mort Abrahams, and based on characters created by Pierre Boulle. (See PLANET OF THE
APES). (W, Q).

217 BENJAMIN. (Paramount-1968-Michel Deville). A film derived
from an original screenplay by Nina Companeez and Michel Deville. (W, Q).

218 BENJI. (Mulberry Square-1974-Joe Camp). Joe Camp wrote
this original screenplay. (V, HR).

THE BERKELEY-TO-BOSTON FORTY-BRICK LOST-BAG
BLUES see DEALING

219 BERSERK! (Columbia-1968-Jim O'Connolly). Story and screenplay by Aben Kandel and Herman Cohen. (FF, NYTFR, FM,
W, LC, AMPAS, Q).

220 THE BEST HOUSE IN LONDON. (MGM-1969-Philip Saville).

An original screenplay written by Denis Norden. (FF, W, LC, AMPAS, Q).

220a THE BEST MAN. (United Artists-1964-Franklin Schaffner). Gore Vidal wrote the screenplay based on his play; Little, Brown & Co., 1960, 168p. (FF, LACOPL, AMPAS, W, Q, NYTFR).

221 BETTER A WIDOW. (Universal-1969-Duccio Tessari). The screenplay by Ennio de Concini, Adriano Baracco, Brian Degas, Tudor Gates, Duccio Tessari, was based on a story by Ennio de Concini. (FF, W, Q).

222 BEWARE OF THE BRETHREN. (Cinerama-1972-Robert Hartford-Davis). An original screenplay by Brian Comport. (FF).

223 BEWARE: THE BLOB. (Jack H. Harris-1972-Larry Hagman). This film was based on a screenplay by Jack Woods and Anthony Harris which was taken from a story by Richard Clair. (W, FF).

224 BEYOND ATLANTIS. (Dimension-1973-Eddie Romero). Charles Johnson is credited with the writing of this original screenplay. (W).

225 BEYOND CONTROL. (Mishkin-1971-Anthony Baker). This original screenplay is attributed to Anthony Baker, Martin Roda-Becher, Charles Niessen, Ed Marcus, Joe Juliano. (W).

226 BEYOND LOVE AND EVIL. (Allied Artists-1971-Jacques Scandelari). An original screenplay written by Jean Stuart, Jean Pierre Deloux, and Jacques Scandelari. (W).

227 BEYOND THE GREAT WALL. (Frank Lee International-1967-Li Han-Hsiang). A documentary with no credit available for script. (W, Q).

228 BEYOND THE LAW. (Grove Press, 1968-Norman Mailer). A screenplay improvised by the actors, from a story outline by Norman Mailer. (FF, NYTFRM, FM, W, Q).

229 BEYOND THE VALLEY OF THE DOLLS. (20th Century-Fox-1970-Russ Meyer). Roger Ebert wrote the screenplay from a story by Roger Ebert and Russ Meyer. (W, Q).

230 THE BIBLE (... IN THE BEGINNING). (20th Century-Fox-1966-John Huston). The screenplay by Christopher Fry with the assistance of Jonathan Griffin, Ivo Perilli, and Vittorio Bonicelli was published by Pocket Books, 1966. It was adapted from episodes in the Old Testament. (FF, NYTFR, McC, LC, AMPAS, W, Q).

231 BIBLE. (Poolemar-1974-Wakefield Poole). No screenplay credit. (V).

232   LES BICHES.   (Jack H. Harris-1968-Claude Chabrol).   An
original screenplay by Paul Gegauff and Claude Chabrol.   (FF,
NYTFR, LC).

233   BIG BAD MAMA.   (New World-1974-Steve Carver).   William
Norton and Frances Doel are credited with this original screenplay.   (V, HR).

234   THE BIG BIRD CAGE.   (New World-1972-Jack Hill).   Jack
Hill wrote this screenplay.   (FF).

235   THE BIG BOUNCE.   (Warner Bros.-7 Arts-1969-Alex March).
A screenplay by Robert Dozier based on a novel by Elmore
Leonard.   (W, FF, LC, AMPAS, NYTFR, Q).

236   THE BIG BUST-OUT.   (New World-1973-Richard Jackson).
Sergio Garrone is credited with this original screenplay.   (W,
Q).

237   THE BIG CITY.   (Edward Harrison-1967-Satyajit Ray).   The
screenplay by Satyajit Ray is based on a story by Narenda
Nath Mitra.   (FF, AMPAS).

238   THE BIG CITY.   (New Yorker-1971-Carlos Diegues).   A
screenplay by Carlos Diegues and Leopoldo Serran.   (W).

239   THE BIG CUBE.   (Warner Bros.-7 Arts-1969-Tito Davison).
An original screenplay by William Douglas Lansford, based on
a story by Tito Davison and Edmundo Baez.   (W, LC, AMPAS,
Q).

240   THE BIG DOLL HOUSE.   (New World-1971-Jack Hill).   An
original screenplay attributed to Don Spencer.   (W).

241   THE BIG GUNDOWN.   (Columbia-1968-Sergio Sollima).   The
film is based on a screenplay by Sergio Donati and Sergio Sollima, based on a story by Franco Solinas and Fernando Mor-
andi.   (FF, NYTFR, FM, W, LC, AMPAS, Q).

242   A BIG HAND FOR THE LITTLE LADY.   (Warner Bros.-1966-
Fielder Cook).   The screenplay by Sidney Carroll was based
on his TV play, Big Deal at Laredo.   (FF, NYTFR, LC,
AMPAS, Q, W).

243   BIG JAKE.   (National General-1971-George Sherman).   The
film was drawn from an original story and screenplay by Harry
Julian Fink and R. M. Fink.   (W, Q).

244   THE BIG MOUTH.   (Columbia-1967-Jerry Lewis).   A screenplay by Jerry Lewis and Bill Richmond, based on a story by
Bill Richmond.   (FF, NYTFR, FM, W, LC, AMPAS, Q).

245   THE BIG T.N.T. SHOW.   (American International-1966-Larry

Peerce). A documentary, no script credit. (LC, W, Q).

246   BIGFOOT. (Ellman Enterprises-1973-Robert F. Slatzer). A
      screenplay by James Gordon White and Robert F. Slatzer. (W,
      FF).

247   THE BIGGEST BUNDLE OF THEM ALL. (MGM-1968-Ken
      Annakin). A screenplay by Josef Shaftel, Sy Salkowitz and Ric-
      cardo Aragno, based on a story by Josef Shaftel. (FF,
      NYTFR, FM, W, LC, Q, AMPAS).

248   BIJOU. (Poolemar-1972-Wakefield Poole). No screenplay
      credit. (W, V).

249   BIKE BOY. (Andy Warhol-1967-Andy Warhol). Written by
      Andy Warhol. (FF, W).

249a BIKINI BEACH. (American International-1964-William Asher).
      The team of William Asher, Leo Townsend, and Robert Dillon
      wrote this original screenplay. (FF, W, Q).

250   BIKINI PARADISE. (Allied Artists-1967-Gregg Tallas). How-
      ard Bert's screenplay was based on a story by Daniel Aubrey.
      (FF, AMPAS).

251   BILLIE. (United Artists-1965-Don Weis). Screenplay by Ron-
      ald Alexander, based on his play Time Out for Ginger; Drama-
      tists Play Service, 1953, 132p. (NYTFR, LC, AMPAS, W,
      LACOPL, Q).

252   BILLION DOLLAR BRAIN. (United Artists-1967-Ken Russell).
      A screenplay by John McGrath based on the novel by Len
      Deighton, Putnam, 1966. (FF, NYTFR, FM, W, AMPAS,
      AMPAS, LACOPL, Q).

253   BILLY JACK. (Warner Bros.-1971-T.C. Frank aka Tom
      Laughlin). Screenplay by Frank and Teresa Christina, pub-
      lished by Avon, 1973, 124p. (W, LACOPL, Q).

254   BILLY THE KID VS. DRACULA. (Embassy-1966-William
      Beaudine). Screenplay by Carl K. Hittleman. (FF, AMPAS,
      W).

255   BILLY TWO HATS. (United Artists-1974-Ted Kotcheff). An
      original screenplay by Alan Sharp. (HR).

256   THE BIRD WITH THE CRYSTAL PLUMAGE. (UMC-1970-
      Dario Argento). An original screenplay by Dario Argento was
      the inspiration for the film. (W, NYTFR).

257   THE BIRDS AND THE BEADS. (1973). No script credit.
      (W).

258 BIRDS DO IT. (Columbia-1966-Andrew Marton). Screenplay
by Arnie Kogen and Art Arthur, based on a story by Leonard
Kaufman. (FF, LC, AMPAS, W, Q).

259 BIRDS IN PERU. (Regional-1968-Romain Gary). A screenplay
by Romain Gary based on his short story. (FF, NYTFR,
AMPAS, Q).

260 THE BIRDS, THE BEES AND THE ITALIANS. (Claridge-
1967-Pietro Germi). The screenplay by Age and Scarpelli,
Luciano Vincenzoni and Pietro Germi, was based on an original story by Pietro Germi and Luciano Vincenzoni. (NYTFR,
W, AMPAS, Q).

261 THE BIRTHDAY PARTY. (Continental-1968-William Friedkin).
Screenplay by Harold Pinter, based on his play, Grove Press,
1961, 120 p. (FF, NYTFR, W, AMPAS, LACOPL, Q).

262 THE BISCUIT EATER. (Buena Vista-1972-Vincent McEveety).
Lawrence Edward Watkin wrote the screenplay based on a story
by James Street. (W, FF).

263 BITTER LOVE. (Alpherat-1974-Florestano Vancini). An original screenplay by Suso Cecchi d'Amico and Florestano Vancini. (V).

264 BLACK BEAUTY. (Paramount-1971-James Hill). Wolf Mankowitz based his screenplay on the novel by Anna Sewell;
World Publishing Co., 1946, 315p. (W, LACOPL, Q).

265 THE BLACK BELLY OF THE TARANTULA. (MGM-1972-
Paolo Cavara). A screenplay by Lucile Laks, based on the
story by Marcello Canon. (FF).

266 BLACK BELT JONES. (Warner Bros.-1974-Robert Clouse).
Oscar Williams based his screenplay on a story by Alex Rose
and Fred Weintraub. (HR).

267 THE BLACK BUNCH. (Entertainment Pyramid-1973-Henning
Schellerup). No screenplay credit available. (W).

268 BLACK CAESAR. (American International-1973-Larry Cohen).
An original screenplay by Larry Cohen. (W, Q).

269 BLACK EYE. (Warner Bros.-1974-Jack Arnold). A screenplay by Mark Haggard and Jim Martin, based on Jeff Jacks'
novel, Murder on the Wild Side. (V).

270 BLACK FANTASY. (Impact-1972-Lionel Rogosin). Dialogue
improvised. (W).

271 BLACK GIRL. (New Yorker-1969-Ousmane Sembene). Screenplay by Ousmane Sembene who based it on his novel of the

same name. (FF, W, NYTFR).

272 BLACK GIRL. (Cinerama-1972-Ossie Davis). Screenplay by
J. E. Franklin, based on her play. (W, FF, Q).

273 BLACK GOD, WHITE DEVIL. (New Yorker-1971-Glauber
Rocha). Story and screenplay by Glauber Rocha. (W).

274 THE BLACK GODFATHER. (Cinemation-1974-John Evans).
An original screenplay by John Evans. (HR, V).

275 BLACK GUNN. (Columbia-1972-Robert Hartford-Davis). Franklin Coen wrote this adaptation based on a screenplay by Robert
Shearer, from an idea by Robert Hartford-Davis. (W, FF, Q).

276 BLACK JACK. (American International-1972-William T. Naud).
A screenplay by Dick Gautier, William T. Naud, based on a
story by William T. Naud and Dick Gautier. (W).

277 BLACK JESUS. (Plaza-1971-Valerio Zurlini). An original
screenplay by Valerio Zurlini and Franco Brusati. (W).

THE BLACK KLANSMAN see I CROSSED THE COLOR LINE

277a BLACK LIKE ME. (Continental-1964-Carl Lerner). Gerda
Lerner and Carl Lerner received screenwriting credit, which
was based on the book by John Howard Griffin; Houghton, 1961,
176p. (FF, LACOPL, NYTFR, W, Q).

278 BLACK MAMA, WHITE MAMA. (American International-1973-
Eddie Romero). A screenplay by H. R. Christian, based on a
story by Joseph Viola and Jonathan Demme. (W, Q).

279 THE BLACK MOSES OF SOUL. (Aquarius-1973-Chuck Johnson). A documentary; no screenwriting credit. (W).

280 BLACK ON WHITE. (Audubon-1969-Tinto Brass). No screen
credits available. (W, Q).

281 BLACK PETER. (Billings-1971-Milos Forman). A screenplay
by Milos Forman, Jaroslav Papousek, and Ivan Passer. (W).

282 BLACK RODEO. (Cinerama-1972-Jeff Kanew). No script
credit. (FF).

282a BLACK SABBATH. (American International-1964-Mario Bava).
A screenplay by Marcello Fondato, with the collaboration of Alberto Bevilacqua and Mario Bava. "The Drop of Water" based
on a story by Anton Chekhov; "The Telephone" is based on a
story by F. G. Snyder. "The Wurdalak" is based on a story
by Leo Tolstoy. (Q, FF).

283 BLACK SAMSON. (Warner Bros.-1974-Charles Bail). A

screenplay written by Warren Hamilton, Jr., based on a story by Daniel B. Cady. (V).

284   BLACK SPURS. (Paramount-1965-R. G. Springsteen). Steve Fisher is credited with this original screenplay. (NYTFR, LC, AMPAS, W).

285   A BLACK VEIL FOR LISA. (Commonwealth United-1969-Massimo Dallamano). A screenplay by Giuseppe Belli, Vittoriano Patrick, Massimo Dallamano, and Audrey Nohra, from a story by Giuseppe Belli. (W).

286   THE BLACK WINDMILL. (Universal-1974-Don Siegel). A screenplay by Leigh Vance, based on a novel Seven Days to a Killing, by Clive Egleton; Coward, 1973, 252p. (V, LACOPL).

287   BLACKBEARD'S GHOST. Buena Vista-1968-Robert Stevenson). Bill Walsh and Don DaGradi authored this screenplay, which they based on the novel by Ben Stahl; Houghton, 1965. (FF, NYTFR, FM, W, LC, AMPAS, LACOPL, Q).

288   BLACKENSTEIN. (Exclusive International-1973-). No credit. (W).

BLACKSNAKE see SWEET SUZY

289   BLACULA. (American International-1972-William Crain). Screenplay by Joan Torres and Raymond Koenig, based on a character created by Bram Stoker. (FF, Q).

290   BLADE. (Joseph Green-1973-George Manasse). An original screenplay by Ernest Pintoff and Jeff Lieberman. (W).

291   BLAZING SADDLES. (Warner Bros.-1974-Mel Brooks). A screenplay by Mel Brooks, Norman Steinberg, Andrew Bergman, Richard Pryor, and Alan Uger, from a story by Andrew Bergman. Original paperback novel based on the screenplay was written by Tad Richards, and published in 1974 by Warner Paperback Library, 175p. (HR, V, LACOPL).

292   BLESS THE BEASTS AND CHILDREN. (Columbia-1971-Stanley Kramer). Screenplay by Mac Benoff, based on the novel by Glendon Swarthout; Doubleday, 1970, 205p. (W, LACOPL, Q).

293   BLINDFOLD. (Universal-1966-Philip Dunne). Screenplay by Philip Dunne and W. H. Menger, based on the novel by Lucille Fletcher; Random House, 1960. (FF, NYTFR, LC, AMPAS, W, LACOPL, Q).

294   BLINDMAN. (20th Century-Fox-1971-Ferdinando Baldi). An original screenplay by Piero Anchisi, Vincenzo Cerami, and Tony Anthony. (FF, Q).

295   THE BLISS OF MRS. BLOSSOM. (Paramount-1968-Joseph Mc-
Grath). A screenplay attributed to Alec Coppel and Denis Norden, based on the play A Bird in the Nest by Alec Coppel,
from a story by Josef Shaftel. (FF, W, LC, AMPAS, Q).

296   BLOOD AND BLACK LACE. (Allied Artists-1965-Mario Bava).
An original story and screenplay by Marcel Fondat, Joe Baril-
la, and Mario Bava. (NYTFR, AMPAS, W, Q).

297   BLOOD AND LACE. (American International-1971-Philip Gilbert). Gil Lasky wrote this original screenplay. (W, Q).

298   BLOOD BATH. (American International-1966-Jack Hill &
Stephanie Rothman). Screenplay by Jack Hill and Stephanie
Rothman. (FF, LC, AMPAS, W, Q).

299   BLOOD BEAST FROM OUTER SPACE. (World Entertainment
Corporation-1968-John Gilling). A screenplay by Jim O'Con-
nolly, based on the novel The Night Callers, by Frank Crisp.
(FF, W, LC).

300   BLOOD FIEND. (Hemisphere-1968-Samuel Gallu). An original screenplay by Ellis Kadison and Roger Marshall. (FF, Q).

301   BLOOD FOR DRACULA. (Bryanston-1974-Paul Morrissey).
Original screenplay by Paul Morrissey. (V).

302   BLOOD FROM THE MUMMY'S TOMB. (American International-
1972-Seth Holt). A screenplay by Christopher Wicking, based
on the novel Jewel of the Seven Stars by Bram Stoker; Harper
& Row, 1904. (FF, LACOPL).

303   BLOOD OF THE CONDOR. (Tricontinental-1973-Jorge Sanjines). An original screenplay written by Oscar Soria and
Jorge Sanjines. (W).

304   BLOOD ON THE ARROW. (Allied Artists-1965-Sidney Salkow).
A screenplay by Robert E. Kent, based on a story by Robert
E. Kent and Mark Hanna. (FF).

305   THE BLOOD ROSE. (Allied Artists-1970-Claude Mulot). An
original screenplay attributed to Claude Mulot. (W).

306   BLOODY MAMA. (American International-1970-Norman Corman). A screenplay by Robert Thom, from a story by Robert
Thom and Don Peters. (W, NYTFR).

307   BLOODY PIT OF HORROR. (Pacemaker Pictures-1967-Mas-
simo Pupillo). An original screenplay by Roberto Natale and
Romano Migliorini. (FF, Q).

308   BLOW-UP. (MGM-1966-Michelangelo Antonioni). A screenplay
by Michelangelo Antonioni, Edward Bond, and Tonino Guerra,

based on a story by Michelangelo Antonioni, inspired by a
short story by Julio Cortazar.   Screenplay published 1971 by
Simon & Schuster, 119p.   (FF, NYTFR, LC, AMPAS, W,
LACOPL, Q, SCH, MCC).

309   BLUE.   (Paramount-1968-Silvio Narizzano).   A screenplay by
Meade Roberts and Ronald M. Cohen, based on a story by
Ronald M. Cohen.   (FF, NYTFR, FM, W, LC, AMPAS, Q).

310   THE BLUE BEAST.   (Toho-1965-Hiromichi Horikawa).   An
original screenplay written by Yoshio Shirasaka.   (W).

311   THE BLUE MAX.   (20th Century-Fox-1966-John Guillermin).
The screenplay written by Gerald Hanley, David Pursall, and
Jack Seddon, was based on the novel by Jack D. Hunter; Dut-
ton, 1964.   (Q, FF, NYTFR, LC, AMPAS, W. LACOPL).

312   BLUE MONEY.   (Crown International-1972-Alain-Patrick Chap-
puis).   An original screenplay by Nick Boretz.   (FF).

313   BLUE MOVIE.   (Andy Warhol-1969-Andy Warhol).   Script improvised by the actors; the scenario by Andy Warhol was published by Grove Press, 1970, 128p.   (SCH, FF, W, NYTFR).

314   BLUE SEXTET.   (Unisphere-1972-David E. Durston).   Written
by David E. Durston.   (FF).

315   BLUE SUMMER.   (Monarch-1973-Chuck Vincent).   Screenplay
by Chuck Vincent.   (W).

316   BLUE SURFARI.   (Excelsior-1970-Milton Blair).   Written by
Milton Blair.   (W).

317   BLUE WATER, WHITE DEATH.   (National General-1971-).
Screenplay by Peter Gimbel.   (W, Q).

318   BLUEBEARD.   (Cinerama-1972-Edward Dmutryk).   Screenplay
by Ennio De Concini, Edward Dmytryk, and Maria Pia Fusco.
(W, FF, Q).

319   BLUES FOR LOVERS.   (20th Century-Fox-1966-Paul Henreid).
The Burton Wohl screenplay was based on an original story by
Paul Henreid and Burton Wohl.   (NYTFR, LC, AMPAS, W, Q).

320   BLUME IN LOVE.   (Warner Bros.-1973-Paul Mazursky).   An
original screenplay by Paul Mazursky.   (W, Q).

321   THE BOATNIKS.   (Buena Vista-1970-Norman Tokar).   Screenstory and screenplay by Arthur Julian, based on a story by
Marty Roth.   (W, NYTFR, Q).

322   BOB & CAROL & TED & ALICE.   (Columbia-1969-Paul Mazursky).   An original screenplay written by Paul Mazursky and

Larry Tucker. (FF, W, AMPAS, NYTFR, Q).

323   BOB & DARYL & TED & ALEX. (Fanrow-1972-Stan Preston).
      No author credit. (W).

324   THE BOBO. (Warner Bros.-7 Arts-1967-Robert Parrish). A
      screenplay by David R. Schwartz, based on his play The Bobo
      and the novel Olimpia by Burt Cole published by Macmillan,
      1959. (Q, FF, NYTFR, FM, W, LC, AMPAS, LACOPL).

325   THE BODY STEALERS. (Allied Artists-1971-Gerry Levy). No
      screenwriting credit available. (W).

326   BOEING BOEING. (Paramount-1965-Edward Anhalt). Based
      on a play by Marc Camoletti. (NYTFR, LC, W, AMPAS, Q).

327   THE BOFORS GUN. (Regional-1968-Jack Gold). Screenplay
      by John McGrath, based on his play Events While Guarding the
      Bofors Gun. (FF, NYTFR, FM, W, AMPAS, Q).

328   LA BOHEME. (Warner Bros.-1965-Franco Zeffirelli). A
      filmed version of the famed opera in four acts by Giuseppe Gi-
      acosa and Luigi Illica, based on the novel Scenes de la Vie de
      Bohème by Henri Murger; Larousse, 1851, and music by Gia-
      como Puccini. (NYTFR, LC, W, LACOPL).

329   LE BONHEUR. (Clover-1966-Agnes Varda). From a screen-
      play by Agnes Varda, this film was produced. (FF, NYTFR,
      W, Q).

329a LA BONNE SOUPE. (20th Century-Fox-1964-Robert Thomas).
      A screenplay by Robert Thomas, based on the play by Felicien
      Marceau. (FF, Q, NYTFR).

330   LES BONNES FEMMES. (Robert and Raymond Hakim Release-
      1966-Claude Chabrol). Screenplay by Paul Gegauff, adaptation
      by Claude Chabrol. (FF, NYTFR).

331   BONNIE AND CLYDE. (Warner Bros.-7 Arts-1967-Arthur
      Penn). An original screenplay by David Newman and Robert
      Benton. The screenplay was published in The Bonnie and Clyde
      Book compiled and edited by S. Wake and Nicola Hayden; Si-
      mon & Schuster, 1972, 223p. (Q, FF, NYTFR, FM, W, LC,
      AMPAS, LACOPL).

332   BONNIE'S KIDS. (General Film Corporation-1972-Arthur Marks).
      An original screenplay by Arthur Marks. (FF).

333   BOOK OF NUMBERS. (AVCO Embassy-1973-Raymond St.
      Jacques). A screenplay by Larry Spiegel, based on a novel by
      Robert Deane Phaar. (W, Q).

334   BOOM! (Universal-1968-Joseph Losey). An original screen-

play by Tennessee Williams, based on his short story "Man
Bring This Up the Road" which is in Knightly Quest, New Di-
rections, 1966; and his play The Milk Train Doesn't Stop Here
Anymore, New Directions, 1964, 118p.   (FF, NYTFR, FM,
W, AMPAS, LACOPL, Q).

335 BOOTLEGGERS.   (Howco-1974-Charles B. Pierce).   An original screenplay written by Earl E. Smith.   (V).

336 BOOTS TURNER.   (Rowland-Williams-1973-J. Edward & J.
Lasko).   An original screenplay by J. Edward and J. Lasko.
(W).

337 BORA BORA.   (American International-1970-Ugo Leberatore).
A film taken from an original screenplay by Ugo Leberatore.
(W, FM, Q).

338 BORN FREE.   (Columbia-1966-James Hill).   A motion picture
screenplay written by Gerald L. C. Copley, based on the book
by Joy Adamson; Pantheon Books, 1960, 220p.   (FF, NYTFR,
LC, W, AMPAS, LACOPL, Q, FM).

339 BORN LOSERS.   (American International-1967-T. C. Frank aka
Tom Laughlin).   Screenplay by E. James Lloyd aka Tom
Laughlin.   (FF, NYTFR, W, LC, AMPAS, Q).

340 BORN TO WIN.   (United Artists-1971-Ivan Passer).   An original screenplay by David Scott Milton.   (W, Q).

341 BORN WILD.   (American International-1968-Maury Dexter).
An original screenplay by James Gordon White.   (FF, NYTFR,
W, AMPAS, LC).

342 BOROM SARRET.   (New Yorker-1969-Ousmane Sembene).   An
original screenplay by Ousmane Sembene.   (W, NYTFR).

343 BORSALINO.   (Paramount-1970-Jacques Deray).   A screenplay
by Jean Cau, Claude Sautet, Jacques Deray, and Jean-Claude
Carrière, adapted from "The Bandits of Marseilles" by Eugene Saccomano.   (W, NYTFR, Q).

344 THE BOSTON STRANGLER.   (20th Century-Fox-1968-Richard
Fleischer).   A screenplay by Edward Anhalt, based on the book
by Gerold Frank; New American Library, 1966, 364p.   (FF
NYTFR, W, LC, AMPAS, Q, LACOPL).

345 LE BOUCHER.   (Cinerama-1971-Claude Chabrol).   An original
work for the screen by Claude Chabrol.   (W, NYTFR, Q).

346 BOUDU SAVED FROM DROWNING.   (Pathe Contemporary-
1967-Jean Renoir).   Screenplay by Jean Renoir, based on the
play by Rene Fauchois.   (FF, NYTFR, W).

347 THE BOUNTY KILLER. (Embassy-1965-Spencer G. Bennet). An original screenplay by R. Alexander and Leo Gordon. (W, AMPAS, Q).

348 BOXCAR BERTHA. (American International-1972-Martin Scorsese). A screenplay by Joyce H. Corrington and John William Corrington, based on characters in Sisters of the Road, the autobiography of Boxcar Bertha Thompson, as told to Dr. Ben L. Reitman. (FF).

349 BOY. (Grove-1970-Nagisa Oshima). Screenplay by Tsutomu Tamura. (W, NYTFR).

350 A BOY ... A GIRL. (Jack Hanson-1969-John Derek). Screenplay authored by John Derek. (W, AMPAS, Q).

351 THE BOY CRIED MURDER. (Universal-1966-George Breakston). A screenplay by Robin Estridge, based on the story by Cornell Woolrich. Also made in 1949 as THE WINDOW. (FF, LC, W, AMPAS, Q).

352 BOY, DID I GET A WRONG NUMBER. (United Artists-1966-George Marshall). A screenplay by Burt Styler, Albert E. Lewin, and George Kennett, based on a story by George Beck. (FF, LC, W, AMPAS, Q).

353 THE BOY FRIEND. (MGM-1971-Ken Russell). A screenplay written by Ken Russell, and based on Sandy Wilson's musical of the same name; Dutton, 1955, 216p. (W, LACOPL)

THE BOY NEXT DOOR see TO FIND A MAN

354 A BOY TEN FEET TALL. (Paramount-1965-Alexander MacKendrick). A screenplay by Denis Cannan, based on the novel Sammy Going South, by W. H. Canaway. (FF, LC, W, AMPAS).

355 THE BOY WHO CRIED WEREWOLF. (Universal-1973-Nathan H. Juran). An original work for the screen by Bob Homel. (W).

356 THE BOYS IN THE BAND. (National General-1970-William Friedkin). Mart Crowley wrote the screenplay adapted from his play of the same name; Farrar, 1968, 182p. (W, LACOPL, NYTFR).

357 BOYS IN THE SAND. (Poolemar-1971-Wakefield Poole). Story by Wakefield Poole, no dialogue. (W).

358 THE BOYS OF PAUL STREET. (20th Century-Fox-1969-Zoltan Fabri). Screenplay by Zoltan Fabri and Endre Bohem, based on the 1927 novel by Ferenc Molnar. (FF, W, AMPAS, NYTFR).

359   THE BRAIN. (Paramount-1969-Gerard Oury). Screenplay, adaptation and dialogue by Gerard Oury, Marcel Julian, and Daniele Thompson. (W, LC, NYTFR).

360   BRAINSTORM. (Warner Bros.-1965-William Conrad). Screenplay by Mann Rubin, based on a story by Larry Marcus. NYTFR, LC, W, AMPAS).

361   BRANCHES. (New Line-1971-Ed Emshwiller). No screenplay credits available. (W).

362   BRANDY IN THE WILDERNESS. (New Line-1971-Stanton Kaye). An original screen work by Stanton Kaye and Michaux French. (W).

362a THE BRASS BOTTLE. (Universal-1964-Harry Keller). Oscar Brodney wrote the screenplay based on the novel by F. Anstey. (FF, NYTFR, Q).

363   O BRAVO GUERREIRO. (New Yorker-1971-Gustavo Dahl). A screenplay by Gustavo Dahl and Roberto Marinho de Azevedo Neto. (W).

363a THE BRAZEN WOMEN OF BALZAC. (Globe-1971-Josef Zachar). An original screenplay by Kurt Nachtman. (W).

      BREAK LOOSE see PARADES

364   BREEZY. (Universal-1973-Clint Eastwood). An original screenplay by Jo Heims. (W).

365   BREWSTER McCLOUD. (MGM-1970-Robert Altman). A screenplay by Doran William Cannon. (W, NYTFR).

      THE BRIDE see THE HOUSE THAT CRIED MURDER

366   THE BRIDE WORE BLACK. (Lopert-1968-Françoise Truffaut). A screenplay by François Truffaut and Jean-Louis Richard, based on the novel The Bride Wore Black by William Irish aka Cornell Woolrich. (FF, NYTFR, W, LC, AMPAS).

367   THE BRIDES OF FU MANCHU. (7 Arts-1966-Don Sharp). A screenplay by Peter Welbeck based on the characters created by Sax Rohmer. (FF, W, AMPAS).

368   THE BRIDGE AT REMAGEN. (United Artists-1969-John Guillerim). Screenplay by Richard Yates, William Roberts and Ray Rigby, based on a story by Roger Hirson and a book by Kenneth Hechler; Ballantine, 1957, 238p. (FF, W, LC, AMPAS, LACOPL, NYTFR).

369   THE BRIDGE IN THE JUNGLE. (United Artists-1971-Pancho Kohner). Screenplay written by Pancho Kohner, based on the

novel by Bruno Traven; Knopf, 1938. (W, LACOPL).

370   THE BRIG. (1965-). Story and screenplay by Kenneth H.
      Brown, based on his play; Hill & Wang, 1965, 107p. (AMPAS,
      LACOPL).

371   No entry.

372   THE BRIGAND OF KANDAHAR. (Columbia-1966-John Gilling).
      An original screenplay by John Gilling. (FF, LC, W,
      (AMPAS).

373   BRIGHTY OF THE GRAND CANYON. (Feature Film Corpora-
      tion of America-1967-Norman Foster). Screenplay by Norman
      Foster, based on the book by Marguerite Henry; Rand Mc-
      Nally & Co. , 1953, 219p. (FF, W, LC, AMPAS, LACOPL).

374   BRING ME THE HEAD OF ALFREDO GARCIA. (United Artists-
      1974-Sam Peckinpah). Screenplay by Gordon Dawson and Sam
      Peckinpah, from a story by Frank Kowalski. (V, HR).

375   THE BROAD COALITION. (August-1972-Simon Nuchtern). An
      original screenplay by William C. Reilly. (W).

376   THE BROKEN WINGS. (Continental-1968-Yusuf Malouf).
      Screenplay by Saeed Akal, based on the novel by Kahlil Gib-
      ran; Citadel Press, 1957, 128p. (FF, NYTFR, W, LACOPL).

377   BRONCO BULLFROG. (New Yorker-1972-Barney Platts-Mills).
      An original work for the screen by Barney Platts-Mills. (FF).

378   BROTHER CARL. (New Yorker-1972-Susan Sontag). An orig-
      inal screenplay by Susan Sontag. (W, FF).

379   BROTHER JOHN. (Columbia-1971-James Goldstone). An
      original screenplay by Ernest Kinoy. (W).

380   BROTHER OF THE WIND. (Sun International-1973-). Screen-
      play by John Mahon and John Champion. (W).

381   BROTHER ON THE RUN. (Southern Star-1973-Herbert Strock).
      An original screenplay by Herbert Strock. (W).

382   BROTHER SUN, SISTER MOON. (Paramount-1973-Franco
      Zeffirelli). An original screenplay by Suso Cecchi d'Amico,
      Kenneth Ross, Lina Wertmuller, and Franco Zefferelli. (W).

383   THE BROTHERHOOD. (Paramount-1969-Martin Ritt). An
      original screenplay by Lewis John Carlino. (FF, W, LC,
      AMPAS, NYTFR).

384   THE BROTHERHOOD OF SATAN. (Columbia-1971-Bernard
      McEveety). An original work for the screen written by

William Welch, based on a story by Sean MacGregor. (W).

385 BROTHERLY LOVE. (MGM-1970-J. Lee Thompson). A
screenplay written by James Kennaway, based on his play
Country Dance, and his novel Household Ghosts, Atheneum,
1961. (W, LACOPL NYTFR, Q).

386 THE BROTHERS O'TOOLE. (CVD-1973-Richard Erdman).
No script credit. (W).

387 THE BRUTE AND THE BEAST. (American International-1968-
Lucio Fulci). Original story and screenplay by Fernando di
Leo. (FF, W, LC).

388 BRUTE CORPS. (General Film Corporation-1972-Jerry Jameson). Screenplay by Mike Kars and Abe Polsky. (FF).

389 THE BUBBLE. (Arch Obler-1967-Arch Obler). A screenplay
attributed to Arch Obler. (W, AMPAS).

390 BUCK AND THE PREACHER. (Columbia-1972-Sidney Poitier).
A screenplay written by Ernest Kinoy, based on a story by
Ernest Kinoy and Drake Walker. (W, Q).

391 BUCKSKIN. (Paramount-1968-Michael Moore). An original
screenplay by Michael Fisher. (FF, W, LC, AMPAS).

392 BUDDHA. (Lopert-1965-Kenji Misumi). A script by Fuji
Yahiro. (NYTFR).

392a BULLET FOR A BADMAN. (Universal-1964-R. G. Springsteen). Mary and Willard Willingham wrote the screenplay
based on a novel by Marvin H. Albert. (AMPAS, FF, W, Q).

393 A BULLET FOR PRETTY BOY. (American International-
1970-Larry Buchanan). A screenplay by Henry Rosenbaum,
from a story by Enrique Touceda and Larry Buchanan. (W,
NYTFR).

394 A BULLET FOR SANDOVAL. (Universal Marion-1970-Julio
Buchs). A screenplay by Ugo Guerro, José Luis Martínez
Molla, and Frederic de Urratia. (W).

395 A BULLET FOR THE GENERAL. (AVCO Embassy-1969-Da-
miano Damiani). A screenplay by Salvatore Laurani, Franco
Solinas, and Damiano Damiani. (FF, W, NYTFR).

396 BULLITT. (Warner Bros.-7 Arts-1968-Peter Yates). A
screenplay by Alan R. Trustman and Harry Kleiner, based on
the novel Mute Witness by Robert L. Fish, Doubleday, 1963.
(FF, NYTFR, FM, W, AMPAS, LACOPL).

397 BUMMER. (Entertainment Ventures-1973-William Allen Castle-

man).   An original screen work by Alvin L. Fast.   (W).

398   BUNNY LAKE IS MISSING.   (Columbia-1965-Otto Preminger).
This screenplay by John and Penelope Mortimer, was based on
the novel by Marriam Modell aka Evelyn Piper, 1957.

399   BUNNY O'HARE.   (American International-1971-).   An original
screenplay by Stanley Z. Cherry and Coslough Johnson, based
on a story by Stanley Z. Cherry.   (W).

400   BUONA SERA, MRS. CAMPBELL.   (United Artists-1969-Mel-
vin Frank).   A screenplay by Melvin Frank, Sheldon Keller,
and Dennis Norden.   (FF, W, LC, AMPAS, NYTFR).

401   THE BURGLARS.   (Columbia-1972-Henri Verneuil).   A screenplay by Henri Verneuil and Vahe Katcha, based on the novel
The Burglar by David Goodis.   (FF, Q).

402   THE BURMESE HARP.   (Brandon-1967-Kon Ichikawa).   A
screenplay by Natto Wada from a story by Michio Takeyama.
(NYTFR, W, AMPAS).

403   BURN.   (United Artists-1970-Gillo Pontecorvo).   A screenplay
by Franco Solinas, Giorgio Arlorio, with a story by Gilo Pontecorvo, Franco Solinas, and Giorgio Arlorio.   (W, NYTFR).

404   BURY ME AN ANGEL.   (New World-1972-Barbara Peeters).
An original screenplay by Barbara Peeters.   (W).

405   BUS RILEY'S BACK IN TOWN.   (Universal-1965-Harvey Hart).
A work for the screen by Walter Gage aka William Inge.   (FF,
Q, LC, W, AMPAS).

406   THE BUSHBABY.   (MGM-1970-John Trent).   A screenplay by
Robert Maxwell and William H. Stevenson, based on a novel by
William H. Stevenson.   (W, AMPAS).

407   BUSHMAN.   (American Film Institute-1971-David Schickele).
An original screenplay by David Schickele.   (W).

408   BUSTER AND BILLIE.   (Columbia-1974-Daniel Petrie).   A
screenplay by Ron Turbeville, from a story by Ron Turbeville
and Ron Baron.   (V).

409   BUSTING.   (United Artists-1974-Peter Hyams).   An original
screenplay by Peter Hyams.   (HR).

410   THE BUSY BODY.   (Paramount-1967-William Castle).   A
screenplay by Ben Starr, based on the novel by Donald E.
Westlake; Random House, 1966.   (FF, W, LC, AMPAS,
LACOPL).

411   BUTCH CASSIDY AND THE SUNDANCE KID.   (20th Century-

Fox-1969-George Roy Hill). A screenplay by William Goldman, published by Bantam Books, 1969, 134p. (FF, AMPAS, NYTFR, Q, W, SCH).

412   BUTLEY. (American Film Theatre-1974-Harold Pinter). A screenplay by Simon Gray, based on his play; Viking, 1971, 78p. (HR, LACOPL, V).

413   BUTTERFLIES ARE FREE. (Columbia-1972-Milton Katselas). A screenplay by Leonard Gershe, based on his play; Random House, 1969, 107p. (FF, LACOPL, W, V, HR).

414   BWANA TOSHI. (Brandon-1970-Susumu Hani). A screenplay by Kunio Shimizu and Susumu Hani, based on a book by Toshishide Katayori. (W, NYTFR).

415   BYE BYE BRAVERMAN. (Warner Bros.-7 Arts-1968-Sidney Lumet). A screenplay by Herbert Sargent, based on the novel, To an Early Grave by Wallace Markfield, Simon & Schuster, 1964. (FF, NYTFR, FM, W, LC, AMPAS, LACOPL).

416   C. C. AND COMPANY. (AVCO Embassy-1970-Seymour Robbie). A screenplay by Roger Smith. (W).

417   CABARET. (Allied Artists-1972-Bob Fosse). A screenplay by Jay Presson Allen, based on the musical play by Jose Masteroff, Random House, 1967, 115p.; the play I Am a Camera by John Van Druten, Random House, 1952, 182p.; and the book Berlin Stories whose story "Goodbye to Berlin" served as the original source for all the above, New Directions, 1954, 207p. (FF, W, Q, LACOPL).

418   CACTUS FLOWER. (Columbia-1969-Gene Saks). A screenplay by I. A. L. Diamond, based on a play by Abe Burrows, based on a French play Fleur de Cactus by Pierre Barillet and Jean-Pierre Gredy. (W, LC, AMPAS, LACOPL).

419   CACTUS IN THE SNOW. (General Film Corp.-1971-Martin Zweiback). An original screenplay by Martin Zweiback. (W, FF).

420   CAGED VIRGINS. (Boxoffice International-1973-Jean Rollins). No credits available. (W).

421   CAHILL, UNITED STATES MARSHAL. (Warner Bros.-1973-Andrew V. McLaglen). Film based on a screenplay by Harry Julian Fink and Rita M. Fink, from a story by Barney Slater. A novelization based on the screenplay was written by Joe Millard, Cahill; published in 1973 by Award Books, 184p. (LACOPL, W, V).

CALIFORNIA HOLIDAY see SPINOUT

422   CALIFORNIA SPLIT.   (Columbia-1974-Robert Altman).   An
original screenplay by Joseph Walsh.   (V).

423   CALLIOPE.   (Moonstone-1971-Matt Cimber).   An original
script by Beth Keele.   (W).

424   CAMELOT.   (Warner Bros.-7 Arts-1967-Joshua Logan).   A
screenplay by Alan Jay Lerner and Frederick Loewe, Random
House, 1961, 115p.; and the book The Once and Future King
by T. H. White, Putnam, 1958.   (FF, NYTFR, W, AMPAS,
Q, LACOPL).

425   THE CAMERONS.   (1974-Freddie Wilson).   A screenplay by
Patricia Latham, based on the novel Camerons on the Train by
Jane Duncan.   (MFB).

426   CAMILLE 2000.   (Audubon-1969-Radley Metzger).   A screenplay by Michael De Forrest, based on the novel Camille, by
Alexandre Dumas, Heritage Press, 1955.   (FF, W, LACOPL).

427   CAMPER JOHN.   (Cinemation-1973-Sean McGregor).   No credits.   (W).

428   CAN HEIRONYMUS MERKIN EVER FORGET MERCY HUMPPE
AND FIND TRUE HAPPINESS?   (Regional-1969-Anthony New-
ley).   An original screenplay written by Herman Raucher and
Anthony Newley.   (W, FF, AMPAS).

429   CANCEL MY RESERVATION.   (Warner Bros.-1972-Paul Bogart).   A screenplay by Arthur Marx and Robert Fisher, based
on the novel, The Broken Gun by Louis L'Amour; Bantam
Books, 1966, 151p.   (W, LACOPL, Q).

430   THE CANDIDATE.   (Warner Bros.-1972-Michael Ritchie).   An
original screenplay by Jeremy Larner.   (FF, W, Q, V).

431   CANDIDATE FOR MURDER.   (Lester Schoenfeld Films-1968-
David Villiers).   A screen adaptation by Lukas Heller, based
on the story "The Best Laid Plans of a Man in Love" by Edgar
Wallace.   (FF)

432   CANDY.   (Cinerama-1968-Christian Marquand).   A screenplay
by Buck Henry, based on the novel by Terry Southern and Ma-
son Hoffenberg; Putnam, 1964.   (FF, FM, NYTFR, W, AMPAS,
LACOPL, Q).

433   THE CANDY SNATCHERS.   (GFC-1973-Guerdon Trueblood). An
original screenplay by Bryan Gindoff.   (W).

434   CANDY STRIPE NURSES.   (New World-1974-Alan Holleb).   An
original screenplay attributed to Alan Holleb.   (HR).

435   CANNIBAL GIRLS.   (American International-1973-Ivan Reitman).

Robert Sandler wrote this original screenplay. (W).

THE CANNIBALS see THE YEAR OF THE CANNIBALS

436 CANNON FOR CORDOBA. (United Artists-1970-Paul Wendkos).
Stephen Kandel wrote this original screenplay. (W).

437 THE CAPER OF THE GOLDEN BULLS. (Embassy-1967-Rus-
sel Rouse). Ed Waters and David Moessinger wrote the screenplay based on the novel by William P. McGivern; Dodd, 1966.
(FF, NYTFR, FM, W, AMPAS, LACOPL).

438 CAPRICE. (20th Century-Fox-1967-Frank Tashlin). An original story by Martin Hale and Jay Jason served as the inspiration for the screenplay by Jay Jason and Frank Tashlin. (FF,
NYTFR, FM, W, LC, AMPAS, Q).

439 CAPRICIOUS SUMMER. (Sigma III-1968-Jiri Menzel). A
screenplay by Jiri Menzel, based on a novel by Vladislav Van-
cura. (FF, NYTFR, W).

440 CAPTAIN APACHE. (Scotia International-1971-Alexander
Singer). Screenplay by Philip Yordan and Milton Sperling,
based on a novel by S. E. Whitman. (W).

441 CAPTAIN KRONOS: VAMPIRE HUNTER. (Paramount-1974-
Brian Clemens). An original screenplay by Brian Clemens.
(V).

442 CAPTAIN MILKSHAKE. (Twi National-1972-Richard Crawford).
An original screenplay by Richard Crawford and Barry Leicht-
ling. (FF).

443 CAPTAIN NEMO AND THE UNDERWATER CITY. (MGM-1970-
James Hill). A screenplay by Pip and Jane Baker, and R.
Wright Campbell, inspired by the work of Jules Verne. (W).

444 CAPTAIN NEWMAN, M. D. (Universal-1964-David Miller).
Richard L. Breen, Phoebe and Henry Ephron wrote this screenplay which was based on a novel by Leo Rosten; Harpers, 1961,
331p. (FF, AMPAS, LACOPL, NYTFR, W, Q).

445 LES CARABINIERS. (West End-1968-Jean-Luc Godard). A
screenplay by Roberto Rossellini, Jean Gruault and Jean-Luc
Godard, based on a play by Benjamin Joppolo. (FF, NYTFR,
W).

446 CARAVAN TO VACCARES. (20th Century-Fox-1974-Geoffrey
Reeve). A screenplay by Paul Wheeler, based on the novel by
Alistair MacLean; Doubleday, 1970, 259p. (MFB, LACOPL,
V).

447 CAREER BED. (Provocative-1973-Joel M. Reed). An original

work for the screen by Joel M. Reed.   (W).

448   CARESSED.   (Brenner-1965-Laurence L. Kent).   No credit.
(W, LC).

449   THE CAREY TREATMENT.   (MGM-1972-Blake Edwards).   A
screenplay by James P. Bonner, based on the novel A Case of
Need by Jeffrey Hudson aka Michael Crichton; World Publishing
Co., 1968.   (W, Q, FF, LACOPL).

450   CARMEN, BABY.   (Audubon-1967-Radley Metzger).   A screen-
play by Jesse Vogel, based on the story by Prosper Merimee,
Carmen & Other Stories; Ginn, 1907.   (FF, NYTFR, W,
LACOPL).

451   CARNAL KNOWLEDGE.   (AVCO Embassy-1971-Mike Nichols).
An original screenplay written by Jules Feiffer; published by
Farrar, Straus and Giroux, 1971, 118p.   (W, Q, LACOPL).

451a THE CARPETBAGGERS.   (Paramount-1964-Edward Dmytryk).
A screenplay written by John Michael Hayes, based on the novel
by Harold Robbins; Simon & Schuster, 1961, 679p.   (FF,
LACOPL, AMPAS W, NYTFR, Q).

452   CARRY ON CABBY.   (Governor-1967-Gerald Thomas).   A
screenplay by Talbot Rothwell, based on an original story by S.
C. Green and R. M. Hills.   (FF, AMPAS).

453   CARRY ON CAMPING.   (American International-1972-Gerald
Thomas).   An original screenplay by Talbot Rothwell.   (FF,
W, AMPAS).

454   CARRY ON CLEO.   (Governor-1965-Gerald Thomas).   An original screenplay by Talbot Rothwell.   (NYTFR, W, AMPAS).

455   CARRY ON DOCTOR.   (American International-1972-Gerald
Thomas).   An original work for the screen by Talbot Rothwell.
(W, AMPAS).

456   CARRY ON HENRY VIII.   (American International-1972-Gerald
Thomas).   Talbot Rothwell is credited with this original screenplay.   (FF).

457   CARRY ON SPYING.   (Governor-1965-Gerald Thomas).   No
screen writing credit available.   (FF)

457a CARTOUCHE.   (Embassy-1964-Philippe De Broca).   Screenplay
by Daniel Boulanger and Philippe De Broca, with the collaboration of Charles Spaak, and dialogue by Daniel Boulanger.   (FF,
NYTFR, W, Q).

458   CASANOVA '70.   (Embassy-1965-Mario Monicelli).   A screenplay by Furio Scarpelli, Agenore Incrocci and Mario Monicelli,

from an original story by Tonino Guerra.   (NYTFR, W,
AMPAS).

THE CASE OF THE MISSING SWITCHBOARD OPERATOR   see
LOVE AFFAIR

459   THE CASE OF THE NAVES BROTHERS. (Europix Internation-
al-1972-Luiz Sergio Person).   A screenplay by Jean-Claude
Bernadet and Luiz Sergio Person, based on the book O Caso
Dos Irmaos Naves by Joao Alamy Filko.   (FF).

460   CASINO ROYALE.   (Columbia-1967-John Huston, Ken Hughes,
Val Guest, Robert Parrish, and Joe McGrath).   A screenplay
written by Wolf Mankowitz, John Law, and Michael Sayers,
suggested by the novel by Ian Fleming; Macmillan, 1953. (FF,
NYTFR, FM, W, LC, AMPAS, Q, LACOPL).

461   CAST A GIANT SHADOW.   (United Artists-1966-Melville Shavelson).   A screenplay by Melville Shavelson, based on the book
by Ted Berkman; Doubleday, 1962, 321p.   (FF, NYTFR, LC,
W, AMPAS, LACOPL).

462   THE CASTAWAY COWBOY.   (Buena Vista-1974-Vincent Mc-
Eveety).   A screenplay by Don Tait, from a story by Don Tait,
Richard Bluel, and Hugh Benson.   (V).

463   THE CASTLE.   (Continental-1969-Rudolf Noelte).   A screenplay
by Rudolf Noelte, based on the novel by Franz Kafka; Knopf,
1954.   (W, FF, LACOPL).

464   CASTLE KEEP.   (Columbia-1969-Sydney Pollack).   A screenplay by Daniel Taradash and David Rayfiel, based on the novel
by William Eastlake; Simon & Schuster, 1965.   (FF, LC,
AMPAS, LACOPL).

465   CASTLE OF EVIL.   (United Picture Corporation-1967-Francis
D. Lyon).   A screenplay by Charles A. Wallace.   (FF, W).

466   CASTLE OF PURITY.   (Azteca-1974-Arturo Ripstein).   An
original screenplay by Jose E. Pacheco and Arturo Ristein.
(HR).

467   THE CAT.   (Embassy-1966-Ellis Kadison).   A screenplay by
William Redlin and Laird Koenig.   (FF, W, AMPAS).

468   CAT AND MOUSE.   (Evergreen-1970-Hansjurgen Pohland).   A
novel by Gunter Grass, published by Harcourt, Brace & World,
1963, 189p., served as inspiration for the screenplay by Hans-
jurgen Pohland.   (W, LACOPL).

469   THE CAT ATE THE PARAKEET.   (KEP-1972-Phillip Pine).
An original work for the screen by Phillip Pine.   (W).

470   CAT BALLOU. (Columbia-1965-Elliot Silverstein). Walter
      Newman and Frank R. Pierson wrote the screenplay which was
      based on the novel by Roy Chanslor. (NYTFR, LC, W,
      AMPAS, Q).

471   CAT IN THE SACK. (Pathe Contemporary-1967-Gilles Groulx).
      An original screenplay by Gilles Groulx. (NYTFR).

472   CATALINA CAPER. (Crown-International-1968-Lee Sholem).
      A screenplay by Clyde Ware, based on a story by Sam Pierce.
      (FF, W, AMPAS).

473   CATCH MY SOUL. (Cinerama-1974-Patrick McGoohan). A
      screenplay by Jack Good, adapted from Shakespeare's Othello.
      (HR, V).

474   CATCH-22. (Paramount-1970-Mike Nichols). A screenplay by
      Buck Henry, based on a novel by Joseph Heller; Simon &
      Schuster, 1961, 484p. (W, LACOPL, Q, V).

475   CATLOW. (MGM-1971-Sam Wanamaker). A screenplay by
      Scot Finch and J. J. Griffith, from the novel by Louis L'-
      Amour. (W).

476   THE CATS. (National Showmanship-1969-Henning Carlsen). A
      screenplay by Sigyn Sahlin, based on a play by Valentin Chor-
      elle. (FF, W).

477   CAULDRON OF BLOOD. (Cannon-1971-Edward Mann). An
      original screenplay by John Melson and Edward Mann. (W).

478   CAVE OF THE LIVING DEAD. (Trans-Lux-1966-Akos V. Ra-
      tony). An original work for the screen by C. V. Rock. (FF).

479   THE CAVERN. (20th Century-Fox-1965-Edgar G. Ulmer).
      This motion picture was based on an original screenplay by
      Michael Pertwee and Jack Davies. (NYTFR, LC, W).

480   CELEBRATION AT BIG SUR. (20th Century-Fox-1971-). A
      documentary; no script credit. (W).

480a THE CEREMONY. (United Artists-1964-Laurence Harvey).
      Ben Barzman authored the original screenplay, with additional
      dialogue by Laurence Harvey. (W, FF, NYTFR, Q).

481   CESAR AND ROSALIE. (Cinema V-1972-Claude Sautet). An
      original screenplay by Jean-Loup Dabadie and Claude Sautet.
      (W, FF).

482   CHAFED ELBOWS. (Impact-1967-Robert Downey). An origi-
      nal script by Robert Downey inspired the film. (FF, NYTFR,
      W).

483   CHAIN GANG WOMEN.   (Crown International-1972-Lee Frost).
An original screenplay by Lee Frost and Wes Bishop.   (W).

484   THE CHAIRMAN.   (20th Century-Fox-1969-J. Lee Thompson).
Ben Maddow based his screenplay on the novel by Jay Richard
Kennedy; World Publishing Co., 1969, 240p.   (FF, W,
AMPAS, LACOPL).

484a THE CHALK GARDEN.   (Universal-1964-Ronald Neame).   A
screenplay by John Michael Hayes, based on the play by Enid
Bagnold; Random House, 1956, 165p.   (AMPAS, W, FF,
LACOPL, NYTFR, Q).

485   A CHALLENGE FOR ROBIN HOOD.   (20th Century-Fox-1969-
C. M. Pennington-Richards).   An original screenplay by Peter
Bryan.   (Q, FF, W, LC).

486   THE CHALLENGES, A TRILOGY.   (Selmier-1973-Dean Selmi-
er).   An original screenplay by Jose Hernandez Miguel.   (W).

487   LA CHAMADE.   (Lopert-1969-Alain Cavalier).   A screenplay
by François Sagan and Alain Cavalier, based on the novel by
Françoise Sagan; E. P. Dutton 1966, 156p.   (FF, W,
LACOPL).

488   CHAMBER OF HORRORS.   (Warner Bros.-1966-Hy Averback).
A screenplay by Stephen Kandel, based on a story by Ray Russell and Stephen Kandel.   (FF, NYTFR, LC, W, AMPAS).

489   THE CHAMPAGNE MURDERS.   (Universal-1968-Claude Chabrol).   An original story by William Benjamin served as the
basis for the screenplay by Claude Brule, Derek Prouse, and
Paul Gegauff.   (FF, NYTFR, W).

490   CHANDLER.   (MGM-1972-Paul Magwood).   A screenplay by
John Sacret Young, based on a story by Paul Magwood.   (FF).

491   A CHANGE OF HABIT.   (Universal-1969-William Graham).   A
screenplay by James Lee and S. S. Schweitzer, based on a
story by Eric Bercovici, John Joseph, and Richard Morris.
(AMPAS, Q, NYTFR, W).

492   CHANGE OF MIND.   (Cinerama Releasing Corporation-1969-
Robert Stevens).   A screenplay written directly for the screen
by Seeleg Lester and Richard Wesson.   (FF, W, AMPAS).

493   CHANGES.   (Cinerama Releasing Corporation-1969-Hal Bartlett).   An original screenplay by Bill E. Kelly and Hall Bartlett.   (FF, W, AMPAS).

494   CHAPPAQUA.   (Regional-1967-Conrad Rooks).   An original
work for the screen by Conrad Rooks.   (FF, Q, NYTFR,
FM, W, LC, AMPAS).

495 THE CHARGE OF THE LIGHT BRIGADE. (United Artists-1968-Tony Richardson). A screenplay by Charles Wood, partly based on the book The Reason Why by Cecil Woodham Smith, McGraw-Hill, 1953, 287p.; and the poem by Alfred Lord Tennyson, in Poetical Works, Oxford University Press, 1953, 867p. (FF, NYTFR, FM, W, LC, AMPAS, LACOPL).

496 CHARLES, DEAD OR ALIVE. (New Yorker-1972-Alain Tanner). An original screenplay by Alain Tanner. (FF).

497 CHARLEY AND THE ANGEL. (Buena Vista-1973-Vincent McEveety). A screenplay by Roswell Rogers, inspired by The Golden Evenings of Summer by Will Stanton. (W).

498 CHARLEY-ONE-EYE. (Paramount-1973-Don Chaffey). An original screenplay by Keith Leonard. (W).

499 CHARLEY VARRICK. (Universal-1973-John Vernon). A screenplay by Howard Rodman, Dean Riesner, from the novel The Looters by John Reese; Random House, 1968. (W, LACOPL, FF).

500 CHARLIE BUBBLES. (Regional-1968-Albert Finney). An original screenplay by Shelagh Delaney. (FF, NYTFR, FM, W, AMPAS).

501 CHARLIE, THE LONESOME COUGAR. (Buena Vista-1967-Winston Hibler). A screenplay by Jack Spiers, based on a story by Jack Spiers and Winston Hibler. (FF, W, LC, AMPAS).

502 CHARLOTTE'S WEB. (Paramount-1973-Charles A. Nichols and Iwao Takamoto). Screenplay by Earl Hamner Jr., based on the book by E. B. White; Harper and Row, 1952, 184p. (W, LACOPL, V).

503 CHARLY. (Cinerama-1968-Ralph Nelson). A screenplay by Stirling Silliphant, based on a short story and novel, Flowers for Algernon, by Daniel Keyes; Harcourt, Brace & World, 1966, 274p. (FF, NYTFR, FM, W, AMPAS, LACOPL).

504 CHARRO! (National General-1969-Charles Marquis Warren). A screenplay by Charles Marquis Warren, based on a story by Frederic Louis Fox. (FF, W, AMPAS, Q).

505 CHARULATA. (1965-Satyajit Ray). A screenplay by Satyajit Ray, from a story by Rabindranath Tagore. (NYTFR).

506 THE CHASE. (Columbia-1966-Arthur Penn). Lillian Hellman wrote the screenplay which was based on the novel and play by Horton Foote; Rinehart, 1956. (FF, NYTFR, LC, W, AMPAS, LACOPL, Q).

507   CHASTITY. (American International-1969-Alessio De Paola).
      An original screenplay attributed to Sonny Bono. (FF, W,
      AMPAS, Q).

508   CHATO'S LAND. (United Artists-1972-Michael Winner). An
      original screenplay by Gerald Wilson. (W, Q).

509   CHE! (20th Century-Fox-1969-Richard Fleischer). A screen-
      play by Michael Wilson and Sy Bartlett, based on a story by
      Sy Bartlett and David Karp. (FF, W, LC, AMPAS).

510   CHECKMATE. (JER-1973-Lem Amero). An original screen-
      play by LaRue Watts. (W).

511   THE CHEERLEADERS. (Cinemation-1973-Paul Glickler). An
      original work for the screen by Paul Glickler, Tad Richards,
      and Ace Baandige. (W).

512   THE CHELSEA GIRLS. (Film-Makers' Distribution Center-
      1966-Andy Warhol). No writing credits; dialogue improvised.
      (W, FF, AMPAS).

513   CHERRY, HARRY, AND RAQUEL. (Russ Meyer-1969-Russ
      Meyer). A screenplay by Russ Meyer and Tom Wolfe, based
      on a story by Russ Meyer. (W, LC).

513a CHEYENNE AUTUMN. (Warner Bros.-1964-John Ford). A
      screenplay credited to James R. Webb, based on the novel by
      Mari Sandoz; McGraw-Hill, 1953, 282p. (AMPAS, LACOPL,
      FF, NYTFR, Q, W).

514   THE CHEYENNE SOCIAL CLUB. (National General-1970-Gene
      Kelly). An original screenplay by James Lee Barrett. (W).

515   CHILDISH THINGS. (Filmworld-1969-John Derek). An origi-
      nal work for the screen written by Don Murray. (W, AMPAS).

516   CHILDREN OF THE DAMNED. (MGM-1964-Anton M. Leader).
      An original screenplay by John Briley. (FF, NYTFR, W, Q).

517   CHILDREN SHOULDN'T PLAY WITH DEAD THINGS. (Geneni
      Films-1972-Benjamin Clark). An original screenplay by Benja-
      min Clark and Alan Ormsby. (FF).

517a CHILD'S PLAY. (Paramount-1972-Sidney Lumet). A screen-
      play by Leon Prochnik, from a play by Robert Marasco; Ran-
      dom House, 1970, 110p. (W, FF, LACOPL).

518   CHINA IS NEAR. (Royal-1968-Marco Bellocchio). A screen-
      play by Marco Bellocchio and Elda Tattoli, based on a story by
      Marco Bellocchio. Screenplay published by Orion Press; 1969,
      160p. (SCH, LACOPL, NYTFR, FM, W).

519 CHINATOWN. (Paramount-1974-Roman Polanski). An original screenplay by Robert Towne. (V, HR, NYT).

520 THE CHINESE IN PARIS. (Cine Qua Non-1974-Jean Yanne). A screenplay by Jean Yanne, and Gerard Sire, from the book by Robert Beauvais. (V).

521 LA CHINOISE. (Leacock Pennebaker-1968-Jean-Luc Godard). An original screenplay written directly for the screen by Jean-Luc Godard. (FF, NYTFR, W).

522 CHISUM. (Warner Bros.-1970-Andrew V. McLaglen). An original screenplay by Andrew J. Fenady. (W).

523 CHITTY CHITTY BANG BANG. (United Artists-1968-Ken Hughes). A screenplay by Roald Dahl and Ken Hughes, based on a collection of stories by Ian Fleming; Scholastic Book Services, 1964, 155p. (FF, NYTFR, W, LC, AMPAS, LACOPL, Q).

524 CHLOE IN THE AFTERNOON. (Columbia-1972-Eric Rohmer). An original screenplay by Eric Rohmer. (W).

525 CHOSEN SURVIVORS. (Columbia-1974-Sutton Roley). A screenplay by H. B. Cross and Joe Reb Moffly, based on a story by H. B. Cross. (V).

526 CHRISTA. (American International-1971-Jack O'Connell). An original screenplay by Jack O'Connell. (W).

527 THE CHRISTIAN LICORICE STORE. (National General-1971-James Frawley). An original screenplay by Floyd Mutrux. (W).

528 THE CHRISTINE JORGENSEN STORY. (United Artists-1970-Irving Rapper). A screenplay by Robert E. Kent and Ellis St. Joseph, based on the book by Christine Jorgensen; Eriksson, 1967, 332p. (W, LACOPL).

529 THE CHRISTMAS KID. (Producers Releasing Organization-1967-Sidney Pink). A screenplay by Jim Henaghan and R. Rivero. (FF, W).

530 THE CHRISTMAS THAT ALMOST WASN'T. (Childhood-1966-Rossano Brazzi). The screenplay and original story is attributed to Paul Tripp. (FF, W, AMPAS, Q).

531 THE CHRISTMAS TREE. (Continental-1969-Terence Young). A screenplay by Terence Young, based on the novel by Michel Bataille; Morrow, 1969, 255p. (FF, W, AMPAS, LACOPL, Q).

532 CHROME AND HOT LEATHER. (American International-1972-Lee Frost). A screenplay by Michael Allen Haynes, David Neibel

and Don Tait, based on a story by Michael Allen Haynes and
David Neibel. (FF, W).

533 CHRONICLE OF A SUMMER. (Pathe Contemporary-1965-Jean
Rouch & Edgar Morin). A documentary; no script credit. (W).

534 CHUBASCO. (Warner Bros.-7 Arts-1969-Allen H. Miner). A
screenplay written directly for the screen by Allen H. Miner.
(FF, LC, AMPAS, Q).

535 CHUKA. (Paramount-1967-Gordon Douglas). A screenplay by
Richard Jessup, based on his novel. (FF, NYTFR, FM, W,
LC, AMPAS, Q).

536 CIAO! MANHATTAN. (Maron-1973-John Palmer & David
Weisman). Written by John Palmer and David Weisman. (W).

537 THE CINCINNATI KID. (MGM-1965-Norman Jewison). A
screenplay by Ring Lardner, Jr., and Terry Southern, based
on the novel by Richard Jessup; Little, Brown & Co., 1963.
(NYTFR, LC, W, AMPAS, LACOPL, Q).

538 CINDERELLA LIBERTY. (20th Century-Fox-1973-Mark Rydell).
A screenplay by Darryl Ponicsan, based on his novel of the
same title; Harper & Row, 1973, 179p. (W, LACOPL, V,
HR).

539 CINERAMA'S RUSSIAN ADVENTURE. (United Roadshow Pre-
sentations-1966-Leonid Kristy, Roman Karmen, Boris Dolin,
Oleg Lebedev, Solomon Kogan, and Vassily Katanian). Narration written by Homer McCoy. (NYTFR, W, AMPAS).

540 CIRCLE OF LOVE. (Walter Reade/Sterling-1965-Roger Vadim). A screenplay by Jean Anouilh, based on the play by
Arthur Schnitzler, La Ronde (Merry Go-Round); Weidenfeld
and Nicolson, 1953, 90p. (FF, W, AMPAS, LACOPL, Q).

540a CIRCUS WORLD. (Paramount-1964-Henry Hathaway). Screenplay attributed to Ben Hecht and Julian Halevy, from an original story by Philip Yordan. (NYTFR, FF, W, Q, AMPAS).

541 CISCO PIKE. (Columbia-1972-Bill L. Norton). A screenplay
written directly for the screen by Bill L. Norton. (FF, Q).

542 CITY OF FEAR. (Allied Artists-1965-Peter Bezencenet). An
original screenplay by Peter Welbeck. (W, AMPAS, Q).

543 CLAIRE'S KNEE. (Columbia-1971-Eric Rohmer). An original
screenplay by Eric Rohmer; Simon & Schuster, 1972. (W,
LACOPL, Q).

544 CLAMBAKE. (United Artists-1967-Arthur H. Nadel). A
screenplay by Arthur Browne, Jr., based on his original story.

(FF, NYTFR, FM, W, LC, AMPAS, Q).

545   CLARENCE THE CROSS-EYED LION. (MGM-1965-Andrew
Marton). A screenplay by Alan Caillou, from a story by Art
Arthur and Marshall Thompson. (NYTFR, LC, W, AMPAS).

CLASH BY NIGHT see ESCAPE BY NIGHT

546   CLASS OF '44. (Warner Bros.-1973-Paul Bogart). Screenplay by Herman Raucher; novelization by Madeleine Shaner
based on the screenplay and published by Warner Paperback
Library, 1973, 255p. (W, LACOPL, Q).

547   THE CLASS OF '74. (Crest-1972-Arthur Marks and Mack
Bing). No screenplay credits given. (FF).

548   CLAUDINE. (20th Century-Fox-1974-John Berry). An original screenplay by Tina and Lester Pine. (HR, V).

549   CLAY PIGEON. (MGM-1971-Tom Stern and Lane Slate). A
screenplay by Ronald Buck, Buddy Ruskin, and Jack Gross,
Jr., based on a story by Buddy Ruskin and Jack Gross, Jr.
(FF, W, Q).

550   CLEOPATRA JONES. (Warner Bros.-1973-Jack Starrett). A
screenplay written by Max Julien, Sheldon Keller, from a story
by Max Julien. (W, Q).

551   THE CLIMAX. (Lopert-1967-Pietro Germi). Screenplay and
story by Pietro Germi, Alfredo Giannetti, Tullio Pinelli, and
Carlo Bernari. (FF, NYTFR, W, AMPAS, Q).

552   CLIMAX. (Sherpix-1971-Jack Genaro). A screenplay by Jack
Genaro, Rick Beaty, from a story by Cal Dunn. (W).

553   A CLOCKWORK ORANGE. (Warner Bros.-1971-Stanley Kubrick). A screenplay by Stanley Kubrick, based on the novel
by Anthony Burgess; Modern Library, 1968, 436p. The screenplay by Mr. Kubrick was also published. (FF, W, LACOPL,
V, HR, Q).

554   THE CLONES. (Filmmakers International-1973-Paul Hunt &
Lumar Card). An original screenplay by Steve Fisher. (W).

555   CLOPORTES. (International Classics-1966-Pierre Granier-
Deferre). Albert Simonin and Michel Audiard wrote the screen-
play, based on a novel by Alphonse Boudard. (FF, NYTFR,
LC, W, Q).

556   CLOSELY WATCHED TRAINS. (Sigma III-1967-Jiri Menzel).
A screenplay by Bohumil Hrabel and Jiri Menzel, based on a
story by Bohumil Hrabel. Screenplay published by Simon &
Schuster; 1971, 144p. (FF, NYTFR, AMPAS, LACOPL, Q).

557   CLOUDS OVER ISRAEL.   (1966-Ivan Lengyel).   A screenplay
      by Moshe Hadar and Ivan Lengyel, based on a story "Sinaia"
      by Moshe Hadar and Ivan Lengyel.   (NYTFR, W, AMPAS, Q).

558   THE CLOWNS.   (Levitt-Pickman-1971-Federico Fellini).   An
      original screenplay by Federico Fellini and Bernardino Zapponi.
      (W, Q).

559   CLUE OF THE TWISTED CANDLE.   (Lester Schoenfeld-1968-
      Allan Davis).   A screenplay by Philip Mackie, based on the
      novel by Edgar Wallace.   (FF).

560   C'MON, LET'S LIVE A LITTLE.   (Paramount-1967-David But-
      ler).   An original screenplay by June Starr.   (FF, NYTFR,
      FM, W, AMPAS, Q).

561   COAST OF SKELETONS.   (7 Arts-1965-Robert Lynn).   A
      screenplay by Anthony Scott Veitch, based on the novel
      Sanders of the River by Edgar Wallace.   (NYTFR, W, Q).

562   THE COBRA.   (American International-1968-Mario Sequi).   A
      screenplay by Cumersindo Mollo, based on a story by Adriano
      Bolzoni.   (FF, NYTFR, FM, W, LC, Q).

563   THE COCKEYED COWBOYS OF CALICO COUNTY.   (Universal-
      1970-Tony Leader).   An original screenplay by Ranald Mac-
      Dougall.   (W, Q).

564   CODE NAME TRIXIE.   (Cambist-1973-George Romero).   No
      credits.   (W).

565   CODE 7 VICTIM 5.   (Universal-1965-Robert Lynn).   An origi-
      nal screenplay by Peter Yeldham from a story by Peter Wel-
      beck.   (W, LC, AMPAS, Q).

566   COFFY.   (American International-1973-Jack Hill).   An original
      screenplay by Jack Hill.   (W).

567   COLD SWEAT.   (Emerson Film Enterprises-1974-Terence
      Young).   Shimon Wincelberg and Albert Simonin wrote the
      screenplay, from a novel by Richard Matheson.   (HR).

568   COLD TURKEY.   (United Artists-1971-Norman Lear).   A
      screenplay by Norman Lear, based on a story by William Price
      Fox, Jr., and Norman Lear.   (W).

569   THE COLLECTOR.   (Columbia-1965-William Wyler).   Stanley
      Mann and John Kohn authored the screenplay, based on the nov-
      el by John Fowles; Little, Brown & Co., 1963, 305p. (NYTFR,
      LC, W, AMPAS, LACOPL, Q).

570   COLOR ME DEAD.   (Commonwealth-1969-Eddie Davis).
      Screenplay originally written for the screen by Russell Rouse

and Clarence Greene. (W, Q).

571   COME BACK BABY. (Film-Makers' Distribution Center-1968-
David Allan Greene). An original screenplay by David Allan
Greene. (FF, NYTFR, W).

572   COME BACK CHARLESTON BLUE. (Warner Bros.-1972-
Mark Warren). A screenplay by Bontche Schweig and Peggy
Elliott, based on the novel The Heat's On by Chester Himes;
Putnam, 1966, 220p. (Q, FF, W, LACOPL).

573   COME HAVE COFFEE WITH US. (Altura-1973-Alberto Lattuada). A screenplay by Tulio Kezich, Alberto Lattuada, Adriano Baroco, and Piero Chiara, based on a novel by Piero
Chiara. (W).

574   COME HOME AND MEET MY WIFE. (Fida-1974-Mario Monicelli). A screenplay by Age, Scarpelli, and Mario Monicelli.
(V).

COME PLAY WITH ME see GRAZIE, ZIA

575   COME SPY WITH ME. (20th Century-Fox-1967-Marshal Stone).
A screenplay by Cherney Berg, based on an original story by
Stuart James. (FF, W, LC, AMPAS, Q).

576   THE COMEDIANS. (MGM-1967-Peter Glenville). A screenplay by Graham Greene, based on his novel; Viking Press,
1966, 309p. (Q, FF, NYTFR, FM, W, LC, AMPAS,
LACOPL).

576a THE COMEDY OF TERRORS. (American International-1964-
Jacques Tourneur). An original screenplay by Richard Matheson. (FF, NYTFR, W, Q).

577   COMETOGETHER. (Allied Artists-1971-Saul Swimmer). An
original screenplay by Saul Swimmer & Tony Anthony. (W).

578   THE COMIC. (Columbia-1969-Carl Reiner). An original
screenplay by Carl Reiner and Aaron Ruben. (W, Q, AMPAS).

579   COMING APART. (Kaleidoscope-1969-Milton Moses Ginsberg).
An original screenplay by Milton Moses Ginsberg; Lancer
Books, 1969, 208p. (Q, W, SCH).

579a COMMANDO. (American International-1964-Frank Wisbar).
This screenplay was written by Giuseppe Mangione, Nino Guerrini, William Demby, Frank Wisbar, and Enrico Bercovic,
and was based on a story by Arturo Tofanelli. (FF).

COMMON LAW CABIN see HOW MUCH LOVING DOES A
NORMAL COUPLE NEED?

580   COMPAÑEROS. (Cinerama-1972-Sergio Corbucci). A screenplay by Dino Maiuri, Massimo de Rita, Fritz Ebert, Sergio
Corbucci, based on an idea by Sergio Corbucci. (FF, Q).

581   COMPANY OF KILLERS. (Universal-1972-Jerry Thorpe).
An original screenplay by E. Jack Neuman. (W, Q).

582   THE COMPUTER WORE TENNIS SHOES. (Buena Vista-1970-
Robert Butler). An original screenplay by Joseph L. Mc-
Eveety. (W, Q).

583   THE CONCERT FOR BANGLADESH. (20th Century-Fox-1972-
Saul Swimmer). A documentary; commentary by Saul Swimmer.
(FF, Q, W).

584   THE CONCUBINES. (Boxoffice International-1969-Kohji Taka-
matsu). Screenplay written by Jiku Yamatoya. (W).

585   EL CONDOR. (National General-1970-John Guillermin). A
screenplay by Larry Cohen and Steven Carabatsos, from a
story by Steven Carabatsos. (W, Q).

586   THE CONFESSION. (Paramount-1970-Costa-Gavras). Adaptation and screenplay by Jorge Semprun, based on a story by
Lise and Artur London. (W, Q).

587   CONFESSIONS OF A WINDOW CLEANER. (Columbia-1974-
Val Guest). A screenplay by Christopher Wood and Val Guest,
based on a book by Timothy Lea. (V).

588   THE CONFORMIST. (Paramount-1971-Bernardo Bertolucci).
A screenplay by Bernardo Bertolucci, based on the novel by
Alberto Moravia. (W, Q).

589   CONQUERED CITY. (American International-1966-Joseph Anthony). No screen credit available. (W, LC, Q).

590   THE CONQUEROR WORM. (American International-1968-
Michael Reeves). A screenplay by Michael Reeves and Tom
Baker, based on the novel Witchfinder General by Ronald Bas-
sett and a poem by Edgar Allan Poe. (FF, NYTFR, FM, W,
LC, AMPAS, Q).

591   THE CONQUEST OF THE PLANET OF THE APES. (20th
Century-Fox-1972-J. Lee Thompson). Screenplay by Paul
Dehn, based on characters created by Pierre Boulle. (FF,
Q).

592   CONRACK. (20th Century-Fox-1974-Martin Ritt). A screen-
play by Irving Ravetch, Harriet Frank Jr., based on the book
The Water Is Wide by Pat Conroy; Houghton, 1972, 306p. (HR,
LACOPL, V).

593 CONTEST GIRL. (Continental-1966-Val Guest). An original
     screenplay by Val Guest and Robert Muller. (W, Q).

594 THE CONVERSATION. (Paramount-1974-Francis Ford Cop-
     pola). An original screen work by Francis Ford Coppola.
     (HR, V).

595 CONVICT STAGE. (20th Century-Fox-1965-Lesley Selander).
     A screenplay by Daniel Mainwaring, from a story by Donald
     Barry. (W, LC, Q, AMPAS).

596 COOGAN'S BLUFF. (Universal-1968-Donald Siegel). A screen-
     play by Herman Miller, Dean Reisner and Howard Rodman,
     based on a story by Herman Miller. (FF, NYTFR, W, LC,
     AMPAS, Q).

597 COOL BREEZE. (MGM-1972-Barry Pollack). A screenplay
     by Barry Pollack, based on the novel The Asphalt Jungle by
     W. R. Burnett; Pocket Books, 1949, 247p. (FF, W, LACOPL,
     Q).

598 COOL HAND LUKE. (Warner Bros.-7 Arts-1967-Stuart Ros-
     enberg). Screenplay by Donn Pearce and Frank R. Pierson,
     based on the novel by Donn Pearce; Scribner, 1965. (FF,
     NYTFR, FM, W, LC, Q, AMPAS).

599 THE COOL ONES. (Warner Bros.-1967-Gene Nelson). Joyce
     Geller wrote the screenplay, from an adaptation by Gene Nel-
     son and Bob Kaufman, based on a story by Joyce Geller. (FF,
     Q, NYTFR, FM, W, LC, AMPAS).

599a THE COOL WORLD. (Cinema V-1964-Shirley Clarke). A
     screenplay written by Shirley Clarke and Carl Lee, based on
     the novel of the same name by Warren Miller; Little, Brown
     & Co., 1959, and the play The Cool World by Warren Miller
     and Robert Rossen. (FF, W, LACOPL, NYTFR, Q, AMPAS).

600 THE COP. (Audubon-1971-Yves Boisset). An original screen-
     play by Claude Veillot and Yves Boisset. (W, Q).

601 COP-OUT. (Cinerama-1968-Pierre Rouve). A screenplay
     written by Pierre Rouve, based on the novel Les Inconnus dans
     la Maison (The Stranger in the House) by Georges Simenon,
     1954. (FF, Q, W, AMPAS, LACOPL).

602 COPS AND ROBBERS. (United Artists-1973-Aram Avakian).
     A original screenplay by Donald E. Westlake based on his
     book; Evans, 1972, 286p. (W, LACOPL).

603 CORKY. (MGM-1972-Leonard Horn). An original screenplay
     by Eugene Price. (W).

604 CORPORATE QUEEN. (Victoria-1969-John and Lem Amero).

An original screenplay by John and Lem Amero. (W).

605   THE CORPSE GRINDERS. (Gemini-1972-Ted V. Mikels).
      Arch Hall and Joseph L. Cranston wrote this original screen-
      play. (FF).

606   THE CORRUPT ONES. (Warner Bros.-1967-James Hill). A
      work for the screen by Brian Clemens, based on a story by
      Ladislaw Fodor. (AMPAS, FF, FM, LC, NYTFR, Q, W).

607   CORRUPTION. (Columbia-1968-Robert Hartford-Davis). An
      original screenplay by Donald Ford and Derek Ford. (FF,
      FM, LC, NYTFR, Q, W).

608   COTTON COMES TO HARLEM. (United Artists-1969-Ossie
      Davis). A screenplay by Arnold Perl and Ossie Davis, based
      on a novel by Chester Himes; Putnam, 1965. (W, Q,
      LACOPL).

609   COTTONPICKIN' CHICKENPICKERS. (Southern Musical Pro-
      ductions-1967-Larry E. Jackson). A screenplay by Bob Baron
      and Larry E. Jackson. (FF).

610   COULD I BUT LIVE. (Toho-1965-Zenzo Matsuyama). An
      original screenplay by Zenzo Matsuyama. (W).

611   COUNT DRACULA. (Crystal Pictures-1972-Jesus Franco). A
      screenplay by Peter Welbeck, Augusto Finochi and Jesus Fran-
      co, based on the novel Dracula by Bram Stoker; Dodd, 1970,
      430p. (FF, LACOPL).

612   COUNT YORGA, VAMPIRE. (American International-1970-
      Bob Kelljan). An original screenplay by Bob Kelljan. (Q, W).

613   COUNTDOWN. (Warner Bros.-7 Arts-1968-Robert Altman).
      A screenplay by Loring Mandel, based on the novel The Pil-
      grim Project by Hank Searls; McGraw-Hill, 1964, 274p. (FF,
      W, NYTFR, FM, LC, AMPAS, LACOPL).

614   THE COUNTERFEIT CONSTABLE. (7 Arts-1966-Robert Dhery).
      An original screenplay by Robert Dhery and Pierre Tchernia.
      (FF, NYTFR, W, Q).

615   THE COUNTERFEIT KILLER. (Universal-1968-Josef Leytes).
      A screenplay by Harold Clements and Steven Bochco based on
      the television production The Faceless Man. (FF, W, AMPAS,
      Q).

616   COUNTERPOINT. (Universal-1968-Ralph Nelson). A screen-
      play by James Lee and Joel Oliansky, based on the novel The
      General by Alan Sillitoe; Knopf, 1960. (FF, NYTFR, FM, W,
      LC, AMPAS, LACOPL).

617 COUNTESS DRACULA. (20th Century-Fox-1972-Peter Sasdy).
A screenplay by Jeremy Paul, based on a story by Alexander
Paul and Peter Sasdy, and an idea by Gabriel Ronay. (FF,
Q).

618 A COUNTESS FROM HONG KONG. (Universal-1967-Charles
Chaplin). An original screenplay by Charles Chaplin. (FF
NYTFR, FM, W, LC, AMPAS, Q).

619 COUNTRY CUZZINS. (Boxoffice International-1972-Bethel G.
Buckalew). An original screenplay by Bethel G. Buckalew.
(FF).

620 A COVENANT WITH DEATH. (Warner Bros.-1967-Lamont
Johnson). A screenplay by Larry Marcus and Saul Levitt,
based upon the novel by Stephen Becker; Atheneum, 1964, 240p.
(FF, NYTFR, Q, FM, LC, W, AMPAS, LACOPL).

621 COVER ME BABE. (20th Century Fox-1970-Noel Black). An
original screenplay by George Wells. (W, Q).

622 THE COWARDS. (Jaylo-1970-Simon Nuchtern). A screenplay
written directly for the screen by Simon Nuchtern. (W)

623 THE COWBOYS. (Warner Bros.-1972-Mark Rydell). A screen-
play by Irving Ravetch, Harriet Frank, Jr., and William Dale
Jennings, based on the novel by William Dale Jennings; Stein
& Day, 1971, 242p. (FF, LACOPL, Q).

624 CRACK IN THE WORLD. (Paramount-1965-Andrew Marton).
An original screenplay by John Marchip White and Julian Halevy. (NYTFR, LC, W, AMPAS, Q).

625 CRAZE. (Warner Bros.-1974-Freddie Francis). A screenplay
by Aben Kandel and Herman Cohen, based on the novel Infernal
Idol by Henry Seymour. (V).

625a CRAZY DESIRE. (Embassy-1964-Luciano Salce). A screenplay
by Luciano Salce, Franco Castellano, and Giuseppe Moccia,
based on the short story "A Girl Named Francesca" by Enrico
Stella. (FF, NYTFR, W, Q).

626 CRAZY JOE. (Columbia-1974-Carlo Lizzani). An original
screenplay by Lewis Carlino. (HR).

627 CRAZY PARADISE. (Sherpix-1965-Gabriel Axel). A screenplay by Gabriel Axel, from a novel by Ole Jule. (NYTFR, W,
Q).

628 CRAZY QUILT. (Continental-1966-John Korty). A screenplay
by John Korty, based on the novel The Illusionless Man and
the Visionary Maid by Allen Wheelis; W. W. Norton, 1966,
206p. (FF, NYTFR, W, AMPAS, LACOPL, Q).

629 THE CRAZY WORLD OF JULIUS VROODER. (20th Century-
Fox-1974-Arthur Hiller). Daryl Henry wrote the screenplay;
a novelization by Ruth Wolff, based on the screenplay, was
published by Dell Publishing Co.; 1974, 173p. (V, HR,
LACOPL).

630 THE CRAZY WORLD OF LAUREL AND HARDY. (Joseph
Brenner Associates-1967-). Scenario by Bill Scott. (FF, W,
AMPAS).

631 LES CREATURES. (New Yorker-1969-Agnes Varda). A work
for the screen by Agnes Varda. (W).

632 THE CREEPING FLESH. (Columbia-1973-Freddie Francis).
An original screenplay by Peter Spenceley and Jonathan Rum-
bold. (W, Q).

633 CRESCENDO. (Warner Bros.-1972-Alan Gibson). A screenplay by Jimmy Sangster and Alfred Shaughnessy. (W, FF, Q).

634 CRIES AND WHISPERS. (New World-1972-Ingmar Bergman).
An original screenplay by Ingmar Bergman. (W, FF, Q).

634a THE CRIMSON BLADE. (Columbia-1964-John Gilling). An
original work for the screen authored by John Gilling. (FF,
W, Q).

635 THE CRIMSON CULT. (American International-1970-Vernon
Sewell). An original screenplay by Mervyn Haisman and Henry
Lincoln. (W, Q).

636 CROMWELL. (Columbia-1970-Ken Hughes). An original
screenplay by Ken Hughes. (W, Q).

637 THE CROOK. (United Artists-1971-Claude Lelouch). An original screenplay attributed to Claude Lelouch, Pierre Uytterhoe-
ven, and Claude Pinoteau. (W, Q).

638 THE CROOKED ROAD. (7 Arts-1965-Don Chaffey). A screenplay by J. Garrison, based on the novel by Morris L. West.
(FF, W, AMPAS).

639 THE CROSS AND THE SWITCHBLADE. (Gateway-1972-Don
Murray). Don Murray and James Bonnet wrote the screenplay,
based on the book by David Wilkerson and John and Elizabeth
Sherrill; Bernard Geis, 1963, 217p. (FF, W, LACOPL, Q).

640 CRUCIBLE OF HORROR. (Cannon-1971-Viktors Ritelis). An
original screenplay by Olaf Pooley. (W).

641 THE CRUCIFIED LOVERS. (New Line Cinema-1971-Kenji
Mizoguchi). A screenplay by Yoshikota Yoda and Matsutaro
Kwaguchi, after a Kabuki drama. (W).

642   CRUNCH. (American International-1970-Marran Gosov).   No
       screenplay credit available.   (W, Q).

643   CRY OF THE BANSHEE. (American International-1970-Gordon
       Hessler).   A screenplay by Tim Kelly and Christopher Wicking.
       (W, Q).

644   CRYPT OF THE LIVING DEAD. (Atlas-1973-Ray Danton).   A
       screenplay by Lou Shaw, from a story by Lois Gibson.   (W).

645   CUL-DE-SAC. (Sigma III-1966-Roman Polanski).   An original
       screenplay by Roman Polanski and Gerard Brach.   (FF,
       NYTFR, W, AMPAS, Q).

646   THE CULPEPPER CATTLE COMPANY.   (20th Century-Fox-
       1972-Dick Richards).   A screenplay by Eric Bercovici and
       Gregory Prentiss, from a story by Dick Richards.   (W, Q).

647   CULT OF THE DAMNED.   (American International-1969-
       Robert Thom).   A screenplay by Robert Thom.   (W, Q).

648   THE CURSE OF THE FLY.   (20th Century-Fox-1966-Don
       Sharp).   A screenplay by Harry Spalding.   (FF, LC, W,
       AMPAS, Q).

648a   THE CURSE OF THE LIVING CORPSE.   (20th Century-Fox-
       1964-Del Tenney).   An original screenplay by Del Tenney.
       (FF, NYTFR, Q, W).

649   THE CURSE OF THE MUMMY'S TOMB.   (Columbia-1965-Mi-
       chael Carreras).   A screenplay written by Henry Younger.
       (W, LC, Q).

650   CURSE OF THE VAMPIRES.   (Marvin-1971-Gerardo De Leon).
       A screenplay by Ben Feleo, Pierre L. Salas, based on a story
       by Ben Feleo.   (W).

651   CURSE OF THE VOODOO.   (Allied Artists-1966-).   A screen-
       play by Tony O'Grady, with additional scenes and dialogue by
       Leigh Vance.   (W, AMPAS).

652   CUSTER OF THE WEST.   (Cinerama-1968-Robert Siodmak).
       A screenplay written by Bernard Gordon and Julian Halevy.
       (FF, NYTFR, W, AMPAS, Q).

653   CYCLE SAVAGES.   (Trans American-1970-Bill Brame).   A
       screenplay authored by Bill Brame.   (W, Q).

654   CYCLES SOUTH.   (DAL Arts-1971-Don Marshall).   An origi-
       nal screenplay by Patrick McNamara.   (W).

655   DADDY'S GONE A-HUNTING.   (National General-1969-Mark
       Robson).   A screenplay by Larry Cohen and Lorenzo Semple,

Jr.; novelization based on the screenplay written by Mike St.
Clair, Bantam Books, 1969, 153p. (FF, W, AMPAS,
LACOPL, Q).

DAGGERS OF BLOOD see INVASION 1700

656 DAGMAR'S HOT PANTS, INC.   (Trans American-1972-Vernon
P. Becker). A screenplay by Vernon P. Becker and Louis M.
Heyward. (FF, Q).

657 DAISIES. (Sigma III-1967-Vera Chytilova). A screenplay by
Vera Chytilova, Ester Krumbachova, from a story by Vera
Chytilova and Ester Krumbachova. (W).

658 DAISY MILLER. (Paramount-1974-Peter Bogdanovich). A
screenplay by Frederic Raphael, from the story by Henry
James, in The Henry James Reader, 1965, Scribner; 626p.
(V, LACOPL).

659 DALEKS--INVASION EARTH 2150 A.D.   (Continental-1968-
Gordon Flemyng). A screenplay by Milton Subotsky, based on
the BBC Television serial by Terry Nation. (FF).

660 THE DAMNED. (Warner Bros.-7 Arts-1969-Luchino Visconti).
A screenplay written directly for the screen by Nicola Bada-
lucco, Enrico Medioli, and Luchino Visconti. (W, AMPAS,
Q).

661 A DANDY IN ASPIC. (Columbia-1968-Anthony Mann). A
screenplay by Derek Marlowe, based on his novel; Putnam,
1966. (Q, FF, NYTFR, FM, W, LC, AMPAS, LACOPL).

662 DANGER: DIABOLIK. (Paramount-1968-Mario Bava). A
screenplay by Dino Maiuri, Adriano Baracco, and Mario Bava,
based on the illustrated feature of Angela and Luciana Gius-
sani. (FF, W, LC, Q).

663 DAREDEVIL IN THE CASTLE. (Frank Lee International-
1969-Hiroshi Inagaki). A screenplay by Hiroshi Inagaki and
Takeshi Kimura, based on an original story by Genzo Murakami. (FF, W).

664 THE DARING DOBERMANS. (Dimension-1973-Byron Ross
Chudnow). No screenplay credit available. (W).

665 DARING GAME. (Paramount-1968-Laslo Benedek). A screenplay by Andy White, based on a story by Art Arthur and Andy
White. (FF, W, AMPAS, Q).

666 DARK DREAMS. (213 Releasing Organization-1971-Roger
Guermontes). An original screenplay by Canidia Ference. (W).

667 DARK INTRUDER. (Universal-1965-Harvey Hart). An origi-

nal screenplay by Barre Lyndon. (NYTFR, LC, W, AMPAS, Q).

668   DARK OF THE SUN. (MGM-1968-Jack Cardiff). A screenplay by Quentin Werty aka Ranald MacDougall, and Adrian Spies, based on the novel Train from Katanga, by Wilbur A. Smith; Viking, 1965, 280p. (Q, FF, NYTFR, FM, W, LC, AMPAS, LACOPL).

669   DARK PLACES. (Cinerama-1974-Don Sharp). An original screenplay written by Ed Brennan and Joseph Van Winkle. (V).

669a   DARK PURPOSE. (Universal-1964-George Marshall). A screenplay by David P. Harmon and Massimo D'Avack, based on the novel by Doris Hume Kilburn. (FF, NYTFR, W, Q, AMPAS).

670   THE DARK SIDE OF TOMORROW. (Able-1970-Barbara Peeters & Jacques Beerson). A screenplay by Barbara Peeters, from a story by Jacques Beerson. (W).

671   DARK STAR. (Jack H. Harris-1974-John Carpenter). A screenplay by John Carpenter and Dan O'Bannon; novelization based on the screenplay written by Alan Dean Foster, published by Ballantine Books; 1974, 183p. (V, LACOPL).

672   DARKER THAN AMBER. (National General-1970-Robert Clouse). A screenplay by Ed Waters, from a novel by John D. MacDonald; Lippincott, 1966, 207p. (W, LACOPL, Q).

673   DARLING. (Embassy-1965-John Schlessinger). A screenplay written directly from the screen by Frederic Raphael. (NYTFR, W, AMPAS, Q).

674   DARLING LILI. (Paramount-1970-Blake Edwards). A screenplay by Blake Edwards and William Peter Blatty. (W, Q).

675   THE DARWIN ADVENTURE. (20th Century-Fox-1972-Jack Couffer). A screenplay by William Fairchild, from a story by Jack Couffer, Robert Crandall, and Ken Middleman. (W, FF, Q).

676   DAUGHTERS OF DARKNESS. (Gemini-Maron-1971-Harry Kumel). An original screenplay by Pierre Drouot and Harry Kumel. (W, Q).

677   DAUGHTERS OF SATAN. (United Artists-1972-Hollingsworth Morse). A screenplay by John C. Higgins, based on a story by John Bushelman. (W, FF, Q).

677a   THE DAY AND THE HOUR. (MGM-1964-Rene Clement). A screenplay written by Rene Clement and Roger Vailland, based on a story by Andre Barret. (FF, NYTFR, Q).

678   DAY FOR NIGHT. (Warner Bros.-1973-François Truffaut).
      An original screenplay by François Truffaut, Jean-Louis Rich-
      ard, and Suzanne Schiffman. (W).

679   A DAY IN COURT. (Ultra-1965-Steno). A screenplay by
      Lucio Fulci, Alberto Sordi, and Alessanoro Continenza, based
      on an idea by Lucio Fulci. (W).

680   A DAY IN THE DEATH OF JOE EGG. (Columbia-1972-Peter
      Medak). A screenplay by Peter Nichols, based on his play;
      Grove Press, 1967, 87 p. (W, LACOPL, FF, Q).

681   DAY OF ANGER. (National General-1970-Tonino Valerii).
      Story and screenplay by Ernesto Gastaldi, Tonino Valerii,
      Renzo Genta, based on the novel Der Tod ritt Dienstags by
      Ron Barker. (W, Q).

682   THE DAY OF THE DOLPHIN. (AVCO Embassy-1973-Mike
      Nichols). Screenplay by Buck Henry from the novel by Robert
      Merle; Simon & Schuster, 1969. (W).

683   DAY OF THE EVIL GUN. (MGM-1968-Jerry Thorpe). A
      screenplay by Charles Marquis Warren and Eric Bercovici,
      based on a story by Charles Marquis Warren. (FF, NYTFR,
      FM, W, LC, AMPAS).

684   THE DAY OF THE JACKAL. (Universal-1973-Fred Zinne-
      mann). A screenplay attributed to Kenneth Ross, from the
      book by Frederick Forsyth; Viking Press, 1971, 380p. (W,
      LACOPL).

685   THE DAY THE FISH CAME OUT. (International Classics-
      1967-Michael Cacoyannis). A screenplay by Michael Cacoyan-
      nis. (FF, NYTFR, FM, W, AMPAS, Q).

686   THE DAY THE SUN ROSE. (Shochiku-1973-Tetsuya Yama-
      nouchi). A screenplay by Hisayuki Suzuki and Kunio Shimizu.
      (W).

687   THE DAYDREAMER. (Embassy-1966-Jules Bass). A screen-
      play by Arthur Rankin, Jr., based on four tales--"The Little
      Mermaid," "The Emperor's New Clothes," "Thumbelina," and
      the "Garden of Paradise" by Hans Christian Andersen; in Com-
      plete Andersen, Heritage Press, 1949, 430p. (FF, W,
      AMPAS, LACOPL, Q).

688   DAYS AND NIGHTS IN THE FOREST. (Pathe Contemporary-
      1973-Satyajit Ray). A screenplay by Satyajit Ray, from a nov-
      el by Sunil Ganguly. (W).

689   DAYTON'S DEVILS. (Commonwealth United Entertainment-
      1968-Jack Shea). A screenplay by Fred De Gorter. (FF, FM,
      NYTFR, W, Q).

690   DE SADE. (American International-1969-Cy Enfield).   A screenplay written directly for the screen by Richard Matheson.
(W, AMPAS, Q).

691   THE DEAD ARE ALIVE.   (National General-1972-Armando
Crispino).   A screenplay by Armando Crispino, Lucio Battis-
trada, Damjanovic and Elsholtz.   (FF, Q).

692   DEAD CERT.   (1974-Tony Richardson).   A screenplay by Tony
Richardson and John Oaksey, based on the novel by Dick Francis; Holt, 1962.   (MFB, LACOPL).

693   DEAD EYES OF LONDON.   (Magna-1966-Alfred Vohrer).   A
screenplay by Trygve Larsen, based on the novel by Edgar
Wallace.   (FF).

694   DEAD HEAT ON A MERRY-GO-ROUND.   (Columbia-1966-
Bernard Girard).   An original screenplay by Bernard Girard.
(FF, LC, NYTFR, W, AMPAS, Q).

DEAD OR ALIVE   see   A MINUTE TO PRAY, A SECOND TO
DIE

694a   DEAD RINGER.   (Warner Bros.-1964-Paul Henreid).   A
screenplay by Albert Beich and Oscar Millard, based on a
story by Rian James.   (FF, NYTFR, W, Q, AMPAS).

695   DEADFALL.   (20th Century-Fox-1968-Bryan Forbes).   A
screenplay by Bryan Forbes, based on the novel by Desmond
Cory; Walker & Co., 1965, 250p.   (Q, FF, NYTFR, FM, W,
LC, AMPAS, LACOPL).

696   DEADLIER THAN THE MALE.   (Universal-1967-Ralph Thomas).
A screenplay by Jimmy Sangster, David Osborn, and Liz
Charles-Williams, based on the novels of H. C. McNeile; Bull-
Dog Drummond, Doran, 1920.   (Q, FF, NYTFR, FM, W,
LC, AMPAS, LACOPL).

697   THE DEADLY AFFAIR.   (Columbia-1967-Sidney Lumet).   A
screenplay by Paul Dehn, based on the novel Call for the Dead
by John Le Carré; Walker, 1962.   (Q, FF, NYTFR, FM, W,
LC, AMPAS, LACOPL).

698   THE DEADLY BEES.   (Paramount-1967-Freddie Francis).   A
screenplay by Robert Bloch and Anthony Marriott, based on
the novel A Taste for Honey by H. F. Heard; in Murder with
a Difference by Christopher Morley; Random House, 1946.   (Q,
FF, FM, NYTFR, W, LC, AMPAS, LACOPL).

699   DEADLY CHINA DOLL.   (MGM-1973-Huang Feng).   A screenplay by Ho Jen.   (W).

700   THE DEADLY TRACKERS.   (Warner Bros.-1973-Barry Shear).

A screenplay by Lukas Heller, based on a story "Riata" by Samuel Fuller. (W).

701 THE DEADLY TRAP. (National General-1972-Rene Clement). A screenplay by Sidney Buchman and Eleanor Perry, based on the novel The Children Are Gone by Arthur Cavanaugh; Simon & Schuster, 1966, 191p. (FF, LACOPL, Q).

702 DEAF SMITH AND JOHNNY EARS. (MGM-1973-Paolo Cavara). An original screenplay by Harry Essex and Oscar Saul. (W, Q).

703 DEALING. (Warner Bros.-1972-Paul Williams). A screenplay by Paul Williams and David Odell, based on the novel by Michael Douglas (aka Michael Crichton); Knopf, 1971, 222p. (W, LACOPL, FF, Q).

704 DEAR BRIGITTE. (20th Century-Fox-1965-Henry Koster). A screenplay written by Hal Kanter, based on the novel Erasmus with Freckles by John Hasse; Simon & Schuster, 1963, 160p. (FF, LC, W, AMPAS, LACOPL, Q).

705 DEAR, DEAD DELILAH. (Southern Star-1972-John Farris). A screenplay by John Farris. (FF).

706 DEAR HEART. (Warner Bros.-1965-Delbert Mann). A screenplay by Tad Mosel, from his own story. (FF, LC, AMPAS, Q).

707 DEAR JOHN. (Sigma III-1966-Lars Magnus Lindgren). A screenplay by Lars Magnus Lindgren, based on a novel by Olle Lansberg; Random House, 1968, 215p. (FF, NYTFR, W, AMPAS, LACOPL, Q).

708 DEATH CURSE OF TARTU. (Thunderbird International Pictures-1967-William Grefe). An original story and screenplay by William Grefe. (FF, LC).

709 DEATH IN VENICE. (Warner Bros.-1971-Luchino Visconti). A screenplay by Luchino Visconti and Nicola Badalucco, from the novel by Thomas Mann; Knopf, 1965, 118p. (W, LACOPL, Q).

710 DEATH OF A GUNFIGHTER. (Universal-1969-Allen Smithee aka Robert Totten and Don Siegel). A screenplay by Joseph Calvelli, based on a novel by Lewis B. Patten; Doubleday, 1968, 162p. (FF, AMPAS, LACOPL, W).

711 DEATH OF A JEW. (Cine Globe-1973-Denys de la Patelliere). A screenplay by Vahe Katcha and Denys de la Patelliere, based on a book by Vahe Katcha. (W, FF).

712 THE DEATH OF TARZAN. (Brandon-1968-Jaroslav Balik).
A screenplay by Josef Nesvadba and Jaroslav Balik, based on
a short story by Josef Nesvadba. (FF, NYTFR, W, Q).

THE DEATH OF THE APE-MAN see THE DEATH OF TAR-
ZAN

713 DEATH RIDES A HORSE. (United Artists-1969-Giulio Petroni).
An original screenplay by Luciano Vincenzoni and Giulio Petroni. (FF, W, Q).

714 DEATH WISH. (Paramount-1974-Michael Winner). A screenplay by Wendell Mayes, based on the novel by Brian Garfield;
McKay, 1972, 184p. (V, LACOPL).

715 THE DEATHMASTER. (American International-1972-Ray Danton). A screenplay written by R. L. Grove. (FF, W).

716 DEATHWATCH. (Beverly-1967-Vic Morrow). A screenplay
by Barbara Turner and Vic Morrow, based on the play by
Jean Genet; Grove Press, 1954, 166p. (FF, NYTFR, FM,
W, LACOPL).

717 THE DEBUT. (Maron-Gemini-1971-Gleb Panfilov). An original screenplay by E. Gavrilovich and Gleb Panfilov. (W).

718 THE DECAMERON. (United Artists-1971-Pier Paolo Pasolini). Pier Paolo Pasolini wrote the screenplay which he
based on the tales by Boccaccio; Stravon, 1946. (W,
LACOPL, Q).

719 THE DECEASED. (New Yorker-1971-Leon Hirszman). An
original work for the screen by Leon Hirszman, Eduardo
Coutinho, and Nelson Rodrigues. (W).

THE DECEIVERS see INTIMACY

720 DECLINE AND FALL OF A BIRD WATCHER. (20th Century-
Fox-1969-John Krish). A screenplay written by Ivan Foxwell,
with additional scenes by Alan Hackney and Hugh Whitmore;
adapted from Evelyn Waugh's Decline and Fall; Dell, 1934,
416p. (W, LC, AMPAS, LACOPL, Q).

721 DEEP END. (Paramount-1971-Jerzy Skolimowski). An original screenplay by Jerzy Skolimowski, J. Gruza, and B. Sulik.
(W, Q).

722 DEEP SLEEP. (Barferd-1973-Alfred Sole). No credit available. (W).

723 DEEP THROAT. (Aquarius Films-1972-Gerard Damiano). An
original screenplay credited to Gerard Damiano. (FF, W).

724 DEEP THRUST. (American International-1973-Heang Feng).
     No screenplay credits available. (W).

725 THE DEFECTOR. (7 Arts-1966-Raoul Levy). A screenplay
     written by Robert Guenette and Raoul Levy, based on the novel
     The Spy, by Paul Thomas. (FF, NYTFR, W, AMPAS, Q).

726 DEFIANCE. (Stu Segall-1974-Armand Weston). An original
     screenplay by Armand Weston. (V).

727 A DEGREE OF MURDER. (Universal-1972-Volker Schlondorff).
     A screenplay written by Volker Schlondorff, Gregor von Rez-
     zori, Niklas Franz, and Arne Boyer. (W).

728 A DELICATE BALANCE. (American Film Theatre-1973-Tony
     Richardson). A screenplay by Edward Albee, from his play;
     Atheneum, 1966, 170p. (W, LACOPL).

729 DELIVERANCE. (Warner Bros.-1972-John Boorman). A
     screenplay by James Dickey, based on his novel; Houghton,
     1970, 278p. (FF, LACOPL, W, Q).

730 THE DELUGE. (Film Polski-1974-Jerzy Hoffman). A screen-
     play by Wojciech Zukrowski, Adam Kerseten, and Jerzy Hoff-
     man, based on the novel by Henryk Sienkiewicz; Little, Brown
     & Co., 1891. (V, LACOPL).

731 LE DEPART. (Pathe Contemporary-1968-Jerzy Skolimowski).
     A screenplay by Jerzy Skolimowski and Andrzej Kostenko.
     (FF, NYTFR, W).

732 DERBY. (Cinerama-1971-Robert Kaylor). A documentary; no
     writing credits given. (W, Q).

733 DESERTER USA. (Kanawha-1969-Lars Lambert and Olle Sjog-
     ren). A screenplay written by Lars Lambert and Olle Sjogren.
     (W).

734 THE DESPERADOS. (Columbia-1969-Henry Levin). A screen-
     play by Walter Brough, from a story by Clarke Reynolds.
     (W, AMPAS, Q).

735 DESPERATE CHARACTERS. (ITC-1971-Frank D. Gilroy). A
     screenplay written by Frank D. Gilroy, based on a novel by
     Paul Fox; Harcourt, Brace, 1970, 156p. (W, LACOPL, Q).

736 DESTINATION INNER SPACE. (Magna-1966-Francis D. Lyon).
     A screenplay attributed to Arthur C. Pierce. (FF, LC, W,
     AMPAS, Q).

737 DESTROY ALL MONSTERS. (American International-1969-
     Ishiro Honda). An original screenplay by Kaoru Mabuchi and
     Ishiro Honda. (FF, W).

738 DESTROY, SHE SAID. (Grove-1970-Marguerite Duras). A screenplay written by Marguerite Duras, from her novel; Grove Press, 1970, 133p. (W, LACOPL).

739 THE DESTRUCTORS. (Feature Film Corporation of America-1968-Francis D. Lyon). A screenplay by Arthur C. Pierce and Larry E. Jackson. (FF, W, AMPAS).

740 THE DESTRUCTORS. (American International-1974-Robert Parrish). A screenplay written by Judd Bernard. (V).

DETAINED WHILE WAITING FOR JUSTICE see WHY

741 THE DETECTIVE. (20th Century-Fox-1968-Gordon Douglas). A screenplay by Abby Mann, based on the novel by Roderick Thorp; Dial Press, 1966. (FF, NYTFR, W, LC, AMPAS, LACOPL, Q).

742 DETECTIVE BELLI. (Plaza-1970-Romolo Guerrieri). A screenplay by Franco Verucci, Alberto Silvestri, Massimo d'Avico, adapted from the novel, Makeup Stains by Ludovico Dentice. (W, Q).

DETECTIVE GERONIMO see THE POLICE CONNECTION

743 DETOUR. (Brandon-1969-Grisha Ostrovski and Todor Stoyanov). Screenplay and story written by Blaga Dimitrova. (FF, W, Q).

744 DETROIT 9000. (General-1973-Arthur Marks). A screenplay by Orville Hampton, based on a story by Arthur Marks. (W).

745 THE DEVIL BY THE TAIL. (Lopert-1969-Philippe De Broca). A screenplay by Daniel Boulanger. (FF, W, LC, Q).

745a DEVIL DOLL. (Associated-1964-Lindsay Shonteff). A screenplay authored by George Barclay and Lance Z. Hargreaves, based on a story by Frederick E. Smith. (Q, FF, W).

746 THE DEVIL IN LOVE. (Warner Bros.-7 Arts-1968-Ettore Scola). An original story and screenplay written by Ruggero Maccari and Ettore Scola. (FF, NYTFR, W).

747 THE DEVIL IN MISS JONES. (Marvin-1973-Gerard Damiano). A screen work written by Gerard Damiano. (W).

748 THE DEVILS. (Warner Bros.-1971-Ken Russell). A screenplay written by Ken Russell, based on a play by John Whiting; Hill & Wang, 1961, 114p., and the book The Devils of Loudon by Aldous Huxley; Harper & Row, 1952, 340p. (W, LACOPL, Q).

749 DEVIL'S ANGELS. (American International-1967-Daniel Haller).

A screenplay by Charles Griffith. (FF, NYTFR, FM, W, LC, AMPAS, Q).

750   THE DEVIL'S BRIDE. (20th Century-Fox-1968-Terrence Fisher). A screenplay by Richard Matheson, based on the novel, The Devil Rides Out by Dennis Wheatley. (FF, FM, NYTFR, W, LC, Q).

751   THE DEVIL'S BRIGADE. (United Artists-1968-Andrew W. Mc-Laglen). William Roberts wrote the screenplay based on the book by Robert H. Anderson and Colonel George Walton. (FF, NYTFR, FM, W, LC, AMPAS, Q).

752   THE DEVIL'S DAFFODIL. (Goldstone Film Enterprises-1967-Akos von Rathony). A screenplay by Basil Dawson and Donald Taylor, based on the novel The Daffodil Mystery by Edgar Wallace. (FF).

753   DEVIL'S DUE. (Norman Arno-1973-Ernest Danna). A screenplay by Gerry Pound. (W).

754   THE DEVIL'S 8. (American International-1969-Burt Topper). A screenplay by James Gordon White, Willard Hyuck, and John Milius, from a story by Larry Gordon. (W, LC, AMPAS, Q).

THE DEVIL'S IMPOSTER see POPE JOAN

755   DEVILS OF DARKNESS. (20th Century-Fox-1966-Lance Comfort). A screenplay and original story by Lyn Fairhurst. (FF, W).

756   THE DEVIL'S OWN. (20th Century-Fox-1967-Cyril Frankel). A screenplay by Nigel Kneale, based on the novel The Devil's Own by Peter Curtis; Doubleday, 1960, 279p. (FF, NYTFR, FM, W, LC, AMPAS, Q, LACOPL).

757   THE DEVIL'S WIDOW. (American International-1972-Roddy McDowall). A screenplay by William Spier. (W, Q).

757a DEVIL-SHIP PIRATES. (Columbia-1964-Don Sharp). Jimmy Sangster wrote this original screenplay. (FF, Q, W).

758   THE DIABOLICAL DR. Z. (U.S. Films-1967-Jesus Franco). A screenplay authored by Jesus Franco and Jean-Claude Carrière, based on a novel by David Kuhne. (FF).

759   DIALOGUE. (Lionel Rogosin-1967-Janos Hersko). An original screenplay by Janos Hersko. (FF, NYTFR).

760   DIAMONDS ARE FOREVER. (United Artists-1971-Guy Hamilton). A screenplay by Richard Maibaum, Tom Mankiewicz, based on the novel by Ian Fleming; in More Gilt-Edged Bonds, Macmillan, 1965, 661p. (W, LACOPL, Q).

761   DIAMONDS OF THE NIGHT.   (Impact-1968-Jan Nemec).   A
screenplay by Arnost Lustig and Jan Nemec, based on a story
by Arnost Lustig.   (FF, NYTFR, W).

762   DIARIES, NOTES AND SKETCHES.   (Film Makers-1970-Jonas
Mekas).   No author credit available.   (W).

762a   DIARY OF A BACHELOR.   (American International-1964-Sandy
Howard).   An original screenplay credited to Ken Barnett.   (FF,
Q).

763   DIARY OF A CHAMBERMAID.   (International Classics-1965-
Luis Buñuel).   A screenplay by Luis Buñuel and Jean-Claude
Carrière, based on the novel by Octave Mirbeau.   (FF, W,
AMPAS, Q).

764   DIARY OF A MAD HOUSEWIFE.   (Universal-1970-Frank Perry).
A screenplay written by Eleanor Perry, based on a novel by
Sue Kaufman; Random House, 1967.   (W, LACOPL, Q).

765   DIARY OF A SCHIZOPHRENIC GIRL.   (Allied Artists-1970-
Nelo Risi).   A work for the screen written by Nelo Risi, and
Fabio Carpi, based on the book of the same name by Marguer-
ite Andree Sechehaye.   (W, Q).

766   DIARY OF A SHINJUKU BURGLAR.   (Grove-1973-Nagisa Oshima).   An original screenplay written by Tsutomu Tamura,
Mamoru Sasaki, Masao Adachi, and Nagisa Oshima.   (W).

767   DIARY OF A SWINGER.   (Boxoffice International-1967-John and
Lem Amero).   A screenplay written by Robert Parker.   (FF).

DIARY OF AN INNOCENT YOUNG BOY   see   BENJAMIN

768   DID YOU HEAR THE ONE ABOUT THE TRAVELING SALES-
LADY?   (Universal-1968-Don Weis).   A screenplay by John
Fenton Murray, based on a story by Jim Fritzell and Everett
Greenbaum.   (FF, W, AMPAS).

769   DIE! DIE! MY DARLING!   (Columbia-1965-Silvio Narizzano).
A screenplay by Richard Matheson, based on the novel Night-
mare, by Anne Blaisdell; Harper & Row, 1961.   (FF, LC, W,
AMPAS, LACOPL).

770   DIE, MONSTER, DIE!   (American International-1965-Daniel
Haller).   A screenplay by Jerry Sohl, from the story Colour
Out of Space by H. P. Lovecraft; Lancer Books, 1967.   (W,
LC, AMPAS, LACOPL).

771   DIGBY, THE BIGGEST DOG IN THE WORLD.   (Cinerama-
1974-Joseph McGrath).   A screenplay by Ted Key.   (V).

772   DILLINGER.   (American International-1973-John Milius).   A

screenplay by John Milius; original novelization based on the
screenplay was written by Henry Clement, and published by
Curtis Books, 1973, 157p. (W, LACOPL, Q).

772a DIMKA. (Artkino-1964-Ilya Frez). Wolf Dolgy authored this
original screenplay. (FF, NYTFR).

773 DINAH EAST. (Emerson-1970-Gene Nash). A screenplay written by Gene Nash. (W).

774 DINGAKA. (Embassy-1965-Jamie Uys). An original screenplay by Jamie Uys. (NYTFR, W).

775 THE DION BROTHERS. (Columbia-1974-Jack Starrett). A
screenplay by Bill Kerby and David Whitney aka Terence Mal-
ick. (V).

776 DIONYSUS IN 69. (Sigma III-1970-Richard Schechner). Por-
tions of text adapted by William Arrowsmith from Euripides'
The Bacchae. (W, Q).

777 THE DIRT GANG. (American International-1972-Jerry Jameson). An original screenplay by William Mercer and Michael
C. Healy. (W).

778 THE DIRTIEST GIRL I EVER MET. (American International-
1973-Pete Walker). No screenplay credit available. (W).

779 DIRTY DINGUS MAGEE. (MGM-1970-Burt Kennedy). A
screenplay written by Tom Waldman, Frank Waldman, and
Joseph Heller, based on The Ballad of Dingus Magee by David
Markson; Bobbs, Merrill, 1965. (W, LACOPL, Q).

780 THE DIRTY DOZEN. (MGM-1967-Robert Aldrich). A screenplay by Nunnally Johnson and Lukas Heller, based on the novel
by E. M. Nathanson; Random House, 1965, 498p. (FF,
NYTFR, FM, W, LC, AMPAS, Q).

781 THE DIRTY GAME. (American International-1966-Terence
Young, Christian-Jaque and Carlo Lizzani). Screenplay by Jo
Eisinger, based on a screenplay by Jacques Remy, Christian-
Jaque, Ennio de Concini and Philippe Bouvard. (FF, W,
AMPAS, Q).

782 DIRTY HARRY. (Warner Bros.-1971-Don Siegel). A screenplay by Harry Julian Fink, R. M. Fink, and Dean Riesner,
from a story by the Finks. (W, Q).

783 THE DIRTY HEROES. (NMD-1971-Alberto de Martino). A
screenplay written by Dino Verdo, Vincenzo Flamini, Alberto
Verucci, Franco Silvestri, and Alberto de Martino. (W).

784 DIRTY LITTLE BILLY. (Columbia-1972-Stan Dragoti). An

original screenplay written by Charles Moss and Stan Dragoti. (W, Q).

785   DIRTY MARY, CRAZY LARRY. (20th Century-Fox-1974-John Hough). A screenplay by Leigh Chapman and Antonio Santean, from a novel The Chase by Richard Unekis. (V).

786   DIRTY O'NEIL. (American International-1974-Howard Freen and Lewis Teague). An original screenplay by Howard Freen. (V, HR, MFB).

787   THE DIRTY OUTLAWS. (Transvue-1972-Franco Rossetti). Ugo Guerra, Franco Rossetti, and Vincenzo Cerami authored this original screenplay. (W, FF).

788   DIRTYMOUTH. (Superior-1971-Herbert S. Altman). An original script by Herbert S. Altman. (W).

789   THE DISCREET CHARM OF THE BOURGEOISIE. (20th Century-Fox-1972-Luis Buñuel). An original screenplay by Luis Buñuel and Jean-Claude Carrière. (FF, W, Q).

790   DISK-O-TEK HOLIDAY. (Allied Artists-1966-Vince Scarza). No writing credits. (FF).

790a   DISORDER. (Pathe Contemporary-1964-Franco Brusati). The original screenplay is attributed to Franco Brusati and Francesco Ghedini. (FF, NYTFR, Q).

791   THE DISORDERLY ORDERLY. (Paramount-1964-Frank Tashlin). Frank Tashlin wrote the screenplay based on a story by Norm Liebmann and Ed Haas. (FF, AMPAS, NYTFR, W, Q).

791a   A DISTANT TRUMPET. (Warner Bros.-1964-Raoul Walsh). The screenplay was authored by John Twist, adapted by Richard Fielder and Albert Beich, and based on the novel by Paul Horgan; Farrar, 1960, 629p. (FF, LACOPL, NYTFR, W, Q, AMPAS).

DITES-LE AVEC DES FLEURS see SAY IT WITH FLOWERS

792   DIVORCE AMERICAN STYLE. (Columbia-1967-Bud Yorkin). A screenplay by Norman Lear, based on a story by Robert Kaufman. (FF, NYTFR, FM, LC, AMPAS, Q).

792a   DO NOT DISTURB. (20th Century-Fox-1965-Ralph Levy). A screenplay by Milt Rosen and Richard Breen, based on a play by William Fairchild. (NYTFR, LC, W, AMPAS, Q).

793   DO YOU KEEP A LION AT HOME? (Brandon-1966-Pavel Hobl). No screenwriting credits available. (W, Q).

794   THE DOBERMAN GANG. (Dimension-1972-Byron Chudnow).

A screenplay by Louis Garfinkle and Frank Ray Perilli, from their original story. (FF).

795 DR. ?? COPPELIUS!! (Childhood-1968-Ted Kneeland). A work written by Ted Kneeland, based on the ballet Coppelia, music by Leo Delibes and a libretto by Charles Nuitter. (FF, NYTFR, Q, W).

795a DR. CRIPPEN. (Warner Bros.-1964-Robert Lynn). Leigh Vance wrote the screenplay based upon an actual event. (FF, NYTFR, W, Q).

796 DOCTOR DEATH: SEEKER OF SOULS. (Cinerama-1973-Eddie Saeta). An original screenplay by Sal Ponti. (W).

797 DOCTOR DOLITTLE. (20th Century-Fox-1967-Richard Fleischer). A screenplay by Leslie Bricusse, based on the stories by Hugh Lofting; Lippincott, 1967. (FF, NYTFR, FM, W, LC, AMPAS, LACOPL).

798 DOCTOR FAUSTUS. (Columbia-1968-Richard Burton & Nevill Coghill). A screenplay by Nevill Coghill, from the play The Tragical History of Doctor Faustus by Christopher Marlowe; Methuen, 1949, 221p. (FF, NYTFR, FM, W, LC, AMPAS, LACOPL).

799 DOCTOR GLAS. (20th Century-Fox-1969-Mai Zetterling). A screen work by Mai Zetterling and David Hughes, based on the 1905 novel by Hjalmar Söderberg; Little, Brown & Co., 1963, 150p. (FF, LACOPL, Q).

800 DR. GOLDFOOT AND THE BIKINI MACHINE. (American International-1966-Norman Taurog). A screenplay written by Elwood Ulman and Robert Kaufman, from a story by James Hartford. (FF, NYTFR, LC, W, AMPAS, Q).

801 DR. GOLDFOOT AND THE GIRL BOMBS. (American International-1967-Mario Bava). A screenplay by Louis M. Heyward and Robert Kaufman, based on a story by James Hartford. (FF, LC, W, AMPAS, Q).

801a DOCTOR IN DISTRESS. (Governor-1964-Ralph Thomas). A screenplay written by Nicholas Phipps and Ronald Scott Thorn, based on characters created by Richard Gordon. (FF, NYTFR, W, Q).

802 DR. JEKYLL AND SISTER HYDE. (American International-1972-Roy Ward Baker). A screenplay by Biran Clemens, based on the novel, The Strange Case of Dr. Jekyll and Mr. Hyde and Other Stories, by Robert Louis Stevenson; MacDonald, 1950, 525p. (FF, LACOPL, Q).

803 DR. PHIBES RISES AGAIN. (American International-1972-

Robert Fuest). A screenplay by Robert Fuest and Robert
Blees, based on characters created by James Whiton, and
William Goldstein; an original novelization based on the motion
picture screenplay was written by William Goldstein, and published by Award Books, 1972. (W, Q, LACOPL).

803a DR. STRANGELOVE: OR, HOW I LEARNED TO STOP
WORRYING AND LOVE THE BOMB. (Columbia-1964-Stanley
Kubrick). Stanley Kubrick, Terry Southern, and Peter George
wrote the screenplay, based on the novel Red Alert by Peter
George; Bantam Books, Inc., 1963. (AMPAS, FF, LACOPL,
NYTFR, W, Q).

804 DR. TERROR'S HOUSE OF HORRORS. (Paramount-1965-
Freddie Francis). An original screenplay written by Milton
Subotsky. (W, LC, Q).

805 DR. WHO AND THE DALEKS. (Continental-1967-Gordon
Flemyng). A screenplay by Milton Subotsky, based on the
BBC television serial by Terry Nation. (FF, W, Q).

806 DOCTOR, YOU'VE GOT TO BE KIDDING! (MGM-1967-Peter
Tewksbury). A screenplay by Phillip Shuken, based on the
novel Three for a Wedding by Patte Wheat Mahan; McKay,
1965. (Q, FF, NYTFR, FM, W, LC, AMPAS, LACOPL).

807 DOCTOR ZHIVAGO. (MGM-1965-David Lean). A screenplay
by Robert Bolt, based on the novel by Boris Pasternak; Pantheon, 1958. Screenplay published by Random House, 1965,
224p. (W, LACOPL, Q, MCC, V, FF, AMPAS).

808 DOCTORS' WIVES. (Columbia-1971-George Schaefer). A
screenplay by Daniel Taradash, based on the novel by Frank
G. Slaughter; Doubleday, 1967. (W, Q, LACOPL).

808a THE DOLL. (Kanawha-1964-Arne Mattson). A screenplay by
Eva Seeberg, based on themes by Lars Forsell. (FF,
NYTFR, W).

809 DOLLARS. (Columbia-1971-Richard Brooks). An original
screenplay written by Richard Brooks. (W, Q).

810 A DOLL'S HOUSE. (Paramount-1973-Patrick Garland). A
screenplay by Christopher Hamilton, based on the play by Henrik Ibsen; Washington Square Press, 1968, 54p. (W, Q,
LACOPL).

811 A DOLL'S HOUSE. (Tomorrow Entertainment-1973-Joseph
Losey). A screenplay by David Mercer, from Michael Meyer's
English translation of Henrik Ibsen's play. (W).

812 THE DON IS DEAD. (Universal-1973-Richard Fleischer). A
screenplay by Marvin H. Albert, based on his novel. (W).

813   DON'T CRY WITH YOUR MOUTH FULL.   (1974-Pascal Thomas).   A screenplay by Pascal Thomas, Roland Duval, and Suzanne Schiffman.   (NYT).

814   DON'T DRINK THE WATER.   (AVCO Embassy-1969-Howard Morris).   A screenplay by R. S. Allen, Harvey Bullock, based on a play by Woody Allen; Random House, 1967, 112p.   (W, LACOPL, Q).

815   DON'T JUST LAY THERE.   (Mattis-Pine-1970-Phillip Pine). A work written directly for the screen by Phillip Pine.   (W).

816   DON'T JUST STAND THERE!   (Universal-1968-Ron Winston). A screenplay by Charles Williams, based on his novel The Wrong Venus.   (FF, NYTFR, W, AMPAS, Q).

817   DON'T LOOK BACK.   (Leacock-Pennebaker-1967-D. A. Pennebaker).   A documentary written by D. A. Pennebaker. (NYTFR, W, LC, AMPAS, Q).

818   DON'T LOOK IN THE BASEMENT.   (Hallmark-1973-S. F. Brownrigg).   An original screenplay by Tim Pope.   (W).

819   DON'T LOOK NOW.   (Buena Vista-1969-Gerard Oury).   An original work for the screen by Gerard Oury.   (FF, W, Q).

820   DON'T LOOK NOW.   (Paramount-1973-Nicholas Roeg).   A screenplay by Alan Scott and Chris Bryant, from a story by Daphne du Maurier.   (W).

821   DON'T MAKE WAVES.   (MGM-1967-Alexander Mackendrick). A screenplay by Ira Wallach and George Kirgo, based on the novel Muscle Beach by Ira Wallach; Little, Brown & Co., 1959, 236p.   (Q, FF, NYTFR, FM, W, LC, AMPAS, LACOPL).

822   DON'T RAISE THE BRIDGE, LOWER THE RIVER.   (Columbia-1968-Jerry Lewis).   A screenplay by Max Wilk, based on his novel: Macmillan, 1960.   (Q, FF, NYTFR, FM, W, LC, AMPAS, LACOPL).

822a DON'T TEMPT THE DEVIL.   (United Motion Picture Organization-1964-Christian Jaque).   A screenplay by Henri Jeanson with Umberto Orsini, based on a novel by Jean Laborde, adapted by Paul Andreota, Christian Jaque, and Henri Jeanson. (FF, NYTFR, W, Q).

823   DON'T TURN THE OTHER CHEEK.   (International Amusement Corp.-1974-Duccio Tessari).   A screenplay by Dino Maiuri, Massimo de Rita, Juan de Orduna y Fernández, Gunter Eber, based on Lewis B. Patten's novel, The Killer from Yuma. (V).

824   DON'T WORRY, WE'LL THINK OF A TITLE. (United Artists-
      1966-Harmon Jones). An original screenplay by John Hart and
      Morey Amsterdam. (FF, Q, LC, W, AMPAS).

825   DOOMSDAY VOYAGE. (Futurama International-1972-John
      Vidette). A screenplay by John Vidette. (W).

826   DOOR-TO-DOOR MANIAC. (American International-1966-Bill
      Karn). A screenplay by M. K. Forester, based on a story by
      Palmer Thompson, adapted by Robert Joseph. (W, AMPAS).

827   DORIAN GRAY. (American International-1970-Massimo Dalla-
      mano). A screenplay written by Marcello Coscia and Mas-
      simo Dallamano; based on a novel by Oscar Wilde, The Pic-
      ture of Dorian Gray, World Book Co., 1946. (W, LACOPL,
      Q).

828   DOUBLE INITIATION. (Hollywood International-1970-Carlos
      Tobalina). A work written by Carlos Tobalina. (W).

829   THE DOUBLE MAN. (Warner Bros.-7 Arts-1968-Franklin J.
      Schaffner). Authoring credits for this screenplay go to Frank
      Tarloff and Alfred Hayes, who based it on the novel Legacy
      of a Spy by Henry S. Maxfield; 1958, Harper, 248p. (FF,
      NYTFR, W, LC, AMPAS, LACOPL, Q).

830   DOUBLE-STOP. (World Entertainment-1968-Gerald Seth Sin-
      dell). An original screenplay by Roger and Gerald Sindell.
      (W).

831   DOUBLE TROUBLE. (MGM-1967-Norman Taurog). A screen-
      play by Jo Heims, based on a story by Marc Brandel. (FF,
      NYTFR, FM, W, LC, AMPAS, Q).

831a DOULOS--THE FINGER MAN. (Pathe-Contemporary-1964-
      Jean-Pierre Melville). A screenplay by Jean-Pierre Melville,
      based on the novel by Pierre Lesou. (FF, W, NYTFR, Q).

832   THE DOVE. (Paramount-1974-Charles Jarrott). A screenplay
      by Peter Beagle and Adam Kennedy, based on the book by Rob-
      in Lee Graham with Derek Gill; Harper & Row, 1972. (V,
      LACOPL).

833   THE DOWNHILL RACER. (Paramount-1969-Michael Ritchie).
      A screenplay by James Salter, based on The Downhill Racers
      by Oakley Hall; Viking Press, 1963. (W, Q, LC, AMPAS,
      LACOPL).

834   DRACULA A. D. 1972. (Warner Bros.-1972-Alan Gibson). A
      screenplay written by Don Houghton. (FF, Q).

835   DRACULA HAS RISEN FROM THE GRAVE. (Warner Bros.-7
      Arts-1969-Freddie Francis). A screenplay by John Elder,

based on the character created by Bram Stoker. (FF, W, Q).

836   DRACULA--PRINCE OF DARKNESS. (20th Century-Fox-1966-
       Terence Fisher). A screenplay by John Sansom, based on an
       idea by John Elder and the characters created by Bram Stoker.
       (FF, LC, W, Q, AMPAS).

837   DRACULA VS. FRANKENSTEIN. (Independent International-
       1973-Al Adamson). An original story and screenplay by Willi-
       am Pugsley and Samuel M. Sherman. (W).

838   THE DRAGON DIES HARD. (American International-1974-).
       No screenwriter credits available. (V).

838a   DRAGON SKY. (Lopert-1964-Marcel Camus). A screenplay
       by Jacques Viot, adapted by Jacques Viot and Marcel Camus.
       (FF, NYTFR, W, Q).

       A DRAMA OF JEALOUSY (AND OTHER THINGS) see THE
       PIZZA TRIANGLE

839   THE DREAM MAKER. (Universal-1964-Don Sharp). An origi-
       nal work for the screen written by Leigh Vance. (FF,
       NYTFR, Q, W).

839a   A DREAM OF KINGS. (National General-1969-Daniel Mann).
       A screenplay authored by Harry Mark Petrakis, Ian Hunter,
       based on the novel by Harry Mark Petrakis; McKay, 1966,
       180p. (W, AMPAS, Q).

840   THE DREAMER. (Cannon-1970-Dan Wolman). An original
       screenplay by Dan Wolman. (W, Q).

841   DREAMS OF GLASS. (Universal-1970-Robert Clouse). An
       original screenplay written by Robert Clouse. (W, Q).

842   THE DRIFTER. (Filmmakers' Distribution Center-1967-Alex
       Matter). Alex Matter wrote this original screenplay. (FF,
       NYTFR, W).

843   DRIVE, HE SAID. (Columbia-1971-Jack Nicholson). A screen-
       play by Jeremy Larner and Jack Nicholson, from the novel by
       Jeremy Larner; Dial Press, 1964, 190p. (Q, W, LACOPL).

844   THE DRUMS OF TABU. (PRO-1967-Javier Seto). No author
       credit available. (W).

845   DUCK, YOU SUCKER. (United Artists-1972-Sergio Leone). A
       screenplay by Luciano Vincenzoni, Sergio Donati, and Sergio
       Leone. (Q, FF).

846   DUEL AT DIABLO. (United Artists-1966-Ralph Nelson). A
       screenplay by Marvin H. Albert and Michael M. Grilikhes,

based on the novel <u>Apache Rising</u> by Marvin H. Albert.   (FF, LC, W, Q, AMPAS)

847   DUET FOR CANNIBALS. (Grove Press-1969-Susan Sontag). An original screenplay by Susan Sontag.   (W).

848   DUFFY. (Columbia-1968-Robert Parrish).   A screenplay by Donald Cammell and Harry Joe Brown, Jr., based on a story by Donald Cammell, Harry Joe Brown, Jr., and Pierrre De La Salle.   (FF, NYTFR, Q, AMPAS, W, LC).

849   DULCIMA. (Cinevision Films Ltd.-1972-Frank Nesbitt).   A screenplay by Frank Nesbitt, from a story by H. E. Bates. (FF, Q, W).

850   THE DUNWICH HORROR.   (American International-1970-Daniel Haller).   A screenplay by Curtis Lee Hanson, Henry Rosenbaum, and Ronald Silkosky, based on stories by H. P. Lovecraft; Arkham House, 1963.   (Q, W, LACOPL).

851   DUSTY AND SWEETS McGEE.   (Warner Bros.-1971-Floyd Mutrux).   An original screenplay by Floyd Mutrux.   (W, Q).

852   DUTCHMAN.   (Continental-1967-Anthony Harvey).   No screenplay credit available.   Based on the play by LeRoi Jones; Morrow, 1964, 88p.   (Q, FF, NYTFR, FM, W, AMPAS, LACOPL).

853   DYNAMITE.   (Distribpix-1972-John and Lem Amero).   An original screenplay attributed to John and Lem Amero.   (W).

854   DYNAMITE CHICKEN.   (EYR Programs-1972-Ernie Pintoff). An original work for the screen by Ernie Pintoff.   (FF).

855   EAGLE IN A CAGE.   (National General-1972-Fielder Cook). A screenplay by Millard Lampell.   (W, FF, Q).

856   EAGLE OVER LONDON.   (Cine Globe-1973-Enzo G. Castellari). No author credit available.   (W).

857   EARLY SPRING.   (New Yorker-1974-Yasujiro Ozu).   An original screenplay by Yasujiro Ozu and Kogo Noda.   (NYT).

858   THE EARTH DIES SCREAMING.   (20th Century-Fox-1966-Terence Fisher).   An original screenplay by Henry Cross. (W, LC, AMPAS).

859   EARTHQUAKE.   (Universal-1974-Mark Robson).   An original work for the screen by George Fox and Mario Puzo; a novelization based on the screenplay was written by George Fox, Signet, 1974, 128p.   (V, LACOPL).

860   EAST OF SUDAN.   (Columbia-1965-Nathan Juran).   An origi-

nal screenplay written by Jud Kinberg. (W, LC; FF gives
date as 1964).

861   EASY COME, EASY GO. (Paramount-1967-John Rich). An
      original screenplay by Allan Weiss and Anthony Lawrence.
      (FF, NYTFR, FM, W, LC, AMPAS, Q).

862   EASY RIDER. (Columbia-1969-Dennis Hopper). This original
      screenplay was written by Peter Fonda, Dennis Hopper, and
      Terry Southern; Signet, 1969, 191p. (W, Q, LACOPL).

863   THE EAVESDROPPER. (Royal-1966-Leopoldo Torre Nilsson).
      An original screenplay by Beatriz Guido, Joe Goldberg, Mabel
      Itzcovich, Edmundo Eidhelbaum, and Leopoldo Torre Nilsson.
      (W).

864   THE EDGE. (Film-Makers' Distribution Center-1968-Robert
      Kramer). An original screenplay authored by Robert Kramer.
      (FF, NYTFR, W, Q).

865   THE EDUCATION OF SONNY CARSON. (Paramount-1974-
      Michael Campus). A screenplay by Fred Hudson, based on a
      book by Sonny Carson; Norton, 1972, 203p. (V, LACOPL).

866   THE EFFECT OF GAMMA RAYS ON MAN-IN-THE-MOON
      MARIGOLDS. (20th Century-Fox-1972-Paul Newman). A
      screenplay by Alvin Sargent, based on the play by Paul Zindel;
      Harper & Row, 1971, 108p. (W, FF, LACOPL).

867   EIGHT ON THE LAM. (United Artists-1967-George Marshall).
      A screenplay by Albert E. Lewin and Burt Styler, based on a
      story by Bob Fisher and Arthur Marx. (FF, NYTFR, FM,
      W, LC, AMPAS, Q).

868   EIGHTEEN IN THE SUN. (Goldstone Film Enterprises-1966-
      Camillo Mastrocinque). An original screenplay by Franco
      Castellano and Pipolo aka Giuseppe Moccia. (FF).

869   80 STEPS TO JONAH. (Warner Bros.-1969-Gerd Oswald).
      Frederic Louis Fox wrote the screenplay based on a story by
      Frederic Louis Fox and Gerd Oswald. (W, Q).

870   EL DORADO. (Paramount-1967-Howard Hawks). A screenplay
      by Leigh Brackett, based on the novel, The Stars in Their
      Courses by Harry Brown; Knopf, 1960, 362p. (Q, FF, NYTFR,
      FM, W, LC, AMPAS, LACOPL).

871   EL GRECO. (20th Century-Fox-1967-Luciano Salce). A screen-
      play by Guy Elmes, Massimo Franciosa, Luigi Magni, and Lu-
      ciano Salce. (FF, NYTFR, W, Q, AMPAS).

872   EL TOPO. (ABK-1971-Alexandro Jodorowsky). An original
      screenplay by Alexandro Jodorowsky, published by Douglas

Book Corp., 1971, 173p. (W, LACOPL, Q).

873 ELECTRA GLIDE IN BLUE. (United Artists-1973-James William Guercio). A screenplay by Robert Boris, from a story by Robert Boris and Rupert Hitzig. (W).

874 11 HARROWHOUSE. (20th Century-Fox-1974-Aram Avakian). A screenplay by Jeffrey Bloom, based on a novel by Gerald A. Browne; Arbor House, 1972, 286p. (V, LACOPL).

875 ELVIRA MADIGAN. (Cinema V-1967-Bo Widerberg). An original screenplay by Bo Widerberg. (FF, NYTFR, W, Q).

876 THE EMBALMER. (Europix Consolidated-1966-Dino Tavello). No screenplay credit available. (FF).

877 EMBASSY. (Hemdale-1973-Gordon Hessler). A screenplay by William Fairchild. (W).

878 THE EMBRACERS. (Joseph Brenner-1967-Gary Graver). Gary Graver authored the screenplay. (FF).

EMERGENCY WARD see THE CAREY TREATMENT

879 THE EMIGRANTS; (Warner Bros.-1972-Jan Troell). A screenplay by Jan Troell and Bengt Forslung, based on a series of novels by Vilhelm Moberg: The Emigrants, Simon & Schuster, 1951, 366p.; Unto a Good Land, Simon & Schuster, 1954; Last Letter Home, Simon & Schuster, 1961. (FF, LACOPL, Q).

880 EMITAI. (New Yorker-1973-Ousmane Sembene). No author credit. (W).

881 EMMANUELLE. (1974-Just Jaeckin). A screenplay by Jean-Luis Richard, from the book by Emmanuelle Arsan. (V).

882 EMPEROR OF THE NORTH POLE. (20th Century-Fox-1973-Robert Aldrich). An original screenplay by Christopher Knopf. (W, Q).

883 EMPRESS WU. (Shaw Brothers-1965-Li Han-hsiang). Wang Yueh-ting wrote the original screenplay. (W).

883a THE EMPTY CANVAS. (Embassy-1964-Damiano Damiani). A screenplay by Damiano Damiani, Tonino Guerra, and Ugo Liberatore, based on the novel by Alberto Moravia; Farrar, Straus, and Cudahy; 1961, 306p. (FF, W, LACOPL, NYTFR, AMPAS, Q).

884 THE END OF SUMMER. (Toho-1970-Yasujiro Ozu). An original screenplay by Yasujiro Ozu and Kogo Noda. (W).

885   END OF THE ROAD. (Allied Artists-1970-Aram Avakian). A
      screenplay authored by Dennis McGuire, Terry Southern, and
      Aram Avakian, based on the novel by John Barth; Doubleday,
      1967, 188p. (W, LACOPL, Q).

886   THE ENDLESS SUMMER. (Cinema V-1966-Bruce Brown).
      Written by Bruce Brown. (FF, W, AMPAS, Q).

887   ENGAGEMENT ITALIANO. (Sedgeway-1966-Alfredo Giannetti).
      A screenplay written by Alfredo Giannetti. (FF, NYTFR, W,
      Q).

888   ENGLAND MADE ME. (Cine Globe-1973-Peter Duffell). A
      screenplay by Desmond Cory, and Peter Duffell, based on a
      novel by Graham Greene; Doubleday, 1935, 274p. (W,
      LACOPL).

889   ENOUGH ROPE. (Artixo-1966-Claude Autant-Lara). A screen-
      play by Jean Aurenche and Pierre Bost, based on the novel
      The Blunderer by Patricia Highsmith; 1954. (FF, NYTFR, W,
      LACOPL).

889a ENSIGN PULVER. (Warner Bros.-1964-Joshua Logan). A
      screenplay by Joshua Logan and Peter S. Feibleman, based on
      a play by Thomas Heggen and Joshua Logan, Dramatists Play
      Service, 1948, 79p.; and from a novel by Thomas Heggen,
      Houghton, 1946. (FF, LACOPL, AMPAS, W, Q, NYTFR).

890   ENTER LAUGHING. (Columbia-1967-Carl Reiner). A screen-
      play by Joseph Stein and Carl Reiner, based on the play by
      Joseph Stein, as adapted from the novel by Carl Reiner, 1958,
      Simon & Schuster, 214p. (Q, FF, NYTFR, FM, W, LC,
      AMPAS, LACOPL).

891   ENTER THE DRAGON. (Warner Bros.-1973-Robert Clouse).
      An original screenplay by Michael Allin; a novelization based
      on the screenplay was written by Mike Roote, and published by
      Award Books, 1973. (W, LACOPL).

892   ENTERTAINING MR. SLOANE. (Continental-1970-Douglas
      Hickox). A screenplay by Clive Exton, from the play of the
      same name by Joe Orton. (W, Q).

893   ERIC SOYA'S "17." (Peppercorn-Wormser-1967-Annelise
      Meineche). A screenplay by Bob Ramsing, based on the novel
      by Carl Eric Soya. (FF, NYTFR, W, Q).

894   EROICA. (Amerpole-1966-Andrzej Munk). An original screen-
      play by Jerzy Stefan Stawinski. (FF, NYTFR, W, Q).

895   THE EROTIC ADVENTURES OF ZORRO. (Entertainment Ven-
      tures-1973-Robert Freeman). An original screenplay by Mona
      Lott, Joy Boxe, and David F. Friedman. (W, FF).

896 THE EROTIC MEMOIRS OF A MALE CHAUVINIST PIG. (Mature-1973-John Butterworth). An original screenplay by Ray Hoersch. (W).

897 THE EROTIC THREE. (Cannon-1972-Alex Matter). An original screenplay by Steve Winsten and Alex Matter. (FF).

898 EROTICON. (Adelphia-1971-Richard Lacey). An original screenplay by Bernard L. Sackett and Richard Lacey. (W).

899 EROTIKUS. (Hand-in-Hand-1973-Nicholas Grippo). A documentary narrated by Fred Halsted. No script credit available. (W).

900 ESCAPE BY NIGHT. (Allied Artists-1965-Montgomery Tully). A screenplay by Maurice J. Wilson and Montgomery Tully, based on the novel Clash by Night by Rupert Croft-Cooke. (FF, W).

901 ESCAPE FROM THE PLANET OF THE APES. (20th Century-Fox-1971-Don Taylor). An original screenplay by Paul Dehn, based on the characters created by Pierre Boulle. (See also PLANET OF THE APES). (W, Q).

902 ESCAPE TO NOWHERE. (Peppercorn-Wormser-1974-Claude Pinoteau). An original screenplay by Jean-Loup Dabadie and Claude Pinoteau. (HR).

903 ESCAPE TO THE SUN. (Cinevision-1972-Menahem Golan). An original screenplay by Menahem Golan and Joseph Gross. (W, FF, Q).

904 EUGENIE. (Distinction-1970-Jess Franco). A screenplay by Peter Welbeck, based on Philosophy in the Boudoir by the Marquis de Sade, in Complete Justine, Philosophy in the Bedroom and Other Writings, Grove Press, 1965, 753p. (W, LACOPL).

905 EVA. (Times Film Corporation-1965-Joseph Losey). A screenplay authored by Hugo Butler and Evan Jones, from the novel by James Hadley Chase, Come Easy--Go Easy. (NYTFR, W, AMPAS).

906 EVE. (Commonwealth United Entertainment-1968-Jeremy Summers). An original screenplay by Peter Welbeck. (FF, Q).

907 EVEN DWARFS STARTED SMALL. (New Line Cinema-1971-Werner Herzog). An original screenplay by Werner Herzog. (W).

908 AN EVENING WITH THE ROYAL BALLET. (Sigma III-1965-Anthony Asquith and Anthony Havelock-Allan). A documentary; no script credit. (W).

909   AN EVENT. (Continental-1970-Vatroslav Mimica). A screenplay by Zelijko Senecic and Vatroslav Mimica and Kruno Quien,
based on a short story by Anton Chekhov. (W).

910   EVERY BASTARD A KING. (Continental-1970-Uri Zohar). An
original screenplay by Uri Zohar and Eli Tavor. (W, Q).

911   EVERY DAY IS A HOLIDAY. (Columbia-1966-Mel Ferrer).
An original screenplay by Mel Ferrer and José Maria Palacio,
from a screen story by Mel Ferrer. (W, AMPAS, Q).

912   EVERY LITTLE CROOK AND NANNY. (MGM-1972-Cy Howard).
Cy Howard, Jonathan Axelrod, and Robert Klane authored this
screenplay from a novel by Evan Hunter aka Ed McBain;
Doubleday, 1972, 229p. (W, LACOPL, Q).

EVERY MAN'S WOMAN see A ROSE FOR EVERYONE

913   EVERYTHING YOU ALWAYS WANTED TO KNOW ABOUT SEX*
... *BUT WERE AFRAID TO ASK. (United Artists-1972-
Woody Allen). A screenplay by Woody Allen, based on the
book by Dr. David Reuben; McKay, 1969, 342p. (FF,
LACOPL, Q).

913a EVIL OF FRANKENSTEIN. (Universal-1964-Freddie Francis).
An original screenplay by John Elder. (W, FF, NYTFR, Q).

914   THE EXECUTIONER. (Columbia-1970-Sam Wanamaker). A
screenplay by Jack Pulman, from a story by Gordon McDonell.
(W, Q).

915   EXECUTIVE ACTION. (National General-1973-David Miller).
Dalton Trumbo wrote the screenplay from a story by Donald
Freed and Mark Lane. (W).

916   THE EXORCIST. (Warner Bros.-1973-William Friedkin).
William Peter Blatty wrote the screenplay, based on his novel;
Harper, 1971, 340p. (W, LACOPL).

917   THE EXPERIMENT. (Jaguar-1973-Gorton Hall). An original
screenplay written by Gorton Hall. (W).

918   EXPLOSION. (American International-1970-). No author credit available. (W, Q).

919   EXQUISITE CADAVER. (Wheeler-1973-Vicente Aranda). An
original screenplay by Vicente Aranda and A. Radinad. (W).

920   THE EXTERMINATING ANGEL. (Altura-1967-Luis Buñuel).
Screenplay written by Luis Buñuel, adapted from the play Los
Naufragos de la Calle de la Providencia by Jose Bergamin;
screenplay published by Simon & Schuster, 1972, 299p. (Q,
FF, NYTFR, W, AMPAS, LACOPL).

921 EXTREME CLOSE-UP. (National General-1973-Jeannot
Szwarc). An original screenplay by Michael Crichton. (W,
Q).

922 AN EYE FOR AN EYE. (Embassy-1966-Michael Moore). An
original screenplay written by Bing Russell and Sumner Williams. (FF, W, AMPAS).

923 EYE OF THE CAT. (Universal-1969-David Lowell Rich).
Joseph Stefano authored the original screenplay. (FF, W,
AMPAS, Q).

924 EYE OF THE DEVIL. (MGM-1967-J. Lee Thompson). An
original screenplay by Robin Estridge and Dennis Murphy,
based on the novel Day of the Arrow by Philip Loraine; Mill-
Morrow, 1964, 186p. (FF, NYTFR, W, LC, AMPAS, Q,
LACOPL).

925 THE EYE OF THE NEEDLE. (Eldorado-1965-Marcello Andrei).
A screenplay written by G. Mangione, A. Bevilacqua, T. Dem-
bi, and M. Andrei, based on a story by G. Berto and D. Troi-
si. (NYTFR, Q).

925a THE EYES OF ANNIE JONES. (20th Century-Fox-1964-Regi-
nald Le Borg). A screenplay by Louis Vittes, based on a story
by Henry Slesar. (FF, NYTFR, Q, W).

926 FBI CODE 98. (Warner Bros.-1964-Leslie H. Martinson). An
original screenplay written by Stanley Niss. (FF, NYTFR, Q,
W).

926a F. T. A. (American International-1972-Francine Parker). An
original screenplay by Robin Menken, Michael Alaimo, Rita
Martinson, Holly Near, Len Chandler, Pamala Donegan, Jane
Fonda, Donald Sutherland, and Dalton Trumbo. (FF, Q).

927 A FABLE. (MFR-1971-Al Freeman, Jr.). A screenplay by
LeRoi Jones, from his play Slave; Morrow, 1964, 88p. (W,
LACOPL).

928 THE FABULOUS BASTARD FROM CHICAGO. (Walnut Interna-
tional-1969-Greg Corarito). An original screenplay by Richard
Compton. (W).

929 THE FACE OF FU MANCHU. (7 Arts-1965-Don Sharp). A
screenplay written by Peter Welbeck, based on the Sax Rohmer
novel. (NYTFR, W, AMPAS, Q).

930 FACES. (Continental-1968-John Cassavetes). An original
screenplay by John Cassavetes, published by New American Library, 1970, 319p. (FF, A, NYTFR, W, AMPAS, LACOPL).

931 THE FACTS OF MURDER. (7 Arts-1965-Pietro Germi). An

original screenplay by Pietro Germi, Alfred Gianetti, and Ennio Concini. (NYTFR).

932   FAHRENHEIT 451. (Universal-1966-François Truffaut).
François Truffaut and Jean-Louis Richard authored the screenplay, based on a novel by Ray Bradbury; Simon & Schuster, 1967. (Q, FF, NYTFR, LC, W, AMPAS, LACOPL).

932a FAIL SAFE. (Columbia-1964-Sidney Lumet). A screenplay by Walter Bernstein, based on the novel by Eugene Burdick and Harvey Wheeler; McGraw-Hill, 1962, 284p. (FF, LACOPL, NYTFR, AMPAS, Q, W).

933   THE FALL OF THE ROMAN EMPIRE. (Paramount-1964-Anthony Mann). A screenplay by Ben Barzman, Basilio Franchina, and Philip Yordan. (FF, NYTFR, W, Q, AMPAS).

933a FALSTAFF. (Peppercorn-Wormser-1967-Orson Welles). An original screen presentation by Orson Welles, based on five plays by William Shakespeare: Henry IV (Parts I and II), Richard II, Henry V, The Merry Wives of Windsor, in Complete Plays and Poems; Houghton Mifflin Co., 1942, 1420p. (W, Q, LACOPL).

934   THE FAMILY. (International Coproduction-1973-Sergio Sollima). No script credits given. (W).

935   FAMILY HONOR. (Cinerama-1973-Clark Worswick). Louis Pastore wrote this original screenplay. (W, Q).

936   THE FAMILY JEWELS. (Paramount-1965-Jerry Lewis). An original work for the screen by Jerry Lewis and Bill Richmond. (NYTFR, Q, LC, W, AMPAS).

FAMILY LIFE see WEDNESDAY'S CHILD

937   THE FAMILY WAY. (Warner Bros.-7 Arts-1967-Roy Boulting). A screenplay written by Bill Naughton, based on the play he wrote, All In Good Time; Samuel French, 1964, 86p. (Q, FF, NYTFR, FM, W, AMPAS, LACOPL).

938   FANDO AND LIS. (Cannon-1970-Alejandro Jodorowsky). Screenplay and dialogue by Fernando Arrabel and Alejandro Jodorowsky. (W, Q).

939   FANNY HILL. (Pan World Distributing-1965-Russ Meyer). A screen work by Robert Hill, based on the novel by John Cleland; G. P. Putnam's Sons, 1963, 228p. (W).

940   FANNY HILL. (Cinemation-1969-Mac Ahlberg). A screenplay by Mac Ahlberg, based on the novel Memoirs of a Woman of Pleasure by John Cleland; Putnam, 1963, 228p. (W, Q, LACOPL).

941   FANTASTIC VOYAGE. (20th Century-Fox-1966-Richard Flei-
       scher). A screenplay by Harry Kleiner, adaptation by David
       Duncan, based on a story by Otto Klement and Jay Lewis
       Bixby. (FF, NYTFR, LC, W, AMPAS, Q).

942   FANTOMAS. (Lopert-1966-André Hunebelle). An original
       screenplay by Jean Halain. (FF, NYTFR, W, Q).

943   FAR FROM THE MADDING CROWD. (MGM-1967-John Schles-
       inger). A screenplay by Frederic Raphael, based on the novel
       by Thomas Hardy; Dodd, Mead & Co., 1968. (Q, FF,
       NYTFR, W, LC, AMPAS, LACOPL).

944   THE FASCIST. (Embassy-1965-Luciano Salce). A screenplay
       by Castellano-Pippolo and Luciano Salce. (NYTFR, W, Q).

945   FASTER, PUSSYCAT! KILL! KILL! (Eve Productions-1966-
       Russ Meyer). A screenplay by Jack Moran, from an original
       story by Russ Meyer. (FF, LC, W, AMPAS).

946   THE FASTEST GUITAR ALIVE. (MGM-1968-Michael Moore).
       An original screenplay by Robert E. Kent. (FF, NYTFR, FM,
       W, LC, AMPAS, Q).

947   FAT CITY. (Columbia-1972-John Huston). A screenplay by
       Leonard Gardner, based on his novel; Farrar, 1969, 183p.
       (W, LACOPL, Q).

948   THE FAT SPY. (Magna-1966-Joseph Cates). An original
       screenplay by Matthew Andrews. (FF, W, AMPAS).

948a   FATE IS THE HUNTER. (20th Century-Fox-1964-Ralph Nel-
       son). A screenplay by Harold Medford, based on the book by
       Ernest K. Gann; Simon & Schuster, 1961, 390p. (FF,
       AMPAS, LACOPL, NYTFR, W, Q).

949   FATHER. (Continental-1967-Istvan Szabo). An original screen-
       play written by Istvan Szabo. (FF, NYTFR, W).

950   FATHER OF A SOLDIER. (Artkino-1966-Rezo Chkeidze). An
       original screenplay by Suliko Zhgeidze. (FF, NYTFR, W, Q).

951   FATHOM. (20th Century-Fox-1967-Leslie Martinson). A
       screenplay by Lorenzo Semple, Jr., based on a novel by Larry
       Forester. (FF, FM, NYTFR, W, LC, AMPAS, Q).

952   THE FEAR. (Trans-Lux-1967-Costas Manoussakis). An origi-
       nal screenplay written by Costas Manoussakis. (FF, W, Q).

953   FEAR IS THE KEY. (Paramount-1973-Michael Tuchner). A
       screenplay authored by Robert Carrington, based on the novel
       by Alistair MacLean; Doubleday, 1961. (W, LACOPL).

954 FEARLESS FRANK. (American International-1970-Philip Kaufman). A screenplay by Philip Kaufman. (W, Q).

955 THE FEARLESS VAMPIRE KILLERS. (MGM-1967-Roman Polanski). An original screenplay and story by Roman Polanski and Gerard Brach. (FF, NYTFR, FM, W, LC, AMPAS, Q).

956 FELLINI SATYRICON. (United Artists-1970-Federico Fellini). A screenplay by Federico Fellini and Bernardino Zapponi; published by Ballantine Books, 1970, 280p. (W, LACOPL, Q).

957 FELLINI'S ROMA. (United Artists-1972-Federico Fellini). A screenplay by Federico Fellini and Bernardino Zapponi. (FF, Q).

958 FEMALE ANIMAL. (Cinemation-1970-Juan Carlo Grinella). An original screenplay by Octavio Bellini and Marcello Lazarino. (W).

959 THE FEMALE BUNCH. (Gilbreth-1972-Al Adamson & John Cardos). A screenplay by Jale Lockwood and Brent Nimrod, based on a story by Raphael Nussbaum. (W, FF).

960 THE FEMALE RESPONSE. (Trans-American-1973-Tim Kincaid). An original screenplay by Tim Kincaid and David Newburge. (W).

961 UNE FEMME DOUCE. (New Yorker-1971-Robert Bresson). Screenplay authored by Robert Bresson, adapted from "The Gentle Woman" by Fyodor Dostoyevsky, in Letters from the Underworld, Dutton. (W, LACOPL).

962 LA FEMME INFIDELE. (Allied Artists-1969-Claude Chabrol). A screenplay by Claude Chabrol. (W).

963 FEMMES AU SOLEIL. (Albina-1974-Lilane Dryfust). An original screenplay by Lilane Dryfust. (V).

964 FERRY CROSS THE MERSEY. (United Artists-1965-Jeremy Summers). A screenplay by David Franden, from a story by Tony Warren. (FF, LC, W, Q).

965 FESTIVAL. (Peppercorn-Wormser-1967-Murray Lerner). A documentary, with commentary written by Murray Lerner. (W, AMPAS, Q).

966 FEVER. (Variety-1971-Armando Bo). An original screenplay by Armando Bo. (W).

967 FEVER HEAT. (Paramount-1968-Russell S. Doughton, Jr.). A screenplay by Henry Gregor Felsen, based on his novel written under the pseudonym of Angus Vicker). (FF, W, LC, AMPAS, Q).

968   THE FEVERISH YEARS.   (1967-Dragoslav Lazic).   An original
screenplay by Liubisa Kozomara and Goraidan Mihic.
(NYTFR).

968a THE FIANCES.   (Janus-1964-Ermanno Olmi).   A screenplay
written by Ermanno Olmi.   (FF, NYTFR, W).

969   THE FICKLE FINGER OF FATE.   (Producers Releasing Organ-
ization-1967-Richard Rush).   An original screenplay written by
Jim Henaghan.   (FF, W).

970   FIDDLER ON THE ROOF.   (United Artists-1971-Norman Jewison).   Joseph Stein wrote the screenplay which was based on
the musical of the same name, and the stories of Sholem
Aleichem; Crown, 1964, 116p.   (W, LACOPL, Q).

THE FIEND see BEWARE OF THE BRETHREN

971   15 FROM ROME.   (McAbee-1968-Dino Risi).   A screenplay by
Age and Scarpelli aka Agenore Incrocci and Furio Scarpelli,
Elio Petri, Ettore Scola, Ruggero Maccari, and Dino Risi.
(FF, NYTFR, W, AMPAS).

972   THE FIFTH HORSEMAN IS FEAR.   (Sigma III-1968-Zbynek
Brynych).   A screenplay by Zbynek Brynych based on a story
by Jana Belehradska, "Without the Beauty, Without the Collar."
(FF, NYTFR, W, AMPAS, Q).

973   THE FIGHTING PRINCE OF DONEGAL.   (Buena Vista-1966-
Michael O'Herlihy).   A screenplay by Robert Westerby, based
on the book Red Hugh, Prince of Donegal by Robert T. Reilly;
Farrar, 1957.   (FF, NYTFR, LC, W, AMPAS, LACOPL, Q).

974   FIGURES IN A LANDSCAPE.   (National General-1971-Joseph
Losey).   A screenplay by Robert Shaw, and Joseph Losey,
based on a novel by Barry England; Random House, 1968.   (W,
LACOPL, Q).

975   THE FILE ON THE GOLDEN GOOSE.   (United Artists-1969-
Sam Wanamaker).   An original screenplay by John C. Higgins
and James B. Gordon, based on a story by John C. Higgins.
(FF, W, LC, Q).

976   THE FILTHIEST SHOW IN TOWN.   (William Mishkin-1973-
Rick and Bob Endelson).   An original screenplay by Rick Endelson.   (W).

977   THE FILTHY FIVE.   (William Mishkin-1968-Andy Milligan).   A
screenplay authored by Gerald Jacuzzo and Andy Milligan.   (FF).

978   THE FINAL COMEDOWN.   (New World-1972-Oscar Williams).
An original screenplay by Oscar Williams.   (FF).

979   FINDERS KEEPERS.   (United Artists-1967-Sidney Hayers).   A
screenplay by Michael Pertwee, based on a story by George H.
Brown.   (FF, W, AMPAS, Q).

980   FINDERS KEEPERS, LOVERS WEEPERS.   (Eve-1969-Russ
Meyer).   A screenplay by Richard Zachary, based on a story
by Russ Meyer.   (FF, W, LC).

981   A FINE MADNESS.   (Warner Bros.-1966-Irvin Kershner).   A
work for the screen authored by Elliott Baker, based on his
novel of the same name; Putnam, 1964.   (Q, FF, NYTFR, LC,
W, AMPAS, LACOPL).

982   A FINE PAIR.   (National General-1969-Francesco Maselli).   A
screenplay by Francesco Maselli, Luisa Montagnana, Larry
Gelbart, and Virgil C. Leone, based on a story by Luisa Montagnana.   (FF, W, Q).

982a THE FINEST HOURS.   (Columbia-1964-Peter Baylis).   Victor
Wolfson based his screenplay on The Second World War by
Sir Winston Churchill; Time, 1959, 2 vols.   (FF, LACOPL,
NYTFR, W, Q).

983   FINGER ON THE TRIGGER.   (Allied Artists-1966-Sidney Pink).
An original screenplay by Luis De Los Arcos and Sidney Pink.
(FF, W, AMPAS, Q).

984   FINIAN'S RAINBOW.   (Warner Bros.-7 Arts-1968-Francis
Ford Coppola).   A screenplay by E. Y. Harburg and Fred
Saidy, based on their musical play; Random House, 1947, 143p.
(Q, FF, NYTFR, W, LC, AMPAS, LACOPL).

985   FINNEGANS WAKE.   (Brandon-1966-Mary Ellen Bute).   The
shooting script authored by Mary Ellen Bute, T. J. Nemeth,
Jr., and Romana Javitz, based on a play by Mary Manning
and the novel by James Joyce; Viking, 1958.   (W, LACOPL).

986   FINNEY.   (Gold Coast-1969-Bill Hare).   An original screenplay by Bill Hare.   (W).

987   THE FIRE WITHIN.   (Governor-1964-Louis Malle).   A screenplay by Louis Malle, based on a novel by Drieu La Rochelle.
(W, FF, Q, NYTFR).

988   FIREBALL 500.   (American International-1966-William Asher).
Screenplay by William Asher and Leo Townsend.   (FF,
NYTFR, W, AMPAS, Q).

989   FIRECREEK.   (Warner Bros.-7 Arts-1968-Vincent McEveety).
An original screenplay by Calvin Clements.   (FF, NYTFR,
FM, W, LC, AMPAS, Q).

990   THE FIREMEN'S BALL.   (Cinema V-1968-Milos Forman).

Milos Forman, Ivan Passer and Jaroslav Papousek wrote this original screenplay. (FF, NYTFR, Q, W, AMPAS).

991   THE FIRST CIRCLE. (Paramount-1973-Aleksander Ford). A screenplay by Aleksander Ford, from a novel by Aleksander I. Solzhenitsyn; Harper, 1968. (W, LACOPL, FF, Q).

992   FIRST LOVE. (UMC-1970-Maximilian Schell). A screenplay by Maximilian Schell and John Gould, based on the novel by Ivan Turgenev; Norton, 1968, 334p. (W, LACOPL, Q).

992a FIRST MEN IN THE MOON. (Columbia-1964-Nathan Juran). A screenplay by Nigel Kneale and Jan Read, from the story by H. G. Wells. (FF, Q, NYTFR, W).

993   THE FIRST TIME. (United Artists-1969-James Neilson). Jo Heims and Roger Smith wrote the screenplay, based on a story by Bernard Bassey. (FF, W, LC, AMPAS, Q).

994   FIRST TIME ROUND. (Kingsway-1972-J. Brian). Script by J. Brian. (W).

995   FIRST TO FIGHT. (Warner Bros.-1967-Christian Nyby). An original screenplay by Gene L. Coon. (FF, W, LC, AMPAS, Q).

996   FISHKE GOES TO WAR. (Moishe Baruch-1972-George Ovadia). An original screenplay by Michael Shvili. (W).

997   FIST IN HIS POCKET. (Peppercorn-Wormser-1968-Marco Bellocchio). An original screenplay by Marco Bellocchio. (FF, NYTFR, W, Q).

998   A FISTFUL OF DOLLARS. (United Artists-1967-Sergio Leone aka Bob Robertson). Screenplay by Sergio Leone and Duccio Tessari, based on a story by Toni Palombi. (FF, NYTFR, LC, Q).

999   FISTS OF FURY. (National General-1973-Lo Wei). An original screenplay attributed to Lo Wei. (W, Q).

1000 FITZWILLY. (United Artists-1967-Delbert Mann). A screenplay by Isobel Lennart, based on the novel A Garden of Cucumbers by Poyntz Tyler; Random House, 1960. (Q, FF, NYTFR, FM, W, LC, AMPAS, LACOPL).

1001 FIVE BLOODY GRAVES. (Independent International-1971-Al Adamson). An original story and screenplay by Robert Dix. (W).

1002 FIVE CARD STUD. (Paramount-1968-Henry Hathaway). Marguerite Roberts wrote the screenplay, based on a novel by Ray Gaulden, Glory Gulch. (FF, NYTFR, FM, W, LC, AMPAS, Q).

1003   FIVE EASY PIECES. (Columbia-1970-Bob Rafelson). Screenplay written by Adrien Joyce, adapted from a story by Bob
Rafelson and Adrien Joyce. (W, Q).

1004   FIVE FINGERS OF DEATH. (Warner Bros.-1973-Cheng
Chang Ho). An original screenplay by Chiang Yang. (W, Q).

1005   FIVE GENTS' TRICK BOOK. (Toho-1966-Sayo Marubayashi).
An original screenplay by Ryozo Kasahara. (W).

1006   THE FIVE MAN ARMY. (MGM-1970-Don Taylor). An original screenplay by Dario Argento and Marc Richards. (W,
Q).

1007   FIVE MILLION YEARS TO EARTH. (20th Century-Fox-
1968-Roy Ward Baker). An original story and screenplay by
Nigel Kneale. (FF, NYTFR, W, LC, Q).

1008   FIVE ON THE BLACK HAND SIDE. (United Artists-1973-
Oscar Williams). A screenplay by Charles L. Russell, based
on his play of the same title. (W).

1009   FIVE THE HARD WAY. (Fantascope-1969-Gus Trikonis). A
work written for the screen by Tony Huston and Larry Billman, from a story by Larry Billman. (W).

1010   THE FIXER. (MGM-1968-John Frankenheimer). Dalton
Trumbo wrote the screenplay for this film, from the novel by
Bernard Malamud; Farrar, 1966. (FF, NYTFR, W, LC,
AMPAS, LACOPL, Q).

1011   FLAME OVER VIETNAM. (Producers Releasing Organiza-
tion-1967-Joe Lacy). A screenplay by Ralph Salvia, John
Hart and Joe Lacy, based on a story by Ralph Salvia. (FF,
W).

1012   FLAMING FRONTIER. (Warner Bros.-7 Arts-1968-Alfred
Vohrer). Eberhard Keindorff, Johanna Sibelius and Fred
Denger authored this screenplay, based on a novel by Karl
May. (FF, W, Q).

1013   THE FLANDERS AND ALCOTT REPORT ON SEX RESPONSE.
(Films International-1971-Eric Jeffrey Haims). Film is
based on a story by Dr. Ann Foster. (W).

1014   FLAP. (Warner Bros.-1970-Carol Reed). A screenplay
written by Clair Huffaker, based on the novel Nobody Loves
a Drunken Indian by Clair Huffaker; McKay, 1967. (W,
LACOPL, Q).

1015   FLAREUP. (MGM-1969-James Neilson). An original screenplay by Mark Rodgers. (W, LC, Q).

1016   THE FLAVOR OF GREEN TEA OVER RICE. (New Yorker-
        1973-Yasujiro Ozu). An original screenplay by Yasujiro Ozu
        and Kogo Noda. (W).

1017   A FLEA IN HER EAR. (20th Century-Fox-1968-Noel Howard).
        John Mortimer authored the screenplay based on his English
        language stage adaptation of the play La Puce a L'Oreille by
        Georges Feydeau. (FF, NYTFR, FM, W, LC, AMPAS, Q).

1017a   DIE FLEDERMAUS. (Casino-1964-Geza von Cziffra). A
        screenplay by Geza von Cziffra, based on the operetta by Jo-
        hann Strauss. (FF, NYTFR).

1018   FLESH. (Factory-1968-Paul Morrissey). An original screen-
        play by Paul Morrissey. (FF, NYTFR, W, Q).

        FLESH FOR FRANKENSTEIN see FRANKENSTEIN

1019   FLESH GORDON. (Mammoth-1974-Howard Ziehm and Mi-
        chael Benveniste). An original screenplay by Michael Ben-
        veniste. (V, HR).

1020   FLESHPOT ON 42ND STREET. (William Mishkin-1972-Andy
        Milligan). An original script written by Andy Milligan. (FF,
        W).

        THE FLIGHT see LA FUGA

1020a   FLIGHT FROM ASHIYA. (United Artists-1964-Michael And-
        erson). Elliott Arnold and Waldo Salt co-authored the screen-
        play based on the novel by Elliott Arnold; Knopf, 1959, 273p.
        (FF, W, Q, AMPAS, LACOPL, NYTFR).

1021   FLIGHT OF THE DOVES. (Columbia-1971-Ralph Nelson). A
        screenplay by Frank Gabrielson and Ralph Nelson, based on
        a book by Walter Macken; Macmillan, 1968. (W, LACOPL,
        Q).

1022   THE FLIGHT OF THE PHOENIX. (20th Century-Fox-1966-
        Robert Aldrich). A screenplay by Lukas Heller, from the
        novel by Elleston Trevor; Harper, 1964. (FF, NYTFR, LC,
        W, AMPAS, LACOPL, Q).

1023   FLIGHT TO FURY. (Harold Goldman Associates-1967-Jack
        Nicholson). A screenplay by Monte Hellman, based on a
        story by Monte Hellman. (FF, W).

1024   THE FLIM-FLAM MAN. (20th Century-Fox-1967-Irvin Ker-
        shner). A screenplay by William Rose, based on the novel
        The Ballad of the Flim-Flam Man by Guy Owen; Macmillan,
        1965. (Q, FF, NYTFR, FM, W, LC AMPAS, LACOPL).

1024a   FLIPPER'S NEW ADVENTURE. (MGM-1964-Leon Benson).

A screenplay written by Art Arthur, based on characters created by Ricou Browning and Jack Cowden. (FF, NYTFR, W, AMPAS, Q).

1025   FLOATING WEEDS. (Altura-1970-Yasujiro Ozu). A screenplay written by Kogo Noda and Yasujiro Ozu, from a story by Yasujiro Ozu. (W).

1026   FLOWER THIEF. (Film-Makers-1969-Ron Rice). An original screenplay by Ron Rice. (W).

1027   FLUFFY. (Universal-1965-Earl Bellamy). An original work for the screen written by Samuel Roeca. (NYTFR, LC, W, AMPAS).

1028   FLY ME. (New World-1973-Cirio Santiago). An original screenplay by Miller Drake. (W).

1029   THE FLYING MATCHMAKER. (National Showmanship-1970-Israel Becker). A screenplay by Israel Becker and Alex Maimon, adapted into English by Paulette Rubinstein, based on The Two Lemels by Abraham Goldfaden. (W).

1030   THE FOLKS AT RED WOLF INN. (Scope III-1972-Bud Townsend). An original screenplay by Allen J. Actors. (W).

1031   FOLLOW ME. (Cinerama-1969-Gene McCabe). An original screenplay written by Stanley Ralph Ross. (W, AMPAS, Q).

1032   FOLLOW ME, BOYS! (Buena Vista-1966-Norman Tokar). Louis Pelletier wrote the screenplay based on the book God and My Country by MacKinlay Kantor; World, 1954. (Q, FF, NYTFR, LC, W, AMPAS, LACOPL).

1033   THE FOOL KILLER. (Landau-1965-Servando Gonzalez). Morton Fine and David Friedkin wrote the screenplay based on the novel by Helen Eustis; Doubleday, 1954. (FF, W, AMPAS, LACOPL).

1034   FOOLS. (Cinerama-1970-Tom Gries). An original work for the screen written by Robert Rudelson. (W, Q).

1035   FOOLS' PARADE. (Columbia-1971-Andrew V. McLaglen). A work for the screen written by James Lee Barrett, adapted from the novel by Davis Grubb; World Publishing Co., 1969, 306p. (W, LACOPL, Q).

1036   FOR A FEW DOLLARS MORE. (United Artists-1967-Sergio Leone). An original screenplay written by Luciano Vincenzoni and Sergio Leone. (FF, NYTFR, FM, W, LC, Q).

1037   FOR LOVE OF IVY. (Cinerama-1968-Daniel Mann). Robert Alan Arthur wrote this screenplay, based on an original story by Sidney Poitier. (FF, NYTFR, W, AMPAS, Q).

1038 FOR PETE'S SAKE. (Columbia-1974-Peter Yates). A screenplay by Stanley Shapiro and Maurice Richlin; a novelization
based on the screenplay was written by Bradford Street; Avon
Books, 1974, 192p. (V, LACOPL).

1039 FOR SINGLES ONLY. (Columbia-1968-Arthur Dreifuss). A
screenplay by Hal Collins and Arthur Dreifuss, based on a
story by Arthur Hoerl and Albert Derr. (FF, NYTFR, FM,
W, LC, AMPAS, Q).

1039a FOR THOSE WHO THINK YOUNG. (United Artists-1964-Les-
lie H. Martinson). James O'Hanlon, George O'Hanlon and
Dan Beaumont wrote the screenplay from an original story by
Dan Beaumont. (FF, NYTFR, AMPAS, Q, W).

1040 FORBIDDEN UNDER THE CENSORSHIP OF THE KING.
(Lemming-1973-Barry R. Kerr). Script written by Barry R.
Kerr. (W).

1041 THE FORBIN PROJECT. (Universal-1970-Joseph Sargent).
James Bridges wrote the screenplay based on the novel Co-
lossus by D. F. Jones; Putnam, 1966. (W, LACOPL, Q).

1042 FORT COURAGEOUS. (20th Century-Fox-1965-Lesley Selander). An original screenplay by Richard Landau. (FF,
LC, W, AMPAS, Q).

1043 FORT UTAH. (Paramount-1967-Lesley Selander). A screenplay written directly for the screen by Steve Fisher and Andrew Craddock. (Q, FF, NYTFR, FM, W, LC, AMPAS).

1044 FORTUNA. (Trans American-1969-Menahem Golan). A
screenplay by Volodja Semitjov, Alexander Ramati and Joseph
Gross, based on a story by Menahem Talmi. (W).

1045 FORTUNE AND MEN'S EYES. (MGM-1971-Harvey Hart). A
screenplay by John Herbert and based on his play of the same
name; Grove Press, 1967, 96 p. (W, LACOPL, Q).

1046 THE FORTUNE COOKIE. (United Artists-1966-Billy Wilder).
A screenplay by Billy Wilder and I. A. L. Diamond. The
screenplay was published as The Apartment and The Fortune
Cookie: Two Screenplays by Billy Wilder and I. A. L. Dia-
mond; Praeger, 1971, pp. 119-191. (FF, NYTFR, W,
AMPAS, Q).

1047 40 CARATS. (Columbia-1973-Milton Katselas). A screenplay
by Leonard Gershe, based on a play adapted by Jay Allen
from Barillet and Gredy; Random House, 1969, 119p. (W,
LACOPL, Q).

1048   40 GUNS TO APACHE PASS. (Columbia-1967-William Witney).
       A screenplay by Willard and Mary Willingham. (FF, LC,
       AMPAS, Q).

1049   THE FOUNTAIN OF LOVE. (Crown International-1969-Ernst
       Hofbauer). An original screenplay by Walter Schneider.
       (W).

1050   FOUR CLOWNS. (20th Century-Fox-1970-). Narration writ-
       ten by Robert Youngson. (W, Q).

1050a FOUR DAYS IN NOVEMBER. (United Artists-1964-Mel Stu-
       art). Narration written by Theodore Strauss. (FF, NYTFR,
       W, Q).

1051   FOUR FLIES ON GREY VELVET. (Paramount-1972-Dario
       Argento). A screenplay by Dario Argento, based on a story
       by Dario Argento, Luigi Cozzi, and Mario Foglietti. (FF,
       Q).

1052   FOUR NIGHTS OF A DREAMER. (New Yorker-1972-Robert
       Bresson). An original screenplay by Robert Bresson. (W,
       FF).

1053   491. (Janus-1967-Vilgot Sjöman). A screenplay by Lars
       Görling, based on his novel; Grove Press, 1966, 282p. (FF,
       NYTFR, W, LACOPL).

1054   FOUR STARS. (Filmmakers' Distribution Center-1967-Andy
       Warhol). A screenplay by Andy Warhol. (FF, W).

1055   THE FOX. (Warner Bros.-7 Arts-1968-Mark Rydell). A
       screenplay by Lewis John Carlino and Howard Koch, based on
       the novella by D. H. Lawrence; Bantam Books, 1951, 105p.
       (Q, FF, NYTFR, FM, W, AMPAS, LACOPL).

1056   FOXY BROWN. (American International-1974-Jack Hill). An
       original screenplay by Jack Hill. (HR, V).

1057   FRAGMENT OF FEAR. (Columbia-1971-Richard C. Sarafian).
       An original screenplay by Paul Dehn. (W, Q).

1058   FRANKENSTEIN. (Bryanston-1974-Paul Morrissey). A
       screenplay by Paul Morrissey. (HR).

       FRANKENSTEIN AND THE GIANT LIZARD see FRANKEN-
       STEIN CONQUERS THE WORLD

1059   FRANKENSTEIN AND THE MONSTER FROM HELL. (Para-
       mount-1974-Terence Fisher). An original screenplay by John
       Elder. (V).

1060   FRANKENSTEIN CONQUERS THE WORLD. (American International-1966-Inoshiro Honda). A screenplay by Reuben Bercovitch, based on his original story. (FF, LC, W, AMPAS, Q).

1061 FRANKENSTEIN CREATED WOMAN. (20th Century-Fox-1967-Terence Fisher). A screenplay by John Elder. (FF, W, LC, AMPAS, Q).

1062 FRANKENSTEIN MEETS THE SPACE MONSTER. (Allied Artists-1966-Robert Gaffney). An original screenplay by George Garret. (FF, LC, W, AMPAS, Q).

1063 FRANKENSTEIN MUST BE DESTROYED! (Warner Bros. - 1970-Terence Fisher). A screenplay by Bert Batt, from a story by Anthony Nelson Keys and Bert Batt. (W, Q).

1064 FRANKENSTEIN'S BLOODY TERROR. (Independent-International Pictures-1972-Henry L. Egan). An original screenplay by Jacinto Molina. (W).

1065 FRANKIE AND JOHNNY. (United Artists-1966-Frederick De Cordova). A screenplay by Alex Gottlieb, from a story by Nat Perrin. (FF, NYTFR, LC, W, AMPAS, Q).

1066 FRASIER, THE SENSUOUS LION. (LCS-1973-Pat Shields). A work for the screen by Jerry Kobrin, based on a story by Sandy Dore. (W).

1067 FRAULEIN DOKTOR. (Paramount-1969-Alberto Lattuada). An original screenplay by Duilio Coletti, Vittoriano Petrilli, Stanley Mann, H. C. Craig, and Alberto Lattuada. (FF, W, LC, Q).

FREE THE ARMY see F. T. A.

1068 FREEBIE AND THE BEAN. (Warner Bros. -1974-Richard Rush). Robert Kaufman authored the screenplay from a story by Floyd Mutrux. Original novel based on screenplay by Paul Ross; Warner Paperback Library, 1974, 172p. (V).

1069 THE FRENCH CONNECTION. (20th Century-Fox-1971-William Friedkin). A screenplay by Ernest Tidyman, based on a novel by Robin Moore; Little, Brown & Co., 1969, 309p. (W, LACOPL, Q).

1070 THE FRENCH CONSPIRACY. (Cine Globe-1973-Yves Boisset). A screenplay by Ben Barzman and Basilio Franchina, with adaptation and dialogue by Jorge Semprun. (W).

1071 FRENZY. (Universal-1972-Alfred Hitchcock). A screenplay by Anthony Shaffer, based on the novel Goodbye Piccadilly, Farewell Leicester Square by Arthur La Bern; Stein, 1966. (FF, LACOPL, Q).

1072   FRIDAY ON MY MIND.   (Continental-1970-Wayne A. Schotten).   Script written by Wayne A. Schotten.   (W).

1073   FRIEND OF THE FAMILY.   (International Classics-1965-
Robert Thomas).   A screenplay by Robert Thomas, adapted
from the play Patate by Marcel Achard.   (NYTFR, LC, Q).

1074   FRIENDS.   (Paramount-1971-Lewis Gilbert).   An original
screenplay by Jack Russell and Vernon Harris.   (W, Q).

1075   THE FRIENDS OF EDDIE COYLE.   (Paramount-1973-Peter
Yates).   A screenplay by Paul Monash, based on the novel
by George V. Higgins; Knopf, 1971, 183p.   (W, LACOPL,
Q).

1076   FRIGHT.   (Allied Artists-1972-Peter Collinson).   Original
screenplay written by Tudor Gates.   (FF).

1077   FRITZ THE CAT.   (Cinemation-1972-Ralph Bakshi).   A
screenplay by Ralph Bakshi, based on the comic strip by Robert Crumb.   (FF, Q).

1078   FROGS.   (American International-1972-George McCowan).   A
work for the screen written by Robert Hutchison and Robert
Blees, from a story by Robert Hutchison.   (W, Q).

1079   FROM EAR TO EAR.   (Cinemation-1971-Louis Soulanes).   No
author credits available.   (W, Q).

1079a   FROM RUSSIA WITH LOVE.   (United Artists-1964-Terence
Young).   The screenplay by Richard Maibaum and Joanna Harwood, was based on a novel by Ian Fleming; Signet, 1959,
191p.   (FF, AMPAS, LACOPL, NYTFR, Q, W).

1080   FROM THE MIXED-UP FILES OF MRS. BASIL E. FRANK-
WEILER.   (Cinema V-1973-Fielder Cook).   A screenplay by
Blanche Hanalis, based on a novel by E. L. Konigsburg;
Atheneum, 1967.   (W, LACOPL).

1081   THE FRONT PAGE.   (Universal-1974-Billy Wilder).   A
screenplay by Billy Wilder and I. A. L. Diamond, based on
the play by Ben Hecht and Charles MacArthur; in 50 Best
Plays of the American Theatre, Vol. I, by Clive Barnes;
Crown Publishers, pp. 295-345.   (V, LACOPL).

1082   FRONTIER HELLCAT.   (Columbia-1966-Alfred Vohrer).   A
screenplay by Eberhard Keindorff and Johanna Sibelius, based
on the novel by Karl May.   (FF, AMPAS, Q).

1083   FROZEN ALIVE.   (Magna-1966-Bernard Knowles).   No screenplay credits available.   (FF).

1084   THE FROZEN DEAD.   (Warner Bros.-7 Arts-1967-Herbert J.

Leder).   An original screenplay written by Herbert J. Leder. (FF, Q, NYTFR, FM, W, LC, AMPAS, Q).

FUCK   see   BLUE MOVIE

FUCK THE ARMY   see   F. T. A.

1085   FUEGO.   (Haven International-1969-Armando Bo).   An original screenplay by Armando Bo.   (W, Q).

1086   LA FUGA.   (International Classics-1966-Paolo Spinola).   A work for the screen by Sergio Amidei, in collaboration with Prof. Piero Bellanova, based on an idea by Paolo Spinola and Carla Conti.   (FF, NYTFR, LC, W).

1087   A FULL LIFE.   (New Yorker-1972-Susumu Hani).   Susumu Hani is credited with the screenplay, from a story by Tatsuzo Ishikawa.   (W).

FUN AND GAMES   see   1,000 CONVICTS AND A WOMAN

1088   FUN AND GAMES.   (Audubon-1973-Mervyn Nelson).   No screenplay credits available.   (W).

1088a   FUN IN ACAPULCO.   (Paramount-1964-Richard Thorpe). Allan Weiss wrote the original screenplay.   (Q, W, AMPAS, NYTFR, FF).

1089   FUNERAL IN BERLIN.   (Paramount-1966-Guy Hamilton).   A screenplay by Evan Jones, based on the novel by Len Deighton; Putnam, 1964.   (Q, FF, NYTFR, LC, W, AMPAS, LACOPL).

1090   FUNERAL PARADE OF ROSES.   (New Yorker-1973-Toshio Matsumoto).   An original screenplay by Toshio Matsumoto. (W).

1091   THE FUNNIEST MAN IN THE WORLD.   (Evergreen-1969-Vernon P. Becker).   An original screenplay by Vernon P. Becker.   (W, Q).

1092   FUNNY GIRL.   (Columbia-1968-William Wyler).   A screenplay by Isobel Lennart, based on her musical play with music by Jule Styne and lyrics by Bob Merrill; Random House, 1964, 134p.   (Q, FF, NYTFR, W, LC, AMPAS, LACOPL).

1093   A FUNNY THING HAPPENED ON THE WAY TO THE FORUM. (United Artists-1966-Richard Lester).   A screenplay by Melvin Frank and Michael Pertwee, based on the musical comedy by Burt Shevelove and Larry Gelbart; Dodd, 1963, 107p.   (Q, FF, NYTFR, LC, W, AMPAS, LACOPL).

1094   FUNNYMAN.   (1971-John Korty).   An original screenplay by John Korty and Peter Bonerz.   (NYTFR, W, AMPAS).

1095   THE FURTHER PERILS OF LAUREL AND HARDY. (20th
        Century-Fox-1968). Commentary written by Robert Youngson.
        (FF, W, LC, Q).

1096   FUTZ. (Commonwealth United-1969-Tom O'Horgan). A
        screenplay by Joseph Stefano, based on a play by Rochelle
        Owens; in New American Plays, V. 2, Hill and Wang. (W,
        LACOPL, Q).

1097   FUZZ. (United Artists-1972-Richard A. Colla). A screen-
        play by Evan Hunter, based on the novel by Ed McBain aka
        Evan Hunter; Doubleday, 1968. (W, LACOPL, Q).

1098   LE GAI SAVOIR. (EYR-1970-Jean-Luc Godard). A screen-
        play by Jean-Luc Godard, based on Emile by Jean Jacques
        Rousseau; Dutton, 1957, 444p. (W, LACOPL).

1099   GAILY, GAILY. (United Artists-1969-Norman Jewison). A
        work for the screen by Abram S. Ginnes, based on Ben
        Hecht's book; Doubleday, 1963, 227p. (W, AMPAS, LACOPL,
        Q).

1100   GALIA. (Zenith International-1966-Georges Lautner). A
        screenplay by Vahe Katcha and Georges Lautner, based on an
        original story by Vahe Katcha. (FF, NYTFR, W, Q).

1101   GAMBIT. (Universal-1966-Ronald Neame). A screenplay by
        Jack Davies and Alvin Sargent, based on a story by Sidney
        Carroll, "Who Is Mr. Dean?" (FF, NYTFR, LC, AMPAS,
        Q).

1102   THE GAMBLER. (Paramount-1974-Karel Reisz). An origi-
        nal screenplay by James Toback. (V, HR).

1103   THE GAMBLERS. (UM-1970-Ron Winston). A screenplay
        written by Ron Winston, based on a play by Nikolai Gogol;
        Macaulay, 1927, 210p. (W, LACOPL, Q).

1104   THE GAME IS OVER. (Royal-1967-Roger Vadim). A screen-
        play by Jean Cau, Roger Vadim, and Bernard Frechtman,
        based on the novel La Curée by Emile Zola. (FF, NYTFR,
        W, Q).

1105   GAMES. (Universal-1967-Curtis Harrington). A screenplay
        by Gene Kearney, based on a story by Curtis Harrington and
        George Edwards. (FF, NYTFR, FM, W, AMPAS, Q).

1106   THE GAMES. (20th Century-Fox-1970-Michael Winner). A
        screenplay by Erich Segal, from the book by Hugh Atkinson;
        Simon & Schuster, 1967. (W, LACOPL, Q).

1107   THE GAMES MEN PLAY. (Joseph Brenner Associates-1968-
        Daniel Tinayre). A screenplay by Eduardo Borras, based on

a novel by Dante Sierra. (FF, NYTFR, W, AMPAS).

1108   GAMES OF DESIRE. (Times Films-1968-Hans Albin & Peter
        Berneis). A screenplay by Peter Berneis. (FF, LC).

1109   GAMMERA THE INVINCIBLE. (World Entertainment-1967-
        Noriaki Yuasa). A screenplay by Nizo Takahashi, from an
        idea of Yonejiro Saito's, with additional dialogue by Richard
        Kraft. (W).

1110   THE GANG THAT COULDN'T SHOOT STRAIGHT. (MGM-
        1971-James Goldstone). A screenplay by Waldo Salt, from the
        novel by Jimmy Breslin; Viking, 1969, 249p. (W, LACOPL,
        Q).

1111   GANGA ZUMBA. (New Yorker-1972-Carlos Diegues). A
        screenplay by Carlos Diegues, Leopoldo Serran, Ruben Rocha
        Filho, from a novel by João Felicio dos Santos. (W).

1112   GANJA AND HESS. (Kelly-Jordan-1973-Bill Gunn). An origi-
        nal screenplay by Bill Gunn. (W).

1113   THE GARDEN OF DELIGHTS. (Perry-Fleetwood-1971-Carlos
        Saura). An original screenplay written by Rafael Azcona and
        Carlos Saura. (W).

1114   THE GARDEN OF THE FINZI-CONTINIS. (Cinema V-1971-
        Vittorio De Sica). A screenplay by Cesare Zavattini, Vittorio
        Bonicelli, and Ugo Pirro, based on the novel by Giorgio Bas-
        sani; Atheneum, 1965. (W, LACOPL, Q).

1115   THE GARNET BRACELET. (Artkino-1966-Abram Room). A
        screenplay by A. Granberg and Abram Room, based on the
        novel by Alexander Kuprin. (FF, NYTFR, W, Q).

1116   GAS-S-S-S! (American International-1970-Roger Corman).
        An original screenplay by George Armitage. (W).

1117   THE GATLING GUN. (Ellman Enterprises-1973-Robert Gor-
        dan). An original screenplay by Mark Hanna, and Joseph
        Van Winkle. (W).

1118   THE GAY DECEIVERS. (Fanfare-1969-Bruce Kessler). A
        screenplay by Jerome Wish, based on a story by Abe Polsky
        and Gil Lasky. (FF, W, AMPAS, Q).

1119   THE GENESIS CHILDREN. (Lyric-1972-Anthony Aikman). An
        original screenplay by Billy Byars and Anthony Aikman. (W).

1120   GENGHIS KHAN. (Columbia-1965-Henry Levin). A screen-
        play by Clarke Reynolds and Beverly Cross, based on an
        original story by Berkely Mather. (NYTFR, LC, W,
        AMPAS).

1121   GENTLE GIANT. (Paramount-1968-James Neilson). A
        screenplay by Edward J. Lakso and Andy White, based on the
        novel Gentle Ben by Walt Morey; Dutton, 1965. (Q, FF, FM,
        NYTFR, W, LC, AMPAS, LACOPL).

1122   THE GENTLE PEOPLE AND THE QUIET LAND. (Commer-
        cial-1972-Richard H. Bartlett). A screenplay by Richard H.
        Bartlett, based on the photographic works of James Warner.
        (W).

1123   THE GENTLE RAIN. (Comet-1966-Burt Balaban). An origi-
        nal screenplay by Robert Cream. (FF, W, Q).

1124   GEORGE! (Capital-1972-Wallace C. Bennett). A screenplay
        by Wallace C. Bennett, based on a story by Marshall Thomp-
        son. (FF, W).

1125   GEORGIA, GEORGIA. (Cinerama-1972-Stig Bjorkman). An
        original screenplay by Maya Angelou. (FF, Q).

1126   GEORGY GIRL. (Columbia-1966-Silvio Narizzano). A screen-
        play by Margaret Forster and Peter Nichols, based on the
        novel by Margaret Forster; Berkley, 1965. (Q, FF, NYTFR,
        LC, W, AMPAS, LACOPL).

1127   GERTRUD. (Pathe Contemporary-1966-Carl Dreyer). A
        screenplay by Carl Dreyer, based on a play by Hjalmar Söd-
        erberg. (FF, NYTFR).

1128   GET CARTER. (MGM-1971-Mike Hodges). A screenplay by
        Mike Hodges, based on the novel Jack's Return Home by Ted
        Lewis; Doubleday, 1970, 206p. (W, LACOPL, Q).

1129   GET ON WITH IT! (Governor-1965-C. M. Pennington-
        Richards). An original screenplay by Hazel Adair and Hugh
        Woodhouse. (W, Q).

1130   GET TO KNOW YOUR RABBIT. (Warner Bros.-1972-Brian
        De Palma). An original screenplay by Jordan Crittenden.
        (W, Q).

1131   GET YOURSELF A COLLEGE GIRL. (MGM-1965-Sidney Mil-
        ler). An original screenplay by Robert E. Kent. (FF, LC,
        AMPAS, Q).

1132   THE GETAWAY. (National General-1972-Sam Peckinpah).
        A work for the screen by Walter Hill, based on the novel by
        Jim Thompson; Bantam Books, 1973, 184p. (W, FF, Q,
        LACOPL).

1133   GETTING STRAIGHT. (Columbia-1970-Richard Rush). A
        screenplay by Robert Kaufman, based on a novel by Ken
        Kolb; Chilton, 1967. (W, LACOPL, Q).

1134 GHIDRA, THE THREE-HEADED MONSTER. (Continental-
1966-Inoshiro Honda). An original screenplay by Shinichi
Sekizawa. (W).

1135 THE GHOST. (Magna-1966-Riccardo Freda aka Robert Hampton). A screenplay by Robert Davidson and Riccardo Freda.
(FF, AMPAS).

1136 THE GHOST AND MR. CHICKEN. (Universal-1966-Alan Rafkin). A screenplay by James Fritzell and Everett Greenbaum. (FF, NYTFR, LC, W, AMPAS, Q).

1137 GHOST IN THE INVISIBLE BIKINI. (American International-
1966-Don Weis). A screenplay by Louis M. Heyward and Elwood Ullman based on a story by Louis M. Heyward. (FF,
LC, W, AMPAS, Q).

1138 GHOSTS--ITALIAN STYLE. (MGM-1969-Renato Castellani).
A screenplay by Renato Castellani, Tonino Guerra, Adriano
Baracco, and Piero De Bernardi. (FF, W, LC, Q).

1139 GINGER. (Joseph Brenner-1971-Don Schain). An original
screenplay by Don Schain. (W).

1140 THE GIRL AND THE BUGLER. (Artkino-1967-Alexander Mit-
ta). An original screenplay by Alexander Volodin. (W).

1141 THE GIRL AND THE GENERAL. (MGM-1967-Pasquale Festa
Campanile). An original screenplay by Luigi Malerba, based
on a story by Pasquale Festa Campanile and Massimo Franciosa. (FF, W, LC, AMPAS, Q).

1142 THE GIRL FROM PETROVKA. (Universal-1974-Robert Ellis
Miller). A screenplay by Allan Scott, and Chris Bryant,
from a book by George Feifer; Viking, 1971, 252p. (V,
LACOPL).

1143 THE GIRL-GETTERS. (American International-1966-Michael
Winner). A screenplay by Peter Draper. (FF, NYTFR, W,
Q).

1144 GIRL HAPPY. (MGM-1965-Boris Sagal). An original screenplay by Harvey Bullock and R. S. Allen. (NYTFR, LC, W,
AMPAS, Q).

1145 THE GIRL IN BLUE. (Cinerama-1974-George Kaczender). An
original screenplay by Douglas Bowie. (HR).

1146 THE GIRL ON A MOTORCYCLE. (Claridge-1968-Jack Cardiff). A screenplay by Ronald Duncan, based on the novel
Motorcycle, by Andre Pieyre De Mandiargues; Grove Press,
1965. (FF, NYTFR, Q, W, AMPAS, LACOPL).

1147   THE GIRL WHO COULDN'T SAY NO.   (20th Century-Fox-1970-
        Franco Brusati).   An original screenplay by Franco Brusati
        and Ennio de Concini.   (W, Q).

1148   THE GIRL WHO KNEW TOO MUCH.   (Commonwealth-1969-
        Francis D. Lyon).   An original screenplay by Charles Wal-
        lace.   (W, Q).

1149   THE GIRL WITH HUNGRY EYES.   (Boxoffice International-
        1966-William Rotsler).   William Rotsler wrote this original
        screenplay.   (FF).

1149a   THE GIRL WITH THE GREEN EYES.   (Lopert-1964-Desmond
        Davis).   Edna O'Brien's screenplay was based on her novel
        The Lonely Girl; Random House, 1962.   (W, FF, Q, LACOPL,
        NYTFR).

1150   THE GIRL WITH THE HATBOX.   (Artkino-1970-Boris Bar-
        net).   An original screenplay by V. Turkin and V. Shershen-
        evich.   (W).

1151   THE GIRL WITH THREE CAMELS.   (Continental-1968-Vaclav
        Krska).   A screenplay by Miloslav Stehlik and Vaclav Krska,
        based on a story by Miloslav Stehlik.   (FF, NYTFR, W).

1152   THE GIRLS.   (New Line Cinema-1972-Mai Zetterling).   A
        screenplay by Mai Zetterling and David Hughes, including
        passages from Lysistrata by Aristophanes.   (FF).

1153   GIRLS ARE FOR LOVING.   (Continental-1973-Don Schain).
        Don Schain is credited with the writing of this screenplay.
        (W).

        THE GIRLS OF 42ND STREET   see   FLESHPOT ON 42ND
        STREET

1154   THE GIRLS ON THE BEACH.   (Paramount 1965 William N.
        Witney).   An original screenplay by David Malcolm.   (W,
        LC, AMPAS, Q).

1155   GIRLY.   (Cinerama-1970-Freddie Francis).   A screenplay by
        Brian Comport, based on the play by Maisie Mosco.   (W).

1156   GIT!   (Embassy-1965-Ellis Kadison).   A screenplay by Homer
        McCoy, based on a story by Homer McCoy and Ellis Kadison.
        (W, AMPAS, Q).

1157   GIVE HER THE MOON.   (United Artists-1970-Philippe de
        Broca).   Daniel Boulanger and Philippe de Broca wrote this
        original screenplay.   (W).

1157a   THE GIVEN WORD.   (Lionex-1964-Anselmo Duarte).   Ansel-
        mo Duarte authored this original screenplay.   (FF, NYTFR).

1158 GLADIATORS SEVEN. (MGM-1964-Pedro Lazaga). An original work for the screen written by Sandro Continenza, Bruno Corbucci, Alberto De Martino, and Giovanni Grimaldi. (Q, W, NYTFR, FF).

1158a THE GLASS BOTTOM BOAT. (MGM-1966-Frank Tashlin). An original screenplay written by Everett Freeman. (FF, LC, W, AMPAS, Q).

1159 GLASS HOUSES. (Columbia-1972-Alexander Singer). This original screenplay was written by Alexander Singer and Judith Singer. (W).

1160 THE GLASS SPHINX. (American International-1968-Luigi Scattini). An original screenplay written by Adalberto Albertino, Camas Gil, and Jose A. Cascales. (FF).

1161 GLEN AND RANDA. (UMC-1971-Jim McBride). Lorenzo Mans, Rudolph Wurliter and Jim McBride authored this original screenplay. (W, Q).

1161a A GLOBAL AFFAIR. (MGM-1964-Jack Arnold). A screenplay by Arthur Marx and Bob Fisher and Charles Lederer, from a story by Eugene Vale. (FF, NYTFR, W, Q).

GLORY BOY see MY OLD MAN'S PLACE

1162 THE GLORY GUYS. (United Artists-1965-Arnold Laven). A Sam Peckinpah screenplay, based on a novel The Dice of God by Hoffman Birney; Holt, 1956. (W, LC, AMPAS, LACOPL, Q).

1163 THE GLORY STOMPERS. (American International-1968-Anthony Lanza). A screenplay by James Gordon White and John Lawrence. (FF, NYTFR, W, LC, AMPAS, Q).

1164 THE GNOME-MOBILE. (Buena Vista-1967-Robert Stevenson). A screenplay by Ellis Kadison, taken from the novel The Gnomobile by Upton Sinclair; Bobbs-Merrill, 1962. (FF, W, LC, AMPAS, LACOPL, Q).

1165 THE GO-BETWEEN. (Columbia-1971-Joseph Losey). A screenplay by Harold Pinter, based on a novel by L. P. Hartley; Knopf, 1953. (W, LACOPL, Q).

1166 GOD FORGIVES--I DON'T! (American International-1969-Giuseppe Colizzi). An original story and screenplay by Giuseppe Colizzi. (W, LC).

1167 THE GODFATHER. (Paramount-1972-Francis Ford Coppola). A screenplay by Mario Puzo and Francis Ford Coppola, based on the novel by Mario Puzo; Putnam, 1969, 446p. (FF, LACOPL, Q).

1168   THE GODFATHER, PART II.   (Paramount-1974-Francis Ford
       Coppola).   A screenplay by Francis Ford Coppola and Mario
       Puzo, based on the latter's novel; Putnam, 1969, 446p.   (V,
       NYT, LACOPL).

1169   THE GODSON.   (Artists International-1972-Jean-Pierre Mel-
       ville).   A screenplay by Jean-Pierre Melville, based on the
       novel The Ronin, by Joan McLeod.   (FF).

1170   GODSPELL.   (Columbia-1973-Joh-Michael Tebelak).   An orig-
       inal screenplay by David Greene and John-Michael Tebelak,
       based on the stage production.   (W, Q).

1171   GODZILLA VS. THE SMOG MONSTER.   (American Interna-
       tional-1972-Yoshimitu Banno).   An original screenplay by
       Kaoru Mabuchi and Yoshimitu Banno.   (FF).

1171a GODZILLA VS. THE THING.   (American International-1964-
       Inoshiro Honda).   An original screenplay by Shinichi Seki-
       zawa.   (FF, NYTFR, Q).

1172   GO-GO BIGBEAT!   (Eldorado-1965-Kenneth Hume).   A docu-
       mentary; no writers credits given.   (W).

1173   GO GO MANIA.   (American International-1965-Frederic
       Goode).   An original screenplay by Roger Dunton.   (FF, LC,
       W, Q).

1174   GOIN' DOWN THE ROAD.   (Chevron-1970-Donald Shebib).   An
       original screenplay written by William Fruet.   (W, Q).

1175   GOING HOME.   (MGM-1971-Herbert B. Leonard).   This orig-
       inal screenplay was written by Lawrence B. Marcus.   (W,
       Q).

1176   GOLD.   (Allied Artists-1974-Peter Hunt).   A screenplay by
       Wilbur Smith and Stanley Price, from the novel Goldmine by
       Wilbur Smith; Doubleday, 1970, 240p.   (V, HR, LACOPL).

1176a GOLD FOR THE CAESARS.   (MGM-1964-Andre De Toth and
       Sabatino Ciuffini).   A screenplay by Arnold Perl and Sabatino
       Ciuffini, based on the novel by Florence A. Seward; Prentice-
       Hall, 1962.   (W, AMPAS, LACOPL, FF, Q).

1177   THE GOLDEN ARROW.   (MGM-1964-Antonio Margheriti).   A
       screenplay by Bruno Vailati, Augusto Frassineti, Filippo San-
       just, Giorgio Prosperi, and Giorgio Arlorio, with dialogue
       written and directed by George Higgins III.   (Q, FF).

1177a GOLDEN NEEDLES.   (American International-1974-Robert
       Clouse).   An original screenplay by S. Lee Pogostin and
       Sylvia Schneble.   (V).

1178 THE GOLDEN VOYAGE OF SINBAD. (Columbia-1974-Gordon Hessler). A screenplay written directly for the screen by Brian Clemens. (V).

1178a GOLDFINGER. (United Artists-1964-Guy Hamilton). Richard Maibaum and Paul Dehn based their screenplay on a novel by Ian Fleming; Macmillan, 1959. (FF, LACOPL, NYTFR, AMPAS, W, Q).

1179 GOLDSTEIN. (Altura-1965-Philip Kaufman and Benjamin Monaster). An original screenplay by Philip Kaufman and Benjamin Monaster. (NYTFR, W, AMPAS, Q).

1179a GOLIATH AND THE SINS OF BABYLON. (American International-1964-Michele Lupo). Original story and screenplay by Roberto Gianviti and Francesco Scardamaglia. (FF, NYTFR).

1180 GOLIATH AND THE VAMPIRES. (American International-1964-Giacomo Gentilomo and Sergio Corbucci). An original screenplay by Sergio Corbucci and Duccio Tessari. (FF, W, Q).

1180a GONE IN 60 SECONDS. (H. B. Halicki International-1974-H. B. Halicki). An original screenplay by H. B. Halicki. (V).

1181 GONE WITH THE WIND. (MGM-1967-Victor Fleming). A screenplay credited to Sidney Howard, based on the novel by Margaret Mitchell; Macmillan, 1961. (NYTFR, W, AMPAS, LACOPL, Q).

A GOOD DAY FOR FIGHTING see CUSTER OF THE WEST

1182 THE GOOD GUYS AND THE BAD GUYS. (Warner Bros.-7 Arts-1969-Burt Kennedy). An original screenplay by Ronald M. Cohen and Dennis Shryack. (W, AMPAS, Q).

1183 GOOD MORNING AND GOODBYE! (Eve-1968-Russ Meyer). An original work for the screen by John E. Moran. (FF, NYTFR, W, LC).

1183a GOOD NEIGHBOR SAM. (Columbia-1964-David Swift). James Fritzell, Everett Greenbaum, and David Swift wrote the screenplay, based on a novel by Jack Finney; Simon & Schuster, 1963, 190p. (FF, LACOPL, W, Q, AMPAS, NYTFR).

1184 THE GOOD, THE BAD AND THE UGLY. (United Artists-1968-Sergio Leone). A screenplay by Luciano Vincenzoni and Sergio Leone, based on a story by Age & Scarpelli, Luciano Vincenzoni, and Sergio Leone. (FF, NYTFR, FM, W, LC, AMPAS, Q).

1185 GOOD TIMES. (Columbia-1967-William Friedkin). A screenplay by Tony Barrett, based on a story by Nicholas Hyams. (FF, NYTFR, W, LC, AMPAS, Q).

1185a GOODBYE CHARLIE.   (20th Century-Fox-1964-Vincente Min-
       nelli).   A screenplay by Harry Kurnitz, based on the play by
       George Axelrod.   (FF, Q, NYTFR, W, AMPAS).

1186   GOODBYE, COLUMBUS.   (Paramount-1969-Larry Peerce).   A
       screenplay by Arnold Schulman, based on the novella by Phil-
       ip Roth; Houghton, 1959.   (FF, W, LC, AMPAS, LACOPL,
       Q).

1187   GOODBYE GEMINI.   (Cinerama-1970-Alan Gibson).   A screen-
       play by Edmund Ward, from a novel Ask Agamemnon by Jenni
       Hall.   (W, Q).

1188   GOODBYE, MR. CHIPS.   (MGM-1969-Herbert Ross).   A
       screenplay by Terence Rattigan, based on the novel by James
       Hilton; Little, Brown & Co., 1962.   (W, LC, AMPAS,
       LACOPL, Q).

1189   GORDON'S WAR.   (20th Century-Fox-1973-Ossie Davis).   An
       original screenplay by Howard Friedlander and Ed Spielman.
       (W).

1190   THE GORGON.   (Columbia-1965-Terence Fisher).   An origi-
       nal screenplay by John Gilling, based on a story by J. Lle-
       wellyn Devine.   (W, Q).

1191   GOSH!   (Tom Scheuer-1974-Tom Scheuer).   An original
       screenplay by Tom Scheuer.   (V).

1192   THE GOSPEL ACCORDING TO ST. MATTHEW.   (Continental
       1966-Pier Paolo Pasolini).   Screenplay by Pier Paolo Pasolini,
       adopted from the Gospel of St. Matthew.   (FF, NYTFR, W,
       AMPAS, Q).

1193   GOSPEL ROAD.   (20th Century-Fox-1973-Robert Elfstrom).
       An original screenplay by Johnny Cash and Larry Murray.
       (W, Q).

1194   GOYOKIN.   (Toho-1970-Hideo Gosha).   A screenplay by Hideo
       Gosha and Kei Tasaka.   (W).

1195   GRACE'S PLACE.   (L.A.C.-1973-Chuck Vincent).   No screen-
       play credits available.   (W).

1196   THE GRADUATE.   (Embassy-1967-Mike Nichols).   A screen-
       play by Calder Willingham and Buck Henry, based on the novel
       by Charles Webb; New American Library, 1963, 160p.   (Q,
       FF NYTFR, FM, W, AMPAS, LACOPL).

1197   GRAND PRIX.   (MGM-1966-John Frankenheimer).   An original
       screenplay by Robert Alan Arthur.   (FF, NYTFR, LC, W,
       AMPAS, Q).

1198   GRAND SLAM. (Paramount-1968-Giuliano Montaldo). A
screenplay written directly for the screen by Mino Roli, Marcello Fondato, Antonio De La Loma and Caminito. (Q, FF,
FM, NYTFR, W).

1199   THE GRAND SUBSTITUTION. (Frank Lee International-1965-
Yen Chun). An original screenplay by Chen E-Hsin.
(NYTFR, Q).

1200   LA GRANDE BOUFFE. (ABKCO-1973-Marco Ferreri). An
original work for the screen by Marco Ferreri and Rafael
Azcona. (W).

1201   THE GRAPEDEALER'S DAUGHTER. (Filmmakers-1970-
Walter Gutman). An original screenplay by Walter Gutman.
(W).

1202   THE GRASSHOPPER. (National General-1970-Jerry Paris).
A screenplay by Jerry Belson and Garry Marshall, from the
novel The Passing of Evil by Mark McShane. (W, Q).

THE GRAVY TRAIN   see   THE DION BROTHERS

1203   GRAZIE, ZIA. (AVCO Embassy-1969-Salvatore Samperi). A
screenplay by Sergio Bazzini, Pier Giuseppe Murgia and Salvatore Samperi, based on an original story by Salvatore
Samperi. (FF, W, Q).

1204   GREASER'S PALACE. (Cinema V-1972-Robert Downey). An
original work for the screen written by Robert Downey. (FF).

1205   THE GREAT AMERICAN COWBOY. (Sun International-1974-
Keith Merrill). An original screen work by Douglas Kent Hall.
(V).

1205a THE GREAT ARMORED CAR SWINDLE. (Falcon-1964-Lance
Comfort). A Peter Lambert script, based on a novel by
Laurence Meynell. (FF, W).

1206   THE GREAT BANK ROBBERY. (Warner Bros.-7 Arts-1969-
Hy Averback). A screenplay by William Peter Blatty, based
on the novel by Frank O'Rourke; New American Library, 1961,
128p. (FF, W, AMPAS, LACOPL, Q).

1207   THE GREAT BRITISH TRAIN ROBBERY. (Peppercorn-Worm-
ser-1967-John Olden & Claus Peter Witt). An original story
and screenplay by Henry Kolarz. (W, Q).

1208   GREAT CATHERINE. (Warner Bros.-7 Arts-1969-Gordon
Flemyng). A screenplay by Hugh Leonard, based on the play
Whom Glory Still Adores by George Bernard Shaw; in Complete
Plays, Dodd, 1962, 6 vols. (FF, LC, AMPAS, LACOPL, Q).

1209   THE GREAT GATSBY.   (Paramount-1974-Jack Clayton).   A
screenplay by Francis Ford Coppola, from the novel by F.
Scott Fitzgerald; Scribner, 1925.   (V, MFB, LACOPL).

1210   THE GREAT NORTHFIELD, MINNESOTA RAID.   (Universal-
1972-Philip Kaufman).   An original screenplay by Philip Kaufman.   (W, Q).

1211   THE GREAT RACE.   (Warner Bros.-1965-Blake Edwards).   A
screenplay by Arthur Ross, from a story by Arthur Ross and
Blake Edwards.   (NYTFR, Q, LC, W, AMPAS).

1212   THE GREAT SIOUX MASSACRE.   (Columbia-1965-Sidney Salkow).   A screenplay by Fred C. Dobbs, from a story by Sidney Salkow and Marvin Gluck.   (W, AMPAS, Q).

1213   THE GREAT SPY CHASE.   (American International-1966-
Georges Lautner).   An original screenplay by Michel Audiard
and Albert Simonin.   (FF, NYTFR, LC, W, Q).

1214   THE GREAT WALL.   (Magna-1965-Shigeo Tanaka).   An original screenplay by Fuji Yahiro.   (NYTFR, W).

1215   THE GREAT WALTZ.   (MGM-1972-Andrew L. Stone).   An
original story and screenplay by Andrew L. Stone.   (W, FF,
Q).

1216   THE GREAT WHITE HOPE.   (20th Century-Fox-1970-Martin
Ritt).   Howard Sackler wrote the screenplay, which was taken
from his play of the same name; in Best Plays of the Sixties
(edited by Stanley Richards), Doubleday, 1970, pp. 901-1036.
(W, Q).

1217   THE GREATEST STORY EVER TOLD.   (United Artists-1965-
George Stevens).   A screenplay by James Lee Barrett and
George Stevens, based on the books of the Old and New Tes-
taments, other ancient writings, and the book The Greatest
Story Ever Told by Fulton Oursler and writings by Henry
Denker; Doubleday, 1949, 299p.   (FF, LC, W, AMPAS, Q).

1218   THE GREEN BERETS.   (Warner Bros.-7 Arts-1968-John
Wayne & Ray Kellogg).   A screenplay by James Lee Barrett,
based on the novel by Robin Moore; Crown, 1965, 341p.   (Q,
FF, NYTFR, FM, W, LC, AMPAS, LACOPL).

1219   THE GREEN SLIME.   (MGM-1969-Kinji Fukasaku).   An original screenplay by Charles Sinclair, William Finger and Tom
Rowe.   (FF, W, LC, Q).

1220   THE GREEN WALL.   (Altura-1972-Armando Robles Godoy).
An original screenplay by Armando Robles Godoy.   (FF).

1221   GREETINGS.   (Sigma III-1968-Brian De Palma).   Charles

Hirsch and Brian De Palma wrote this original screenplay.
(FF, NYTFR, W, AMPAS, Q).

1222   GRIMMS' FAIRY TALES FOR ADULTS ONLY. (Cinemation-
1970-Rolf Thiel & Helen Gary). An original screenplay by
Rolf Thiel and Tom Baum. (W, Q).

1223   THE GRISSOM GANG. (Cinerama-1971-Robert Aldrich). A
screenplay by Leon Griffiths from a novel by James Hadley
Chase. (W, Q).

1224   THE GROUNDSTAR CONSPIRACY. (Universal-1972-Lamont
Johnson). A screenplay by Matthew Howard, based on the
novel The Alien by L. P. Davies; Doubleday, 1968. 182p.
(FF, LACOPL, Q).

1225   THE GROUP. (United Artists-1966-Sidney Lumet). A screen-
play written by Sidney Buchman, based on the novel by Mary
McCarthy; Harcourt, 1963. (Q, FF, NYTFR, LC, W,
AMPAS, LACOPL).

1226   GROUP MARRIAGE. (Dimension-1973-Stephanie Rothman).
No credit for screenplay available. (W).

1227   GROUPIES. (Maron-1970-Ron Dorfman & Peter Nevard). No
writing credits available; documentary.

1228   LA GUERRE EST FINIE. (Brandon-1967-Alain Resnais). Screenplay and dialogue by Jorge Semprun. Screenplay published by
Grove Press, 1967, 192p. (LACOPL, SCH, FF, NYTFR, W).

1229   GUESS WHAT WE LEARNED IN SCHOOL TODAY? (Cannon-
1970-John G. Avildsen). An original screenplay by Eugene
Price. (W, Q).

1230   GUESS WHO'S COMING TO DINNER. (Columbia-1967-Stanley
Kramer). An original screenplay by William Rose. (Q, FF,
NYTFR, FM, W, LC, AMPAS).

1230a   THE GUEST. (Janus-1964-Clive Donner). Harold Pinter
wrote the screenplay based on his play, The Caretaker; Grove
Press, 1960, 121p. (FF, W, Q, NYTFR, LACOPL).

1231   GUESTS ARE COMING. (Mitchell Kowal-1967-Gerard Zalew-
ski, Jan Rutkiewicz & Romuald Drobacynski). An original
screenplay by Jan J. Szcepanski. (W, Q).

1232   THE GUIDE. (Stratton International-1965-Tad Danielewski).
A screenplay by Pearl S. Buck and Tad Danielewski, based on
the novel by R. K. Narayan; Viking, 1958. (FF, LC, W,
LACOPL, Q).

1233   A GUIDE FOR THE MARRIED MAN. (20th Century-Fox-

1967-Gene Kelly). A screenplay by Frank Tarloff, based on
his book; Price, Stern & Sloan, 1967, 186p. (Q, FF, FM,
NYTFR, W, LC, AMPAS, LACOPL).

1234   GUILT. (Crown International-1967-Lars Görling). A screenplay by Lars Görling. (FF, NYTFR, W, Q).

1235   GUMSHOE. (Columbia-1972-Stephen Frears). An original
screenplay by Neville Smith. (FF, Q).

1236   A GUNFIGHT. (Paramount-1971-Lamont Johnson). An original screenplay by Harold Jack Bloom. (W, Q).

1237   GUNFIGHT AT COMANCHE CREEK. (Allied Artists-1964-
Frank McDonald). An original screenplay by Edward Bernds.
(FF, W, Q).

1238   GUNFIGHT IN ABILENE. (Universal-1967-William Hale). A
screenplay by Berne Giler and John D. F. Black, based on the
novel by Clarence Upson Young. (FF, W, LC, AMPAS, Q).

1239   GUNFIGHTERS OF CASA GRANDE. (MGM-1965-Roy Rowland).
A screenplay by Borden and Patricia Chase and Clark Reyn-
olds, from a story by Borden and Patricia Chase. (NYTFR,
LC, W, AMPAS, Q).

1240   GUNMEN OF THE RIO GRANDE. (Allied Artists-1965-Tulio
Demicheli). A screenplay by Gene Luotto, based on a story
by Chen Morrison. (W, AMPAS).

1241   GUNN. (Paramount-1967-Blake Edwards). A screenplay by
Blake Edwards and William Peter Blatty, based on a story
and characters created by Blake Edwards. (FF, NYTFR, FM,
LC, AMPAS, Q).

1242   GUNPOINT. (Universal-1966-Earl Bellamy). A screenplay
written directly for the screen by Mary and Willard Willingham. (FF, LC, W, AMPAS, Q).

1242a GUNS AT BATASI. (20th Century-Fox-1964-John Guillermin).
A screenplay by Robert Hollis, based on his novel Siege of
Battersea. (Q, FF, NYTFR, W).

1243   GUNS FOR SAN SEBASTIAN. (MGM-1968-Henri Verneuil).
A screenplay by James R. Webb, based on the novel A Wall
for San Sebastian by William Barby Faherty, S.J.; Academy
Guild Press, 1962. (Q, FF, NYTFR, FM, W, LC, AMPAS,
LACOPL).

1243a GUNS OF THE MAGNIFICENT SEVEN. (United Artists-1969-
Paul Wendkos). An original screenplay by Herman Hoffman.
(FF, W, LC, AMPAS, Q).

1244 THE GURU. (20th Century-Fox-1969-James Ivory). An original screenplay written by Ruth Prawer Jhabvala and James Ivory. (FF, W, LC, Q).

1245 GYPSY GIRL. (Continental-1967-John Mills). A screenplay by Mary Hayley Bell and John Prebble, based on the original story Bats with Baby Faces by Mary Hayley Bell. (FF, W, Q).

1246 THE GYPSY MOTHS. (MGM-1969-John Frankenheimer). A work for the screen by William Hanley, based on the novel by James Drought; Skylight Press, 1964. (FF, W, LC, AMPAS, LACOPL, Q).

1247 HAGBARD AND SIGNE. (Steve Prentoulis-1968-Gabriel Axel). A screenplay by Gabriel Axel and Frank Jaeger, based on a Scandinavian legend. (FF, NYTFR, W).

1248 HAIL, HERO! (National General-1969-David Miller). A screenplay by David Manber, from a novel by John Weston; McKay, 1968. (W, AMPAS, LACOPL, Q).

1249 HAIL! MAFIA. (7 Arts-1967-Raoul J. Levy). Screenplay adapted by Raoul J. Levy, from a story by Pierre-Vial Lesou. (W).

1250 HAIL TO THE CHIEF. (Cine-Globe-1973-Fred Levinson). An original screenplay and story by Larry Spiegel and Ohil Dusenberry. (W).

1251 HALF A SIXPENCE. (Paramount-1968-George Sidney). A screenplay by Beverley Cross, adapted by Dorothy Kingsley, based on the musical play by Beverley Cross and the novel Kipps by H. G. Wells; Longmans, 1962. (Q, FF, NYTFR, W, LC, AMPAS, LACOPL).

1252 THE HALLELUJAH TRAIL. (United Artists-1965-John Sturges). A screenplay by John Gay, based on the novel by Bill Gulick; Doubleday, 1963. (NYTFR, LC, W, AMPAS, LACOPL, Q).

1253 HALLS OF ANGER. (United Artists-1970-Paul Bogart). An original screenplay by John Shaner and Al Ramrus. (W, Q).

1254 HALLUCINATION GENERATION. (American International-1966-Edward Mann). An original screenplay by Edward Mann). An original screenplay by Edward Mann. (FF, LC, W).

1254a HAMLET. (Warner Bros.-1964-Bill Colleran). A filmed version of the play by William Shakespeare; American Book Co., 1906, 350p. (FF, LACOPL, W, NYTFR).

1255   HAMLET. (Lopert-1966-Grigori Kozintsev). A screenplay
        by Grigori Kozintsev, based on the Russian language transla-
        tion by Boris Pasternak of the play by William Shakespeare.
        (Q, FF, NYTFR, W, AMPAS, LACOPL).

1256   HAMLET. (Columbia-1969-Tony Richardson). Adapted for
        the screen by Tony Richardson, from the play by William
        Shakespeare; American Book Co., 1906, 350p. (W, LACOPL,
        Q).

1257   HAMMER. (United Artists-1972-Bruce Clark). An original
        screenplay by Charles Johnson. (FF, Q).

1258   HAMMERHEAD. (Columbia-1968-David Miller). A screen-
        play by William Bast and Herbert Baker, based on the novel
        by James Mayo; Morrow, 1964. (Q, FF, NYTFR, FM, W,
        LC, AMPAS, LACOPL).

1259   HAMMERSMITH IS OUT. (Cinerama-1972-Peter Ustinov).
        An original screenplay by Stanford Whitmore. (FF, Q, W).

1259a   THE HANDS OF ORLAC. (Continental-1964-Edmond T. Gre-
        ville). John Baines and Edmond T. Greville co-authored the
        screenplay, based on a novel by Maurice Renard. (FF, Q,
        W).

1260   HANDS OF THE RIPPER. (Universal-1972-Peter Sasdy). A
        screenplay by L. W. Davidson, based on a short story by Ed-
        ward Spencer Shew. (FF).

1261   HANG 'EM HIGH. (United Artists-1968-Ted Post). An origi-
        nal screenplay written by Leonard Freeman and Mel Goldberg.
        (FF, Q, LC, AMPAS).

1262   HANNIBAL BROOKS. (United Artists-1969-Michael Winner).
        A screenplay by Dick Clement and Ian La Frenais, based on
        an original story by Michael Winner and Tom Wright. (FF,
        W, LC, AMPAS, Q).

1263   HANNIE CAULDER. (Paramount-1972-Burt Kennedy). An
        original screenplay by Z. X. Jones aka Burt Kennedy and
        David Haft. (FF, Q).

1264   THE HAPPENING. (Columbia-1967-Elliot Silverstein). A
        screenplay by Frank R. Pierson, James D. Buchanan, and
        Ronald Austin, based on a story by James D. Buchanan and
        Ronald Austin. (Q, FF, AMPAS, LC, W, FM, NYTFR).

1265   THE HAPPIEST MILLIONAIRE. (Buena Vista-1967-Norman
        Tokar). A screenplay by A. J. Carothers, based on the book
        My Philadelphia Father by Kyle Crichton and Cordelia Drexel
        Biddle; Doubleday, 1955, 256p., and the stage play, The Hap-
        piest Millionaire; Dramatists Play Service, 1957, 89p. (Q,
        FF, NYTFR, W, LC, AMPAS, LACOPL).

1266   HAPPINESS. (New Yorker-1973-Alexandre Medvedkine).   An
        original screenplay by Alexandre Medvedkine.   (W).

1267   THE HAPPINESS CAGE.   (Cinerama-1972-Bernard Girard).
        A screenplay by Ron Whyte, based on the play by Dennis
        Reardon.   (Q, W).

1268   HAPPY AS THE GRASS WAS GREEN.   (Martin-1973-Charles
        Davis).   A screenplay written by Charles Davis, based on the
        novel by Merle Good.   (W).

1269   HAPPY BIRTHDAY, DAVY.   (Zenith-1970-Richard Fontaine).
        An original screenplay written by Chuck Roy.   (W).

1270   HAPPY BIRTHDAY, WANDA JUNE.   (Columbia-1971-Mark
        Robson).   A screenplay by Kurt Vonnegut, Jr. , from his play
        of the same name; Delacorte, 1971, 199p.   (W, LACOPL, Q).

1271   HAPPY DAYS.   (Anonymous Releasing Triumvirate-1974-
        Beau Buchanan).   An original screenplay by Trixie Morris
        and Beau Buchanan.   (V).

1272   HAPPY END.   (Continental-1968-Oldrich Lipsky).   A screen-
        play by Milos Macourek and Oldrich Lipsky, based on an orig-
        inal story by Milos Macourek.   (FF, NYTFR, W, Q).

1273   THE HAPPY ENDING.   (United Artists-1969-Richard Brooks).
        An original screenplay by Richard Brooks.   (W, AMPAS, Q).

1274   HAPPY MOTHER'S DAY--LOVE, GEORGE.   (Cinema V-1973-
        Darren McGavin).   An original screenplay by Robert Clouse.
        (W, FF).

1275   HAPPY NEW YEAR.   (AVCO Embassy-1973-Claude Lelouch).
        An original screenplay by Claude Lelouch.   (W).

1275a   HARAKIRI.   (Toho-1964-Masaki Kobayashi).   A screenplay by
        Shinobu Hashimoto, based on a novel by Yasuhiko Takiguchi.
        (FF, NYTFR, W, Q).

1276   HARBOR LIGHTS.   (20th Century-Fox-1964-Maury Dexter).
        An original screenplay by Henry Cross.   (FF, Q, W, NYTFR).

1276a   HARD CONTRACT.   (20th Century-Fox-1969-S. Lee Pogostin).
        An original screenplay by S. Lee Pogostin.   (FF, W, LC,
        AMPAS, Q).

1277   A HARD DAY'S NIGHT.   (United Artists-1964-Richard Lester).
        An original screenplay by Alun Owen.   (Q, FF, NYTFR, W,
        AMPAS).

1277a   THE HARD RIDE.   (American International-1971-Burt Topper).
        An original screenplay by Burt Topper.   (W, Q).

1278   THE HARDER THEY COME. (New World-1973-Perry Henzell). An original screenplay by Perry Henzell and Trevor
D. Rhone. (W).

1279   HARLOT. (Graffitti-1971-Howard Ziehm and Mike Light).
An original screenplay by Lester Romano. (W).

1280   HARLOW. (Magna-1965-Alex Segal). An original screenplay
written by Karl Tunberg. (NYTFR, W, AMPAS, Q).

1281   HARLOW. (Paramount-1965-Gordon Douglas). A screenplay
by John Michael Hayes, based on the book by Irving Shulman;
Bernard Geis, 1964, 408p. (NYTFR, LC, W, AMPAS, Q).

1282   HAROLD AND MAUDE. (Paramount-1971-Hal Ashby). An
original screenplay by Colin Higgins. (W, Q).

1283   HARPER. (Warner Bros.-1966-Jack Smight). A screenplay
by William Goldman, based on the novel The Moving Target
by Ross MacDonald; Knopf, 1949. (Q, FF, NYTFR, LC, W,
AMPAS, LACOPL).

1284   THE HARRAD EXPERIMENT. (Cinerama-1973-Ted Post). A
screenplay by Michael Werner, Ted Cassedy, based on a novel
by Robert H. Rimmer; Bantam Books, 1973. (W, LACOPL,
Q).

1285   THE HARRAD SUMMER. (Cinerama-1974-Steven H. Stern).
An original screenplay by Mort Thaw and Steven Zacharias.
(V).

1286   HARRY AND TONTO. (20th Century-Fox-1974-Paul Mazursky).
A screenplay by Paul Mazursky and Josh Greenfeld, based on
the novel by Josh Greenfeld; Saturday Review Press, 1974,
183p. (V, LACOPL).

1287   HARRY IN YOUR POCKET. (United Artists-1973-Bruce Geller). An original screenplay by James David Buchanan, and
Ron Austin. (V, W).

1288   HARUM SCARUM. (MGM-1965-Gene Nelson). An original
screenplay by Gerald Drayson Adams. (NYTFR, LC W,
AMPAS, Q).

1289   HARVEY MIDDLEMAN, FIREMAN. (Columbia-1965-Ernest
Pintoff). Ernest Pintoff wrote the original screenplay.
(NYTFR, LC, W, AMPAS).

1289a THE HAUNTED PALACE. (American International-1964-Roger
Corman). A screenplay written by Charles Beaumont, based
on the story by Edgar Allan Poe and a story by H. P. Lovecraft; in Complete Tales and Poems by Edgar Allan Poe;
Doubleday, 1966. (FF, LACOPL, W, Q, NYTFR).

1290   HAVING A WILD WEEKEND. (Warner Bros.-1965-John
Boorman). An original screenplay by Peter Nichols.
(NYTFR, LC, W, AMPAS, Q).

1291   HAWAII. (United Artists-1966-George Roy Hill). A screenplay by Dalton Trumbo and Daniel Taradash, based on the
novel by James A. Michener; Random House, 1959. (Q, FF,
NYTFR, LC, W, AMPAS, LACOPL).

1292   THE HAWAIIANS. (United Artists-1970-Tom Gries). A
screenplay by James R. Webb, based on the novel Hawaii
by James A. Michener; Random House, 1959. (W, Q,
LACOPL).

1293   THE HAWKS AND THE SPARROWS. (Brandon-1967-Pier
Paolo Pasolini). An original screenplay by Pier Paolo Pasolini. (FF, NYTFR, W, Q).

1293a HE RIDES TALL. (Universal-1964-R. G. Springsteen). A
screenplay by Charles W. Irwin and Robert Creighton Williams, based on a story by Charles W. Irwin. (FF, NYTFR,
W, Q).

1294   HE WHO RIDES A TIGER. (Sigma III-1968-Charles Crichton). An original screenplay by Trevor Peacock. (FF,
NYTFR, W).

1295   HEAD. (Columbia-1968-Bob Rafelson). An original screenplay by Bob Rafelson and Jack Nicholson. (Q, FF, NYTFR,
FM, W, LC, AMPAS).

1296   HEAD OF THE FAMILY. (GGP-1973-Nanni Loy). No author
credit. (W).

1297   HEAD ON. (Leon-1971-Edward Lakso). An original screenplay by Edward Lakso. (W).

A HEART AS BIG AS THAT   see   THE WINNER

1298   THE HEART IS A LONELY HUNTER. (Warner Bros.-7 Arts
-1968-Robert Ellis Miller). A screenplay by Thomas C.
Ryan, based on the novel by Carson McCullers; Houghton Mifflin Co., 1940, 273p. (Q, FF, NYTFR, FM, W, LACOPL,
LC, AMPAS).

1299   THE HEARTBREAK KID. (20th Century-Fox-1972-Elaine May).
A screenplay by Neil Simon, based on the story by Bruce Jay
Friedman, "A Change of Plan," in Black Angels, Simon &
Schuster, 1966. (W, FF, LACOPL, Q).

1300   HEAT. (Levitt-Pickman-1972-Paul Morrissey). Paul Morrissey wrote the screenplay from an original idea by John
Hallowell. (FF, Q).

1301   HEAT OF MADNESS.   (William Mishkin-1966-Harry Wuest).
        An original screenplay by Eliza McCormick.   (FF, AMPAS).

1302   HEAVEN WITH A GUN.   (MGM-1969-Lee H. Katzin).   An
        original screenplay written by Richard Carr.   (FF, W, LC,
        AMPAS, Q).

1303   HEAVY TRAFFIC.   (American International-1973-Ralph Bak-
        shi).   Ralph Bakshi wrote the original screenplay.   (W).

1304   HEIDI.   (Warner Bros.-7 Arts-1968-Werner Jacobs).   A
        screenplay by Richard Schweizer, adapted by Michael Haller,
        based on the novel by Johanna Spyri; Macmillan, 1962.   (FF,
        NYTFR, W, LACOPL, Q).

1305   HELGA.   (American International-1968-Erich F. Bender).   An
        original screenplay by Erich F. Bender.   (FF, NYTFR, W,
        LC).

1306   HELL IN THE PACIFIC.   (Cinerama-1969-John Boorman).   A
        screenplay by Alexander Jacobs and Eric Bercovici, based on
        a story by Reuben Bercovitch.   (FF, W, AMPAS, Q).

1307   HELL ON WHEELS.   (Crown International-1967-Will Zens).
        An original screenplay by Wesley Cox.   (FF, W, AMPAS).

1308   HELL UP IN HARLEM.   (American International-1973-Larry
        Cohen).   Larry Cohen wrote this original screenplay.   (W).

1309   THE HELL WITH HEROES.   (Universal-1968-Joseph Sargent).
        A screenplay by Halsted Welles and Harold Livingston, based
        on a story by Harold Livingston.   (FF, NYTFR, FM, W,
        AMPAS, Q).

1310   THE HELLBENDERS.   (Embassy-1967-Sergio Corbucci).   Al-
        bert Band and Ugo Liberatore wrote their screenplay, which
        was taken from an original story by Virgil C. Gerlach.   (FF,
        W, AMPAS).

1311   THE HELLCATS.   (Crown International-1969-Robert F. Slatz-
        er).   An original screenplay by Tony Houston and Robert F.
        Slatzer, based on an original story by James Gordon White and
        John Zila, Jr.   (FF, W).

1312   HELLFIGHTERS.   (Universal-1969-Andrew V. McLaglen).   An
        original screenplay by Clair Huffaker.   (FF, LC, AMPAS, Q).

1313   HELLO, DOLLY!   (20th Century-Fox-1969-Gene Kelly).   A
        screenplay by Ernest Lehman, based on the stage musical by
        Michael Stewart; DBS Publications, 1966, 117p.; on the play by
        Thornton Wilder, The Matchmaker, in Three Plays, Harper,
        1957, 401p.; and on the play The Merchant of Yonkers, also
        by Thornton Wilder; Harper, 1939, 180p.   (AMPAS, LACOPL,
        Q, W, V).

1314   HELLO DOWN THERE.   (Paramount-1969-Jack Arnold).   A
screenplay by Frank Telford and John McGreevey, based on
a story by Ivan Tors and Art Arthur.   (FF, LC, AMPAS,
Q).

1315   HELLO-GOODBYE.   (20th Century-Fox-1970-Jean Negulesco).
An original screenplay by Roger Marshall.   (W, Q).

1316   HELL'S ANGELS '69.   (American International-1969-Lee Madden).   A screenplay by Don Tait, based on a story by Tom
Stern and Jeremy Slate.   (FF, W, AMPAS, Q).

1317   HELLS ANGELS ON WHEELS.   (U.S. Films-1967-Richard
Rush).   An original screenplay by R. Wright Campbell.   (FF,
NYTFR, FM, W, AMPAS).

1318   HELL'S BELLES.   (American International-1969-Maury Dexter).   An original screenplay by James Gordon White and Robert McMullen.   (W, Q, LC, AMPAS, V).

1319   HELL'S BLOODY DEVILS.   (Independent-International-1970-
Al Adamson).   Jerry Evans wrote this original screenplay.
(W).

1320   THE HELLSTROM CHRONICLE.   (Cinema V-1971-Walon
Green).   A screenplay written by David Seltzer.   (W, Q).

1321   HELP! (United Artists-1965-Richard Lester).   A screenplay
by Marc Behm and Charles Wood, from a story by Marc
Behm.   (NYTFR, LC, W, AMPAS, Q).

1322   HENRY VIII AND HIS SIX WIVES.   (Anglo-EMI-1973-Waris
Hussein).   A screenplay by Ian Thorne; an original novel
based on the screenplay was written by Maureen Peters; Ballantine Books, 1972, 222p.   (W, FF, HR, LACOPL).

1323   HER AND SHE AND HIM.   (Rochambeau-1970-Max Pecas).
Film is based on an original story written by Michele Rossi.
(W).

1324   HERBIE RIDES AGAIN.   (Buena Vista-1974-Robert Stevenson).
Bill Walsh wrote this screenplay, taken from a story by Gordon Buford.   (V).

1325   HERCULES IN THE HAUNTED WORLD.   (Woolner Bros. -
1965-Mario Bava).   An original screenplay by Mario Bava,
Alessandro Continenza, Giorgio Prosperi, and Duccio Tessari.
(FF, Q).

1326   HERCULES, SAMSON AND ULYSSES.   (MGM-1965-Pietro
Francisci).   An original screenplay by Pietro Francisci.
(NYTFR, LC, W, Q).

1327   HERE WE GO ROUND THE MULBERRY BUSH. (Lopert-
        1968-Clive Donner). A screenplay by Hunter Davies, based
        on his novel; Little, Brown & Co., 1965. (Q, FF, NYTFR,
        W, LC, AMPAS, LACOPL).

1328   HERE'S YOUR LIFE. (Brandon-1968-Jan Troell). A screen-
        play by Jan Troell and Bengst Forslund, based on the novel
        Romanen Om Olof (The Story of Olaf) by Eyvind Johnson.
        (FF, NYTFR, W).

1329   THE HERO. (AVCO Embassy-1972-Richard Harris). A
        screenplay by Wolf Mankowitz, from a story by Joseph Gross.
        (W, Q).

1330   THE HEROES OF TELEMARK. (Columbia-1966-Anthony
        Mann). Screenplay written by Ivan Moffat and Ben Barzman,
        based on "Skis Against the Atom" by Knut Haukelid and "But
        for These Men" by John Drummond. (FF, NYTFR, LC, W,
        AMPAS, Q).

1331   HEROINA. (Royal-1965-Jeronimo Mitchell Melendez). The
        original screenplay by Enrique de la Torre, is taken from an
        original story by Jeronimo Mitchell Mclendez. (NYTFR, W).

1332   HEX. (20th Century-Fox-1973-Leo Garen). A screenplay by
        Leo Garen and Steve Katz, from a story by Doran Willian
        Cannon and Vernon Zimmerman. (W).

1333   HI, MOM! (Sigma III-1970-Brian De Palma). A screenplay
        by Brian De Palma, from a story by Brian De Palma and
        Charles Hirsch. (W, Q).

1334   HICKEY AND BOGGS. (United Artists-1972-Robert Culp).
        An original screenplay by Walter Hill. (W, FF, Q).

1334a   HIDE AND SEEK. (Universal-1964-Cy Endfield). A screen-
        play by David Stone, based on a story by Harold Greene,
        adapted by Robert Foshko. (FF, NYTFR).

1335   HIGH. (Joseph Brenner Associates-1969-Laurence L. Kent).
        An original screenplay by Laurence L. Kent. (FF, W, LC,
        Q).

1336   THE HIGH COMMISSIONER. (Cinerama-1968-Ralph Thomas).
        A screenplay by Wilfred Greatorex, based on the novel by
        Jon Cleary; Morrow, 1966. (FF, NYTFR, W, AMPAS,
        LACOPL, Q).

1337   HIGH INFIDELITY. (Magna-1965-Franco Rossi, Elio Petri,
        Luciano Salce, Mario Monicelli). This episodic comedy drama
        was written by Age and Scarpelli, Scola and Maccari. (NYTFR,
        W, AMPAS, Q).

1338   HIGH PLAINS DRIFTER.   (Universal-1973-Clint Eastwood).
       An original screenplay by Ernest Tidyman.   (W, Q).

1339   HIGH PRIESTESS OF SEXUAL WITCHCRAFT.   (Triumvirate-
       1973-Beau Buchanan).   An original screenplay by Beau Bu-
       chanan.   (W).

1340   HIGH RISE.   (Maturpix-1973-Danny Stone).   An original
       screenplay written by Danny Stone.   (W).

1341   A HIGH WIND IN JAMAICA.   (20th Century-Fox-1965-Alex-
       ander Mackendrick).   A screenplay by Stanley Mann, Ronald
       Harwood, and Denis Cannan, from the novel by Richard
       Hughes; Harper, 1957, 212p.   (Q, NYTFR, LC, W, AMPAS,
       LACOPL).

1342   THE HILL.   (MGM-1965-Sidney Lumet).   A screenplay based
       on an original play by Ray Rigby and R. S. Allen; Day, 1965.
       (Q, NYTFR, LC, W, AMPAS, LACOPL).

1343   THE HILLS RUN RED.   (United Artists-1967-Lee W. Beaver
       aka Carlo Lizzani).   An original screenplay by Dean Craig.
       (FF, NYTFR, FM, W, AMPAS, Q).

1344   THE HIRED HAND.   (Universal-1971-Peter Fonda).   An origi-
       nal screenplay by Alan Sharp.   (W, Q).

1345   THE HIRED KILLER.   (Paramount-1967-Frank Shannon).   An
       original work for the screen by Frank Shannon.   (FF, NYTFR,
       FM, W, AMPAS, Q).

1346   THE HIRELING.   (Columbia-1973-Alan Bridges).   A screen-
       play written by Wolf Mankowitz, based on a novel by L. P.
       Hartley; Rinehart, 1957.   (W, LACOPL, Q).

1347   HISTORY LESSONS.   (New Yorker-1973-Jean-Marie Straub).
       An original story and screenplay by Jean-Marie Straub and
       Daniele Huillet.   (W).

1348   HIT! (Paramount-1973-Sidney J. Furie).   An original screen-
       play by Alan R. Trustman and David M. Wolf.   A novelization
       based on the screenplay was written by Arthur Stackman; Ban-
       tam Books, 1973.   (W, LACOPL).

1349   HIT MAN.   (MGM-1972-George Armitage).   Screenplay by
       George Armitage, based on Jack's Return Home by Ted Lewis;
       Doubleday, 1970.   (LACOPL, W).

1350   THE HITCHHIKERS.   (Entertainment Ventures-1973-Ferd and
       Beverly Sebastian).   An original screenplay by Ann Cawthorne.
       (W, FF).

1351   HITLER: THE LAST TEN DAYS.   (Paramount-1973-Ennie de

Concini).   A screenplay by Ennio de Concini, Marie Pia Fusco, and Wolfgang Reinhardt.   English screenplay adaptation by Ivan Moffat.   Based on Gerhard Boldt's Last Days of the Chancellery; Coward, 1973, 224p.   (W, LACOPL).

1352   HOA-BINH.   (Transvue-1971-Raoul Coutard).   A screenplay by Raoul Coutard, based on the novel The Column of Ashes by Françoise Lorrain.   (W, Q).

1353   HOFFMAN.   (Levitt-Pickman-1971-Alvin Rakoff).   A screenplay by Ernest Gebler, based on his novel; Doubleday, 1969, 191p.   (W, LACOPL).

1354   HOLD ON!   (MGM-1966-Arthur Lubin).   An original screenplay by James P. Gordon.   (FF, LC, W, AMPAS, Q).

1355   HOLLYWOOD BABYLON.   (Aquarius-1972-Van Guilder).   No author credit.   (W).

1356   THE HOLY MOUNTAIN.   (ABKCO Films-1974-Alejandro Jodorowsky).   An original screenplay by Alejandro Jodorowsky.   (HR).

1357   HOMBRE.   (20th Century-Fox-1967-Martin Ritt).   A screenplay by Irving Ravetch and Harriet Frank, Jr., based on the novel by Elmore Leonard.   (FF, NYTFR, FM, W, LC, AMPAS, Q).

1358   HOMEBODIES.   (AVCO Embassy-1974-Larry Yust).   A screenplay by Larry Yust, Howard Kaminsky and Bennett Sims.   (V, HR).

1359   THE HOMECOMING.   (American Film Theatre-1973-Peter Hall).   A screenplay by Harold Pinter, based on his play; Grove Press, 1966, 82p.   (W, LACOPL).

1360   HOMER.   (National General-1970-John Trent).   A screenplay by Claude Harz, from a story by Claude Harz and Matt Clark.   (W, Q).

1361   L'HOMME SANS VISAGE.   (Terra Film-SOAT-1974-Georges Franju).   An original screenplay by Jacques Champreux.   (V).

1362   HOMO EROTICUS.   (CIDIF-1973-Marco Vicario).   An original screenplay by Piero Chiara and Marco Vicario.   (W).

1363   THE HONEY POT.   (United Artists-1967-Joseph L. Mankiewicz).   A screenplay authored by Joseph L. Mankiewicz, based on the play Mr. Fox of Venice by Frederick Knott; adapted from the novel The Evil of the Day by Thomas Sterling; Simon & Schuster, 1955; and based in part on the play Volpone by Ben Jonson, University of California Press, 1968, 150p.   (FF, Q, NYTFR, FM, W, LC, AMPAS, LACOPL).

1364   HONEYBABY, HONEYBABY. (Kelly-Jordan-1974-Michael
        Schultz). An original screenplay by Brian Phelan, from a
        story by Leonard Kantor. (V).

1365   HONEYCOMB. (Cine Globe-1972-Carlos Saura). An original
        screenplay by Geraldine Chaplin, Carlos Saura, and Rafael
        Azcona. (W, FF).

1365a   HONEYMOON HOTEL. (MGM-1964-Henry Levin). A screen-
        play by R. S. Allen and Harvey Bullock. (FF, NYTFR, W,
        Q, AMPAS).

1366   THE HONEYMOON KILLERS. (Cinerama-1969-Leonard
        Kastle). An original screenplay by Leonard Kastle. (W, Q).

1367   THE HONKERS. (United Artists-1972-Steve Ihnat). An origi-
        nal screenplay by Steve Ihnat and Stephen Lodge. (W, Q).

1368   HONKY. (Jack H. Harris-1971-William A. Graham). A
        screenplay by Will Chaney, based on the novel Sheila by Gun-
        ard Selberg. (W).

1369   HOOK, LINE AND SINKER. (Columbia-1969-George Marshall).
        A screenplay by Rod Amateau, based on a story by Rod Ama-
        teau and David Davis. (FF, W, LC, AMPAS, Q).

1370   THE HOOKED GENERATION. (Allied Artists-1969-William
        Grefe). An original screenplay by Quinn Morrison, Ray
        Preston, and William Grefe. (W, Q).

1371   HORNETS' NEST. (United Artists-1970-Phil Karlson). A
        screenplay written by S. S. Schweitzer, from a story by S. S.
        Schweitzer and Stanley Colbert. (W, Q).

1371a   THE HORRIBLE DR. HICHCOCK. (Sigma III-1964-Robert
        Hampton aka Riccardo Freda). Julyan Perry authored this
        original screenplay. (FF, NYTFR).

1372   HORROR CASTLE. (Zodiac-1965-Anthony Dawson). A screen-
        play by Anthony Dawson, Gaston Green, and Edmund Greville,
        based on the novel, The Virgin of Nuremberg by Frank Bo-
        gart. (FF, LC, AMPAS).

1373   HORROR HOUSE. (American International-1970-Michael Arm-
        strong). An original screenplay by Michael Armstrong. (W,
        Q).

1374   THE HORROR OF FRANKENSTEIN. (American Continental-
        1971-Jimmy Sangster). A screenplay by Jimmy Sangster,
        Jeremy Burnham, based on characters created by Mary Shel-
        ley. (W).

1375   THE HORROR OF IT ALL. (20th Century-Fox-1965-Terence

Fisher).   A screenplay by Ray Russell.   (FF, LC, AMPAS).

1375a   THE HORROR OF PARTY BEACH.   (20th Century-Fox-1964-
Del Tenney).   A work written directly for the screen by
Richard L. Hilliard.   (FF, NYTFR, AMPAS, W, Q).

1376   HORROR OF THE BLOOD MONSTERS.   (Independent Interna-
tional-1971-Al Adamson).   An original screenplay by Sue Mc-
Nair.   (W).

1377   HORROR ON SNAPE ISLAND.   (Fanfare-1972-Jim O'Connolly).
A screenplay by Jim O'Connolly, based on a story by George
Baxt.   (FF).

1378   THE HORSE IN THE GRAY FLANNEL SUIT.   (Buena Vista-
1968-Norman Tokar).   A screenplay by Louis Pelletier, based
on the novel The Year of the Horse by Eric Hatch; Crown,
1965.   (Q, FF, NYTFR, FM, W, LC, AMPAS, LACOPL).

1379   THE HOSPITAL.   (United Artists-1971-Arthur Hiller).   An
original story and screenplay by Paddy Chayefsky.   (W, Q).

1380   THE HOSTAGE.   (Crown International-1968-Russell S. Dough-
ten, Jr.).   A screenplay by Robert Laning, based on the novel
by Henry Farrell.   (FF, AMPAS).

1381   HOSTILE GUNS.   (Paramount-1967-R. G. Springsteen).   Steve
Fisher and Sloan Nibley wrote this original screenplay, from
a story by Sloan Nibley and James Edward Grant.   (FF, W,
LC, AMPAS, Q).

1382   THE HOT BOX.   (New World-1972-Joe Viola).   An original
screenplay by Joe Viola and Jonathan Demme.   (FF).

1383   HOT CHANNELS.   (Distribpix-1973-R. G. Benjamin).   An original screenplay by Alan Frybach and Paul Williams.   (W).

1384   HOT CIRCUIT.   (Sherpix-1972-Paul Glickler and Richard Lerner).   An original screenplay by Paul Glickler and Richard
Lerner.   (W).

1385   HOT MILLIONS.   (MGM-1968-Eric Till).   A screenplay by Ira
Wallach and Peter Ustinov.   (FF, NYTFR, W, AMPAS, Q).

1385a   HOT MONEY GIRL.   (United Producers Releasing Organization-
1964-Alvin Rakoff).   A screenplay by Jack Andrews, based on
a story by Jeffrey Dell.   (FF).

1386   HOT PANTS HOLIDAY.   (AVCO Embassy-1972-Edward Mann).
A screenplay by Edward Mann, from a story by Robin Moore.
(W).

1387   THE HOT ROCK.   (20th Century-Fox-1972-Peter Yates.)   A

novel by Donald E. Westlake; Simon & Schuster, 1970, 249p.,
served as the inspiration for the screenplay by William Goldman. (W, Q, LACOPL).

1388   HOT ROD HULLABALOO. (Allied Artists-1966-William Naud).
An original story and screenplay by Stanley Schneider. (FF).

1389   HOT RODS TO HELL. (MGM-1967-John Brahm). A screenplay by Robert E. Kent, based on a short story by Alex Gaby.
(Q, FF, NYTFR, FM, W, LC, AMPAS).

1390   HOT SUMMER WEEK. (Fanfare-1973-Thomas J. Schmidt).
An original screenplay by Larry Bischof and David Kaufman.
(W).

1391   HOT TIMES. (William Mishkin-1974-Jim McBride). An original screenplay by Jim McBride. (V).

1392   HOTEL. (Warner Bros.-1967-Richard Quine). A screenplay
by Wendell Mayes, based on the novel by Arthur Hailey;
Doubleday, 1965. (Q, FF, NYTFR, FM, W, LC, AMPAS,
LACOPL).

1393   HOTEL PARADISO. (MGM-1966-Peter Glenville). A screenplay by Peter Glenville and Jean-Claude Carrière, based on
the play L'Hotel du Libre Echange by Georges Feydeau and
Maurice Desvallieres. (FF, NYTFR, LC, W, AMPAS, Q).

1394   THE HOUR AND TURN OF AUGUSTO MATRAGA. (New
Yorker-1971-Roberto Santos). A work by Roberto Santos,
based on a story by João Guimarães Rosa, in Sagarana; Knopf,
1966. (W, LACOPL).

1395   HOUR OF THE GUN. (United Artists-1967-John Sturges). A
screenplay by Edward Anhalt, based on the novel Tombstone's
Epitaph by Douglas D. Martin. (FF, NYTFR, FM, LC,
AMPAS, Q).

1396   HOUR OF THE WOLF. (Lopert-1968-Ingmar Bergman). An
original screenplay by Ingmar Bergman. (FF, NYTFR, W,
Q).

1397   HOURS OF LOVE. (Cinema V-1965-Luciano Salce). An original screenplay by Luciano Salce and Castellano and Pipolo.
(W, Q, NYTFR).

1398   HOUSE IN NAPLES. (UM-1970-Peter Savage). No screenplay
credits available. (W).

1398a   A HOUSE IS NOT A HOME. (Embassy-1964-Russell Rouse).
A screenplay by Russell Rouse and Clarence Greene, based on
the book by Polly Adler; Rinehart, 1953. (FF, LACOPL,
NYTFR, AMPAS, W, Q).

1399   HOUSE OF DARK SHADOWS.   (MGM-1970-Dan Curtis).   An
original screenplay by Sam Hall and Gordon Russell.   (W, Q).

1400   HOUSE OF 1,000 DOLLS.   (American International-1968-
Jeremy Summers).   An original screenplay by Peter Welbeck.
(FF, NYTFR, W, AMPAS, Q).

1401   HOUSE OF WHIPCORD.   (1974-Pete Walker).   A screenplay
by David McGillivray, from a story by Pete Walker.   (MFB).

1402   THE HOUSE ON CHELOUCHE STREET.   (Productions Un-
limited-1974-Moshe Mizrahi).   An original screenplay by
Moshe Mizrahi and Rachel Fabien.   (HR).

1403   THE HOUSE ON SKULL MOUNTAIN.   (20th Century-Fox-
1974-Ron Honthaner).   An original screenplay by Mildred
Pares.   (V, HR).

1404   THE HOUSE THAT CRIED MURDER.   (Unisphere-1973-Jean-
Marie Pelissie).   An original screenplay by John Grissmer
and Jean-Marie Pelissie.   (W).

1405   THE HOUSE THAT SCREAMED.   (American International-
1971-Narcisco Ibanez Serrador).   An original screenplay by
Luis Verna Penafiel, based on a story by Juan Tebar.   (W,
Q).

1406   THE HOUSE WITH AN ATTIC.   (Artkino-1966-).   No author
credit.   (W).

1407   HOW DO I LOVE THEE.   (Cinerama-1970-Michael Gordon).
A screenplay by Everett Freeman and Karl Tunberg, from the
novel Let Me Count the Ways by Peter De Vries; Little,
Brown & Co., 1965.   (W, LACOPL, Q).

1408   HOW I WON THE WAR.   (United Artists-1967-Richard Lester).
A screenplay by Charles Wood, based on the novel by Patrick
Ryan; Morrow, 1963.   (Q, FF, NYTFR, FM, W, LC, AMPAS,
LACOPL).

1409   HOW LOW CAN YOU FALL?   (Titanus-1974-Luigi Comencini).
A screenplay by Luigi Comencini and Ivo Perilli.   (V).

1410   HOW MUCH LOVING DOES A NORMAL COUPLE NEED?   (Eve
Productions-1967-Russ Meyer).   An original screenplay by
John E. Moran.   (FF, LC).

1411   HOW NOT TO ROB A DEPARTMENT STORE.   (Artixo-1965-
Pierre Grimblat).   A screenplay written by Clarence Weff and
Pierre Grimblat, based on a novel by Clarence Weff.   (NYTFR,
W, Q).

1412   HOW SWEET IT IS!   (National General-1968-Jerry Paris).   A screenplay by Garry Marshall and Jerry Belson, based on the novel <u>The Girl in the Turquoise Bikini</u> by Muriel Resnick. (FF, NYTFR, FM, LC, AMPAS, Q).

1413　HOW TASTY WAS MY LITTLE FRENCHMAN. (New Yorker-1973-Nelson Pereira dos Santos). An original screenplay by Nelson Pereira dos Santos. (W).

1414　HOW TO COMMIT MARRIAGE. (Cinerama-1969-Norman Panama). An original screenplay by Ben Starr and Michael Kanin. (FF, W, AMPAS).

1415　HOW TO MURDER YOUR WIFE. (United Artists-1965-Richard Quine). An original screenplay by George Axelrod. (FF, LC, W, AMPAS, Q).

1416　HOW TO SAVE A MARRIAGE--AND RUIN YOUR LIFE. (Columbia-1968-Fielder Cook). An original screenplay by Stanley Shapiro and Nate Monaster. (FF, NYTFR, FM, W, LC, AMPAS, Q).

1417　HOW TO SEDUCE A PLAYBOY. (Chevron-1968-Michael Pfleghar). A screenplay by Klaus Munro and Michael Pfleghar, based on a story by Anatol Bratt. (FF, NYTFR, W).

1418　HOW TO SEDUCE A WOMAN. (Cinerama-1974-Charles Martin). An original screenplay by Charles Martin. (HR).

1419　HOW TO STEAL A MILLION. (20th Century-Fox-1966-William Wyler). A screenplay by Harry Kurnitz, based on a story by George Bradshaw. (FF, NYTFR, LC, W, AMPAS, Q).

1420　HOW TO STUFF A WILD BIKINI. (American International-1965-William Asher). An original screenplay by William Asher and Leo Townsend. (W, LC, AMPAS, Q).

1421　HOW TO SUCCEED IN BUSINESS WITHOUT REALLY TRYING. (United Artists-1967-David Swift). An original screenplay by David Swift, based on the musical play by Abe Burrows, Jack Weinstock, and Willie Gilbert, and the novel by Shepherd Mead; 1952, Simon & Schuster, 148p. (Q, FF, NYTFR, W, LC, AMPAS, LACOPL).

1422　HOW TO SUCCEED WITH SEX. (Medford-1970-Bert I. Gordon). An original screenplay by Bert I. Gordon. (W).

1423　HOWZER. (URI-1973-Ken Laurence). An original screenplay by Ken Laurence. (W).

1424　HUCKLEBERRY FINN. (United Artists-1974-J. Lee Thompson). A screenplay by Richard M. Sherman, from the novel by Mark Twain; Watts, 1969, 387p.   (HR, V, LACOPL).

1425   HUGO AND JOSEPHINE.   (Warner Bros.-7 Arts-1968-Kiell
       Grede).   A screenplay by Maria Gripe and Kiell Grede,
       based on the book by Maria Gripe.   (NYTFR).

1426   HUGS AND KISSES.   (AVCO Embassy-1968-Jonas Cornell).
       An original screenplay by Jonas Cornell.   (FF, NYTFR, W,
       Q).

1427   THE HUMAN DUPLICATORS.   (Woolner Bros.-1965-Hugo
       Grimaldi).   An original screenplay written by Arthur C.
       Pierce.   (FF, Q, LC, W, AMPAS).

1428   HUNGER.   (Sigma III-1968-Henning Carlsen).   A screenplay
       by Henning Carlsen and Peter Seeberg, based on the novel by
       Knut Hamsun; Farrar, 1967, 231p.   (FF, NYTFR, W,
       LACOPL).

1429   HUNGER FOR LOVE.   (Pathe Contemporary-1973-Nelson
       Pereira dos Santos).   No author credit available.   (W).

1430   HUNGRY WIVES.   (Jack H. Harris-1973-George A. Romero).
       An original screenplay by George A. Romero.   (W).

1431   THE HUNT.   (Trans-Lux-1967-Carlos Saura).   An original
       screenplay by Angelino Fons and Carlos Saura.   (NYTFR, W,
       Q).

1432   THE HUNTED SAMURAI.   (Toho-1971-Keiichi Ozawa).   An
       original work for the screen written by Seiji Hoshikawa.   (W).

1433   THE HUNTERS ARE THE HUNTED.   (Radim-1973-Peter
       Fleischman).   An original screenplay by Peter Fleischman.
       (W).

1434   THE HUNTING PARTY.   (United Artists-1971-Don Medford).
       An original screenplay by William Norton, Gilbert Alexander,
       and Lou Morheim, from a story by Gilbert Alexander and Lou
       Morheim.   (W, Q).

1435   HURRY SUNDOWN.   (Paramount-1967-Otto Preminger).   A
       screenplay by Thomas C. Ryan and Horton Foote, based on
       the novel by K. B. Gilden; Doubleday, 1964.   (Q, FF,
       NYTFR, FM, W, LC, AMPAS, LACOPL).

1436   HURRY UP, OR I'LL BE 30.   (AVCO Embassy-1973-Joseph
       Jacoby).   An original screenplay by David Wiltse and Joseph
       Jacoby.   (W).

1437   HUSBANDS.   (Columbia-1970-John Cassavetes).   An original
       screenplay by John Cassavetes.   (W, Q).

1438 HUSH ... HUSH, SWEET CHARLOTTE. (20th Century-Fox-
1965-Robert Aldrich). An original screenplay by Henry Farrell and Lukas Heller. (FF, LC, W, AMPAS, Q).

1439 HYSTERIA. (MGM-1965-Freddie Francis). An original
screenplay by Jimmy Sangster. (NYTFR, LC, W, AMPAS,
Q).

1440 I. F. STONE'S WEEKLY. (Bruck-1973-Jerry Bruck, Jr.).
A documentary interview with I. F. Stone; no screenplay. (W).

1441 I, A LOVER. (Crown International-1968-Borje Nyberg). A
work for the screen by Peer Guldbrandsen, based on a novel
by Stig Holm. (FF, NYTFR, W).

1442 I, A MAN. (Andy Warhol Film-1967-Andy Warhol). Dialogue
improvised from ideas by Andy Warhol. (FF, NYTFR, W,
AMPAS).

1443 I, A WOMAN. (Audubon-1966-Mac Ahlberg). A screenplay
by Peer Guldbrandsen, based on the novel Jeg--En Kvinde
by Siv Holm. (FF, NYTFR).

I, A WOMAN part 2 see "2"

1444 I, A WOMAN, part 3 (THE DAUGHTER). (Chevron-1970-
Mac Ahlberg). An original screenplay by Peer Guldbrandsen.
(W).

1445 I AM A DANCER. (Anglo-EMI-1973-Pierre Jourdan). A documentary; no screenplay credits. (W).

1446 I AM A GROUPIE. (Trans American-1970-Derek Ford). An
original script by Derek Ford and Suzanne Mercer. (W).

1447 I AM CURIOUS (BLUE). (Grove-1970-Vilgot Sjoman). An
original screenplay by Vilgot Sjoman; published by Grove
Press, 1970, 219p. (SCH, W, Q).

1448 I AM CURIOUS (YELLOW). (Grove Press-1969-Vilgot Sjoman).
An original screenplay by Vilgot Sjoman; published by Grove
Press, 1968, 254p. (SCH, FF, W, Q).

I AM CURIOUS GAY see HAPPY BIRTHDAY, DAVY

1449 I AM FRIGID ... WHY? (Audubon-1973-Max Pecas). No
screenplay credits available. (W).

I CALL FIRST see WHO'S THAT KNOCKING AT MY DOOR?

1450 I COULD NEVER HAVE SEX WITH ANY MAN WHO HAS SO
LITTLE REGARD FOR MY HUSBAND. (Cinema V-1973-Ro-
bert McCarty). A screenplay credited to Dan Greenburg,

based on his novel Chewsday; Stein & Day, 1968, 188p. (W, LACOPL).

1451   I CROSSED THE COLOR LINE. (U. S. Films-1966-Ted V. Mikels). An original screenplay by John T. Wilson and Arthur A. Namew. (FF, AMPAS).

1452   I DEAL IN DANGER. (20th Century-Fox-1966-Walter Grauman). An original screenplay by Larry Cohen. (FF, LC, W, AMPAS, Q).

1453   I DRINK YOUR BLOOD. (Cinemation-1970-David Durston). An original screenplay by David Durston. (W).

1454   I ESCAPED FROM DEVIL'S ISLAND. (United Artists-1973- William Witney). An original screenplay by Richard L. Adams. (W).

1455   I EVEN MET HAPPY GYPSIES. (Prominent Films-1968- Aleksandar Petrovic). An original screenplay by Aleksandar Petrovic. (FF, NYTFR, W, AMPAS).

1456   I LIVE IN FEAR. (Brandon-1967-Akira Kurosawa). An original screenplay by Akira Kurosawa, Shinobu Hashimoto, and Hideo Oguni. (FF, W, Q).

1457   I LOVE MY WIFE. (Universal-1970-Mel Stuart). An original screenplay by Robert Kaufman. (W, Q).

1458   I LOVE YOU, ALICE B. TOKLAS! (Warner Bros. -7 Arts- 1968-Hy Averback). An original screenplay by Paul Mazursky and Larry Tucker. (FF, NYTFR, FM, W, LC, AMPAS, Q).

1459   I LOVE YOU, I KILL YOU. (New Yorker-1972-Uwe Brandner). This original screenplay was written by Uwe Brandner. (FF).

1460   I LOVE YOU, ROSA. (Leisure Media-1973-Moshe Mizrahi). An original screenplay written by Moshe Mizrahi. (W).

1461   I MARRIED YOU FOR FUN. (AVCO Embassy-1972-Luciano Salce). A screenplay written by Agenore Incrocci, Furio Scarpelli, Sandro Continenza, Natalia Ginzburg, and Luciano Salce; from a play by Natalia Ginzburg. (W).

1462   I NEVER SANG FOR MY FATHER. (Columbia-1970-Gilbert Cates). A screenplay by Robert Anderson, based on his play of the same name; Random House, 1968, 115p. (W, Q, LACOPL).

1463   I SAW WHAT YOU DID. (Universal-1965-William Castle). An authored work for the screen by William McGivern, based on the novel Out of the Dark by Ursula Curtiss; Dodd, Mead

& Co., 1964, 183p. (NYTFR, LACOPL, LC, W, AMPAS, Q).

I, THE BODY see MORIANNA

1464 I WALK THE LINE. (Columbia-1970-John Frankenheimer). A screenplay by Alvin Sargent, based on a novel An Exile, by Madison Jones; Viking Press, 1967. (W, Q, LACOPL).

1465 I WANT WHAT I WANT. (Cinerama-1972-John Dexter). A screenplay by Gillian Freeman, based on the novel by Geoff Brown, with additional material and dialogue by Gavin Lambert; Putnam, 1966. (W, LACOPL, Q).

1466 I WAS ALL HIS. (Casino-1965-Wolfgang Becker). An original screenplay by Kurt Heuser. (W).

I WAS HAPPY HERE see TIME LOST AND TIME REMEMBERED

1467 ICE STATION ZEBRA. (MGM-1968-John Sturges). A screenplay by Douglas Heyes, based on a screen story by Harry Julian Fink, from the novel by Alistair MacLean; Doubleday, 1963, 176p. (Q, FF, NYTFR, FM, W, LC, AMPAS, LACOPL).

1468 THE ICEMAN COMETH. (American Film Theatre-1973-John Frankenheimer). Screenplay taken from the play by Eugene O'Neill; Random House, 1946, 260p. (W, LACOPL).

1468a I'D RATHER BE RICH. (Universal-1964-Jack Smight). A screenplay by Oscar Brodney, Norman Krasna, and Leo Townsend. (FF, NYTFR, W AMPAS, Q).

1469 IDENTIFICATION MARKS: NONE. (New Yorker-1969-Jerzy Skolimowski). An original screenplay by Jerzy Skolimowski. (W).

1470 THE IDOL. (Embassy-1966-Daniel Petrie). An original screenplay by Millard Lampell, taken from an original story by Ugo Liberatore. (FF, NYTFR, W, AMPAS, Q).

1471 IF ... (Paramount-1969-Lindsay Anderson). A screenplay by David Sherwin, based on the original script Crusaders by David Sherwin and John Howlett; Simon & Schuster, 1969, 167p. (FF, W, LC, MCC, AMPAS, LACOPL, Q, SCH).

1472 IF HE HOLLERS, LET HIM GO! (Cinerama Releasing Corporation-1968-Charles Martin). An original screenplay by Charles Martin. (FF, NYTFR, W, AMPAS, Q).

1473 IF I HAD A GUN. (Ajay-1973-Stefan Uher). A screenplay by Milan Ferko and Stefan Uher, based on a novel by Milan Ferko. (W).

1474   IF IT'S TUESDAY, THIS MUST BE BELGIUM. (United Art-
       ists-1969-Mel Stuart). An original screenplay by David Shaw.
       (FF, W, LC, AMPAS, Q).

1475   I'LL NEVER FORGET WHAT'S'ISNAME. (Regional-1968-
       Michael Winner). An original screenplay by Peter Draper.
       (FF, Q, NYTFR, FM, W, AMPAS, V).

1476   I'LL TAKE SWEDEN. (United Artists-1965-Frederick De
       Cordova). An original screenplay by Nat Perrin, Bob Fisher,
       and Arthur Marx. (NYTFR, LC, W, AMPAS, Q).

1477   THE ILLIAC PASSION. (FilmMaker's Cooperative-1968-Greg-
       ory Markopoulos). An original screenplay by Gregory Marko-
       poulos. (FF, NYTFR, W).

1478   ILLUSION OF BLOOD. (Toho-1968-Shiro Toyoda). A screen-
       play by Toshio Yasumi, based on an 1826 Kabuki drama by
       Namboku Tsuruya. (FF, NYTFR, W).

1479   THE ILLUSTRATED MAN. (Warner Bros.-7 Arts-1969-Jack
       Smight). A screenplay by Howard B. Kreitsek, based on the
       book including three short stories, "The Veldt," "The Long
       Rain," and "The Last Night of the World" by Ray Bradbury;
       Doubleday, 1951. (FF, W, LC, AMPAS, LACOPL, Q).

1480   IMAGE, FLESH AND VOICE. (FilmMakers-1970-Ed Emsch-
       willer). An original screenplay by Ed Emschwiller. (W).

1481   IMAGES. (Columbia-1972-Robert Altman). An adaptation of
       "In Search of Unicorns" by Susannah York, written for the
       screen by Robert Altman. (W, FF, Q).

1482   IMAGO. (Emerson-1970-Ned Bosnick). An original screen-
       play by Ned Bosnick. (W).

1483   IMITATION OF CHRIST. (FilmMakers-1970-Andy Warhol).
       No screenplay credit; dialogue improvised. (W).

1484   THE IMMORTAL STORY. (Fleetwood Films-1969-Orson
       Welles). An original screenplay by Orson Welles, based on
       the story The Immortal Story by Isak Dinesen (Karen Blixen),
       in Anecdotes of Destiny; Random House, 1958, 244p. (FF,
       NYTFR, FM, W, LACOPL, Q).

1485   L'IMMORTELLE. (Grove-1969-Alain Robbe-Grillet). An
       original screenplay by Alain Robbe-Grillet. (W).

1486   IMPASSE. (United Artists-1969-Richard Benedict). An origi-
       nal screenplay by John C. Higgins. (FF, W, LC, Q).

1487   IMPOSSIBLE ON SATURDAY. (Magna-1966-Alex Joffe).
       Story and screenplay by Jean Ferry, Pierre Levy-Corti,

Shabatai-Tevet, and Alex Joffe.   (FF, NYTFR, W, AMPAS, Q).

1488   THE IMPOSSIBLE YEARS. (MGM-1968-Michael Gordon).
An original work by George Wells, based on the play by Bob
Fisher and Arthur Marx. (FF, NYTFR, FM, W, LC, AMPAS, Q).

1489   IN COLD BLOOD. (Columbia-1967-Richard Brooks). A
screenplay by Richard Brooks, based on the book by Truman
Capote; Random House, 1965, 343p. (Q, FF, NYTFR, FM,
W, LC, AMPAS, LACOPL).

1490   IN ENEMY COUNTRY. (Universal-1968-Harry Keller). A
screenplay by Edward Anhalt, based on a story by Sy Bartlett. (FF, W, AMPAS, Q).

1491   IN HARM'S WAY. (Paramount-1965-Otto Preminger). A
screenplay by Wendell Mayes, based on the novel by James
Bassett; World Publishing Co., 1962, 510p. (FF, LC, W,
AMPAS, LACOPL, Q).

1492   IN LIKE FLINT. (20th Century-Fox-1967-Gordon Douglas).
An original screenplay written by Hal Fimberg. (FF, NYTFR,
FM, W, LC, AMPAS, Q).

1493   IN SEARCH OF GREGORY. (Universal-1970-Peter Wood).
An original screenplay by Tonino Guerra, and Lucile Laks,
adapted by Ken Levison. (W, Q).

1494   IN THE HEAT OF THE NIGHT. (United Artists-1967-Norman
Jewison). A screenplay by Stirling Silliphant, based on the
novel by John Ball; Harper & Row, 1965. (Q, FF, NYTFR,
FM, W, LC, AMPAS, LACOPL).

1495   IN THE NAME OF THE FATHER. (Vides-1971-Marco Bellochio). An original screenplay by Marco Bellochio. (W).

1496   INADMISSIBLE EVIDENCE. (Paramount-1968-Anthony Page).
A screenplay by John Osborne, based on his play; Grove
Press, 1965, 115p. (Q, FF, NYTFR, W, LC, AMPAS,
LACOPL).

1497   THE INBREAKER. (Robert G. Elliott-1974-George McCowan).
An original screenplay by Jacob Zilber and William Sigurgeir-
son. (V).

1498   THE INCIDENT. (20th Century-Fox-1967-Larry Pearce). A
screenplay and original story by Nicholas E. Baehr. (FF,
NYTFR, FM, W, LC, AMPAS).

1499   INCIDENT AT PHANTOM HILL. (Universal-1966-Earl Bellamy). A screenplay by Frank Nugent and Ken Pettus, based

on a story by Harry Tatelman. (FF, LC, W, AMPAS, Q).

1499a   THE INCREDIBLE MR. LIMPET. (Warner Bros.-1964-
Arthur Lubin). Jameson Brewer and John C. Rose wrote this
original screenplay. (FF, Q, W, AMPAS, NYTFR).

1500   THE INCREDIBLE TWO-HEADED TRANSPLANT. (American
International-1971-Anthony M. Lanza). An original screenplay
by James Gordon White and John Lawrence. (W, Q).

1501   THE INCREDIBLY STRANGE CREATURES WHO STOPPED
LIVING AND BECAME MIXED-UP ZOMBIES. (Hollywood
Star-1965-Ray Dennis Steckler). A screenplay by Gene Pollock
and Robert Silliphant, based on a story by E. M. Kevke. (W,
AMPAS, Q).

1502   INDIAN PAINT. (Eagle-International-1966-Norman Foster).
An inspiration by Norman Foster, taken from the novel by
Glenn Balch. (W, LC, AMPAS, Q).

INFERNO OF FIRST LOVE see NANAMI

1503   INGA. (Cinemation-1968-Joseph W. Sarno). A screenplay
written by Joseph W. Sarno. (FF, NYTFR, W).

1504   THE INHERITOR. (Hera-1973-Philippe Labro). An original
screenplay by Philippe Labro. (W).

1505   INN OF EVIL. (Toho-1971-Masaki Kobayashi). A screenplay
by Tomoe Ryu, from a story by Shuoroo Yamamoto. (W).

1506   INNOCENT BYSTANDERS. (Paramount-1973-Peter Collinson).
A screenplay by James Mitchell, based on the novel by James
Munro; Knopf, 1969, 243p. (W, Q).

1506a   THE INSECT WOMAN. (Jerome Balsam-1964-Shohei Imamura).
A screenplay by Keiji Hasebe and Shohei Imamura. (FF,
NYTFR, W, Q).

1507   INSIDE DAISY CLOVER. (Warner Bros.-1966-Robert Mulligan). A screenplay written by Gavin Lambert, based on his
novel; Viking Press, 1963. (Q, FF, NYTFR, LC, W,
AMPAS, LACOPL).

1508   INSPECTOR CLOUSEAU. (United Artists-1968-Bud Yorkin).
A screenplay by Tom Waldman and Frank Waldman, based on
a character created by Blake Edwards and Maurice Richlin.
(NYTFR, FF, FM, LC, AMPAS, Q).

1509   INTERLUDE. (Columbia-1968-Kevin Billington). An original
screenplay by Lee Langley and Hugh Leonard, from their original story. (FF, NYTFR, FM, W, LC, AMPAS, Q).

1510   THE INTERNECINE PROJECT. (Allied Artists-1974-Ken
        Hughes). A screenplay by Barry Levinson, and Jonathan
        Lynn, from the novel by Mort W. Elking, Internecine.
        (HR, V).

1511   INTERVAL. (AVCO Embassy-1973-Daniel Mann). An origi-
        nal work for the screen by Gavin Lambert. (W, Q).

1512   INTIMACY. (Goldstone Film Enterprises-1966-Victor Stol-
        off). A screenplay by Eva Wolas, based on an idea by Stan-
        ley Z. Cherry. (FF, W, Q).

1513   INTIMATE LIGHTING. (Altura-1969-Ivan Passer). An origi-
        nal screenplay by Vaclav Sasek, Jaroslav Papousek, and Ivan
        Passer. (W).

1514   INVASION OF THE BEE GIRLS. (Centaur-1973-Denis Sand-
        ers). An original screenplay written by Nicholas Meyer.
        (FF).

1515   INVASION 1700. (Medallion-1965-Fernando Cerchio). A
        screenplay by Henry Sienkiewicz, based on the novel The
        Elite of the Crowd. (W).

1516   INVESTIGATION OF A CITIZEN ABOVE SUSPICION. (Colum-
        bia-1970-Elio Petri). An original screenplay and story by
        Ugo Pirro and Elio Petri. (W, Q).

1517   THE INVITATION. (1974-Claude Goretta). An original
        screenplay by Claude Goretta and Michel Viala). (HR).

1517a   INVITATION TO A GUNFIGHTER. (United Artists-1964-Rich-
        ard Wilson). A screenplay by Elizabeth and Richard Wilson,
        adaptation by Alvin Sapinsley, based on a story by Hal Good-
        man and Larry Klein. (Q, W, NYTFR, AMPAS, FF).

1518   THE IPCRESS FILE. (Universal-1965-Sidney J. Furie). A
        work for the screen by Bill Canaway and James Doran, from
        the novel by Len Deighton; Simon & Schuster, 1962. (NYTFR,
        LC, W, AMPAS, LACOPL, Q).

1519   IS PARIS BURNING? (Paramount-1966-Rene Clement). A
        screenplay by Gore Vidal, Francis Ford Coppola, Jean Aur-
        enche, Pierre Bost, and Claude Brule; based on the book by
        Larry Collins and Dominique Lapierre; Simon & Schuster,
        1965, 376p. (FF, NYTFR, LC, W, AMPAS, LACOPL, Q).

1520   IS THERE SEX AFTER DEATH. (Abel-Child-1971-Jeanne and
        Alan Abel). An original screenplay by Jeanne and Alan Abel.
        (W).

1521   ISABEL. (Paramount-1968-Paul Almond). An original screen-
        play by Paul Almond. (FF, NYTFR, W, AMPAS, Q).

ISADORA see LOVES OF ISADORA

1522   ISLAND AT THE TOP OF THE WORLD. (Buena Vista-1974-
        Robert Stevenson). An original screenplay by John Whedon,
        based on the novel The Lost Ones by Ian Cameron; Morrow,
        1968. (V, LACOPL).

1523   ISLAND OF TERROR. (Universal-1967-Terence Cooper). A
        screenplay by Edward Andrew Mann and Alan Ramsen. (FF,
        W, AMPAS, Q).

1523a   ISLAND OF THE BLUE DOLPHINS. (Universal-1964-James
        B. Clark). A screenplay by Ted Sherdeman and Jane Klove,
        based on the novel by Scott O'Dell; Houghton, 1960. (FF,
        LACOPL, AMPAS, W, Q, NYTFR).

1524   ISLAND OF THE BURNING DAMNED. (Maron-1973-Terence
        Fisher). A screenplay by Ronald Liles, based on a novel by
        John Lymington, with additional dialogue and scenes by Pip
        and Jane Baker. (W, FF).

1525   ISLAND OF THE DOOMED. (Allied Artists-1968-Mel Welles).
        A screenplay by Stephen Schmidt, based on a story by Ira
        Meltcher and E. V. Theumer. (FF, W).

1526   IT. (Warner Bros.-7 Arts-1967-Herbert J. Leder). An orig-
        inal screenplay by Herbert J. Leder. (FF, NYTFR, FM, W,
        LC, AMPAS, Q).

1527   IT AIN'T EASY. (Dandelion-1972-Maury Hurley). An origi-
        nal screenplay written by Mary Olson. (W).

1528   IT HAPPENED HERE. (Lopert-1966-Kevin Brownlow and An-
        drew Molio). An original screenplay by Kevin Brownlow and
        Andrew Molio. (NYTFR, W, Q).

1529   IT HAPPENED IN HOLLYWOOD. (Screw-1973-Peter Lockc).
        An original script attributed to Peter Locke. (W).

1530   IT ONLY HAPPENS TO OTHERS. (GSF-1971-Nadine Trintig-
        nant). An original screenplay by Nadine Trintignant. (W, Q).

1531   IT TAKES ALL KINDS. (Commonwealth-1969-Eddie Davis).
        Eddie Davis and Charles E. Savage wrote this screenplay.
        (W).

        IT WON'T RUB OFF BABY see SWEET LOVE, BITTER

1532   THE ITALIAN CONNECTION. (American International-1973-
        Fernando di Leo). A screenplay written directly for the
        screen by Augusto Finocchi, Ingo Hermess and Fernando di
        Leo. (W).

1533   THE ITALIAN JOB. (Paramount-1969-Peter Collinson).   An
       original work for the screen by Troy Kennedy Martin.   (W,
       LC, AMPAS, Q).

1534   ITALIANO BRAVA GENTE. (Embassy-1966-Giuseppe de San-
       tis).   A screenplay by Ennio de Concini, Augusto Frassinetti,
       Gindomenico Giagni, Serghei Smirnov and Giuseppe de Santis,
       based on a story by Ennio de Concini and Giuseppe de Santis.
       (FF, NYTFR, W, Q).

1535   IT'S A BIKINI WORLD. (Trans American-1967-Stephanie
       Rothman).   An original screenplay by Charles S. Swartz and
       Stephanie Rothman.   (FF, W, LC).

1536   IT'S ALIVE. (Warner Bros.-1974-Larry Cohen).   Larry
       Cohen wrote this original screenplay.   (V, HR).

1537   J. C. (AVCO Embassy-1972-William F. McGaha).   An origi-
       nal screenplay by William F. McGaha and Joe Thirty.   (W).

1538   J. W. COOP. (Columbia-1972-Cliff Robertson).   An original
       screenplay by Cliff Robertson.   (W, Q).

1539   JACK FROST. (Embassy-1966-Alexander Row).   Mikhail Vol-
       pin and Nikolai Erdman are credited with this original screen-
       play.   (W, Q).

1540   JACK OF DIAMONDS. (MGM-1967-Don Taylor).   An original
       work for the screen by Jack De Witt and Sandy Howard. (FF,
       NYTFR, FM, W, LC, AMPAS, Q).

1541   JAMILYA. (Artkino-1972-Irina Poplavskaya).   This screenplay
       was based on a story by Chinghiz Aitmatov.   (W).

1542   JANIS. (Universal-1974-Howard Alk & Seaton Findlay).   A
       documentary; no screenwriting credits available.   (V).

1543   JE T'AIME, JE T'AIME. (New Yorker-1972-Alain Resnais).
       An original screenplay by Jacques Sternberg and Alain Res-
       nais.   (FF).

1544   JENNIFER ON MY MIND. (United Artists-1971-Noel Black).
       A screenplay by Erich Segal, based on the novel Heir by Roger
       L. Simon; Macmillan, 1968, 147p.   (W, LACOPL, Q).

1545   JENNY. (Cinerama-1970-George Bloomfield.   A screenplay by
       Martin Lavut and George Bloomfield, from a story by Diana
       Gould.   (Q, W).

1546   JEREMIAH JOHNSON. (Warner Bros.-1972-Sydney Pollack).
       A screenplay by John Milius and Edward Anhalt, based on the
       novel Mountain Man by Vardis Fisher; Morrow, 1965, 372p.,
       and the story "Crow Killer" by Raymond W. Thorp and Robert
       Bunker.   (W, FF, LACOPL, Q).

1547   JEREMY. (United Artists-1973-Arthur Barron). Arthur Bar-
        ron wrote the screenplay from a novel by John Minahan;
        Bantam Books, 1973, 114p. (W).

1548   THE JERUSALEM FILE. (MGM-1972-John Flynn). An origi-
        nal screenplay by Troy Kennedy Martin. (Q, FF).

1549   JESSE JAMES MEETS FRANKENSTEIN'S DAUGHTER. (Em-
        bassy-1966-William Beaudine). Carl H. Hittleman wrote the
        original screenplay. (Q, FF, W, AMPAS).

1550   JESUS CHRIST SUPERSTAR. (Universal-1973-Norman Jewi-
        son). A screenplay by Melvyn Bragg and Norman Jewison,
        based on the rock opera with book and lyrics by Tim Rice
        and Andrew Lloyd Webber. (W, Q).

1551   THE JESUS TRIP. (EMCO-1971-Russ Mayberry). An origi-
        nal screenplay by Dick Poston. (W).

1552   JIG SAW. (Beverly-1965-Val Guest). A screenplay written
        by Val Guest, based on Sleep Long, My Love by Hillary
        Waugh. (AMPAS, Q).

1553   JIGSAW. (Universal-1968-James Goldstone). A screenplay by
        Quentin Werty [aka Ranald MacDougall], based on a screenplay
        by Peter Stone and the novel Fallen Angel by Howard Fast;
        Little, Brown & Co., 1951. (FF, NYTFR, FM, W, AMPAS,
        LACOPL).

1554   JIMI PLAYS BERKELEY. (New Line Cinema-1973-Peter Pala-
        fian). A documentary; no screenwriting credits given. (W).

1555   JOANNA. (20th Century-Fox-1968-Michael Sarne). An origi-
        nal screenplay by Michael Sarne. (FF, NYTFR, FM, W, LC,
        Q).

1556   JOE. (Cannon-1970-John G. Avildsen). An original screen-
        play by Norman Wexler; Avon, 128p., 1970. (W, MCC,
        LACOPL, Q, SCH).

1557   JOE COCKER/ MAD DOGS AND ENGLISHMEN. (MGM-1971-
        Pierre Adidge). A rock documentary; no author credits. (W,
        Q).

1558   JOE HILL. (Paramount-1971-Bo Widerberg). An original
        screenplay by Bo Widerberg. (W, Q).

1559   JOE KIDD. (Universal-1972-John Sturges). An original
        screenplay written by Elmore Leonard. (FF, Q).

1560   JOHN AND MARY. (20th Century-Fox-1969-Peter Yates).
        John Mortimer wrote this screenplay, which was taken from
        the novel by Mervyn Jones; Atheneum, 1966, 216p. (W,
        AMPAS, LACOPL, Q).

1561   JOHN GOLDFARB, PLEASE COME HOME. (20th Century-
       Fox-1965-J. Lee Thompson). An original screenplay by Wil-
       liam Peter Blatty. (FF, LC, W, AMPAS, Q).

1562   JOHNNY CASH! THE MAN, HIS WORLD, HIS MUSIC. (Con-
       tinental-1970-Robert Elfstrom). No screenplay credits avail-
       able. (W, Q).

1563   JOHNNY GOT HIS GUN. (Cinemation-1971-Dalton Trumbo).
       A work by Dalton Trumbo, based on his novel of the same
       name; Bantam Books, 1970, 243p. (W, Q).

1564   JOHNNY HAMLET. (Transvue-1972-Enzo G. Castellari aka
       Enzo Girolami). A screenplay by Tito Carpi, Francesco
       Scardamaglia and Enzo G. Castellari, based on a story by
       Sergio Corbucci, adapted from William Shakespeare's Hamlet;
       Norton, 1963, 270p. (FF, LACOPL).

1565   JOHNNY MINOTAUR. (Impact-1971-Charles Henri Ford). No
       author credits available. (W).

1566   JOHNNY NOBODY. (Medallion Pictures Corporation-1965-
       Noel Patrick). A screenplay by Patrick Kirwin, based on a
       story "The Trial of Johnny Nobody" by Albert Z. Carr.
       (NYTFR, W, AMPAS, Q).

1567   JOHNNY RENO. (Paramount-1966-R. G. Springsteen). A
       screenplay by Steve Fisher, based on a story by Steve Fisher
       and A. C. Lyles. (FF, NYTFR, LC, Q, W, AMPAS).

1568   JOHNNY TIGER. (Universal-1966-Paul Wendkos). A screen-
       play by Paul Crabtree and R. John Hugh, based on an origi-
       nal story by R. John Hugh. (FF, NYTFR, Q, W, LC,
       AMPAS).

1569   JOHNNY YUMA. (Clover-1967-Romolo Guerrieri). A screen-
       play by Scavolini, George Simonelli, Mario di Leo and Rom-
       olo Guerrieri. (FF, W).

1570   THE JOKERS. (Universal-1967-Michael Winner). A screen-
       play by Dick Clement and Ian La Frenais, based on an origi-
       nal story by Michael Winner. (FF, NYTFR, FM, W,
       AMPAS).

1571   JONATHAN. (New Yorker-1973-Hans W. Geissendorfer). An
       original screenplay by Hans W. Geissendorfer. (W).

1572   JONATHAN LIVINGSTON SEAGULL. (Paramount-1973-Hall
       Bartlett). A screenplay by Richard Bach and Hall Bartlett,
       from the novel by Richard Bach; Macmillan, 1970, 93p. (W,
       LACOPL).

1573   JORY. (AVCO Embassy-1973-Jorge Fons). A screenplay by

Gerald Herman and Robert Irving, based on a novel by Milton R. Bass; Putnam, 1969, 255p. (W, LACOPL, Q).

1574   JOSEPH KILIAN. (1966-Pavel Juracek & Jan Schmidt). An original screenplay authored by Pavel Juracek. (NYTFR).

1575   JOURNEY THROUGH ROSEBUD. (GSF-1972-Tom Gries). An original screenplay by Albert Ruben. (W, Q).

1576   JOURNEY TO SHILOH. (Universal-1968-William Hale). A screenplay attributed to Gene Coon, based on the novel Fields of Honor by Will Henry. (FF, W, AMPAS, Q).

1577   JOURNEY TO THE FAR SIDE OF THE SUN. (Universal-1969-Robert Parrish). A screenplay by Gerry and Sylvia Anderson and Donald James, from a story by Gerry and Sylvia Anderson. (W, Q).

1578   JOVITA. (Altura-1970-Janusz Morgenstern). A screenplay by Tadeusz Konwicki, based on the novel Disneyland by Stanislaw Dygat. (W).

1579   JOY HOUSE. (MGM-1965-Rene Clement). A screenplay by Rene Clement, Pascal Jardin, and Charles Williams, based on the novel by Day Keene. (FF, LC, AMPAS, Q).

1580   JOY IN THE MORNING. (MGM-1965-Alex Segal). A screenplay by Sally Benson, Alfred Hayes, and Norman Lessing, based on the novel by Betty Smith; Harper, 1963, 308p. (NYTFR, LC, W, AMPAS, LACOPL, Q).

1581   JUD. (Maron-1971-Gunther Collins). An original screenplay by Gunther Collins. (W).

1582   JUDEX. (Continental-1966-Georges Franju). A screenplay by Francis Lacassin and Jacques Champreux, based on original scenarios by Louis Feuillade and Arthur Bernede. (FF, NYTFR, W, Q).

1583   JUDITH. (Paramount-1966-Daniel Mann). A screenplay by John Michael Hayes, based on a story by Lawrence Durrell. (FF, NYTFR, LC, W, Q, AMPAS).

1584   JUGGERNAUT. (United Artists-1974-Richard Lester). An original screenplay by Richard De Koker. (V, NYT).

JULES VERNE'S ROCKET TO THE MOON see THOSE FANTASTIC FLYING FOOLS

1585   JULIET OF THE SPIRITS. (Rizzoli-1965-Federico Fellini). A screenplay by Federico Fellini, Tullio Pinelli, Ennio Flaiano, Brunello Rondi, from an original story by Federico Fellini and Tullio Pinelli; Orion Press, 1965, 181p. (NYTFR, MCC, W, Q, AMPAS, LACOPL, SCH).

1586   JULIETTE DE SADE. (Haven International-1969-William Kiefer). No author credits available. (W).

1587   JULIUS CAESAR. (American International-1971-Sturat Burge). A screenplay by Robert Furnival from the play by William Shakespeare; Cambridge University Press, 1968, 219p. (W, Q).

1588   JUMP. (Cannon-1971-Joe Manduke). An original screenplay by Richard Wheelwright. (W, Q).

1589   THE JUNGLE BOOK. (Buena Vista-1967-Wolfgang Reitherman). A screenplay by Ralph Wright, Ken Anderson, and Vance Gerry, inspired by Rudyard Kipling's "Mowgli" stories; Macmillan, 1964, 371p. (W, LC, AMPAS, Q).

1590   JUNIOR BONNER. (Cinerama-1972-Sam Peckinpah). An original screenplay by Jeb Rosebrook. (W, Q).

1591   JUST BEFORE NIGHTFALL. (Columbia-1974-Claude Chabrol). An original screenplay by Claude Chabrol. (HR).

1592   JUST LIKE A WOMAN. (Emerson-1968-Robert Fuest). An original screenplay written by Robert Fuest. (FF).

1593   JUSTINE. (20th Century-Fox-1969-George Cukor). A screenplay by Lawrence B. Marcus, based on four novels known as The Alexandria Quartet (Justine, Balthazar, Mountolive, and Clea) by Lawrence Durrell; E. P. Dutton, 1962, 884p. (FF, W, AMPAS, Q).

1594   KALEIDOSCOPE. (Warner Bros.-1966-Jack Smight). A screenplay written directly for the screen by Robert and Jen-Howard Carrington. (FF, NYTFR, LC, W, AMPAS, Q).

1595   KANCHENJUNGHA. (Harrison-1966-Satyajit Ray). An original screenplay by Satyajit Ray). NYTFR, W, Q).

1596   KANSAS CITY BOMBER. (MGM-1972-Jerrold Freedman). A screenplay by Thomas Rickman and Calvin Clements, based on a story by Barry Sandler. (FF, Q).

1596a   KAPO. (Lionex-1964-Gillo Pontecorvo). A screenplay by Franco Solinas and Gillo Pontecorvo. (FF, NYTFR, W, Q).

1597   KATERINA ISMAILOVA. (Artkino-1969-Mikhail Shapiro). A screenplay by Mikhail Shapiro, based on the opera Katerina Ismailova by Dimitri Shostakovich. (FF).

1598   KAYA, I'LL KILL YOU! (Altura-1969-Vatroslav Mimica). An original screenplay by Vatroslav Mimica and Kruno Quien. (W).

1599   KEEP ON ROCKIN'. (Pennebaker-1973-). A rock music
documentary; no screenplay credit. (W).

1600   KELLY'S HEROES. (MGM-1970-Brian G. Hutton). An original screenplay by Troy Kennedy Martin. (W).

1601   KENNER. (MGM-1969-Steve Sekely). An original screenplay
by Harold Clemins and John R. Loring, based on a story by
Mary Phillips Murray. (FF, W, LC, AMPAS, Q).

1602   KES. (United Artists-1970-Kenneth Loach). A screenplay by
Barry Hines, Kenneth Loach, and Tony Garnett, from the
book A Kestrel for a Knave by Harry Hines. (W, Q).

1603   KHARTOUM. (United Artists-1966-Basil Dearden). A screenplay by Robert Ardrey, based on the life of Sir Charles Gordon. (FF, NYTFR, LC, W, AMPAS, Q).

1604   KID BLUE. (20th Century-Fox-1973-James Frawley). An
original screenplay by Edwin Shrake. (Q, W).

1605   KID RODELO. (Paramount-1966-Richard Carlson). A screenplay by Jack Natteford, from a story by Louis L'Amour.
(FF, NYTFR, LC, W, AMPAS, Q).

1606   KIDNAPPED. (American International-1971-Delbert Mann).
A screenplay by Jack Pulman, based on Kidnapped; Scribner's
1929, 289p.; and David Balfour; Scribner's, 1893, 406p., two
novels by Robert Louis Stevenson. (W, LACOPL, Q).

1607   KILL! (Frank Lee International-1969-Kihachi Okamoto). A
screenplay by Akira Murao and Kihachi Okamoto, based on
the novel Torideyama No Jushichinin by Shugoro Yamamoto.
(W).

1608   KILL A DRAGON. (United Artists-1967-Michael Moore). An
original screenplay by George Schenck and William Marks.
(FF, NYTFR, FM, W, LC, AMPAS, Q).

1609   KILL BABY KILL. (Europix Consolidated-1967-Mario Bava).
A screenplay by Romano Migliorini, Roberto Natale, and
Mario Bava. (FF, W).

1610   KILL OR BE KILLED. (Rizzoli-1968-Amerigo Anton). An
original screenplay by Mario Amendola. (FF, AMPAS).

1610a THE KILLERS. (Universal-1964-Donald Siegel). A screenplay by Gene L. Coon, based on the short story by Ernest
Hemingway; in The Short Stories of Ernest Hemingway; Scrib-
ners, 1965, 499p. (FF, NYTFR, Q, W, AMPAS, LACOPL).

1611   THE KILLING GAME. (Regional-1968-Alain Jessua). A
work for the screen written by Alain Jessua. (FF, NYTFR,
W, Q).

1612   THE KILLING OF SISTER GEORGE. (Cinerama-1968-Robert
        Aldrich). A screenplay by Lukas Heller, based on the play
        by Frank Marcus; Random House, 1965, 117p. (Q, FF,
        NYTFR, FM, W, AMPAS, LACOPL).

1613   KIMBERLEY JIM. (Embassy-1965-Emil Nofal). An original
        story and screenplay by Emil Nofal. (W, AMPAS, Q).

1614   KING, MURRAY. (Iconographic-1969-David Hoffman). An
        original work for the screen by David Hoffman. (FF, W).

1615   KING AND COUNTRY. (American International-1966-Joseph
        Losey). A screenplay by Evan Jones, based on the play by
        John Wilson and a story by James Lansdale Hodson. (FF,
        NYTFR, W, Q).

1616   A KING IN NEW YORK. (Classic Entertainment-1973-
        Charles Chaplin). An original screenplay by Charles Chap-
        lin. (W, AMPAS).

1617   KING KONG ESCAPES. (Universal-1968-Inoshiro Honda).
        An original screenplay by Kaoru Mabuchi. (FF, NYTFR, W,
        LC, Q).

1618   KING LEAR. (Altura-1971-Peter Brook). A screen adapta-
        tion by Peter Brook, from the play by William Shakespeare;
        Methuen, 1963, 260p. (W).

1619   KING OF HEARTS. (Lopert-1967-Philippe De Broca). An
        original screenplay by Daniel Boulanger. (FF, NYTFR, W,
        AMPAS, Q).

1620   THE KING OF MARVIN GARDENS. (Columbia-1972-Bob
        Rafelson). Jacob Brackman wrote the screenplay based on a
        story by Bob Rafelson and Jacob Brackman. (W, FF, Q).

1621   KING OF THE GRIZZLIES. (Buena Vista-1970-Ron Kelly).
        A screenplay authored by Jack Speirs, adapted by Rod Peter-
        son and Norman Wright from Biography of a Grizzly by
        Ernest Thompson Seton. (W, Q).

1622   KING RAT. (Columbia-1965-Bryan Forbes). A screenplay
        by Bryan Forbes, based on a novel by James Clavell; Little,
        Brown & Co., 1962. (Q, NYTFR, LC, W, AMPAS,
        LACOPL).

1623   KINGDOM IN THE CLOUDS. (Xerox-1972-Elisabeta Bostan).
        A screenplay by Elisabeta Bostan, based on an idea by Petre
        Ispirescu. (FF).

1624   KING'S PIRATE. (Universal-1967-Don Weis). A screenplay
        by Paul Wayne, Aeneas MacKenzie, and Joseph Hoffman,
        based on a story by Aeneas MacKenzie. (FF, W, AMPAS, Q).

1625   A KING'S STORY. (Continental-1967-Harry Booth). A screen-
        play and documentary by Glyn Jones, based on the book by
        the Duke of Windsor; Putnam, 1951, 435p. (NYTFR, W,
        AMPAS, LACOPL, Q).

1626   KISS ME, KISS ME, KISS ME! (Extraordinary-1967-Andy
        Milligan). A screenplay by Josef Bush, based on a story by
        William Mishkin. (FF, W).

1626a   KISS ME, STUPID. (Lopert-1964-Billy Wilder). A screen-
        play by Billy Wilder and I. A. L. Diamond, based on the
        play L'Ora della Fantasia by Anna Bonacci. (FF, NYTFR,
        W, AMPAS, Q).

1627   KISS THE GIRLS AND MAKE THEM DIE. (Columbia-1967-
        Henry Levin). A screenplay by Jack Pulman and Dino Mai-
        uri, based on a story by Dino Maiuri. (FF, NYTFR, LC,
        W, AMPAS, Q).

1628   KISS THE OTHER SHEIK. (MGM-1968-Luciano Salce & Ed-
        uardo de Filippo). A screenplay by Goffredo Parise, Renato
        Castellano, Pipolo aka Giuseppe Moccia, Luciano Salce, Ed-
        uardo de Filippo and Isabella Quarantotti. (FF, NYTFR, FM,
        W, LC, Q).

1628a   KISSES FOR MY PRESIDENT. (Warner Bros. -1964-Curtis
        Bernhardt). A screenplay by Claude Binyon and Robert G.
        Kane, based on a story by Robert G. Kane. (FF, AMPAS,
        W, Q, NYTFR).

1629   KISSIN' COUSINS. (MGM-1964-Gene Nelson). A screenplay
        by Gerald Drayson Adams and Gene Nelson, based on a story
        by Gerald Drayson Adams. (FF, NYTFR, W, AMPAS, Q).

1629a   KITTEN WITH A WHIP. (Universal-1964-Douglas Heyes). A
        screenplay by Douglas Heyes, based on a book by Wade Mil-
        ler. (FF, W, Q, NYTFR, AMPAS).

1630   THE KLANSMAN. (Paramount-1974-Terence Young). A
        screenplay by Millard Kaufman and Samuel Fuller, based on
        a novel by William Bradford Huie; Delacorte Press, 1967.
        (V, HR, LACOPL).

1630a   THE KNACK--AND HOW TO GET IT. (Lopert-1965-Richard
        Lester). A screenplay by Charles Wood, based on the play
        by Ann Jellicoe; Dell Publishing Co., 1962, 87p. (NYTFR,
        W, AMPAS, LACOPL, Q).

1631   KNIVES OF THE AVENGER. (World Entertainment Corpora-
        tion-1968-John Hold aka Mario Bava). A screenplay by Al-
        berto Liberati, George Simonelli, and Mario Bava. (FF, W).

1632   KOJIRO. (Toho-1968-Hiroshi Inagaki). A screenplay by

Yoshio Shirasaka, Kendo Matsuura, and Hiroshi Inagaki, based on a story by Genzo Murakami. (FF, NYTFR).

1633   KONA COAST. (Warner Bros.-7 Arts-1968-Lamont Johnson). A screenplay written by Gil Ralston, based on a story by John D. MacDonald. (FF, W, LC, AMPAS, Q).

1634   KONGI'S HARVEST. (Tam Communications-1973-Ossie Davis). A screenplay by Wole Soyinka, based on his play. (W).

1635   KOTCH. (Cinerama-1971-Jack Lemmon). A screenplay by John Paxton, from the novel by Katharine Topkins; McGraw-Hill, 1965. (W, LACOPL, Q).

1636   KOVACS. (Stone-Galanoy-1971-B. Ziggy Stone). A screenplay by Terry Galanoy, with the assistance of Edie Adams. (W).

1637   KRAKATOA, EAST OF JAVA. (Cinerama-1969-Bernard Kowalski). A screenplay by Clifford Newton Gould and Bernard Gordon. (FF, W, AMPAS, Q).

1638   THE KREMLIN LETTER. (20th Century-Fox-1970-John Huston). A screenplay by John Huston and Gladys Hill, based on the novel by Noel Behn; Simon & Schuster, 1966, 284p. (W, Q, LACOPL).

1639   KWAIDAN. (Continental-1965-Masaki Kobayashi). A screenplay by Yoko Mizuki, from the original stories by Lafcadio Hearn; Houghton, 1904. (NYTFR, W, AMPAS, LACOPL, Q).

LSD, I HATE YOU! see MOVIE STAR, AMERICAN STYLE

1640   LACOMBE, LUCIEN. (20th Century-Fox-1974-Louis Malle). A screenplay by Louis Malle and Patrick Modiano. (HR, MFB).

1641   LADIES AND GENTLEMEN, THE ROLLING STONES. (Dragon Aire-1974-Rollin Binzer). A rock documentary; no screenplay credits. (V).

1642   LADY CAROLINE LAMB. (United Artists-1973-Robert Bolt). A screenplay by Robert Bolt. (W, Q).

1643   LADY FRANKENSTEIN. (New World-1973-Mel Welles). No author credits given. (W).

1644   LADY ICE. (National General-1974-Tom Gries). A screenplay by Alan Trustman, Harold Clemens, from a story by Alan Trustman. (W, Q).

1644a   LADY IN A CAGE. (Paramount-1964-Walter Grauman). An original screenplay attributed to Luther Davis. (FF, W, Q, AMPAS, NYTFR).

1645   LADY IN CEMENT. (20th Century-Fox-1968-Gordon Douglas).
A screenplay by Marvin H. Albert and Jack Guss, based on
the novel by Marvin H. Albert. (FF, NYTFR, FM, W, LC,
AMPAS, Q).

1646   THE LADY IN THE CAR WITH GLASSES AND A GUN.
(Columbia-1970-Anatole Litvak). A screenplay by Richard
Harris and Eleanor Perry, based on a novel by Sebastien
Japrisot; Simon & Schuster, 1967, 240p. (W, LACOPL, Q).

1647   THE LADY-KILLER OF ROME. (Manson-1966-Elio Petri).
A screenplay by Elio Petri, Tonino Guerra, Pasquale Festa
Campanile, and Massimo Franciosa. (FF).

1648   LADY KUNG-FU. (National General-1973-Huang Feng). No
author credits given. (W).

1649   LADY L. (MGM-1966-Peter Ustinov). A screenplay by Peter
Ustinov, based on the novel by Romain Gary; Simon & Schuster, 1958. (FF, NYTFR, LC, W, AMPAS, LACOPL, Q).

1650   LADY LIBERTY. (United Artists-1972-Mario Monicelli). A
screenplay by Leonard Melfi, Suso Cecchi d'Amico, Don Carlos Dunaway, R. W. Spera, Mario Monicelli, and Ring Lardner, Jr., based on an original story by Leonard Melfi. (FF,
Q).

1651   THE LADY OF MONZA. (Tower-1970-Eriprando Visconti).
A screenplay by Eriprando Visconti and Giampiero Bona.
(W, Q).

1652   THE LADY ON THE TRACKS. (Royal Films International-
1968-Ladislav Rychman). A screenplay by Vratislav Blazek.
(FF, NYTFR, W).

1653   LADY SINGS THE BLUES. (Paramount-1972-Sidney J. Furie).
A screenplay by Terence McCloy, Chris Clark, and Suzanne
De Passe, based on the book by Billie Holiday and William
Dufty; Lancer Books, 1965, 191p. (FF, LACOPL, Q).

1654   LAKE OF DRACULA. (Toho-1973-Michio Yamamoto). Author credits not available. (W).

1655   LANCELOT OF THE LAKE. (1974-Robert Bresson). An
original screenplay by Robert Bresson. (HR, NYT, V).

1656   LAND RAIDERS. (Columbia-1970-Nathan Juran). An original screenplay by Ken Pettus. (W, Q).

1657   THE LANDLORD. (United Artists-1970-Hal Ashby). A
screenplay by Bill Gunn, based on a novel by Kristin Hunter;
Scribner, 1966, 338p. (W, LACOPL, Q).

1658   LAS VEGAS HILLBILLYS. Woolner Bros.-1966-Arthur C.
Pierce). A screenplay written directly for the screen by
Larry E. Jackson. (RR, AMPAS).

1659   THE LAST ADVENTURE. (Universal-1969-Robert Enrico).
A screenplay by Jose Giovanni, Pierre Pellegri and Robert
Enrico, based on a book by Jose Giovanni. (FF).

1660   THE LAST AMERICAN HERO. (20th Century-Fox-1973-La-
mont Johnson). A screenplay by William Roberts, based on
articles by Tom Wolfe. (W, Q).

1661   THE LAST CHALLENGE. (MGM-1967-Richard Thorpe). A
screenplay by John Sherry and Robert Emmett Ginna, based
on the novel Pistolero's Progress by John Sherry. (FF,
NYTFR, FM, W LC, AMPAS, Q).

1662   LAST DAYS OF MUSSOLINI. (Paramount-1974-Carlo Lizzani). A screenplay by Carlo Lizzani and Fabio Pittorru.
(V).

1663   THE LAST DETAIL. (Columbia-1973-Hal Ashby). A screenplay by Robert Towne, based on the novel by Darryl Ponicsan; Dial Press, 1973, 281p. (W, LACOPL).

1664   THE LAST ESCAPE. (United Artists-1970-Walter Grauman).
A screenplay by Herman Hoffman, based on a story by John
C. Champion and Barry Trivers. (W, Q).

1665   LAST FOXTROT IN BURBANK. (Federated-1973-Charles
Band). A screenplay by Bill Haggard and Sam Vaughn.
(W).

1666   THE LAST GRENADE. (Cinerama-1970-Gordon Flemyng).
Kenneth Ware wrote the screenplay from an adaptation by
James Mitchell and John Sherlock, of the novel The Ordeal
of Major Grigsby by John Sherlock; William Morrow, 1964,
284p. (W, LACOPL, Q).

1667   THE LAST MAN ON EARTH. (American International-1964-
Sidney Salkow). A screenplay written by Logan Swanson and
William P. Leicester, from the novel I Am Legend by Rich-
ard Matheson; Walker, 1954, 122p. (FF, AMPAS, W, Q,
NYTFR, LACOPL).

1668   THE LAST MERCENARY. (Excelsior-1970-Dieter Muller).
No screenplay credits available. (W).

1668a THE LAST MOVIE. (Universal-1971-Dennis Hopper). A
screenplay by Stewart Stern, from a story by Stewart Stern
and Dennis Hopper. (W, Q).

1669   THE LAST OF SHEILA. (Warner Bros.-1973-Herbert Ross).

A screenplay by Anthony Perkins and Stephen Sondheim.   (W, Q, V).

1670   THE LAST OF THE MOBILE HOT-SHOTS.   (Warner Bros.-1970-Sidney Lumet).   A screenplay written by Gore Vidal, based on the play The Seven Descents of Myrtle by Tennessee Williams; New Directions, 1968, 111p.   (W, Q, LACOPL, V).

1671   LAST OF THE RED HOT LOVERS.   (Paramount-1972-Gene Saks).   A screenplay by Neil Simon from his play; Random House, 1970, 92p.   (W, FF, LACOPL, Q).

1672   THE LAST OF THE SECRET AGENTS.   (Paramount-1966-Norman Abbott).   A screenplay by Mel Tolkin, based on an original story by Norman Abbott and Mel Tolkin.   (FF, NYTFR, LC, W, AMPAS, Q).

1673   LAST OF THE SKI BUMS.   (U-M-1969-Dick Barrymore).   No author credits available; narration by Dick Barrymore.   (W, Q).

1674   THE LAST PICTURE SHOW.   (Columbia-1971-Peter Bogdanovich).   A screenplay by Larry McMurtry and Peter Bogdanovich, based on the novel by Larry McMurtry; Dell, 1966, 220p.   (W, LACOPL, Q).

1675   THE LAST RUN.   (MGM-1971-Richard Fleischer).   An original screenplay by Alan Sharp.   (W, Q).

1676   THE LAST SAFARI.   (Paramount-1968-Henry Hathaway).   A screenplay by John Gay, based on the novel Gilligan's Last Elephant by Gerald Hanley; World Publishing Co., 1962.   (FF, W, LC, AMPAS, LACOPL, Q).

1677   THE LAST SHOT YOU HEAR.   (20th Century-Fox-1969-Gordon Hessler).   A screenplay by Tim Shields, based on the play The Sound of Murder by William Fairchild.   (FF, W, LC).

1678   LAST SUMMER.   (Allied Artists-1969-Frank Perry).   A screenplay by Eleanor Perry, based on the novel by Evan Hunter; Doubleday, 1968.   (FF, W, AMPAS, LACOPL, Q).

1679   LAST TANGO IN PARIS.   (United Artists-1973-Bernardo Bertolucci).   A screenplay by Bernardo Bertolucci and Franco Arcalli, published by Delacorte Press, 1972, 224p.   Also, an original novel based on the screenplay, was written by Robert Alley, and published by Dell Publishing Co., 1972, 220p.   (W, LACOPL, FF, Q).

1680   THE LAST VALLEY.   (Cinerama-1971-James Clavell).   An original screenplay written by James Clavell.   (W, Q).

1681   LATE AUTUMN. (New Yorker-1973-Yasujiro Ozu). An original screenplay by Kogo Noda and Yasujiro Ozu. (W).

1682   THE LATE LIZ. (Gateway-1972-Dick Ross). A screenplay
by Bill Rega, based on the autobiography by Gert Behanna
aka Elizabeth Burns; Meredith, 1968, 342p. (FF, W,
LACOPL).

1683   LATE SPRING. (New Yorker-1972-Yasujiro Ozu). A screenplay by Yasujiro Ozu and Kogo Noda. (W).

1684   LATITUDE ZERO. (National General-1970-Ishiro Honda). An
original screenplay by Ted Sherdeman, from a story by Ted
Sherdeman. (W, Q).

1685   THE LAUGHING POLICEMAN. (20th Century-Fox-1973-Stu-
art Rosenberg). A screenplay by Thomas Rickman, based
on a novel by Per Wahloo and Maj Sjowall; Pantheon, 1970,
211p. (W, LACOPL).

1686   LAUGHTER IN THE DARK. (Lopert-1969-Tony Richardson).
A screenplay by Edward Bond, adapted from the novel by
Vladimir Nabokov; New Directions, 1960. (W, AMPAS,
LACOPL, Q).

1687   LAW AND DISORDER. (Columbia-1974-Ivan Passer). A
screenplay by Ivan Passer, William Richert, and Kenneth
Harris Fishman. (V, HR).

1687a   LAW OF THE LAWLESS. (Paramount-1964-William F. Claxton). An original screenplay by Steve Fisher. (FF, AMPAS,
W, Q, NYTFR).

1688   LAWMAN. (United Artists-1971-Michael Winner). A screenplay by Gerald Wilson. (W, Q).

1689   THE LAWYER. (Paramount-1970-Sidney J. Furie). A screenplay by Sidney J. Furie and Harold Buchman. (W, Q).

1690   THE LEARNING TREE. (Warner Bros.-7 Arts-1969-Gordon
Parks). A screenplay by Gordon Parks, based on his novel;
Harper, 1963. (FF, W, AMPAS, LACOPL, Q).

1691   THE LEATHER BOYS. (R. Lee Platt-1965-Sidney J. Furie).
A screenplay by Gillian Freeman, based on the novel by Eliot
George. (NYTFR, W, AMPAS, Q).

1692   LEFT-HANDED. (Hand-in-Hand-1972-Jack Deveau & Jaap
Penraat). No screenplay credits available. (W).

1693   THE LEGEND OF FRENCHY KING. (SNC-1973-Christian-
Jacque). A screenplay by Marie-Ange Anies, Jean Nemours,
Guy Casaril, Clement Bywood, and Daniel Boulanger. (W).

1694   THE LEGEND OF HELL HOUSE.   (20th Century-Fox-1973-
       John Hough).   A screenplay by Richard Matheson, based on
       his novel Hell House; Viking, 1971, 279p.   (W, LACOPL, Q).

1695   THE LEGEND OF LYLAH CLARE.   (MGM-1968-Robert Ald-
       rich).   A screenplay by Hugo Butler and Jean Rouverol,
       based on the teleplay by Robert Thom and Edward De Blasio.
       (FF, NYTFR, LC, AMPAS, Q).

1696   THE LEGEND OF NIGGER CHARLEY.   (Paramount-1972-
       Martin Goldman).   A screenplay by Larry G. Spangler and
       Martin Goldman.   (W, Q).

1697   LEMONADE JOE.   (Allied Artists-1967-Oldrich Lipsky).   A
       work for the screen by Jiri Brdeca and Oldrich Lipsky,
       based on a story by Jiri Brdeca.   (FF, NYTFR, W, AMPAS,
       Q).

1698   LEO THE LAST.   (United Artists-1970-John Boorman).   A
       screenplay by Bill Stair and John Boorman.   (W, Q).

1699   LET IT BE.   (United Artists-1970-Michael Lindsay-Hogg).
       No author credits; a musical documentary.   (W, Q).

1700   LET THE GOOD TIMES ROLL.   (Columbia-1973-Sid Levin,
       Hyman Kaufman, & Bud Friedgen, Yeu-Bun-Yee).   A rock
       music documentary, no author credits available.   (W).

1701   LET'S KILL UNCLE.   (Universal-1966-William Castle).   A
       screenplay by Mark Rodgers, based on the novel by Rohan
       O'Grady; Macmillan, 1963.   (Q, FF, NYTFR, LC, W,
       AMPAS, LACOPL).

1702   LET'S SCARE JESSICA TO DEATH.   (Paramount-1971-John
       Hancock).   A screenplay by Norman Jonas and Ralph Rose.
       (W, Q).

1702a LET'S TALK ABOUT WOMEN.   (Embassy-1964-Ettore Scola).
       Original stories and screenplay by Ruggero Maccari and Et-
       tore Scola.   (FF, W, Q, NYTFR).

1703   THE LEXINGTON EXPERIENCE.   (Corda-1971-Lawrence
       Schiller).   A screenplay by L. M. Kit Carson.   (W).

1704   THE LIBERATION OF L. B. JONES.   (Columbia-1970-William
       Wyler).   A screenplay by Stirling Silliphant and Jesse Hill
       Ford; based on the novel The Liberation of Lord Byron Jones
       by Jesse Hill Ford; Little, Brown & Co., 1965.   (W,
       LACOPL, Q).

1705   THE LIBERTINE.   (Audubon-1969-Pasquale Festa Campanile).
       A screenplay by Nicolo Ferrari and Ottavio Jemma, based
       on a story by Nicolo Ferrari.   (FF, Q).

1706   THE LICKERISH QUARTET. (Audubon-1970-Radley Metz-
        ger). A screenplay by Michael De Forrest, based on the
        story "Hide and Seek" by Michael De Forrest and Radley
        Metzger. (W, Q).

1707   LICKITY SPLIT. (MSW-1974-Carter Stevens). No screen-
        play credit available. (V).

1708   LIEBELEI. (Elite Tonfilm-1974-Max Ophuls). A screenplay
        by Hans Wilhelm and Curt Alexander, from the play by Ar-
        thur Schnitzler, Liebelei. (NYT).

1709   LT. ROBIN CRUSOE, U.S.N. (Buena Vista-1966-Byron
        Paul). A screenplay by Bill Walsh and Don DaGradi, based
        on a story by Retlaw Yensid (Disney spelled backwards).
        (FF, NYTFR, LC, W, AMPAS, Q).

1710   THE LIFE AND TIMES OF JUDGE ROY BEAN. (National
        General-1972-John Huston). An original screenplay by John
        Milius. (W, FF, Q).

1711   THE LIFE AND TIMES OF XAVIERA HOLLANDER. (Mature-
        1974-Larry G. Spangler). A screenplay by Lawrence Pick-
        wick and David Loin. (V).

1712   LIFE AT THE TOP. (Royal-1965-Ted Kotcheff). A screen-
        play by Mordecai Richler, based on the novel by John Braine;
        Houghton, 1962. (NYTFR, LC, W, AMPAS, LACOPL, Q).

1713   LIFE LOVE DEATH. (Lopert-1969-Claude Lelouch). A
        screenplay by Pierre Uytterhoeven and Claude Lelouch. (FF,
        W).

1714   LIFE STUDY. (Nebbia-1973-Michael Nebbia). A screenplay
        written by Arthur Birnkrant, based on a story by Michael
        Nebbia. (W).

1715   LIFE UPSIDE DOWN. (Allied Artists-1965-Alain Jessua).
        An original screenplay by Alain Jessua. (NYTFR, W).

1716   THE LIGHT AT THE EDGE OF THE WORLD. (National
        General-1971-Kevin Bilington). A screenplay by Tom Row,
        based on the novel by Jules Verne; Watts, 1924. (W,
        LACOPL).

1717   THE LIGHT FROM THE SECOND STORY WINDOW. (Jaguar-
        1973-David L. Allen). A screenplay by David L. Allen, from
        his novel of the same name; Exposition Press, 1972. (W,
        LACOPL).

1718   LIGHTNING BOLT. (Woolner Bros.-1967-Anthony Dawson
        aka Antonio Margheriti). A screenplay by Alfonso Balcazar
        and Jose Antonio De La Loma. (FF, W, AMPAS).

1718a   LILITH. (Columbia-1964-Robert Rossen).   Robert Rossen
        wrote the screenplay based upon the novel by J. R. Sala-
        manca; Simon & Schuster, 1961, 381p. (LACOPL, NYTFR,
        AMPAS, W, Q, FF).

1719   LIMBO. (Universal-1972-Mark Robson).   A screenplay by
        Joan Silver, James Bridges, from a story by Joan Silver.
        (W, FF, Q).

1720   THE LIMIT. (Cannon-1972-Yaphet Kotto).   A screenplay by
        Sean Cameron, from a story by Yaphet Kotto.   (W, FF).

1721   THE LION IN WINTER. (AVCO (Embassy-1968-Anthony Har-
        vey).   A screenplay by James Goldman, based on his play;
        Random House, 1966, 110p. (Q, FF, NYTFR, FM, W,
        AMPAS, LACOPL).

1722   LIONS LOVE. (Raab-1969-Agnes Varda).   An original
        screenplay by Agnes Varda.   (W, Q).

1723   THE LIQUIDATOR. (MGM-1966-Jack Cardiff).   Peter Yeld-
        ham wrote this screenplay based on the novel by John Gard-
        ner; Viking, 1964.   (FF, NYTFR, LC, W, LACOPL, Q).

1724   LISTEN, LET'S MAKE LOVE. (Lopert-1969-Vittorio Capri-
        oli).   A screenplay by Vittorio Caprioli, Franca Valeri and
        Enrico Medioli.   (FF, W, Q).

1725   THE LITTLE ARK. (National General-1972-James B. Clark).
        A screenplay by Joanna Crawford, from the novel by Jan De
        Hartog; Harper, 1953.   (W, FF, LACOPL, Q).

1726   LITTLE BIG MAN. (National General-1970-Arthur Penn).
        A screenplay by Calder Willingham, based on the novel by
        Thomas Berger; Dial Press, 1964.   (W, LACOPL, Q).

1727   LITTLE CIGARS. (American International-1973-Chris Chris-
        tenberry).   A screenplay by Louis Garfinkle and Frank Ray
        Perilli.   (W, Q).

1728   LITTLE FAUSS AND BIG HALSY. (Paramount-1970-Sidney
        J. Furie).   A screenplay by Charles Eastman; Farrar, Straus
        & Giroux, 1969, 164p. (W, SCH, MCC, Q, LACOPL).

1729   LITTLE LAURA AND BIG JOHN. (Crown International-1973-
        Luke Moberly & Bob Woodburn).   A screenplay by Luke Mob-
        erly and Bob Woodburn, based on a story by Philip Weidling.
        (W).

1730   LITTLE MALCOLM. (Multicetera-1974-Stuart Cooper).   A
        screenplay by Derek Woodward, from Hail Scrawdyke! (Little
        Malcolm and His Struggle Against the Eunuchs) by David Hall-
        well; Grove Press, 1966, 143p. (V, LACOPL).

1731   LITTLE MOTHER. (Audubon-1973-Radley Metzger). An
        original screenplay by Brian Phelan. (W, Q).

1732   LITTLE MURDERS. (20th Century-Fox-1971-Alan Arkin).
        A screenplay by Jules Feiffer, based on his play of the same
        name; Random House, 1968, 111p. (W, LACOPL, Q).

1733   THE LITTLE NUNS. (Embassy-1966-Luciano Salce). A
        screenplay by Franco Castellano and Giuseppe Moccia. (FF,
        NYTFR, W, Q).

1734   THE LITTLE ONES. (Columbia-1965-Jim O'Connolly). A
        screenplay written directly for the screen by Jim O'Connolly.
        (NYTFR, AMPAS0.

1735   THE LITTLE PRINCE. (Paramount-1974-Stanley Donen).
        Alan Jay Lerner wrote the screenplay which was based on a
        book by Antoine de Saint-Exupéry; Reynal, 1943. (V,
        LACOPL).

        THE LITTLE SOLDIER see LE PETIT SOLDAT

1736   LIVE A LITTLE, LOVE A LITTLE. (MGM-1968-Norman
        Taurog). A screenplay by Michael A. Hoey and Dan Green-
        berg, based on the novel Kiss My Firm But Pliant Lips by
        Dan Greenburg; Grossman Publishers, 1965. (FF, W, LC,
        AMPAS, LACOPL, Q).

1737   LIVE AND LET DIE. (United Artists-1973-Guy Hamilton).
        A screenplay written by Tom Mankiewicz, based on the novel
        by Ian Fleming; Macmillan, 1954. (W, LACOPL).

1738   LIVE FOR LIFE. (United Artists-1967-Claude Lelouch). A
        screenplay by Pierre Uytterhoeven and Claude Lelouch. (FF,
        NYTFR, FM, W, LC, AMPAS, Q).

1739   LIVE IN FEAR. (Brandon-1967-Akira Kurosawa). Shinobu
        Hashimoto, Hideo Oguni and Akira Kurosawa were responsible
        for this original screenplay. (NYTFR, W).

1739a   THE LIVELY SET. (Universal-1964-Jack Arnold). A screen-
        play by Mel Goldberg and William Wood, from a story by Wil-
        liam Alland and Mel Goldberg. (W, Q, FF, NYTFR).

1740   LIVING FREE. (Columbia-1972-Jack Couffer). A screenplay
        written by Millard Kaufman, based on books by Joy Adamson
        Forever Free; Harcourt, 1962, 179p. (FF, LACOPL, Q).

1741   LIZARD IN A WOMAN'S SKIN. (American International-1972-
        Lucio Fulci). A screenplay by Lucio Fulci, Roberto Gianviti,
        Jose Luis Martinez Molla, and Andre Tranche. (FF).

1742   LOCK UP YOUR DAUGHTERS! (Columbia-1969-Peter Coe).

A screenplay based on the Lionel Bart-Laurie Johnson musical that was based on Henry Fielding's Rape Upon Rape and
Sir John Vanbrugh's The Relapse. (W, Q).

1743   LOLA. (American International-1972-Richard Donner). An
       original story and screenplay written by Norman Thaddeus
       Vane. (FF).

1744   LOLA MONTES. (Brandon-1969-Max Ophuls). A screenplay
       by Max Ophuls, Annette Wademant and Franz Geiger, based
       on La Vie Extraordinaire de Lola Montes by Cecil St. Laur-
       ent. (FF, NYTFR).

1745   LOLLY-MADONNA XXX. (MGM-1973-Richard C. Sarafin).
       A screenplay written by Rodney Carr-Smith, Sue Grafton,
       based on the novel Lolly Madonna War by Sue Grafton. (W,
       Q).

1746   THE LONERS. (Fanfare-1972-Sutton Roley). A screenplay
       by John Lawrence and Barry Sandler, based on a story by
       John Lawrence. (FF).

1747   LONESOME COWBOYS. (Sherpix-1969-Andy Warhol). An
       original screenplay by Andy Warhol. (FF, W).

1748   LONG AGO, TOMORROW. (Cinema V-1971-Bryan Forbes).
       Bryan Forbes wrote the screenplay which was based on the
       novel by Peter Marshall, The Raging Moon; Bobbs-Merrill,
       1966. (W, LACOPL, Q).

1749   THE LONG DARKNESS. (Toho-1973-Kei Kumai). A screen-
       play by Keiji Hasebe and Kei Kumai, from a story by Tetsuro
       Miura. (W).

1750   THE LONG DAY'S DYING. (Paramount-1968-Peter Collinson).
       A screenplay by Charles Wood, based on a novel by Alan
       White; Death Finds the Day; Harcourt, 1965. (FF, NYTFR,
       W. Q, LC, LACOPL).

1751   THE LONG DUEL. (Paramount-1967-Ken Annakin). A
       screenplay by Peter Yeldham, based on a story by Ranveer
       Singh. (FF, W, LC, AMPAS, Q).

1752   THE LONG GOODBYE. (United Artists-1973-Robert Altman).
       A screenplay written by Leigh Brackett, based on a novel by
       Raymond Chandler; in The Midnight Raymond Chandler,
       Houghton, 1971, 734p. (W, LACOPL).

1753   A LONG RIDE FROM HELL. (Cinerama-1970-Alex Burks).
       A screenplay by Roberto Natale, and Steve Reeves, based on
       the novel Judas Gun by Gordon Shirreffs. (W, Q).

THE LONG RIDE HOME see   A TIME FOR KILLING

1753a THE LONG SHIPS. (Columbia-1964-Jack Cardiff). A screenplay by Berkely Mather and Beverley Cross, from a novel by
Frans Bengtsson. (FF, NYTFR, W, AMPAS, Q).

1754 THE LONGEST YARD. (Paramount-1974-Robert Aldrich).
A screenplay by Tracy Keenan Wynn, from a story by Albert
S. Ruddy. (V).

1754a LOOKING FOR LOVE. (MGM-1964-Don Weis). A screenplay by Ruth Brooks Flippen. (FF, Q, W).

1755 THE LOOKING GLASS WAR. (Columbia-1970-Frank R. Pierson). A screenplay by Frank R. Pierson, based on the book
by John Le Carré; Coward, 1965. (W, LACOPL, Q).

LOOKING GOOD see CORKY

1756 LOOT. (Cinevision-1972-Silvio Narizzano). A screenplay by
Ray Galton and Alan Simpson, based on the play by Joe Or-
ton; Grove Press, 1967, 87p. (W, LACOPL, Q).

1757 LORD JIM. (Columbia-1965-Richard Brooks). A screenplay
by Richard Brooks, based on the novel by Joseph Conrad;
Norton, 1968, 486p. (FF, LC, W, AMPAS, LACOPL, Q).

1758 LORD LOVE A DUCK. (United Artists-1966-George Axelrod). A screenplay by Larry H. Johnson and George Axelrod, based on the novel by Al Hine. (FF, NYTFR, LC, W,
AMPAS, Q).

1759 LORDS OF FLATBUSH. (Columbia-1974-Stephen F. Verona
& Martin Davidson). A screenplay by Stephen F. Verona,
Gayle Gleckler, and Martin Davidson. (V).

1760 LORNA. (Eve-1965-Russ Meyer). A screenplay by James
Griffith, from a story by Russ Meyer. (W, LC, AMPAS).

1761 L[OS] A[NGELES] PLAYS ITSELF. (Halsted-1972-Fred Halsted). A screenplay written by Fred Halsted. (W).

1762 THE LOSERS. (Fanfare-1970-Jack Starrett). A screenplay
by Alan Caillou. (W, Q).

1763 LOST COMMAND. (Columbia-1966-Mark Robson). A screen-
play by Nelson Gidding, based on the novel The Centurions by
Jean Larteguy; Dutton, 1961. (FF, LC, W, AMPAS,
LACOPL, Q).

1764 THE LOST CONTINENT. (20th Century-Fox-1968-Michael
Carreras). A screenplay by Michael Nash, based on the nov-
el Uncharted Seas by Dennis Wheatley. (FF, NYTFR, W,
LC, AMPAS, Q).

1765   LOST HORIZON. (Columbia-1973-Charles Jarrott).   A
        screenplay written by Larry Kramer, from the novel by
        James Hilton; Morrow, 1933. (W, LACOPL, Q).

1766   LOST IN THE STARS. (American Film Theatre-1974-Daniel
        Mann). A screenplay by Alfred Hayes, adapted from the mu-
        sical play by Maxwell Anderson; Sloane, 1949, 86p.   (HR,
        LACOPL).

1767   THE LOST MAN. (Universal-1969-Robert Alan Aurthur).   A
        work for the screen by Robert Alan Aurthur, based on the
        novel Odd Man Out by Frederick Laurence Green; Reynal,
        1947. (FF, W, AMPAS, LACOPL).

1768   LOST SEX. (Chevron-1968-Kaneto Shindo).   A screenplay by
        Kaneto Shindo. (FF, NYTFR, W).

1769   THE LOST WORLD OF SINBAD.   (American International-
        1966-Senkichi Taniguchi). A screenplay by Takeshi Kimura.
        (W, LC, Q).

1770   LOTNA. (Pol-Ton-1966-Andrzej Wajda).   A screenplay by
        Wojciech Zukrowski and Andrzej Wajda, based on a novel by
        Wojciech Zukrowski. (FF, NYTFR).

1771   LOVE. (Ajay-1973-Karoly Makk).   An original screenplay by
        Tibor Dery. (W).

1772   LOVE A LA CARTE. (Promenade-1965-Antonio Pietrangeli).
        A screenplay written by Ruggero Maccari, Ettore Scola, An-
        tonio Pietrangeli, and Tullio Pinelli. (FF, W, AMPAS, Q).

1773   LOVE AFFAIR. (Brandon-1968-Dusan Makavejev).   A screen-
        play by Dusan Makavejev. (FF, W, Q).

1774   LOVE AND ANARCHY. (Steinmann-Baxter-1974-Lina Wert-
        muller). An original screenplay written by Lina Wertmuller.
        (HR).

1775   LOVE AND KISSES. (Universal-1965-Ozzie Nelson).   A
        screenplay by Ozzie Nelson, based on a play by Anita Rowe
        Block. (W, LC, AMPAS, Q).

1776   LOVE AND MARRIAGE. (Embassy-1966-Gianni Puccini and
        Mino Guerrini). An original screenplay by Bruno Baratti,
        Oreste Biancoli, Eliana de Sabata, Jaja Fiastri, Mino Guer-
        rini, Gianni Puccini and Ennio de Concini. (NYTFR, W, Q).

1777   LOVE AND PAIN AND THE WHOLE DAMN THING. (Colum-
        bia-1973-Alan J. Pakula). An original screenplay by Alvin
        Sargent. (W, Q).

1778   THE LOVE BUG. (Buena Vista-1969-Robert Stevenson).   A

screenplay by Bill Walsh and Don Da Gradi, based on the
story "Car--Boy--Girl" by Gordon Buford. (FF, W, LC,
AMPAS, Q).

1779 LOVE COMES QUIETLY. (Film-Makers International-1974-
Nikolai van der Heyde). A screenplay written directly for
the screen by Nikolai van der Heyde. (HR).

1780 THE LOVE GOD? (Universal-1969-Nat Hiken). An original
screenplay by Nat Hiken. (FF, W, AMPAS, Q).

1781 LOVE HAS MANY FACES. (Columbia-1965-Alexander Singer).
Marguerite Roberts wrote this original screenplay. (FF,
LC, W, AMPAS, Q).

1782 LOVE IN 4 DIMENSIONS. (Eldorado-1965-Massimo Mida,
Jacques Romain, Gianni Puccini, and Mino Guerrini). This
film consists of four screenplays written separately by Bruno
Baratti, Mino Guerrini, Massimo Mida, and Gianni Puccini.
(W, Q).

1783 LOVE IS A FUNNY THING. (United Artists-1970-Claude Lelouch). An original screenplay by Claude Lelouch. (Q, W).

1784 THE LOVE MACHINE. (Columbia-1971-Jack Haley, Jr.).
Screenplay written by Jacqueline Susann and Samuel Taylor,
based on the novel by Jacqueline Susann; Simon & Schuster,
1969, 511p. (LACOPL, Q, V, W).

1785 LOVE ME LIKE I DO. (Hollywood Cinemart-1970-J. Van
Hearn). An original screenplay by J. Van Hearn. (W).

1786 LOVE ME--LOVE MY WIFE. (Cimber-1971-Enzo Battaglia).
An original screenplay by Enzo Battaglia. (W, FF).

1787 THE LOVE MERCHANT. (General Studios-1966-Joe Sarno).
Joe Sarno wrote this original screenplay. (FF).

1788 LOVE STORY. (Paramount-1970-Arthur Hiller). Erich Segal
wrote the screenplay which was based on his novel of the
same name; Harper, 1970, 131p. (LACOPL, Q, W).

1789 LOVE, SWEDISH STYLE. (Screencom International-1972-
Maurice Smith). A screenplay written by Maurice Smith,
based on an original story by John Harris and Marvin Rothman. (FF).

1790 THE LOVED ONE. (MGM-1965-Tony Richardson). A screenplay by Terry Southern and Christopher Isherwood, based on
the novel by Evelyn Waugh; Little, Brown & Co., 1948.
(AMPAS, LC, LACOPL, NYTFR, W, Q).

1791 LOVE-IN '72. (Mishkin-1972-Sidney Knight and Karl Hansen).

Jay Robins wrote this original screenplay. (FF).

1792   THE LOVE-INS. (Columbia-1967-Arthur Dreifuss). Hal Col-
       lins and Arthur Dreifuss were responsible for this screen-
       play written directly for the screen. (FF, FM, LC, NYTFR,
       Q, W, AMPAS).

1793   LOVELAND. (Illustrated-1973-Richard Franklin). An origi-
       nal screenplay by Harriet Rhodes. (W).

1794   A LOVELY WAY TO DIE. (Universal-1968-David Lowell
       Rich). An original screenplay authored by A. J. Russell.
       (FF, FM, NYTFR, W, LC, AMPAS, Q).

1795   LOVERS AND OTHER STRANGERS. (Cinerama-1970-Cy How-
       ard). Renee Taylor, Joseph Bologna and David Z. Goodman
       wrote this original screenplay. (W, Q).

1796   LOVES OF A BLONDE. (Prominent-1966-Milos Forman). An
       original screenplay by Jaroslav Papousek, Milos Forman and
       Ivan Passer. (FF, NYTFR, W, AMPAS, Q).

1797   THE LOVES OF ISADORA. (Universal-1969-Karel Reisz). A
       screenplay by Melvyn Bragg and Clive Exton, based on the
       books Isadora Duncan, An Intimate Portrait by Sewell Brooks,
       and My Life by Isadora Duncan; Boni and Liveright, 1927,
       359p. (FF, W, AMPAS, LACOPL, Q).

1798   THE LOVES OF ONDINE. (Factory-1968-Andy Warhol). A
       scenario written by Andy Warhol. (FF, W, Q).

1799   LOVIN' MOLLY. (Columbia-1974-Sidney Lumet). An origi-
       nal work for the screen by Stephen Friedman. (HR).

1800   LOVING. (Columbia-1970-Irvin Kershner). An original
       screenplay by Don Devlin, based on the novel by J. M. Ryan.
       (W, Q).

1801   LOVING COUPLES. (Prominent-1966-Mai Zetterling). A
       screenplay by Mai Zetterling and David Hughes, based on the
       novel The Misses Von Pahlen by Agnes Von Krusenstjerna.
       (FF, NYTFR, W, Q).

1802   LOVING FEELING. (U-M Film Distributors-1969-Norman J.
       Warren). A screenplay by Robert Hewison, Bachoo Sen, and
       Norman J. Warren. (FF, W).

1803   THE LOVING TOUCH. (Medford-1970-Robert Vincent O'Neil).
       An original screenplay by Robert Vincent O'Neil. (W).

       LSD, I HATE YOU! see MOVIE STAR, AMERICAN STYLE

1803a THE LUCK OF GINGER COFFEY. (Continental-1964-Irvin

Kershner). A screenplay by Brian Moore, based on his own
novel; Little, Brown & Co., 1960, 243p. (FF, LACOPL,
AMPAS, NYTFR, W, Q).

1804   LUDWIG. (MGM-1973-Luchino Visconti). A screenplay by
Luchino Visconti, Enrico Medioli, and Suso Cecchi d'Amico.
(W, Q).

1805   LUDWIG: REQUIEM FOR A VIRGIN KING. (TMS Film-
1974-Hans-Jurgen Syberberg). An original screenplay by
Hans-Jurgen Syberberg. (V).

1806   LUMINOUS PROCURESS. (New Line-1972-Steven Arnold).
A screenplay written by Steven Arnold. (W).

1807   LUPO. (Cannon-1971-Menahem Golan). An original screenplay by Menahem Golan. (W).

1808   LUST FOR A VAMPIRE. (American Continental-1971-Jimmy
Sangster). An original story and screenplay by Tudor Gates,
based on characters created by J. Sheridan Le Fanu. (W).

1809   LUV. (Columbia-1967-Clive Donner). Elliott Baker authored
this screenplay based on the play by Murray Schisgal; Coward, 1965, 98p. (FF, NYTFR, FM, W, LC, AMPAS,
LACOPL).

1809a MGM'S BIG PARADE OF COMEDY. (MGM-1964-). Narration written by Robert Youngson. (FF, NYTFR, W, Q).

1810   MACBETH. (Columbia-1971-Roman Polanski). A screenplay
by Roman Polanski and Kenneth Tynan, based on a play by
William Shakespeare; Yale University Press, 1954, 138p.
(W, LACOPL).

1811   McGUIRE, GO HOME. (Continental-1966-Ralph Thomas).
An original screenplay by Ian Stuart Black. (W, AMPAS, Q).

1811a McHALE'S NAVY. (Universal-1964-Edward J. Montagne). A
screenplay by Frank Gill, Jr., and G. Carleton Brown, from
a story by Si Rose. (NYTFR, FF, AMPAS, W, Q).

1812   McHALE'S NAVY JOINS THE AIR FORCE. (Universal-1965-
Edward J. Montagne). John Fenton Murray wrote the screen-
play from a story by William J. Lederer. (W, LC, AMPAS,
Q).

1813   MACHIBUSE. (Toho-1971-Hiroshi Inagaki). Kyu Fujiki and
Hideo Oguni were responsible for writing this screenplay.
(W).

1814   MACHINE GUN McCAIN. (Columbia-1970-Giuliano Montaldo).
A story and screenplay by Mino Roli, freely based on the

novel Candyleg by Ovid Demaris, English adaptation by Israel Horovitz. (W).

1815   MACHO CALLAHAN. (AVCO Embassy-1970-Bernard L. Kowalski). A screenplay by Clifford Newton Gould, based on a story by Richard Carr. (W).

1816   THE MACK. (Cinerama-1973-Michael Campus). Robert J. Poole wrote this original screenplay. (W, V).

1817   MacKENNA'S GOLD. (Columbia-1969-J. Lee Thompson). A screenplay by Carl Foreman, based on the novel by Will Henry; Random House, 1963. (FF, LC, AMPAS, LACOPL).

1818   THE McKENZIE BREAK. (United Artists-1970-Lamont Johnson). A screenplay by William Norton, from the novel by Sidney Shelley, The Bowmanville Break, Delacorte Press, 1968, 242p. (LACOPL, Q).

1819   THE MACKINTOSH MAN. (Warner Bros.-1973-John Huston). A Walter Hill screenplay, based on the novel The Freedom Trap by Desmond Bagley; Doubleday, 1971, 254p. (W, LACOPL).

1820   MACON COUNTY LINE. (American International-1974-Richard Compton). A screenplay by Max Baer and Richard Compton, from a story by Max Baer. (V).

1821   McQ. (Warner Bros.-1974-John Sturges). A screenplay by Lawrence Roman; original novelization based on the screenplay written by Alexander Edwards, Warner Paperback Library, 1974. (HR, V).

1822   MACUNAIMA. (New Line Cinema-1972-Joaquim Pedro de Andrade). A screenplay by Joaquim Pedro de Andrade, based on the novel by Mario de Andrade. (FF).

1823   THE MAD BOMBER. (Cinemation-1973-Bert I. Gordon). A screenplay written by Bert I. Gordon, from a story by Marc Behm. (W).

MAD DOGS AND ENGLISHMEN see JOE COCKER/MAD DOGS AND ENGLISHMEN

1824   THE MAD EXECUTIONERS. (Paramount-1965-Edwin Zbonek). R. A. Stemmie authored this screenplay which was taken from White Carpet by Bryan Edgar Wallace. (W, AMPAS).

MAD LOVE see L'AMOUR FOU

1825   MAD MONSTER PARTY. (Embassy-1967-Jules Bass). A screenplay by Len Korobkin and Harvey Kurtzman. (W).

1826   THE MAD ROOM. (Columbia-1969-Bernard Girard).   A
       screenplay by Bernard Girard and A. Z. Martin, based on
       a screenplay by Garrett Fort and Reginald Denham, from
       the play Ladies in Retirement by Reginald Denham and Ed-
       ward Percy. (FF, LC, AMPAS, Q).

1827   MADAME BUTTERFLY.   (Rizzoli-1966-Carmine Gallone).
       A screen adaptation of the opera, based on the book by John
       L. Long and the play by David Belasco, with music by Gia-
       como Puccini. (W).

1828   MADAME X.   (Universal-1966-David Lowell Rich).   A screen-
       play by Jean Holloway, based on the play by Alexandre Bis-
       son. (FF, NYTFR, LC, W, AMPAS, Q).

1829   MADAME ZENOBIA.   (Screencom-1973-Eduardo Cemano).
       No screenplay credits available. (W).

1830   MADDALENA.   (Rand & Co.-1971-Jerzy Kawalerowicz).   An
       original screenplay by Sergio Bazina and Jerzy Kawalero-
       wicz. (W, Q).

1831   MADE FOR EACH OTHER.   (20th Century-Fox-1971-Robert
       B. Bean).   A screenplay by Renee Taylor and James Bolog-
       na. (W, Q).

1832   MADE IN ITALY.   (Royal-1967-Nanni Loy).   A screenplay by
       Ettore Scola, Ruggero Maccari, and Nanni Loy, based on
       stories by Ettore Scola and Ruggero Maccari. (FF, NYTFR,
       Q, W. AMPAS).

1833   MADE IN PARIS.   (MGM-1966-Boris Sagal).   Stanley Roberts
       wrote this original screenplay. (FF, NYTFR, LC, W,
       AMPAS, Q).

1834   MADE IN U.S.A.   (Pathe Contemporary-1967-Jean-Luc God-
       ard).   A screenplay by Jean-Luc Godard, from The Jugger by
       Richard Stark; screenplay published by Lorrimer Publishing
       Co., 1967, 87p. (MCC, NYTFR, V).

1835   MADEMOISELLE.   (Lopert-1966-Tony Richardson).   A screen-
       play written by Jean Genet. (FF, NYTFR, W, AMPAS, Q).

1836   MADHOUSE.   (American International-1974-Jim Clark).   Greg
       Morrison wrote this original screenplay from an adaptation by
       Ken Levison. (HR, V).

1837   MADIGAN.   (Universal-1968-Don Siegel).   A screenplay by
       Henri Simoun and Abraham Polonsky, based on the novel The
       Commissioner by Richard Dougherty; Doubleday, 1962. (Q,
       FF, NYTFR, FM, W, AMPAS, LACOPL).

1838   MADIGAN'S MILLIONS.   (American International-1970-Stanley

Prager). A screenplay by James Henaghan and J. L. Bay-
onas. (W, Q).

1839   THE MADWOMAN OF CHAILLOT. (Warner Bros.-7 Arts-
1969-Bryan Forbes). A screenplay by Edward Anhalt, based
on the play by Jean Giraudoux; in A Treasury of the Theatre,
V. 3; Simon & Schuster, 1951, pp. 1177-1203. (W, AMPAS,
LACOPL, Q).

1840   MAEDCHEN IN UNIFORM. (7 Arts-1965-Geza Radvanyi). A
screenplay by F. D. Anam and Dr. Franz Hollering, based
on a play by Christa Winsloe. (NYTFR, W, Q).

1841   MAFIA. (American International-1970-Damiano Damiani).
A screenplay by Ugo Pirro and Damiano Damiani, based on
Mafia Vendetta by Leonardo Sciascia; Knopf, 1963. (W,
LACOPL).

1842   MAFIOSO. (Zenith International-1964-Alberto Lattuada). A
screenplay by Marco Ferreri, Rafael Azcona and Age and
Scarpelli, which was based on an idea by Bruno Caruso.
(FF, Q, Q, NYTFR).

1842a   THE MAGIC CHRISTIAN. (Commonwealth-1970-Joseph Mc-
Grath). A screenplay by Terry Southern, Joseph McGrath
and Peter Sellers, based on a novel by Terry Southern; Random House, 1960. (W, LACOPL, Q).

1843   THE MAGIC GARDEN OF STANLEY SWEETHEART. (MGM-
1970-Leonard Horn). A screenplay written by Robert T.
Westbrook, based on his novel; Crown, 1969, 247p. (W,
LACOPL, Q).

1844   THE MAGNIFICENT CONCUBINE. (Frank Lee-1966-Li Han-
hsiang). An original screenplay by Wang Chih-po. (W, Q).

1845   THE MAGNIFICENT CUCKOLD. (Continental-1965-Antonio
Pietrangeli). A screenplay by Diego Fabbri, Ruggero Mac-
cari, Ettore Scola and Stefano Strucchi, based on the play
Le Cocu Magnifique by Fernand Crommelynck. (FF, W,
AMPAS, Q).

1846   THE MAGNIFICENT SEVEN RIDE! (United Artists-1972-
George McGowan). An original screenplay by Arthur Rowe.
(FF, W).

1847   MAGNUM FORCE. (Warner Bros.-1973-Ted Post). A
screenplay by John Milius, Michael Cimino, based on a story
by John Milius, from original material by Harry Julian Fink
and R. M. Fink. (W).

1848   THE MAGUS. (20th Century-Fox-1968-Guy Green). A
screenplay by John Fowles, based on his novel; Little,

Brown & Co., 1965, 606p. (Q, FF, NYTFR, FM, W, LC, AMPAS, LACOPL).

1849   MAHLER. (1974-Ken Russell). An original screenplay by Ken Russell. (V).

1850   MAID IN SWEDEN. (Cannon-1971-Floch Johnson). An original screenplay by Ronnie Friedland and George Norris. (W).

1851   A MAIDEN FOR THE PRINCE. (Royal Films International-1968-Pasquale Festa Campanile). A screenplay by Giorgio Prosperi, Stefano Strucchi, Ugo Liberatore and Pasquale Festa Campanile, based on 16th-century letters compiled by Alberto Consiglio. (FF, W, Q).

1852   MAIL ORDER BRIDE. (MGM-1964-Burt Kennedy). A screenplay by Burt Kennedy, based on a short story by Van Cort. (AMPAS, W, Q, LC, FF, NYTFR).

1853   THE MAIN CHANCE. (Embassy-1966-John Knight). A screenplay by Richard Harris, based on the novel by Edgar Wallace. (FF, W, AMPAS, Q).

1854   MAJIN. (Daiei-1968-Kimiyoshi Yasuda). A screenplay by Tetsuo Yoshida. (FF, NYTFR).

1855   MAJOR DUNDEE. (Columbia-1965-Sam Peckinpah). A screenplay by Harry Julian Fink, Oscar Saul, and Sam Peckinpah, based on a story by Harry J. Fink. (FF, LC, W, AMPAS, Q).

1856   MAKE A FACE. (Sperling-1971-Karen Sperling). A screenplay by Karen Sperling and Barbara Connell and Avraham Tau. (W).

1856a   MAKE LIKE A THIEF. (Emerson-1966-Palmer Thompson and Richard Long). An original screenplay by Palmer Thompson. (FF, W, AMPAS).

1857   MAKING IT. (20th Century-Fox-1971-). A screenplay written by Peter Bart, based on the novel What Can You Do? by James Leigh; Harper, 1965. (W, LACOPL, Q).

1858   MALE COMPANION. (International Classics-1966-Philippe de Broca). A screenplay by Henri Lanoe, from the book by Andre Couteaux, Gentleman in Waiting; Houghton, 1963. (Q, FF, NYTFR, LC, W, LACOPL).

1859   MALE HUNT. (Pathe Contemporary-1965-Edouard Molinaro). A screenplay and adaptation by France Roche, from an idea by Yvon Guezel and stories by Albert Simonin and Michel Duran. (FF, W).

1860   MAME. (Warner Bros.-1974-Gene Saks). A screenplay by
        Paul Zindel, based on the musical play by Jerry Herman
        (music & lyrics) with a book by Jerome Lawrence and Ro-
        bert E. Lee; Random House, 1967, 137p. This musical was
        based on the play Auntie Mame by Jerome Lawrence and Ro-
        bert E. Lee; Vanguard, 1957, 182p.; and the novel Auntie
        Mame by Patrick Dennis; Vanguard, 1955, 280p. (MFB, V,
        LACOPL, W).

1861   THE MAN. (Paramount-1972-Joseph Sargent). A screenplay
        by Rod Serling, based on the novel by Irving Wallace; Simon
        & Schuster, 1964. (FF, LACOPL, Q).

1862   A MAN AND A WOMAN. (Allied Artists-1966-Claude Le-
        louch). A screenplay written originally for the screen by
        Claude Lelouch; published by Simon and Schuster, 1971, 116p.
        (FF, Q, NYTFR, LC, W, AMPAS, LACOPL).

1863   MAN AND BOY. (Levitt-Pickman-1972-E. W. Swackhamer).
        A screenplay by Harry Essex and Oscar Saul. (W, Q).

1864   A MAN CALLED ADAM. (Embassy-1966-Leo Penn). Les
        Pine and Tina Rome authored this screenplay. (FF, NYTFR,
        W, AMPAS, Q).

1865   A MAN CALLED DAGGER. (MGM-1968-Richard Rush). A
        screenplay written by James Peatman and Robert S. Weekley,
        based on an idea by W. L. Riffs. (FF, W, LC, AMPAS, Q).

1866   A MAN CALLED GANNON. (Universal-1969-James Gold-
        stone). Gene Kearney, Borden Chase, and D. D. Beauchamp
        based their screenplay upon the novel The Man Without a
        Star by Dee Linford; Morrow, 1952. (FF, W, AMPAS,
        LACOPL, Q).

1867   A MAN CALLED HORSE. (National General-1970-Elliot
        Silverstein). A screenplay by Jack DeWitt, from a story by
        Dorothy M. Johnson. (W, Q).

1868   THE MAN CALLED NOON. (National General-1973-Peter
        Collinson). A screenplay by Scot Finch, based on the novel
        by Louis L'Amour. (W).

1869   A MAN COULD GET KILLED. (Universal-1966-Ronald
        Neame and Cliff Owen). A screenplay by Richard Breen and
        T. E. B. Clarke, based on the novel Diamonds for Danger by
        David Esdaile Walker; Harper, 1953. (Q, FF, NYTFR, LC,
        W, AMPAS, LACOPL).

1869a   A MAN FOR ALL SEASONS. (Columbia-1966-Fred Zinne-
        mann). Robert Bolt wrote the screenplay which was based
        on his play; in Plays of Our Time edited by Bennett Cerf,
        Random House, 1967, pp. 631-719. (Q, FF, NYTFR, LC,
        W, AMPAS, LACOPL).

1870   THE MAN FROM BUTTON WILLOW. (United Screen Arts-
        1965-David Detiege). An original screenplay by David De-
        tiege. (W, AMPAS, Q).

1871   MAN FROM COCODY. (American International-1966-Chris-
        tian-Jaque). An original screenplay by Claude Rank. (W).

1872   MAN FROM DEEP RIVER. (Brenner-1973-Umberto Lenzi).
        No author credit given for screenplay. (W).

1873   THE MAN FROM GALVESTON. (Warner Bros.-1964-William
        Conrad). An original work for the screen by Dean Riesner
        and Michael Zagor. (W, Q, NYTFR, FF).

1874   THE MAN FROM O.R.G.Y. AND THE REAL GONE GIRLS.
        (Cinemation-1970-James A. Hill). Screenplay & story by Ted
        Marks, from his novel. (W, Q).

1875   MAN IN THE DARK. (Universal-1965-Lance Comfort). A
        screenplay by James Kelly and Peter Miller, based on a story
        by Vivian Kemble. (FF, W, AMPAS, Q).

1876   MAN IN THE MIDDLE. (20th Century-Fox-1964-Guy Hamil-
        ton). Keith Waterhouse and Willis Hall based their screen-
        play on the novel The Winston Affair by Howard Fast; Crown,
        1959. (LACOPL, NYTFR, AMPAS, W, Q, FF).

1877   MAN IN THE WILDERNESS. (Warner Bros.-1971-Richard C.
        Sarafian). Original screenplay written by Jack DeWitt. (W,
        Q).

1877a   MAN OF LA MANCHA. (United Artists-1972-Arthur Hiller).
        A screenplay by Dale Wasserman, based on his play published
        by Random House, 1966, 82p., which was suggested by Mig-
        uel de Cervantes' Don Quixote, Penguin Books, 1950, 940p.
        (W, FF, LACOPL, Q).

1878   MAN OF THE YEAR. (Universal-1973-Marco Vicario). An
        original screenplay by Piero Chiara and Marco Vicario. (W).

1879   MAN ON A SWING. (Paramount-1974-Frank Perry). David
        Zelag Goodman authored this original screenplay. (HR, V).

1880   THE MAN OUTSIDE. (Allied Artists-1969-Samuel Gallu).
        This screenplay by Samuel Gallu was based on the novel
        Double Agent by Gene Stackleborg. (FF, W, Q).

1881   THE MAN WHO FINALLY DIED. (Goldstone Film Enterprises
        -1967-Quentin Lawrence). Original screenplay written by
        Lewis Greifer and Louis Marks, based on a story by Lewis
        Greifer. (FF).

1882   THE MAN WHO HAD POWER OVER WOMEN. (AVCO Em-

bassy-1971-John Krish). A screenplay by Alan Scott and
Chris Bryant, from a novel by Gordon Williams; Stein, 1967.
(W, LACOPL, Q).

1883   THE MAN WHO HAUNTED HIMSELF. (Levitt-Pickman-
1971-Basil Dearden). An original screenplay by Basil Dearden. (W).

1884   THE MAN WHO LIES. (Grove-1970-Alain Robbe-Grillet).
An original screenplay by Alain Robbe-Grillet. (W).

1885   THE MAN WHO LOVED CAT DANCING. (MGM-1973-Rich-
ard C. Sarafian). Eleanor Perry wrote the screenplay which
was based on a novel by Marilyn Durham; Harcourt, 1972,
246p. (W, LACOPL, Q).

1885a   THE MAN WITH CONNECTIONS. (Columbia-1970-Claude
Berri). An original screenplay written by Claude Berri.
(W, Q).

1886   THE MAN WITH THE BALLOONS. (Sigma III-1968-Marco
Ferreri). This story and screenplay were co-authored by
Marco Ferreri and Rafael Azcona. (FF, NYTFR, W, Q).

1887   THE MAN WITH THE GOLDEN GUN. (United Artists-1974-
Guy Hamilton). A screenplay by Richard Maibaum and Tom
Mankiewicz, based on the novel by Ian Fleming; Signet, 1965,
158p. (V, LACOPL).

1888   THE MAN WITH TWO HEADS. (Mishkin-1972-Andy Milligan). This original screenplay was written by Andy Milligan.
(FF).

THE MAN WITHOUT A FACE see L'HOMME SANS VISAGE

1889   MANDRAGOLA. (Europix Consolidated-1966-Alberto Lattuada). A screenplay by Luigi Magni, Stefano Strucchi and
Alberto Lattuada, based on the story by Niccolo Machiavelli,
in Literary Works, Oxford University Press, 1961, 202p.
(FF, NYTFR, W, AMPAS, LACOPL, Q).

1890   MAN'S FAVORITE SPORT? (Universal-1964-Howard Hawks).
John Fenton Murray and Steve McNeil based their screenplay
on the story "The Girl Who Almost Got Away" by Pat Frank.
(AMPAS, W, FF, Q).

1891   MANSON. (American International-1973-Laurence Merrick).
A documentary compiled and written by Joan Huntington. (W).

1892   MARA OF THE WILDERNESS. (Allied Artists-1966-Frank
McDonald). A screenplay by Tom Blackburn, based on a
story by Rod Scott. (FF, LC, W, AMPAS, Q).

1893   MARAT/SADE (THE PERSECUTION AND ASSASSINATION OF
        JEAN-PAUL MARAT AS PERFORMED BY THE INMATES OF
        THE ASYLUM OF CHARENTON UNDER THE DIRECTION OF
        THE MARQUIS DE SADE).   (United Artists-1967-Peter Brook).
        Adrian Mitchell authored this screen adaptation of the play by
        Peter Weiss; Atheneum, 1965, 117p.   (Q, FF, NYTFR, FM,
        W, AMPAS, LACOPL).

1894   THE MARCO MEN. (NMF-1971-Julio Coll).   Howard Berk
        and Santiago Moncado wrote this original screenplay.   (W).

1895   MARCO THE MAGNIFICENT.   (MGM-1966-Denys De La
        Patelliere and Noel Howard).   A screenplay by Jacques
        Remy, J. P. Rappeneau, Denys De La Patelliere and Raoul
        J. Levy.   (FF, NYTFR, LC, W, Q).

1895a   MARJOE.   (Cinema V-1972-Howard Smith & Sarah Kerno-
        chan).   No screenplay credits; a documentary.   (W, FF, Q).

1896   MARK OF THE DEVIL.   (Hallmark-1972-Michael Armstrong).
        Sergio Cassner and Percy Parker co-authored this screen-
        play.   (FF).

1897   MARLOWE.   (MGM-1969-Paul Bogart).   A screenplay by
        Stirling Silliphant, based on the novel by Raymond Chandler
        The Little Sister, in The Midnight Raymond Chandler; Hough-
        ton, 1971, 734p.   (W, LC, AMPAS, LACOPL, Q).

1898   MARNIE.   (Universal-1964-Alfred Hitchcock).   A screenplay
        by Jay Presson Allen, from the novel by Winston Graham;
        Doubleday, 1961, 281p.   (FF, NYTFR, LACOPL, W, Q).

1899   MAROC 7.   (Paramount-1968-Gerry O'Hara).   David Osborn
        wrote this screenplay and original story.   (FF, W, LC,
        AMPAS, Q).

1900   MAROONED.   (Columbia-1969-John Sturges).   A screenplay
        by May Simon, based on a novel by Martin Caidin.   (NYTFR,
        Q).

1901   THE MARRIAGE CAME TUMBLING DOWN.   (Royal Films In-
        ternational-1968-Jacques Poitrenaud).   A screenplay by Al-
        bert Cossery and Jacques Poitrenaud, based on the novel I
        Am Called Jericho by Catherine Paysan.   (FF, NYTFR, Q̄).

1902   MARRIAGE ITALIAN STYLE.   (Embassy-1964-Vittorio De
        Sica).   A screenplay by Eduardo De Filippo, Renato Castella-
        ni, Antonio Guerra, Leo Benvenuto, and Piero De Bernardi,
        based on the play Filomena Marturano by Eduardo De Filip-
        po.   (FF, AMPAS, NYTFR, W, Q).

1903   MARRIAGE ON THE ROCKS.   (Warner Bros.-1965-Jack
        Donohue).   Cy Howard wrote this original screenplay.

(NYTFR, LC, W, AMPAS, Q).

1903a A MARRIED COUPLE. (Aquarius-1970-Allan King). No additional credits. (W, Q).

1904 THE MARRIED WOMAN. (Royal-1965-Jean-Luc Godard). An original screenplay by Jean-Luc Godard. (NYTFR, W, Q).

1905 MARRY ME! MARRY ME! (Allied Artists-1969-Claude Berri). A screenplay by Claude Berri, from his novel; Morrow, 1969, 101p. (FF, W, LACOPL).

1906 MARTYRS OF LOVE. (New Line Cinema-1969-Jan Nemec). An original screenplay by Ester Krumbachova and Jan Nemec. (FF, W).

1906a MARY JANE. (American International-1968-Maury Dexter). A screenplay by Richard Gautier and Peter L. Marshall, based on a story by Maury Dexter. (FF, NYTFR, W, Q).

1907 MARY POPPINS. (Buena Vista-1964-Robert Stevenson). A screenplay by Bill Walsh and Don DaGradi, based on the books by P. L. Travers; Reynal, 1953. (FF, LACOPL, NYTFR, W, Q, AMPAS).

1908 MARY, QUEEN OF SCOTS. (Universal-1971-Charles Jarrott). John Hale wrote this original screenplay. A novelization by John Hale based on the original screenplay was published by Signet, 1972, 142p. (LACOPL, W, Q).

1909 MASCULINE FEMININE. (Royal-1966-Jean-Luc Godard). A screenplay by Jean-Luc Godard, based on two stories by Guy De Maupassant. The script of the film along with the two short stories by De Maupassant upon which the film is based, was published by Grove Press, 1969, 288p. (FF, NYTFR, W, AMPAS, MCC, SCH, LACOPL).

1910 M*A*S*H. (20th Century-Fox-1970-Robert Altman). A screenplay by Ring Lardner, Jr., from a novel by Richard Hooker; Morrow, 1968, 219p. (FF, W, LACOPL, Q).

1911 THE MASQUE OF THE RED DEATH. (American International-1964-Roger Corman). A screenplay by Charles Beaumont and R. Wright Campbell, from a story by Edgar Allan Poe; in Complete Tales and Poems, Doubleday, 1966. (NYTFR, LACOPL, FF, Q, W).

1912 MASQUERADE. (United Artists-1965-Basil Dearden). A screenplay by Michael Relph and William Goldman, based on the novel by Victor Canning, Castle Minerva. (FF, LC, AMPAS, Q).

1913 MASSACRE IN ROME. (National General-1973-George Pan

Cosmatos). A screenplay by Robert Katz, George Pan Cosmatos, based on Death in Rome by Robert Katz; Macmillan,
1967, 334p. (W, LACOPL).

1914   MASTER OF HORROR.   (U. S. Films-1966-Enrique Carreras).
A screenplay by Luis Penafiel, based on two tales "The Case
of Dr. Valdemar" and "The Cask of Amontillado" by Edgar
Allan Poe; in Complete Stories and Poems, Doubleday, 1966.
(FF, LACOPL).

1915   MASTER SPY. (Allied Artists-1964-Montgomery Tully).   A
screenplay by Maurice J. Wilson and Montgomery Tully,
based on the story "They Also Serve" by Gerald Anstruther
and Paul White. (W, Q, FF, NYTFR).

1916   THE MASTER TOUCH. (Warner Bros. -1974-Michele Lupo).
A screenplay by Mino Roli, Franco Bucceri, Roberto Leoni,
and Michele Lupo. (V).

1917   MATCHLESS. (United Artists-1967-Alberto Lattuada).   A
screenplay by Dean Craig, Jack Pulman, Luigi Malerba, Alberto Lattuada, and Ermanno Donati. (FF, NYTFR, FM,
W, AMPAS, Q).

1918   MATCHLESS. (Australian Film Institute-1974-John Papadop-
oulos). An original screenplay by Sally Blake. (V).

1919   THE MATTEI AFFAIR. (Paramount-1973-Francesco Rosi).
An original story and screenplay by Francesco Rosi, Tonino
Guerra, Nerio Minuzzo, and Tito de Stafano. (W, Q).

1920   A MATTER OF DAYS. (Royal-1969-Yves–Ciampi). An original screenplay by Yves Ciampi, Rodolphe M. Arlaud, Vladimir Kalina, and Alena Vostra. (W).

1921   A MATTER OF INNOCENCE. (Universal-1968-Guy Green).
A screenplay by Keith Waterhouse and Willis Hall, based on
the story "Pretty Polly" by Noel Coward, in Pretty Polly and
Other Stories; Doubleday, 1964. (FF, NYTFR, W, AMPAS,
LACOPL, Q).

A MATTER OF RESISTANCE see LA VIE DE CHATEAU

1922   MAURIE. (National General-1973-Daniel Mann).   An original
screenplay by Douglas Morrow. (W).

1923   MAYA. (MGM-1966-John Berry).   A screenplay by John
Fante, adaptation by Gilbert Wright, and based on the story
"The Wild Elephant" by Jalal Din and Lois Roth. (FF,
NYTFR, LC, W, Q, AMPAS).

1923a MAYERLING. (MGM-1969-Terence Young).   A screenplay by
Terence Young, based on the novel Mayerling by Claude

Anet; Grasset, 1930; and the novel The Archduke by Michael
Arnold, Doubleday, 1967. Historical documentation was also
relied upon. (FF, Q, LC, AMPAS, LACOPL).

1924   ME. (Altura-1970-Maurice Pialat).   An original screenplay
        by Maurice Pialat. (W).

1925   ME AND MY BROTHER. (New Yorker-1969-Robert Frank).
        An original screenplay by Sam Sheppard and Robert Frank.
        (FF).

1926   ME, NATALIE. (National General-1969-Fred Coe).   A. Mar-
        tin Zweiback wrote the screenplay from an original story by
        Stanley Shapiro. (FF, W, AMPAS, Q).

1927   MEAN STREETS. (Warner Bros.-1973-Martin Scorsese).
        An original screenplay written by Martin Scorsese and Mar-
        dik Martin.   Michael T. Kaufman wrote an original novel
        based upon the screenplay; Award Books, 1974, 155p.
        (LACOPL, W, Q).

1928   MEAT RACK. (Sherpix-1970-Michael Thomas).   No screen-
        play credit. (W).

1929   THE MECHANIC. (United Artists-1972-Michael Winner).   An
        original screenplay by Lewis John Carlino. (W, FF, Q).

1930   MEDEA. (New Line-1971-Pier Paolo Pasolini).   A screen-
        play by Pier Paolo Pasolini from the play by Euripides;
        Clarendon Press, 1955, 190p. (W, LACOPL).

1931   MEDIUM COOL. (Paramount-1969-Haskell Wexler).   An orig-
        inal work for the screen written by Haskell Wexler.   (FF,
        W, LC, AMPAS, Q).

1932   MEET ME IN MOSCOW. (Cinemasters International-1966-
        Georgi Daniela).   An original screenplay by Gennadi Shapa-
        likov. (FF, NYTFR).

1933   MELINDA. (MGM-1972-Hugh A. Robertson).   A screenplay
        by Lonne Elder III, story by Raymond Cistheri.   (W, FF, Q).

1934   MELODY. (Levitt-Pickman-1971-Waris Hussein).   An origi-
        nal screenplay by Alan Parker. (W, Q).

1935   MEMORIES OF UNDERDEVELOPMENT. (Tricontinental-
        1973-Tomas Gutierrez Alea).   A work for the screen written
        by Tomas Gutierrez Alea, based on the novel by Edmundo
        Desnoes; Inconsolable Memories, New American Library,
        1967. (W, HR, LACOPL).

1936   MEMORIES WITHIN MISS AGGIE. (1974-Gerard Damiano).
        A script by Ron Wertheim and Gerard Damiano.   (V).

1937   MEMORY OF US.   (Cinema Financial of America-1974-H.
        Kaye Dyal).   An original screenplay by Ellen Geer.   (V).

1938   THE MEPHISTO WALTZ.   (20th Century-Fox-1971-Paul
        Wendkos).   A screenplay by Ben Maddow, based on the novel
        by Fred Mustard Stewart; Coward, 1969, 256p.   (W, LACOPL,
        Q).

1939   THE MERCENARY.   (United Artists-1970-Sergio Corbucci).
        Luciano Vicenzoni, Sergio Spina, Sergio Corbucci wrote the
        screenplay, from a story by Franco Solinas and Giorgio Ar-
        lorio.   (W, Q).

1940   THE MERCHANT OF FOUR SEASONS.   (New Yorker-1973-
        Rainer Werner Fassbinder).   An original screenplay by
        Rainer Werner Fassbinder.   (W).

1941   THE MERMAID.   (Lee-1966-Kao Li).   Chang Chien wrote
        this original screenplay.   (W).

1942   THE MERRY WIVES OF WINDSOR.   (Sigma III-1966-George
        Tressler).   The screenplay and English translation by Nor-
        man Foster, was taken from the opera by Otto Nicolai and
        the play by William Shakespeare; Methuen, 1971, 149p.   (FF,
        NYTFR, W, LACOPL, Q).

1943   MICHAEL AND HELGA.   (American International-1969-Erich
        F. Bender).   Erich F. Bender, Dr. Roland Cammerer, and
        Klaus E. R. Von Schwarze wrote this original screenplay.
        (FF, LC, Q).

1944   MICKEY ONE.   (Columbia-1965-Arthur Penn).   An original
        screenplay written by Alan M. Surgal.   (NYTFR, W, AMPAS,
        Q).

1945   MIDAS RUN.   (Cinerama-1969-Alf Kjellin).   A screenplay by
        James D. Buchanan and Ronald Austin, based on a story by
        Berne Giler.   (FF, W, AMPAS, Q).

1946   MIDDLE OF THE WORLD.   (1974-Alain Tanner).   The screen-
        play was written by John Berger and Alain Tanner.   (HR).

1947   MIDNIGHT COWBOY.   (United Artists-1969-John Schlesinger).
        A screenplay by Waldo Salt, based on the novel by James
        Leo Herlihy; Simon & Schuster, 1965.   (FF, W, LC, AMPAS,
        LACOPL, Q).

1948   THE MIDNIGHT MAN.   (Universal-1974-Roland Kibbee and
        Burt Lancaster).   An original screenplay by Roland Kibbee
        and Burt Lancaster.   (HR, V).

1949   MIDNIGHT PLOWBOY.   (Boxoffice International-1973-Bethel
        Buckalew).   No screenplay credit available.   (W).

1950   THE MIKADO. (Warner Bros. -1967-Stuart Burge). No
       screenplay, a filmed musical performance of the play with
       music and lyrics by W. S. Gilbert and Arthur Sullivan. (W,
       AMPAS, Q).

1951   THE MILITARISTS. (Toho-1973-Hiromichi Korikawa). An
       original screenplay by Ryozo Kasahara. (W).

1952   THE MILKY WAY. (UM-1970-Luis Buñuel). Screenplay and
       dialogue by Luis Buñuel and Jean-Claude Carrière. (W,
       AMPAS, Q).

1953   THE MILLION EYES OF SU-MURU. (American International-
       1967-Lindsay Shonteff). A screenplay by Kevin Kavanagh,
       from an original story by Peter Welbeck, based on books and
       characters created by Sax Rohmer. (FF, W, LC, AMPAS,
       Q).

1954   THE MIND OF MR. SOAMES. (Columbia-1970-Alan Cooke).
       A screenplay by John Hale and Edward Simpson, from a
       novel by Charles Eric Maine. (W, Q).

       THE MIND SNATCHERS see   THE HAPPINESS CAGE

1955   MINGUS. (Film-Makers-1968-Thomas Reichman). No screen-
       play credits; a documentary. (W).

1956   THE MINI-SKIRT MOB. (American International-1968-Maury
       Dexter). An original screenplay by James Gordon White.
       (FF, NYTFR, FM, W, LC, AMPAS, Q).

1957   MINNESOTA CLAY. (Harlequin-1966-Sergio Corbucci). Ad-
       riano Bolzoni and Sergio Corbucci wrote the screenplay, from
       a story by Adriano Bolzoni. (FF).

1958   MINNIE AND MOSKOWITZ. (Universal-1971-John Cassavetes).
       A screenplay by John Cassavetes, published by Black Sparrow
       Press, 1973, 116p. (W, LACOPL, Q).

1959   A MINUTE TO PRAY, A SECOND TO DIE. (Cinerama-1968-
       Franco Giraldi). Ugo Liberatore and Louis Garfinkle wrote
       this screenplay, based on a story by Albert Band and Ugo
       Liberatore. (Q, FF, NYTFR, FM, W, AMPAS).

1960   THE MINX. (Cambist-1969-Raymond Jacobs). An original
       screenplay by Raymond Jacobs and Herbert Jaffey. (Q, W).

1961   THE MIRACLE OF LOVE. (Times Film Corporation-1969-
       F. J. Gottlieb). A screenplay by Oswalt Kolle, based on his
       book Sexuality in Marriage. (FF, W, Q).

1962   MIRAGE. (Universal-1965-Edward Dmytryk). Peter Stone
       wrote this screenplay, from a story by Walter Ericson.
       (NYTFR, Q, LC, W, AMPAS).

1962a THE MISADVENTURES OF MERLIN JONES. (Buena Vista-1964-Robert Stevenson). A screenplay by Tom and Helen August, based on a story by Bill Walsh. (FF, NYTFR, W, Q, AMPAS).

1963 MISSION BATANGAS. (Manson-1969-Keith Larsen). A screenplay written by Lew Antonio, based on a story by Keith Larsen. (FF).

1964 MISSION MARS. (Allied Artists-1968-Nick Webster). A screenplay by Mike St. Clair, based on a story by Aubrey Wisberg. (FF, W, LC).

1965 MISSION STARDUST. (Times-1969-Primo Zeglio). No screenplay credits available. (W, Q).

1966 MISSISSIPPI MERMAID. (United Artists-1970-François Truffaut). A screenplay by François Truffaut, based on the novel Waltz into Darkness by Cornell Woolrich. (W, Q).

1967 MR. BROWN. (Andrieux-1972-Roger Andrieux). A screenplay written by Roger Andrieux. (W).

1968 MISTER BUDDWING. (MGM-1966-Delbert Mann). A screenplay by Dale Wasserman, based on the novel by Evan Hunter, Buddwing; Simon & Schuster, 1964. (Q, FF, NYTFR, LC, W, AMPAS, LACOPL).

1969 MISTER FREEDOM. (Grove-1970-William Klein). An original screenplay written by William Klein. (W).

1970 MR. MAJESTYK. (United Artists-1974-Richard Fleischer). A screenplay written directly for the screen by Elmore Leonard. (V).

1971 MISTER MOSES. (United Artists-1965-Ronald Neame). Charles Beaumont wrote the screenplay with Monja Dinischewsky, which they based on the novel by Max Catto; Morrow, 1961. (FF, LC, W, LACOPL, Q).

1972 MRS. BARRINGTON. (Monarch-1974-Chuck Vincent). An original screenplay by Chuck Vincent and James Vidos. (V).

1973 MRS. BROWN, YOU'VE GOT A LOVELY DAUGHTER. (MGM-1968-Saul Swimmer). An original screenplay by Thaddeus Vane. (FF, W, LC, AMPAS, Q).

1974 MRS. POLLIFAX--SPY. (United Artists-1971-Leslie Martinson). A screenplay by C. A. McKnight, based on the novel by Dorothy Gilman, The Unexpected Mrs. Pollifax; Doubleday, 1966. (W, LACOPL, Q).

1975 MIXED COMPANY. (United Artists-1974-Mel Shavelson). A

1975a THE MODEL MURDER CASE.   (Cinema V-1964-Michael Truman).   Vivienne Knight and Patrick Campbell wrote the
screenplay based on the novel The Nose on My Face, by
Laurence Payne; Macmillan, 1961. (NYTFR, LACOPL, Q,
W, AMPAS, FF).

1976   MODEL SHOP.   (Columbia-1969-Jacques Demy).   A screenplay by Jacques Demy.   (FF, LC, AMPAS, Q).

1976a MODERATO CANTABILE.   (Royal-1964-Peter Brook).   A
screenplay by Marguerite Duras, Gerard Jarlot and Peter
Brook, based on a novel by Marguerite Duras.   (FF, NYTFR,
W).

1977   MODESTY BLAISE.   (20th Century-Fox-1966-Joseph Losey).
A screenplay by Evan Jones, based on the Evening Standard
comic strip created by Peter O'Donnell and Jim Holdaway.
(FF, NYTFR, LC, W, AMPAS, Q).

1978   MOLLY AND LAWLESS JOHN.   (Producers Distributing Cor-
poration-1972-Gary Nelson).   An original screenplay by Terry
Kingsley-Smith.   (W).

1979   THE MOLLY MAGUIRES.   (Paramount-1970-Martin Ritt).   A
screenplay by Walter Bernstein.   (W, Q).

1980   MOMENT TO MOMENT.   (Universal-1966-Mervyn LeRoy).
A screenplay by John Lee Mahin and Alec Coppel, based on
the story "Laughs with a Stranger" by Alec Coppel.   (FF,
NYTFR, Q, LC, W, AMPAS).

1981   MONA.   (Sherpix-1971-Bill Osco).   An original screenplay by
Bill Osco.   (W).

1982   MONDO MOD.   (Timely Motion Picture-1967-Peter Perry).
An original work written by Sherman Greene.   (FF).

1983   MONDO TRASHO.   (FilmMakers-1970-John Waters).   An original script written by John Waters.   (W).

1984   No entry.

1985   THE MONEY JUNGLE.   (Commonwealth United Entertainment-
1968-Francis D. Lyon).   An original screenplay by Charles
Wallace.   (FF, W, Q).

1986   MONEY, MONEY, MONEY.   (Cinerama-1973-Claude Lelouch).
An original screenplay written by Claude Lelouch.   (W, Q).

1987   MONEY TALKS.   (United Artists-1972-Allen Funt).   An original script written by Allen Funt.   (FF, Q).

1988   THE MONEY TRAP.   (MGM-1966-Burt Kennedy).   A screen-

play by Walter Bernstein, based on the novel by Lionel White;
Dutton, 1963. (Q, FF, NYTFR, LC, W, AMPAS, LACOPL).

1989 MONIQUE. (AVCO Embassy-1970-John Brown). An original
screenplay written by John Bown. (Q, W).

1990 THE MONITORS. (Commonwealth United-1969-Jack Shea). A
screen work written by Myron J. Gold, from a novel by
Keith Laumer. (W, Q).

1991 MONKEYS, GO HOME! (Buena Vista-1967-Andrew V. Mc-
Laglen). A screenplay by Maurice Tombragel, based on the
book The Monkeys by G. K. Wilkinson; Farrar, 1962. (FF,
W, LC, AMPAS, LACOPL, Q).

1992 THE MONKEY'S UNCLE. (Buena Vista-1965-Robert Stevenson). Tom and Helen August wrote this original screenplay.
(W, LC, NYTFR, AMPAS, Q).

1993 THE MONSTER OF LONDON CITY. (Producers Releasing
Corporation-1967-Edwin Zbonek). A screenplay by Robert A.
Stemmle, based on a story by Bryan Edgar Wallace. (FF,
W).

1994 MONTE WALSH. (National General-1970-William A. Fraker).
A screenplay by David Z. Goodman, Lukas Heller, based on
a novel by Jack Schaefer; Houghton, 1963. (W, LACOPL,
Q).

1995 MOON ZERO TWO. (Warner Bros.-1970-Roy Ward Baker).
A screenplay by Michael Carreras, from a story by Gavin
Lyall, Frank Hardman, and Martin Davison. (W, Q).

1996 MOONLIGHTING WIVES. (Craddock Films-1968-Joe Sarno).
A script written by Joe Sarno. (FF, NYTFR, W).

1997 THE MOONSHINE WAR. (MGM-1970-Richard Quine). A
screenplay by Elmore Leonard from his novel; Doubleday,
1969, 236p. (W, LACOPL, Q).

1997a THE MOON-SPINNERS. (Buena Vista-1964-James Neilson).
A work for the screen written by Michael Dyne and based on
the novel by Mary Stewart; M. S. Mill Co. and William Morrow & Co., 1963, 303p. (LACOPL, NYTFR, AMPAS, W,
FF, Q).

1998 MOONWALK ONE. (NASA-1972-Theo Kamecke). A script
by E. G. Valens, from a story by Peretz W. Johnnes and
Theo Kamecke. (FF).

1999 MOONWOLF. (Allied Artists-1966-Martin Nosseck and George
Freedland). A screenplay written by George Freedland. (FF,
Q).

2000   MORE. (Cinema V-1969-Barbet Schroeder). Paul Gegauff
        and Barbet Schroeder wrote the screenplay which was based
        on an original screen story by Barbet Schroeder. (FF, W,
        Q).

2001   MORE DEAD THAN ALIVE. (United Artists-1969-Robert
        Sparr). An original screenplay by George Schenck. (FF,
        W, LC, Q, AMPAS).

2002   MORE THAN A MIRACLE. (MGM-1967-Francesco Rosi). A
        screenplay by Francesco Rosi, Tonino Guerra, Raffaele La
        Capria and Peppino Patroni Griffi, based on a story by Ton-
        ino Guerra. (FF, NYTFR, FM, W, LC, AMPAS, Q).

2003   MORGAN! (Cinema V-1966-Karel Reisz). A screenplay by
        David Mercer, based on his play. (FF, NYTFR, W, AMPAS,
        Q).

2004   MORIANNA. (Mondial Films-1968-Arne Mattsson). A screen-
        play by Per Wahloo and Arne Mattsson, based on the novel
        by Jan Ekstrom. (FF, W).

2005   THE MORNING AFTER. (Mature-1972-Sidney Knight). An
        original screenplay by Harvey Green. (W).

2006   MORO WITCH DOCTOR. (20th Century-Fox-1965-Eddie Ro-
        mero). Eddie Romero wrote this screenplay which was
        based on an original story by him. (W, LC, AMPAS; FF
        gives date as 1964).

2007   MOSQUITO SQUADRON. (United Artists-1970-Boris Sagal).
        No screenplay author credit. (W, Q.

2008   THE MOST BEAUTIFUL AGE. (Grove-1970-Jaroslav Papou-
        sek). An original screenplay written by Jaroslav Papousek.
        (W).

2009   MOTOR PSYCHO. (Eve-1965-Russ Meyer). An original
        script by Russ Meyer and W. E. Sprague. (W, AMPAS).

2010   MOUCHETTE. (Cinema Ventures-1968-Robert Bresson). A
        Robert Bresson screenplay, based on a novel by George Ber-
        nanos; Holt, 1966. (W, NYTFR, LACOPL).

2011   MOVE. (20th Century-Fox-1970-Stuart Rosenberg). A
        screenplay by Joel Lieber and Stanley Hart, based on a novel
        by Joel Lieber; McKay, 1968. (W, LACOPL, Q).

2012   MOVIE STAR, AMERICAN STYLE. (Famous Players Cor-
        poration-1967-Albert Zugsmith). An original screenplay by
        Albert Zugsmith and Graham Lee Mahin. (FF, LC,
        AMPAS).

2013   MOVING. (Poolemar-1974-Wakefield Poole).   No screenplay credit available. (V).

2014   MOZAMBIQUE. (7 Arts-1966-Robert Lynn).   A screenplay by Peter Yeldham, based on a story by Peter Welbeck. (FF, NYTFR, W, AMPAS).

2015   MUHAIR. (Haven-1970-Armando Bo).   A screenplay written by Armando Bo. (W).

2016   THE MUMMY'S SHROUD. (20th Century-Fox-1967-John Gilling).   A screenplay by John Gilling, based on an original story by John Elder. (FF, W, LC, AMPAS, Q).

       MUMSY, NANNY, SONNY AND GIRLY see GIRLY

2017   MUNSTER, GO HOME. (Universal-1966-Earl Bellamy).   A screenplay by George Tibbles, Joe Connelly, and Bob Mosher, based on characters created by Charles Addams, and the television series, "The Munsters." (FF, LC, W, AMPAS, Q).

2018   MURDER A LA MOD. (Aries Documentaries-1968-Brian De Palma).   An original screenplay by Brian De Palma. (FF, NYTFR, FM, W).

2018a MURDER AHOY. (MGM-1964-George Pollock).   David Pursall and Jack Seddon wrote the screenplay based on characters created by Agatha Christie. (FF, NYTFR, Q, W).

2019   THE MURDER CLINIC. (Europix Consolidated-1968-Michael Hamilton).   A screenplay by Julian Berry aka Ernesto Gastaldi and Martin Hardy aka Sergio Martino. (FF).

2020   MURDER CZECH STYLE. (Royal-1968-Jiri Weiss).   An original story and screenplay by Jan Otcenasek and Jiri Weiss. (FF, Q, NYTFR, W).

2021   THE MURDER GAME. (20th Century-Fox-1966-Sidney Salkow).   A screenplay by Harry Spalding, based on a story by Irving Yergin. (FF, NYTFR, W, AMPAS, Q).

2022   MURDER IN MISSISSIPPI. (Tiger-1965-J. P. Mawra).   An original screenplay by Herbert S. Altman. (W, AMPAS).

2023   MURDER MOST FOUL. (MGM-1965-George Pollock).   A screenplay by David Pursall and Jack Seddon from the novel Mrs. McGinty's Dead by Agatha Christie; Dodd, 1952. (NYTFR, LC, AMPAS, LACOPL).

2024   MURDER ON THE ORIENT EXPRESS. (Paramount-1974-Sidney Lumet).   A screenplay by Paul Dehn, based on Agatha Christie's novel; Ulverscroft, 1934, 253p. (LACOPL, V, HR, MFB).

2025   THE MURDERED HOUSE.   (Creative Film Services-1974-
        Paulo Cesar Saraceni).   A screenplay by Paulo Saraceni,
        based on a novel by Lucio Cardoso.   (V).

2026   MURDERERS' ROW.   (Columbia-1966-Henry Levin).   A
        screenplay by Herbert Baker, based on the novel by Donald
        Hamilton.   (FF, Q, NYTFR, LC, W, AMPAS).

2027   MURDERS IN THE RUE MORGUE.   (American International-
        1972-Gordon Hessler).   A screenplay by Christopher Wicking
        Henry Slesar, based on the story by Edgar Allan Poe, in
        Complete Stories and Poems; Doubleday, 1966.   (LACOPL,
        W, Q).

2028   MURMUR OF THE HEART.   (Walter Reade-1971-Louis
        Malle).   An original screenplay by Louis Malle.   (W, Q).

2029   MURPH THE SURF.   (Caruth C. Byrd-1974-Marvin Chomsky).
        A screenplay by E. Arthur Kean, based on a story by Allan
        Dale Kuhn.   (V).

2030   MURPHY'S WAR.   (Parmount-1971-Peter Yates).   A screen-
        play by Stirling Silliphant, from a novel by Max Catto; Simon
        & Schuster, 1968, 284p.   (W, LACOPL, Q.

2030a   MUSCLE BEACH PARTY.   (American International-1964-
        William Asher).   Robert Dillon wrote the screenplay based on
        a story by himself and William Asher.   (AMPAS, LC, NYTFR,
        FF, W, Q).

2031   THE MUSIC LOVERS.   (United Artists-1971-Ken Russell).   A
        screenplay by Melvyn Bragg, based on Beloved Friend by
        Catherine Drinker Bowen and Barbara Von Meck.   (W, Q).

2032   THE MUTATION.   (Columbia-1974-Jack Cardiff).   A screen-
        play written directly for the screen by Robert D. Weinbach
        and Edward Mann.   (V).

2033   MUTINY IN OUTER SPACE.   (Allied Artists-1965-Hugo Gri-
        maldi).   An original screenplay by Arthur C. Pierce.   (FF,
        LC, W, AMPAS, Q).

2034   MY BLOOD RUNS COLD.   (Warner Bros.-1965-William Con-
        rad).   A screenplay by John Mantley, based on a story by
        John Meredyth Lucas.   (FF, LC, W, AMPAS, Q).

2034a   MY FAIR BABY.   (Arrow-1973-).   No additional credits
        available.   (W).

2035   MY FAIR LADY.   (Warner Bros.-1964-George Cukor).   A
        screenplay by Alan Jay Lerner, based on the musical play
        with book & lyrics by Alan Jay Lerner, music by Frederick
        Loewe; Coward, 1956, 186p.; and, the play Pygmalion by

George Bernard Shaw; Dodd, Mead & Co., 1967, 359p. (LC, AMPAS, NYTFR, W, Q, LACOPL, FF).

2036   MY HUSTLER. (Film-Makers' Distribution Center-1967-Andy Warhol). No screenplay credit available; dialogue improvised. (FF, NYTFR, W, AMPAS).

2037   MY LOVER, MY SON. (MGM-1970-John Newland). A screenplay by William Marchant and Jenni Hall, based on the story "Second Level" by Wilber Stark and the novel Reputation for a Song by Edward Grierson; Knopf, 1952. (W, LACOPL, Q).

2038   MY NAME IS NOBODY. (1974-Tonino Valerii). An original screenplay by Ernesto Gastaldi. (V).

2039   MY NIGHT AT MAUD'S. (Pathe-1970-Eric Rohmer). An original screenplay by Eric Rohmer; Simon & Schuster, 1972. (W, Q, LACOPL).

2040   MY OLD MAN'S PLACE. (Cinerama-1971-Edwin Sherin). A screenplay by Stanford Whitmore, based on a novel by John Sanford. (W).

2041   MY SIDE OF THE MOUNTAIN. (Paramount-1969-James B. Clark). Ted Sherdeman, Jane Klove, and Joanna Crawford wrote this screenplay based on the novel by Jean Craighead George; Dutton, 1959, 178p. (FF, W, LC, AMPAS, LACOPL, Q).

2042   MY SISTER, MY LOVE. (Sigma III-1967-Vilgot Sjoman). A Vilgot Sjoman screenplay, suggested in part by the play 'Tis Pity She's a Whore by John Ford; Hill & Wang, 1968, 97p. (FF, Q, NYTFR, W, LACOPL).

2043   MY SWEET CHARLIE. (Universal-1970-Lamont Johnson). A screenplay by Richard Levinson and William Link, based on a novel and play of the same name by David Westheimer; Doubleday, 1965. (W, LACOPL, Q).

2044   MY UNCLE ANTOINE. (Gendon-1972-Claude Jutra). A screenplay by Clement Perron, adapted by Claude Jutra and Clement Perron. (FF).

2045   MY WIFE'S HUSBAND. (Lopert-1965-Gilles Grangier). A screenplay by Jean Levitte and Pierre Levy-Corti. (FF, W, Q).

2046   MYRA BRECKINRIDGE. (20th Century-Fox-1970-Michael Sarne). A screenplay by Michael Sarne and David Giler, from the novel by Gore Vidal; Little, Brown & Co., 1968. (W, LACOPL, Q).

2047   THE MYSTERY OF THUG ISLAND. (Columbia-1966-Luigi Capuano). A screenplay by Arpad De Riso and Ottavio Poggi,

based on the novel The Mystery of the Black Jungle by Emil-
io Salgari. (FF, LC, W, Q).

2048 NAKED AMONG THE WOLVES. (Lopert-1967-Frank Beyer).
An original story by Bruno Apitz from which was derived
the screenplay by Alfred Hirschmeier. (NYTFR, W).

2049 NAKED ANGELS. (Favorite-1969-Bruce Clark). An original
screenplay by Bruce Clark. (W).

2050 THE NAKED APE. (Universal-1973-Donald Driver/ Charles
Swenson). No author credits. Screenplay based on the book
by Desmond Morris; McGraw-Hill, 1967, 252p. (W, LACOPL).

2051 THE NAKED BRIGADE. (Universal-1965-Maury Dexter). An
original screenplay by Albert J. Cohen and A. Sanford Wolf.
(NYTFR, W, AMPAS).

2052 NAKED CHILDHOOD. (1968-Maurice Pialat). An original
screenplay written by Maurice Pialat. (NYTFR).

2053 THE NAKED COUNTESS. (Crown International-1973-Curt
Nachman). Curt Nachman wrote this original screenplay.
(W).

2054 THE NAKED KISS. (Allied Artists-1965-Samuel Fuller). An
original screen work by Samuel Fuller. (Q, FF, AMPAS).

2055 THE NAKED PREY. (Paramount-1966-Cornel Wilde). Clint
Johnston and Don Peters wrote this original screenplay. (Q,
FF, LC, W, AMPAS).

2056 THE NAKED RUNNER. (Warner Bros.-7 Arts-1967-Sidney J.
Furie). A screenplay by Stanley Mann, based on the novel
by Francis Clifford; Coward, 1966. (FF, NYTFR, Q, FM,
LC, AMPAS, LACOPL).

2057 THE NAME OF THE GAME IS KILL. (Fanfare-1968-Gunnar
Hellstrom). An original screenplay by Gary Crutcher. (FF,
NYTFR, FM, W, AMPAS).

2058 NAMU, THE KILLER WHALE. (United Artists-1966-Laslo
Benedek). Arthur Weiss wrote this original screenplay. (FF,
LC, W, Q, AMPAS).

2059 NANAMI. (Golden Eagle-1969-Susumu Hani). An original
screenplay by Susumu Hani and Shuji Terayama. (Q, FF, W).

2060 THE NANNY. (20th Century-Fox-1965-Seth Holt). A screenplay by Jimmy Sangster, from the novel by Evelyn Piper;
Atheneum, 1964. (NYTFR, Q, LC, W, AMPAS, LACOPL).

2061 NAPOLEON AND SAMANTHA. (Buena Vista-1972-Bernard

McEveety).   A screenplay by Stewart Raffill.   (FF, Q).

2062   NASHVILLE REBEL.   (American International-1966-Jay J.
       Sheridan).   A screenplay by Ira Kerns and Jay J. Sheridan,
       based on an original idea and story by Click Weston.   (FF,
       LC, W, AMPAS).

2063   NAVAJO JOE.   (United Artists-1967-Sergio Corbucci).   A
       screen work by Dean Craig and Fernando Di Leo, based on
       a story by Ugo Pirro.   (FF, NYTFR, W).

2064   NAVAJO RUN.   (American International-1966-Johnny Seven).
       A screenplay by Jo Heims.   (FF, Q, LC, W, AMPAS).

2065   THE NAVY VS. THE NIGHT MONSTERS.   (Realart-1966-
       Michael Hoey).   A screenplay by Michael Hoey, based on a
       novel by Murray Leinster.   (FF, W, Q, LC, AMPAS).

2066   NAZARIN.   (Altura-1968-Luis Buñuel).   A screenplay by Julio
       Alejandro and Luis Buñuel, based on the novel by Benito
       Pérez Galdós; Simon & Schuster, 1972, 299p.   (FF, NYTFR,
       Q, W, AMPAS, LACOPL).

2067   NECROMANCY.   (Cinerama Releasing Corporation-1972-Bert
       I. Gordon).   An original screenplay by Bert I. Gordon.   (FF,
       Q).

2068   NED KELLY.   (United Artists-1970-Tony Richardson).   An
       original screenplay by Tony Richardson and Ian Jones.   (W,
       Q).

2069   NEGATIVES.   (Continental-1968-Peter Medak).   A screenplay
       by Peter Everett and Roger Lowry, based on a novel by Peter
       Everett; Simon & Schuster, 1965.   (FF, LACOPL, W, NYTFR,
       Q).

2070   THE NELSON AFFAIR.   (Universal-1973-James Cellan Jones).
       A screenplay by Terence Rattigan, based on his play A Be-
       quest to the Nation.   (Q, W).

2071   THE NEPTUNE FACTOR.   (20th Century-Fox-1973-Daniel
       Petrie).   An original screenplay by Jack DeWitt.   (W, Q).

2072   NEVADA SMITH.   (Paramount-1966-Henry Hathaway).   A
       screenplay by John Michael Hayes, based on a character in
       The Carpetbaggers by Harold Robbins; Simon & Schuster, 1961,
       679p.   (FF, NYTFR, LC, W, AMPAS, LACOPL, Q).

2073   NEVER A DULL MOMENT.   (Buena Vista-1968-Jerry Paris).
       A. J. Carothers wrote the screenplay based on the novel
       Thrill a Minute by John Godey; Simon & Schuster, 1967.   (FF,
       NYTFR, FM, W, LC, AMPAS, LACOPL, Q).

2073a NEVER PUT IT IN WRITING. (Allied Artists-1964-Andrew
Stone). An original screenplay by Andrew Stone. (Q, FF,
W).

2074 NEVER TOO LATE. (Warner Bros.-1965-Bud Yorkin). A
screenplay by Sumner Arthur Long, based on the play by Mr.
Long; Samuel French, 1963, 111p. (NYTFR, LC, W, AMPAS,
LACOPL, Q).

2075 THE NEW CENTURIONS. (Columbia-1972-Richard Fleischer).
A screenplay by Stirling Silliphant, based on the novel by
Joseph Wambaugh; Little Brown & Co., 1970, 376p. (W, Q,
LACOPL).

2075a THE NEW INTERNS. (Columbia-1964-John Rich). A screen-
play by Wilton Schiller, based upon characters from the novel
The Interns by Richard Frede, Random House, 1960.
(LACOPL, FF, NYTFR, W, Q).

2076 THE NEW LAND. (Warner Bros.-1973-Jan Troell). A
screenplay by Bengt Forslund and Jan Troell, from the novel
by Vilhelm Moberg, Unto a Good Land; Simon & Schuster,
1954. (See also The Emigrants). (W, LACOPL, Q).

2077 A NEW LEAF. (Paramount-1971-Elaine May). A screenplay
by Elaine May, based on the short story by Jack Ritchie,
"The Green Heart." (W, Q).

2078 THE NEW LIFE STYLE. (Dot-1970-Jerry Macc and Peter
Savage). A screenplay by Jurgen Knop, Jerry Macc, and
Peter Savage. (W).

2079 THE NEW YORK EXPERIENCE. (Trans-Lux-1973-Rusty Russell). Script written by Rusty Russell. (W).

2080 THE NEWCOMERS. (Ander-1972-William Logan). An original work for the screen by William Logan. (W).

2081 THE NEWCOMERS. (Melody-1973-Louis Su). No author
credit. (W).

2082 NEWMAN'S LAW. (Universal-1974-Richard Heffron). An
original screenplay by Anthony Wilson. (V).

2083 NEXT. (Maron-Gemini-1971-Luciano Martino). A screenplay
by Eduardo M. Borchero, Ernesto Gastaldi, and Vittorio
Caronia. (W).

2084 A NICE GIRL LIKE ME. (AVCO Embassy-1969-Desmond
Davis). A screenplay by Anne Piper and Desmond Davis,
based on the novel Marry at Leisure by Anne Piper; Norton
1959. (W, AMPAS, LACOPL, Q).

2085   NICHOLAS AND ALEXANDRA. (Columbia-1971-Franklin J.
        Schaffner). A screenplay by James Goldman, from the book
        by Robert K. Massie; Atheneum, 1967, 584p. (W, LACOPL,
        Q).

2086   THE NICKEL RIDE. (20th Century-Fox-1974-Robert Mulli-
        gan). An original screenplay by Eric Roth. A novel based
        on the screenplay was written by Michael T. Kaufman;
        Award Books, 1974, 171p. (V, LACOPL).

2087   THE NIGHT BEFORE. (Hand-in-Hand-1973-Arch Brown).
        An original work by Arch and Bruce Brown. (W).

2088   NIGHT CALL NURSES. (New World-1972-Jonathan Kaplan).
        An original screenplay by George Armitage. (FF).

2089   THE NIGHT DIGGER. (MGM-1971-Alastair Reid). A screen-
        play by Roald Dahl, based on a novel Nest in a Falling Tree
        by Joy Crowley. (W, Q).

2089a   NIGHT ENCOUNTER. (Shawn International-1964-Robert Hos-
        sein). A screenplay by Robert Hossein, Louis Martin, and
        Alan Poire, based on a story by Robert Hossein. (FF).

2090   THE NIGHT EVELYN CAME OUT OF THE GRAVE. (Phase
        One-1972-Emilio P. Miraglia). An original screenplay by
        Fabio Pittoru, Massimo Felisatti, and Emilio P. Miraglia.
        (W).

2091   NIGHT GAMES. (Sandrews-1966-Mai Zetterling). A screen-
        play by Mai Zetterling and David Hughes, based on the novel
        by Mai Zetterling. (FF, NYTFR, W, AMPAS, Q).

2091a   NIGHT MUST FALL. (MGM-1964-Karel Reisz). A screen-
        play by Clive Exton, based on the play by Emlyn Williams;
        Random House, 1936, 144p. (Q, LACOPL, FF, NYTFR).

2092   NIGHT OF DARK SHADOWS. (MGM-1971-Dan Curtis). An
        original screenplay by Sam Hall, based on a story by Sam
        Hall and Dan Curtis. (W).

2093   NIGHT OF THE COBRA WOMAN. (New World-1972-Andrew
        Meyer). An original screenplay by Andrew Meyer and Kerry
        Magness. (FF, V).

        NIGHT OF THE EXECUTIONER see THE COP

2094   NIGHT OF THE FOLLOWING DAY. (Universal-1969-Hubert
        Cornfield). A screenplay by Hubert Cornfield and Robert
        Phippeny, based on the novel The Snatchers by Lionel White.
        (Q, FF, W, AMPAS).

2095   THE NIGHT OF THE GENERALS. (Columbia-1967-Anatole

Litvak). A screenplay by Joseph Kessel and Paul Dehn,
based on the novel by Hans Helmut Kirst; Harper, 1963, and
on an incident written about by James Hadley Chase. (FF,
NYTFR, Q, W, LC, AMPAS, LACOPL).

2096 THE NIGHT OF THE GRIZZLY. (Paramount-1966-Joseph
      Pevney). A screenplay by Warren Douglas. (FF, LC, W,
      AMPAS).

2096a THE NIGHT OF THE IGUANA. (MGM-1964-John Huston).
      A screenplay by Anthony Veiller and John Huston, based on
      the play by Tennessee Williams; New Directions, 1961, 128p.
      (AMPAS, W, NYTFR, LACOPL, FF).

2097 NIGHT OF THE LEPUS. (MGM-1972-William F. Claxton).
      A screenplay by Don Holliday and Gene R. Kearney, based
      on the novel Year of the Angry Rabbit by Russell Braddon;
      Norton, 1964. (W, Q, FF, LACOPL).

2098 NIGHT OF THE LIVING DEAD. (Continental-1968-George A.
      Romero). An original screenplay by John A. Russo. (FF,
      NYTFR, W, Q).

2099 THE NIGHT OF THE SCARECROW. (1974-Sergio Ricardo).
      A screenplay by Sergio Ricardo, Maurice Capovilla, Jean-
      Claude Bernadet, Plineo Pacheco, Nilson Barbosa. (V).

2100 THE NIGHT OF THE SEAGULL. (Toho-1970-Katsumi Iwau-
      chi). A screenplay by Mitsura Majima and Katsumi Iwauchi,
      from a novel Mermaid by Matsutaro Kawaguchi. (W).

2101 THE NIGHT PORTER. (United Artists-1974-Liliana Cavani).
      A screenplay written directly for the screen by Liliana Ca-
      vani and Italo Moscati. (V, NYT).

2102 THE NIGHT THEY RAIDED MINSKY'S. (United Artists-1968-
      William Friedkin). A screenplay by Arnold Schulman and
      Sidney Michaels and Norman Lear, based on the book by Row-
      land Barber; Simon & Schuster, 1960, 351p. (FF, NYTFR,
      FM, W, LC, Q, AMPAS, LACOPL).

2103 NIGHT TRAIN TO MUNDO FINE. (Hollywood Star-1966-Cole-
      man Francis). An original screenplay by Coleman Francis.
      (W).

2103a NIGHT TRAIN TO PARIS. (20th Century-Fox-1964-Robert
      Douglas). An original screenplay written by Henry Cross.
      (AMPAS, W, Q, FF, NYTFR, LC).

2104 THE NIGHT VISITOR. (UMC-1971-Laslo Benedek). A screen-
      play by Guy Elmes, from a story by Samuel Rosecca. (W).

2105 THE NIGHT WALKER. (Universal-1965-William Castle). A

screenplay by Robert Bloch, based upon "Witches' Friday,"
a story and screenplay by Elizabeth Kata. (FF, NYTFR,
LC W, AMPAS, Q).

2105a THE NIGHT WATCH. (Consort/Orion-1964-Jacques Becker).
A screenplay by Jacques Becker, Jose Giovanni, Jean Aurel,
based on the novel by Jose Giovanni, Le Trou. (NYTFR,
FF).

2106 NIGHT WATCH. (AVCO Embassy-1973-Brian G. Hutton). A
screen play by Tony Williamson, with additional dialogue by
Evan Jones, based upon a play by Lucille Fletcher; Random
House, 1972, 113p. (W, LACOPL, Q).

2107 THE NIGHTCOMERS. (AVCO Embassy-1972-Michael Winner).
A screenplay by Michael Hastings, based on the characters
from The Turn of the Screw by Henry James; Norton, 1966.
(FF, LACOPL, Q).

2107a NIGHTMARE. (Universal-1964-Freddie Francis). A screenplay written directly for the screen by Jimmy Sangster. (FF,
NYTFR, Q, W).

2108 NIGHTMARE CASTLE. (Allied Artists-1967-Allan Grunewald
aka Mario Caiano). An original story and screenplay by
Mario Caiano and Fabio De Agostini. (FF, Q).

2109 NIGHTMARE IN THE SUN. (Zodiac-States Rights-1965-Marc
Lawrence). A screenplay by Ted Thomas, Fanya Lawrence,
based on a story by Marc Lawrence and George Fass. (W,
AMPAS, Q).

2109a NINE DAYS OF ONE YEAR. (Artkino-1964-Mikhail Romm).
Mikhail Romm wrote this original screenplay. (FF).

2110 THE NINE LIVES OF FRITZ THE CAT. (American Interna-
tional-1974-Robert Taylor). An original screenplay by Fred
Halliday, Eric Monte, and Robert Taylor. (V).

2111 1900. (Paramount-1974-Bernardo Bertolucci). A screenplay
by Bernardo Bertolucci, Franco Arcalli and Giuseppe Bertolucci. (HR).

2112 90 DEGREES IN THE SHADE. (Landau-Unger-1966-Jiri
Weiss). A screenplay by David Mercer, based on an origi-
nal story by Jiri Weiss and Jiri Mucha. (FF, NYTFR, W,
Q).

2113 99 AND 44/100% DEAD. (20th Century-Fox-1974-John
Frankenheimer). Robert Dillon wrote this original screen-
play. A novel, based upon the screenplay, was written by
Max Franklin; Award Books, 1974, 157p. (V, LACOPL).

2114   99 WOMEN. (Commonwealth United-1969-Jesus Franco). An
original screenplay by Peter Welbeck, Carlo Fadda, Millo
Cuccia, and Jesus Franco. (FF, W, Q).

2115   NO BLADE OF GRASS. (MGM-1970-Cornel Wilde). A
screenplay by Sean Forestal, and Jefferson Pascal, based upon the novel by John Christopher, 1956. (W, LACOPL, Q).

2116   NO DRUMS, NO BUGLES. (Cinerama-1971-Clyde Ware). An
original screenplay by Clyde Ware. (FF, W, Q).

2117   NO MORE EXCUSES. (Rogosin-1968-Robert Downey). An
original screenplay by Robert Downey. (FF, NYTFR, W, Q).

2117a   NO, MY DARLING DAUGHTER! (Zenith International-1964-
Ralph Thomas). Screenplay by Frank Harvey is based on the
play Handful of Tansy by Harold Brooke and Kay Bannerman.
(NYTFR, FF, W, Q).

2118   NO WAY TO TREAT A LADY. (Paramount-1968-Jack Smight).
A screenplay by John Gay, based on the novel by William
Goldman; Harcourt, 1964. (Q, FF, NYTFR, FM, W, LC,
AMPAS, LACOPL).

2119   NOBODY WAVED GOODBYE. (Cinema V-1965-Eldon Rath-
burn). An original screenplay by Don Owen. (FF, LC, W,
Q).

2120   NOBODY'S PERFECT. (Universal-1968-Alan Rafkin). A
screenplay by John D. F. Black, based on the novel The
Crows of Edwina Hill by Allan R. Bosworth. (FF, FM,
NYTFR, W, LC, AMPAS, Q).

A NOITE DO ESPANTALHO see THE NIGHT OF THE
SCARECROW

2121   NONE BUT THE BRAVE. (Warner Bros.-1965-Frank Sinatra).
A screenplay by John Twist and Katsuya Susaki, from a story
by Kikumaru Okuda. (FF, LC, W, AMPAS, Q).

2122   NORWOOD. (Paramount-1970-Jack Haley, Jr.). A screenplay by Marguerite Roberts, based on the novel by Charles
Portis; Simon & Schuster, 1966. (W, LACOPL, Q).

2123   NOT MINE TO LOVE. (Edward Meadows-1969-Uri Zohar).
A work for the screen written by Uri Zohar, based on a
story by A. B. Yehoshua. (FF, Q).

2124   NOT ON YOUR LIFE. (Pathe Contemporary-1965-Luis Berlanga). A screenplay by Luis Berlanga, Rafael Azcona, and
Ennio Flaiano. (FF, W, AMPAS, Q).

2125   NOT WITH MY WIFE, YOU DON'T! (Warner Bros.-1966-

Norman Panama).   A screenplay by Norman Panama, Larry Gelbart, and Peter Barnes, from a story by Norman Panama and Melvin Frank.   (FF, NYTFR, LC, W, AMPAS, Q).

2125a NOTHING BUT THE BEST.   (Royal-1964-Clive Donner).   A screenplay by Frederic Raphael, based on a short story by Stanley Ellin.   (NYTFR, FF, W, Q).

2126   NOW YOU SEE HIM, NOW YOU DON'T.   (Buena Vista-1972-Robert Butler).   A screenplay by Joseph L. McEveety, based on a story by Robert L. King.   (FF, Q).

2127   THE NUDE RESTAURANT.   (Andy Warhol-1967-Andy Warhol). An original work for the screen by Andy Warhol.   (FF, NYTFR, W, AMPAS).

2128   NO. 96.   (Ash-Harmon and 0-10 Network-1974-Peter Bernados).   An original screenplay by David Sale and Johnny Whyte, based on the Australian television series.   (V).

2129   NUMBER ONE.   (United Artists-1969-Tom Gries).   An original screenplay by David Moessinger.   (FF, W, LC, AMPAS, Q).

2130   THE NUN.   (Altura-1971-Jacques Rivette).   A screenplay by Jean Gruault and Jacques Rivette, based on the novel La Religieuse by Denis Diderot, in Oeuvres Romanesques; Libraires Associés, 1964, 793p.   (W, LACOPL).

2131   A NUN AT THE CROSSROADS.   (Universal-1970-Julio Buchs). A screenplay by Federico de Urrutia, Manuel Sebares, Victor Auz, Jose L. H. Marcos, and Julio Buchs, from a story by Jose Frade.   (W, Q).

2132   O LUCKY MAN!   (Warner Bros.-1973-Lindsay Anderson).   A screenplay by David Sherwin, based on an idea by Malcolm McDowell.   (W, Q).

2133   OSS 117--MISSION FOR A KILLER.   (Embassy-1966-André Hunebelle).   A screenplay by Jean Halain, Pierre Foucaud, and André Hunebelle, based on the novel Le Dernier Quart d'Heure (The Last Quarter Hour) by Jean Bruce.   (FF, W, AMPAS, Q).

2134   THE OBLONG BOX.   (American International-1969-Gordon Hessler).   A screenplay by Lawrence Huntingdon, based on the story by Edgar Allan Poe, in Complete Stories and Poems; Doubleday, 1966.   (FF, W, LC, LACOPL, Q).

2135   OBSESSION.   (O. R. P. Company-1968-Gunnar Hoglund).   A screenplay by Bosse Gustafson and Gunnar Hoglund, based on the novel by Bosse Gustafson.   (FF, NYTFR, W).

2136   THE ODD COUPLE. (Paramount-1968-Gene Saks). A
        screenplay by Neil Simon, based on his play; Random House,
        1966, 116p. (Q, FF, NYTFR, FM, W, LC, AMPAS,
        LACOPL).

2137   THE ODESSA FILE. (Columbia-1974-Ronald Neame). A
        screenplay by Kenneth Ross, and George Markstein, based
        on the novel by Frederick Forsyth; Viking, 1972, 337p. (V,
        HR, LACOPL).

2137a   OEDIPUS THE KING. (Universal-1968-Philip Saville). A
        work written for the screen by Michael Luke and Philip Sa-
        ville, based on the play by Sophocles as translated from the
        Greek by Paul Roche; Prentice-Hall, 1970, 178p. (FF,
        NYTFR, FM, W, LACOPL, Q).

2138   OF HUMAN BONDAGE. (MGM-1964-Ken Hughes). A screen-
        play by Bryan Forbes, based on the novel by W. Somerset
        Maugham; Washington Square Press, 1950. (LACOPL,
        NYTFR, LC, Q, W, AMPAS, FF).

2138a   OF WAYWARD LOVE. (Pathe Contemporary-1964-Sergio Sol-
        lima, Alberto Bonucci, Nino Manfredi). "The Women," a
        screenplay written by Piero Continenza and Gino Scola,
        adapted from a story by Ercole Patti; "The Serpent," by Ugo
        Carpi, Ricci Santangelo and Enzo Mainardi, adapted from a
        story by Mario Soldati; "The Soldier" by Nino Manfredi, Ugo
        Carpi and Gino Scola, adapted from a story by Italo Calvino.
        (FF, NYTFR).

2139   THE OFFENSE. (United Artists-1973-Sidney Lumet). An
        original screenplay by John Hopkins. (W, Q).

2140   THE OFFICE PICNIC. (Tom Cowan-1974-Tom Cowan). An
        original screenplay by Tom Cowan. (V).

2141   OII! CALCUTTA! (Cinemation-1972-Jacques Levy). A
        screenplay by Kenneth Tynan, Jules Feiffer, Dan Greenburg,
        John Lennon, David Newman, and Robert Benton; Grove
        Press, 1969, 190p. (W, FF, LACOPL).

2142   OH DAD, POOR DAD, MAMA'S HUNG YOU IN THE CLOSET
        AND I'M FEELIN' SO SAD. (Paramount-1967-Richard Quine).
        A screenplay by Ian Bernard, based on the play by Arthur L.
        Kopit; Hill and Wang, 1960, 89p. (Q, FF, NYTFR, FM, W,
        LC, AMPAS, LACOPL).

2143   OH! THOSE MOST SECRET AGENTS! (Allied Artists-1966-
        Lucio Fulci). A screenplay by Vittorio Metz, Lucio Fulci,
        and Z. Sollazzo. (FF).

2144   OH! WHAT A LOVELY WAR. (Paramount-1969-Richard At-
        tenborough). A screenplay by Len Deighton (uncredited),

based on the musical play by Joan Littlewood/ Theatre Work-
shop. (Q, W, LC, AMPAS, FF).

2145   OHAYO. (Shochiku Films of America-1966-Yasujiro Ozu). A
       screenplay by Kogo Noda and Yasujiro Ozu. (FF, W, Q).

2146   OKAY BILL. (Four Star Excelsior-1971-John Avildsen). An
       original screenplay by John Avildsen. (W).

2147   OKLAHOMA CRUDE. (Columbia-1973-Stanley Kramer). A
       screenplay by Marc Norman, from his novel; Dutton, 1973,
       251p. (W, Q, LACOPL).

2148   THE OLDEST PROFESSION. (VIP-1968-Franco Indovina,
       Mauro Bolognini, Philippe De Broca, Michael Pfleghar, Claude
       Autant-Lara, and Jean-Luc Godard). A screenplay written
       directly for the screen by Ennio Flaiano ("Prehistoric Times"),
       Daniel Boulanger ("Mademoiselle Mimi"), Ennio Flaiano ("Ro-
       man Nights"), Georges and Andre Tabet ("The Gay Nineties"),
       Jean Aurenche ("Present Day"), and Jean-Luc Godard ("Antici-
       pation"). (FF, NYTFR, W, LC, AMPAS).

2149   THE OLIVE TREES OF JUSTICE. (Pathe Contemporary-1967-
       James Blue). A screenplay by Jean Pelegri, Sylvain Dhome,
       and James Blue, from the novel by Jean Pelegri. (NYTFR).

2150   OLIVER! (Columbia-1968-Carol Reed). A screenplay by Ver-
       non Harris, based on the musical play by Lionel Bart, Hollis
       Music Co., 1960, 142p.; as adapted from the novel Oliver
       Twist by Charles Dickens; Dodd, Mead & Co., 1941. (Q,
       FF, NYTFR, W, LC, AMPAS, LACOPL).

2151   THE OMEGA MAN. (Warner Bros.-1971-Boris Sagal). A
       screenplay by John William, Joyce H. Corrington, from a nov-
       el by Richard Matheson. (W, Q).

2152   ON A CLEAR DAY YOU CAN SEE FOREVER. (Paramount-
       1970-Vincente Minnelli). A screenplay with lyrics by Alan Jay
       Lerner, based on a musical play of the same name by Lerner
       and Burton Lane; Random House, 1966, 115p. (W, LACOPL,
       Q).

       ON ANY STREET   see   BAD GIRLS DON'T CRY

2153   ON HER BED OF ROSES. (Famous Players Corporation-1966-
       Albert Zugsmith). A screenplay by Albert Zugsmith. (FF,
       LC).

2154   ON HER MAJESTY'S SECRET SERVICE. (United Artists-
       1969-Peter Hunt). A screenplay by Richard Maibaum, based
       on a novel by Ian Fleming; New American Library, 1963. (W,
       AMPAS, LACOPL, Q).

2155   ON MY WAY TO THE CRUSADES, I MET A GIRL WHO...
       (Warner Bros. -7 Arts-1969-Pasquale Festa Campanile).   A
       screenplay by Luigi Magni and Larry Gelbart.   (W, AMPAS,
       Q).

2156   ONCE A THIEF.   (MGM-1965-Ralph Nelson).   A screenplay
       by Zekial Marko, from his novel.   (NYTFR, LC, W, AMPAS,
       Q).

2157   ONCE BEFORE I DIE.   (Goldstone Film Enterprises-1966-
       John Derek).   A screenplay by Vance Skarstedt.   (FF, W,
       AMPAS).

2158   ONCE UPON A SCOUNDREL.   (Carlyle Films-1974-George
       Shaefer).   A screenplay by Rip Van Ronkel.   (HR).

2159   ONCE UPON A TIME IN THE WEST.   (Paramount-1969-
       Sergio Leone).   A screenplay by Sergio Leone and Sergio Do-
       nati, based on a story by Dario Argento and Bernardo Berto-
       lucci and Sergio Leone.   (FF, W, LC, Q).

2160   ONCE YOU KISS A STRANGER.   (Warner Bros. -7 Arts-1969-
       Robert Sparr).   A screenplay by Frank Tarloff and Norman
       Katkov, based on a novel by Patricia Highsmith.   (W,
       AMPAS, Q).

2161   THE ONE AND ONLY, GENUINE, ORIGINAL FAMILY BAND.
       (Buena Vista-1968-Michael O'Herlihy).   A screenplay by Low-
       ell S. Hawley, based on the autobiography Nebraska 1888, by
       Laura Bower Van Nuys.   (FF, NYTFR, W, LC, AMPAS, Q).

2162   ONE BRIEF SUMMER.   (Cinevision-1972-John MacKenzie).   A
       screenplay by Wendy Marshall, based on a story by Harry
       Tierney and Guido Coen, suggested by the play Valkyrie's
       Armour by Harry Tierney.   (FF).

2163   ONE BY ONE.   (Trans-International-1974-Claude DuBoc).   A
       narrative written by John Crowley.   (HR).

2164   ONE DAY IN THE LIFE OF IVAN DENISOVICH.   (Cinerama-
       1971-Casper Wrede).   Ronald Harwood wrote the screenplay,
       based on a novel by Alexander Solzhenitsyn; Praeger, 1963.
       (FF, LACOPL).

2165   THE ONE-EYED SOLDIERS.   (United Screen Arts-1967-Jean
       Christophe).   A screenplay by Jean Christophe, based on an
       original story by Richard Frank.   (FF).

2166   100 RIFLES.   (20th Century-Fox-1969-Tom Gries).   A screen-
       play by Clair Huffaker and Tom Gries, based on a novel by
       Robert MacLeod.   (FF, LC, AMPAS, Q).

2167   ONE IS A LONELY NUMBER.   (MGM-1972-Mel Stuart).   A

screenplay by David Seltzer, based on a <u>New Yorker</u> short
story, "The Good Humor Man" by Rebecca Morris. (FF).

2168   ONE LITTLE INDIAN. (Buena Vista-1973-Bernard McEveety).
       A screenplay written directly for the screen by Harry Spald-
       ing. (W, Q).

2168a ONE MAN'S WAY. (United Artists-1964-Denis Sanders). A
       screenplay by Eleanore Griffin and John W. Bloch, based on
       the book <u>Minister to Millions</u> by Arthur Gordon. (NYTFR, W,
       Q, LC, AMPAS, FF).

2169 $1,000,000 DUCK. (Buena Vista-1971-Vincent McEveety).
       A screenplay by Roswell Rogers, based on a story by Ted
       Key. (W, Q).

2170   ONE MILLION YEARS B.C. (20th Century-Fox-1967-Don
       Chaffey). A screenplay by Michael Carreras, based on an
       original story by Mickell Novak, George Baker, and Joseph
       Frickert. (FF, NYTFR, FM, W, LC, AMPAS, Q).

2171   ONE MORE TIME. (United Artists-1970-Jerry Lewis). A
       screenplay written directly for the screen by Michael Pert-
       wee. (W, Q).

2172   ONE MORE TRAIN TO ROB. (Universal-1971-Andrew V.
       McLaglen). A screenplay by Don Tait, and Dick Nelson,
       from a story by William Roberts. (W, Q).

2173   ONE NIGHT AT DINNER. (International-1971-Giuseppe Pa-
       troni Griffi). A screenplay by Dario Argento and Giuseppe
       Patroni Griffi, based on a play by Giuseppe Patroni Griffi.
       (W).

2174   ONE OF OUR SPIES IS MISSING. (1966-E. Darrell Hallen-
       beck). An original screenplay by Howard Rodman, from a
       story by Henry Slesar. (W).

2175   ONE ON TOP OF THE OTHER. (GGP-1973-Lucio Fulci).
       An original screenplay by Lucio Fulci and Robert Gianviti.
       (W).

2175a ONE POTATO, TWO POTATO. (Cinema V-1964-Larry
       Peerce). A screenplay written by Raphael Hayes and Orville
       H. Hampton, from a story by Orville H. Hampton. (NYTFR,
       W, Q, LC, AMPAS, FF).

2176   ONE SPY TOO MANY. (MGM-1966-Joseph Sargent). A
       screenplay by Dean Hargrove. (FF, NYTFR, W, Q).

2177   1,000 CONVICTS AND A WOMAN. (American International-
       1971-Ray Austin). A screenplay by Oscar Brodney. (FF,
       W, Q).

2178   1001 DANISH DELIGHTS.   (Cambist-1973-Svend Methling).
       An original screenplay written by Bob Ramsing.   (W).

2179   ONE WAY PENDULUM.   (Lopert-1965-Peter Yates).   A
       screenplay by N. F. Simpson, based on his play; Grove
       Press, 1960, 93p.   (FF, W, LACOPL, Q).

2180   ONE WAY WAHINI.   (Allied Artists-1965-William O. Brown).
       A screenplay written by Rod Larson.   (W).

2181   THE ONLY GAME IN TOWN.   (20th Century-Fox-1970-George
       Stevens).   A screenplay by Frank D. Gilroy, from his play;
       Random House, 1968, 105p.   (W, LACOPL, Q).

2182   ONLY THE WIND.   (Casino-1965-Fritz Umgelter).   A screen-
       play by Kurt Nachmann and H. O. Schroeder.   (W).

2183   THE ONLY WAY HOME.   (Regional-1972-G. D. Spradlin).
       An original screenplay by Jeeds O'Tilbury.   (W).

2184   ONLY WHEN I LARF.   (Paramount-1968-Basil Dearden).   A
       screenplay by John Salmon, based on the novel by Len Deigh-
       ton; Michael Joseph, 1967, 233p.   (Q, FF, NYTFR, FM, W,
       LACOPL).

2185   ONLY YOU KNOW, AND I KNOW.   (Shoeshine-1971-Alan Rus-
       kin).   A screenplay written directly for the screen by Alan
       Ruskin.   (W).

2186   OPEN SEASON.   (Columbia-1974-Peter Collinson).   A screen-
       play by David Osborn and Liz Charles-Williams.   A noveliza-
       tion based upon the screenplay was written by David Osborn;
       Dell, 1974, 251p.   (V, LACOPL).

2186a OPEN THE DOOR AND SEE ALL THE PEOPLE.   (Noel-
       1964-Jerome Hill).   A screenplay by Jerome Hill.   (FF,
       NYTFR).

2187   OPERATION C. I. A.   (Allied Artists-1965-Christian Nyby).
       A screenplay written by Peer J. Oppenheimer and Bill S.
       Ballinger.   (W, AMPAS, Q).

2188   OPERATION CROSSBOW.   (MGM-1965-Michael Anderson).   A
       screenplay by Richard Imrie, Derry Quinn, and Ray Rigby,
       based on a story by Duilio Coletti and Vittoriano Petrilli.
       (FF, LC, W, AMPAS, Q).

2189   OPERATION KID BROTHER.   (United Artists-1967-Alberto
       De Martino).   An original screenplay by Paul Levy and
       Frank Walker.   (FF, FM, NYTFR, W, AMPAS, Q).

2190   OPERATION LEONTINE.   (Macmillan Audio Brandon-1973-
       Michel Audiard).   An original screenplay by Michel Audiard.
       (W).

2191   OPERATION SNAFU.   (American International-1965-Cyril
        Frankel).   A screenplay by Harold Buchman, from the novel
        Stop at a Winner by R. F. Delderfield.   (NYTFR, LC,
        AMPAS, Q).

2192   OPHELIA.   (New Line Cinema-1974-Claude Chabrol).   An
        original screenplay by Claude Chabrol and Martial Matthieu.
        (HR).

2193   THE OPTIMISTS.   (Paramount-1973-Anthony Simmons and
        Tudor Gates).   A screenplay by Anthony Simmons, Tudor
        Gates, based on the novel The Optimists of Nine Elms by
        Anthony Simmons.   (W).

2194   THE ORGANIZATION.   (United Artists-1971-Don Medford).
        A screenplay by James R. Webb, based on characters cre-
        ated by John Ball.   (See IN THE HEAT OF THE NIGHT).
        (W, Q).

2195   THE ORGANIZER.   (Continental-1964-Mario Monicelli).   Story
        and screenplay by Age, Scarpelli, and Mario Monicelli.   (FF,
        NYTFR).

2196   THE OSCAR.   (Embassy-1966-Russell Rouse).   A screenplay
        by Harlan Ellison, Russell Rouse and Clarence Greene, based
        on the novel by Richard Sale; Simon & Schuster, 1963.   (FF,
        NYTFR, W, AMPAS, LACOPL, Q).

2197   OTHELLO.   (Warner Bros.-1966-Stuart Burge).   A production
        staged by John Dexter, from the play by William Shakespeare.
        (FF, NYTFR, LC, W, AMPAS, LACOPL, Q).

2198   THE OTHER.   (20th Century-Fox-1972-Robert Mulligan).   A
        screenplay by Tom Tryon, from his novel; Knopf, 1971, 280p.
        (W, LACOPL).

2199   THE OTHER ONE.   (Continental-1967-Rene Allio).   An origi-
        nal screenplay by Rene Allio.   (NYTFR).

2200   THE OTHER SIDE OF JOEY.   (Jaguar-1972-Gorton Hall and
        Roger Marks).   An original story & screenplay by Gorton
        Hall.   (W).

2201   OTHON.   (1971-Jean-Marie Straub and Daniele Huillet).   An
        original screenplay by Jean-Marie Straub and Daniele Huillet.
        (W).

2202   OTLEY.   (Columbia-1969-Dick Clement).   A screenplay by
        Ian La Frenais and Dick Clement, based on the novel by Mar-
        tin Waddell; Stein & Day, 1966.   (FF, W, LC, AMPAS,
        LACOPL, Q).

2203   OUR MAN FLINT.   (20th Century-Fox-1966-Daniel Mann).   A

screenplay by Hal Fimberg and Ben Starr, based on a story
by Hal Fimberg. (FF, NYTFR, LC, W, AMPAS, Q).

2204   OUR MOTHER'S HOUSE. (MGM-1967-Jack Clayton). A
       screenplay by Jeremy Brooks and Haya Harareet, based on
       the novel by Julian Gloag; Simon & Schuster, 1963. (Q, FF,
       NYTFR, FM, W, LC, AMPAS, LACOPL).

2205   OUR TIME. (Warner Bros.-1974-Peter Hyams). A screen-
       play by Jane C. Stanton. A novel based on the screenplay
       was written by Alexander Edwards; Warner Paperback Li-
       brary, 1974. (HR, V, LACOPL).

2206   OUT OF IT. (United Artists-1969-Paul Williams). An origi-
       nal screenplay by Paul Williams. (W, Q).

2207   OUT OF SIGHT. (Universal-1966-Lennie Weinrib). A
       screenplay by Larry Hovis, from a story by Dave Asher and
       Larry Hovis. (FF, LC, W, AMPAS, Q).

2208   THE OUT-OF-TOWNERS. (Paramount-1970-Arthur Hiller).
       An original screenplay by Neil Simon. (W, Q).

2209   OUT ONE SPECTRE. (Sunchild-1974-Jacques Rivette). A
       screenplay by Jacques Rivette, based on stories by Honore
       de Balzac. (V).

2210   OUTBACK. (United Artists-1972-Ted Kotcheff). A screen-
       play by Evan Jones, based on the novel Wake in Fright by
       Kenneth Cook; St. Martin's, 1961. (W, LACOPL, Q).

2211   THE OUTFIT. (MGM-1973-John Flynn). A screenplay by
       John Flynn, based on a novel by Richard Stark. (W).

2212   THE OUTLAWS IS COMING. (Columbia-1965-Norman Maur-
       er). Elwood Ullman wrote the screenplay based on a story
       by Norman Maurer. (FF, LC, W, AMPAS, Q).

2213   THE OUTRAGE. (MGM-1964-Martin Ritt). A screenplay by
       Michael Kanin, based on the Japanese Daiel film Rashomon by
       Akira Kurosawa, Grove Press, 1969, 255p.; from stories by
       Ryunosuke Akutagawa, Livewright, 1952; and the play Ra-
       shomon by Fay and Michael Kanin, Random House, 1959,
       76p. (LACOPL, FF, W, Q, NYTFR, AMPAS, LC).

2214   OUTSIDE IN. (Robbins International-1972-G. D. Spradlin).
       An original screenplay by Jeeds O'Tilbury. (W, Q).

2215   THE OUTSIDE MAN. (United Artists-1973-Jacques Deray).
       A screenplay by Jean-Claude Carrière, Jacques Deray, Ian
       McLellan Hunter, from a story by Jean-Claude Carrière and
       Jacques Deray. (W).

2216   THE OVERCOAT. (Cinemasters International-1965-Aleksei Batalov). A screenplay by L. Solovyov, based on the story by Nicolai Gogol; Norton, 1965. (FF, W, LACOPL, Q).

2217   THE OWL AND THE PUSSYCAT. (Columbia-1970-Herbert Ross). A screenplay by Buck Henry, based on a play by Bill Manhoff; Doubleday, 1965, 134p. (W, LACOPL, Q).

2218   P. J. (Universal-1968-John Guillermin). A screenplay by Philip Reisman, Jr., based on a story by Philip Reisman, Jr., and Edward J. Montagne. (FF, NYTFR, FM, W, AMPAS, Q).

2219   THE P.O.W. (Dossick-1973-Phillip H. Dossick). An original screenplay by Phillip H. Dossick. (W).

2220   PACIFIC VIBRATIONS. (American International-1971-John Severson). A documentary, no screen writing credits. (W, Q).

2221   THE PAD (AND HOW TO USE IT). (Universal-1966-Brian G. Hutton). A screenplay by Thomas C. Ryan and Ben Starr, based on the play The Private Ear by Peter Shaffer; Stein, 1964, 120p. (FF, LC, NYTFR, W, AMPAS, LACOPL, Q).

2222   PADDY. (Allied Artists-1970-Daniel Haller). A screenplay by Lee Dunne, from his novel Goodbye to the Hill; Houghton 1965. (W, LACOPL, Q).

2223   PAINT YOUR WAGON. (Paramount-1969-Joshua Logan). A screenplay by Alan Jay Lerner, adaptation by Paddy Chayefsky; Coward, 1952, 140p. (W, AMPAS, LACOPL, Q).

2223a   A PAIR OF BRIEFS. (Davis-1964-Ralph Thomas). A screenplay by Nicholas Phipps, based on the play How Say You? by Harold Brooke and Kay Bannerman. (NYTFR, FF).

2224   PAMELA, PAMELA YOU ARE ... (Distribpix Inc.-1968-William L. Rose). A screenplay and story by William L. Rose and Richard B. Shull. (FF, NYTFR, W).

2225   THE PANIC IN NEEDLE PARK. (20th Century-Fox-1971-Jerry Schatzberg). A screenplay by Joan Didion and John Gregory Dunne, based on a book by James Mills; Farrar, 1966. (W, LACOPL, Q).

2226   PANIC IN THE CITY. (Commonwealth United Entertainment-1968-Eddie Davis). An original screenplay by Eddie Davis and Charles E. Savage. (FF, W, AMPAS).

2227   PAPER CHASE. (20th Century-Fox-1973-James Bridges). A screenplay by James Bridges, based on a novel by John Jay Osborn, Jr.; Houghton, 1971, 181p. (W, LACOPL).

2228   PAPER LION. (United Artists-1968-Alex March). A screen-
play by Lawrence Roman, based on the book by George
Plimpton; Harper, 1966, 362p. (Q, FF, NYTFR, FM, W,
LC, AMPAS, LACOPL).

2229   PAPER MOON. (Paramount-1973-Peter Bogdanovich). A
screenplay by Alvin Sargent, based on the novel Addie Pray
by Joe David Brown; Simon & Schuster, 1971, 313p. (W,
LACOPL, FF, Q).

2230   PAPILLON. (Allied Artists-1973-Franklin J. Schaffner). A
screenplay written by Dalton Trumbo and Lorenzo Semple,
Jr., based on a book by Henri Charrière; Morrow, 1970,
434p. (W, LACOPL).

2231   PARADES. (Cinerama-1972-Robert J. Siegel). An original
work for the screen by George Tabori. (FF).

2232   PARADISE, HAWAIIAN STYLE. (Paramount-1966-Michael
Moore). A screenplay by Allan Weiss and Anthony Lawrence,
from an original story by Allan Weiss. (FF, LC, W,
AMPAS, Q).

2233   THE PARALLAX VIEW. (Paramount-1974-Alan J. Pakula).
A screenplay authored by David Giler and Lorenzo Semple,
Jr., based on the novel by Loren Singer; Doubleday, 1970,
185p. (V, LACOPL, W).

2234   PARANOIA. (Commonwealth United-1969-Umberto Lenzi). A
screenplay by Ugo Moretti, Marie Claire Solleville and Umberto Lenzi, based on a story by Umberto Lenzi. (FF, W,
Q).

PARDON ME, BUT YOUR TEETH ARE IN MY NECK see
THE FEARLESS VAMPIRE KILLERS

2235   PARIS IN THE MONTH OF AUGUST. (Trans-Lux-1968-Pi-
erre Granier-Deferre). A screenplay by R. M. Arland and
Pierre Granier-Deferre, based upon a novel by René Fallet.
(FF, NYTFR, W, AMPAS, Q).

2235a   PARIS WHEN IT SIZZLES. (Paramount-1964-Richard Quine).
George Axelrod's screenplay is based on a story by Julien
Duvivier and Henri Jeanson. (FF, NYTFR, AMPAS, W, Q,
LC).

2236   PART-TIME WORK OF A DOMESTIC SLAVE. (1974-Alex-
ander Kluge). An original screenplay by Hans Drawe and H.
D. Muller. (HR).

2237   THE PARTY. (United Artists-1968-Blake Edwards). A
screenplay by Blake Edwards, Tom Waldman and Frank Waldman, based on a story by Blake Edwards. (FF, NYTFR,
FM, W LC, AMPAS, Q).

2238   THE PARTY'S OVER.   (Allied Artists-1967-Guy Hamilton).
        A screenplay by Marc Behm.   (FF, AMPAS, Q).

2239   PASSAGES FROM JAMES JOYCE'S FINNEGANS WAKE.
        (Grove Press-1967-Mary Ellen Bute).   A screen treatment by
        Mary Manning and Mary Ellen Bute, based on the novel by
        James Joyce and a play by Mary Manning.   Viking, 1958.
        (FF, NYTFR, LACOPL, Q).

2240   THE PASSION OF ANNA.   (United Artists-1970-Ingmar Berg-
        man).   An original screenplay by Ingmar Bergman.   (W, Q).

2241   PAT GARRETT AND BILLY THE KID.   (MGM-1973-Sam
        Peckinpah).   An original screenplay by Rudolph Wurlitzer.
        (W, Q).

2242   A PATCH OF BLUE.   (MGM-1965-Guy Green).   A screenplay
        by Guy Green, from the novel Be Ready with Bells and Drums
        by Elizabeth Kata; Popular Library, 1961.   (NYTFR, LC,
        AMPAS, LACOPL, Q).

2242a   THE PATSY.   (Paramount-1964-Jerry Lewis).   An original
        screenplay by Jerry Lewis and Bill Richmond.   (AMPAS, W,
        Q, NYTFR, FF).

2243   PATTON.   (20th Century-Fox-1970-Franklin J. Schaffner).   A
        story and screenplay by Francis Ford Coppola and Edmund H.
        North, based on the book by Ladislas Farago; Obolensky,
        1963, 885p.   (W, LACOPL, Q).

2244   PAUL AND MICHELLE.   (Paramount-1974-Lewis Gilbert).   A
        screenplay written by Angela Huth and Vernon Harris, based
        on an original story by Lewis Gilbert.   (V, W).

2245   THE PAWNBROKER.   (Ely Landau-1965-Sidney Lumet).   A
        screenplay by Morton Fine and David Friedkin, based on the
        novel by Edward Lewis Wallant; Harcourt, 1961.   (FF, LC,
        W, AMPAS, LACOPL, Q).

2246   PAYDAY.   (Cinerama-1973-Daryl Duke).   An original screen-
        play by Don Carpenter.   (W, Q).

2247   PAYMENT IN BLOOD.   (Columbia-1968-E. G. Rowland).   An
        original screenplay by Tito Carpi and E. G. Rowland.   (FF,
        W, LC, Q).

2248   THE PEACE KILLERS.   (Transvue-1971-Douglas Schwartz).
        An original screenplay by Michael Berk, from a story by Di-
        ana Maddox and Joel B. Michaels.   (W).

2249   THE PEACH THIEF.   (Brandon-1969-Vulo Radev).   A screen-
        play by Vulo Radev, based on a story by Emilian Stanev.
        (FF, W, Q).

2250   THE PEDESTRIAN. (Cinerama-1974-Maximilian Schell).   An
original work for the screen by Maximilian Schell. (HR, W).

2251   PEER GYNT. (Brandon-1965-David Bradley). A screenplay
based on Henrik Ibsen's play; Dutton, 1963, 242p. (W, LC,
LACOPL).

2252   PENDULUM. (Columbia-1969-George Schaefer). An original
screenplay by Stanley Niss. (FF, LC, AMPAS, Q).

2253   PENELOPE. (MGM-1966-Arthur Hiller). A screenplay by
George Wells, based on a novel by E. V. Cunningham; Doubleday, 1965. (FF, NYTFR, LC, W, AMPAS, LACOPL, Q).

2254   THE PENTHOUSE. (Paramount-1967-Peter Collinson).   A
screenplay written by Peter Collinson, based on the play The
Meter Man by C. Scott Forbes. (FF, NYTFR, FM, W, LC,
AMPAS, Q).

2255   PEOPLE MEET AND SWEET MUSIC FILLS THE HEART.
(Trans-Lux-1969-Henning Carlsen). A screenplay by Poul Bo-
rum and Henning Carlsen, based on the novel by Jens August
Schade. (FF).

2256   THE PEOPLE NEXT DOOR. (AVCO Embassy-1970-David
Green). A screenplay by J. P. Miller, based on the television drama of the same name. (W, Q).

2257   PERFECT FRIDAY. (Chevron-1970-Peter Hall). A screenplay by Anthony Grenville-Bell, and C. Scott Forbes, from a
story by C. Scott Forbes. (W, Q).

2258   PERFORMANCE. (Warner Bros.-1970-Donald Cammell and
Nicholas Roeg). An original screenplay by Donald Cammell.
(W, Q).

2259   THE PERILS OF PAULINE. (Universal-1967-Herbert B.
Leonard and Joshua Shelley). A screenplay by Albert Beich,
suggested by a story by Charles W. Goddard. (FF, W, LC,
AMPAS, Q).

2260   PERSECUTION. (Fanfare-1974-Don Chaffey). A screenplay
by Robert B. Hutton and Rosemary Wooten, with additional
scenes and dialogue by Frederick Warner. (V).

2261   PERSONA. (Lopert-1967-Ingmar Bergman). A screenplay by
Ingmar Bergman; Grossman, 1972, 191p. (FF, NYTFR, W,
AMPAS, LACOPL, Q).

2262   PETE 'N' TILLIE. (Universal-1972-Martin Ritt). A screenplay by Julius J. Epstein, based on the novella Witch's Milk
by Peter De Vries; Little, Brown & Co., 1968, 303p., in
The Cat's Pajamas and Witch's Milk. (W, FF, LACOPL, Q).

2263   PETER RABBIT AND TALES OF BEATRIX POTTER.   (MGM-
        1971-Reginald Mills).   No screenplay credit.   (W, Q).

2264   LE PETIT SOLDAT.   (West End-1967-Jean-Luc Godard).   A
        screenplay by Jean- Luc Godard; Simon & Schuster, 1967,
        92p.   (FF, NYTFR, LACOPL, MCC, SCH).

2265   PETULIA.   (Warner Bros. -7 Arts-1968-Richard Lester).   A
        screenplay by Lawrence B. Marcus, based on the novel Me
        and the Archkook Petulia by John Haase; Coward, 1966.   (FF,
        FM, NYTFR, AMPAS, W, LACOPL, Q).

2266   THE PHANTOM OF FREEDOM.   (20th Century-Fox-1974-
        Luis Buñuel).   A screenplay by Luis Buñuel in collaboration
        with Jean-Claude Carrière.   (V, W).

2267   THE PHANTOM OF SOHO.   (Producers Releasing Organiza-
        tion-1967-Franz Josef Gottlieb).   A screenplay by Ladislas
        Fodor, based on the novel Murder by Proxy by Bryan Edgar
        Wallace.   (FF, W).

2268   PHANTOM OF THE PARADISE.   (20th Century-Fox-1974-
        Brian de Palma).   An original screenplay by Brian de Palma.
        A novel based on the screenplay was written by Bjarne Ros-
        taing; Dell Publishing Co. , 1975, 140p.   (LACOPL, V, HR,
        W).

2269   PHASE IV.   (Paramount-1974-Saul Bass).   An original screen-
        play by Mayo Simon.   (V, W).

2270   PHEDRE.   (Altura-1973-Pierre Jourdan).   An original screen-
        play by Jean Racine.   (W).

2270a   THE PHONY AMERICAN.   (Signal International-1964-Akos Von
        Rathony).   Screenplay by Michael Krims and Alexander Badal,
        based on a novel by Heinz Gross and Egon G. Schleinitz.
        (FF).

2271   THE PHYNX.   (Warner Bros. -1970-Lee H. Katzin).   An orig-
        inal work for the screen by Stan Cornyn, from a story by
        Bob Booker and George Foster.   (W, Q).

2272   PIAF.   (AMLF-1974-Guy Casaril).   A screenplay by Guy Cas-
        aril and Françoise Ferley, from the book by Simone Berteaut;
        Harper, 1972, 488p.   (V, LACOPL).

2273   PICKPOCKET.   (New Yorker-1969-Robert Bresson).   An origi-
        nal screenplay by Robert Bresson.   (FF, W, Q).

2274   PICKUP ON 101.   (American International-1972-John Florea).
        An original screenplay by Anthony Blake.   (W, FF).

2275   PICTURE MOMMY DEAD.   (Embassy-1966-Bert I. Gordon).

An original screenplay by Robert Sherman. (FF, NYTFR, W, AMPAS, Q).

2276   PIE IN THE SKY. (Allied Artists-1965-Allen Baron). An original screenplay by Allen Baron. (W, AMPAS).

2277   PIECES OF DREAMS. (United Artists-1970-Daniel Haller). A screenplay by Roger O. Hirson, based on the novel The Wine and the Music by William E. Barrett; Doubleday, 1968. (W, LACOPL, Q).

2278   THE PIED PIPER. (Paramount-1972-Jacques Demy). An original screenplay by Andrew Birkin, Jacques Demy and Mark Peploe. (Q, FF).

2279   PIERROT LE FOU. (Pathe Contemporary Films-1969-Jean-Luc Godard). Jean-Luc Godard wrote the screenplay which was based on Lionel White's novel Obsession, Dutton, 1962. The screenplay was also published by Simon & Schuster, 1969, 104p. (FF, Q, W, AMPAS, LACOPL, SCH, MCC).

2280   PIGEONS. (Plaza-1971-John Dexter). A screenplay by Ron Whyte, based on the novel Sidelong Glances of a Pigeon Kicker by David Boyer; Viking, 1968, 119p. (W, LACOPL, Q).

2281   THE PIGKEEPER'S DAUGHTER. (Box Office International-1972-Bethel G. Buckalew). No screenplay credits available. (FF).

2282   PIGPEN. (New Line Cinema-1974-Pier Paolo Pasolini). An original screenplay by Pier Paolo Pasolini. (HR).

2283   PINK FLAMINGOS. (Saliva-1974-John Waters). An original story and screenplay by John Waters. (V, W).

2284   THE PINK JUNGLE. (Universal-1968-Delbert Mann). A screenplay by Charles Williams, based on the novel Snake Water by Alan Williams; Harper, 1965. (Q, FF, NYTFR, FM, W AMPAS, LACOPL).

2285   PINK NARCISSUS. (Sherpix-1971-). No screenplay credit. (W)

2285a   THE PINK PANTHER. (United Artists-1964-Blake Edwards). An original screenplay by Maurice Richlin and Blake Edwards. (AMPAS, W, LC, Q, FF, NYTFR).

2286   THE PINK PUSSY CAT. (Cambist Films-1967-Alberto Du Bois). An original screenplay by Alberto Du Bois and Diego. (FF).

2287   PINOCCHIO IN OUTER SPACE. (Universal-1965-Ray Goos-

sens). A screenplay by Fred Laderman, from the original
tale by Collodi. (NYTFR, LC, W, AMPAS, Q).

2288   PIPPI IN THE SOUTH SEAS. (G. G. Communications-1974-
Alle Hellbom). Screenplay by Astrid Lindgren, based on her
Pippi Longstockings novels. (V, W).

2289   A PISTOL FOR RINGO. (1966-Duccio Tessari). A screenplay by Duccio Tessari. (NYTFR, W, Q).

2290   PIT STOP. (Distributors International-1969-Jack Hill).
Jack Hill wrote this original screenplay. (W).

2291   THE PIZZA TRIANGLE. (Warner Bros.-1970-Ettore Scola).
A screenplay by Age and Scarpelli and Ettore Scola, based
on a story by Age and Scarpelli. (W, Q).

2292   A PLACE CALLED GLORY. (Embassy-1966-Sheldon Reynolds aka Ralph Gideon). A screenplay by Edward Di Lorenzo, Jerold Hayden Boyd, and Fernando Lamas, based on
a novel by Jerold Hayden Boyd. (FF, NYTFR, W, AMPAS,
Q).

2293   A PLACE CALLED TODAY. (AVCO Embassy-1972-Don
Schain). An original screenplay written by Don Schain.
(FF).

2294   A PLACE FOR LOVERS. (MGM-1969-Vittorio De Sica). A
screenplay by Julian Halevy, Peter Baldwin, Ennio de Concini, Tonino Guerra and Cesare Zavattini, based on the play
Amanti by Brunello Rondi and Renaldo Cabieri. (FF, W,
LC, Q).

2295   PLAGUE OF THE ZOMBIES. (20th Century-Fox-1966-John
Gilling). An original screenplay by Peter Bryan. (FF, LC,
W, AMPAS, Q).

2296   THE PLAINSMAN. (Universal-1966-David Lowell Rich). An
original screenplay by Michael Blankfort. (FF, LC, W,
AMPAS, Q).

2297   PLANET OF BLOOD. (American International-1965-Mario
Bava). A screenplay by Ib Melchior, Alberto Bevilaqua,
Callisto Cosulich, Mario Bava, Antonio Roman, and Rafael J.
Salvia, based on a story by Renato Pestriniero. (W).

2298   PLANET OF THE APES. (20th Century-Fox-1968-Franklin
J. Schaffner). A screenplay by Michael Wilson and Rod Ser-
ling, based on the novel by Pierre Boulle; Vanguard, 1963.
(Q, FF, NYTFR, FM, W, LC, AMPAS, LACOPL).

2299   PLANET OF THE VAMPIRES. (American International-1965-
Mario Bava). An original screenplay by Ib Melchior and

Louis M. Heyward. (W, LC, AMPAS, Q).

2300   THE PLANTATION BOY. (New Yorker-1971-Walter Lima,
        Jr.). A screenplay by Walter Lima, Jr., adapted from a
        novel by José Lins de Rego. (W).

2301   PLAY IT AGAIN, SAM. (Paramount-1972-Herbert Ross). A
        screenplay by Woody Allen, from his play of the same name;
        Random House, 1969, 95p. (W, LACOPL, Q).

2302   PLAY IT AS IT LAYS. (Universal-1972-Frank Perry). A
        screenplay by Joan Didion and John Gregory Dunne, based on
        the novel by Joan Didion; Farrar, 1970, 214p. (FF,
        LACOPL, W, Q).

2303   PLAY MISTY FOR ME. (Universal-1971-Clint Eastwood). A
        screenplay by Jo Heims, Dean Riesner, from a story by Jo
        Heims. (W, Q).

2304   PLAY DIRTY. (United Artists-1969-Andre De Toth). A
        screenplay by Lotte Colin and Melvyn Bragg, based on an
        original story by George Marton. (W, LC, AMPAS, Q).

2304a   THE PLAYGIRLS AND THE VAMPIRE. (Fanfare-1964-Piero
        Regnoli). Piero Regnoli wrote this original screenplay. (FF).

2305   THE PLAYGROUND. (Jerand-1965-Richard Hilliard). A
        screenplay by George Garrett, inspired by the book My
        Brother Death by Cyrus L. Sulzberger; Harper, 1961, 225p.
        (NYTFR, W, AMPAS, LACOPL).

2306   PLAYTIME. (Continental-1973-Jacques Tati). An original
        work written for the screen by Jacques Tati and J. Lagrange.
        (W).

2307   PLAZA SUITE. (Paramount-1971-Arthur Hiller). A screen-
        play by Neil Simon, based on his play of the same name;
        Random House, 1969, 115p. (W, LACOPL, Q).

2308   PLEASE DON'T EAT MY MOTHER! (Box-Office Internation-
        al-1972-Carl Monson). No author credit available. (FF).

2309   PLEASE STAND BY. (Milton-1972-Jack & Joanna Milton).
        An original screenplay written by Jack & Joanna Milton. (W).

2310   THE PLEASURE GAME. (Eve-1970-John Vittoli). An origi-
        nal screenplay written by Chase Frank. (W).

2311   THE PLEASURE GIRLS. (Times Film Corp.-1966-Gerry
        O'Hara). Gerry O'Hara wrote this original screenplay. (FF,
        NYTFR).

2312   THE PLEASURE SEEKERS. (20th Century-Fox-1965-Jean

Negulesco). A screenplay by Edith Sommer, based on Three
Coins in the Fountain by John H. Secondari; Lippincott, 1952.
(Q, LACOPL, AMPAS).

2313   THE PLEDGEMASTERS. (Signature-1971-David P. Parrish).
The film was produced from an idea by Bruce Gregory. (W).

2314   POCKET MONEY. (National General-1972-Stuart Rosenberg).
A screenplay by Terry Malik, based on the novel Jim Kane
by J. P. S. Brown, adapted by John Gay; Dial Press, 1970,
432p. (W, LACOPL, Q).

2315   POINT BLANK. (MGM-1967-John Boorman). A screenplay
by Alexander Jacobs, David Newhouse and Rafe Newhouse,
based on the novel The Hunter by Richard Stark. (FF,
NYTFR, FM, W, LC, AMPAS, Q).

2316   POINT OF TERROR. (Crown International-1972-Alex Nicol).
A screenplay by Tony Crechales and Ernest A. Charles,
based on a story by Peter Carpenter and Chris Marconi. (FF).

2317   THE POLICE CONNECTION. (Cinemation-1973-Bert I. Gordon). An original screenplay by Bert I. Gordon. (W).

2318   THE POLICEMAN. (Cinema V-1972-Ephraim Kishon). An
original screenplay by Ephraim Kishon. (FF).

2319   THE POLITICIANS. (Fountain-1970-Derek Ashburne). An
original screenplay by Derek Ashburne. (W).

2320   POOR COW. (National General-1968-Kenneth Loach). Nell
Dunn and Kenneth Loach wrote this screenplay based on the
novel by Nell Dunn; Doubleday, 1967. (FF, NYTFR, W,
AMPAS, LACOPL, Q).

POP GEAR see GO GO MANIA

2321   POPCORN. (Sherpix-1969-Peter Clifton). A documentary,
no screenplay credit. (W, Q).

2322   POPE JOAN. (Columbia-1972-Michael Anderson). An original screenplay by John Briley. (W, FF).

2323   POPI. (United Artists-1969-Arthur Hiller). Tina and Lester
Pine wrote this original screenplay. (FF, W, LC, AMPAS,
Q).

2324   THE POPPY IS ALSO A FLOWER. (Comet-1967-Terence
Young). A screenplay written by Jo Eisinger, based on a
story idea by Ian Fleming. (FF, NYTFR, FM, Q, W,
AMPAS).

PORCILE see PIGPEN

2325   PORTNOY'S COMPLAINT. (Warner Bros.-1972-Ernest Lehman). A screenplay by Ernest Lehman, based on the novel
by Philip Roth; Random House, 1969, 274p. (FF, Q,
LACOPL, W).

2326   PORTRAIT OF HELL. (Toho-1972-Shiro Toyoda). A screenplay by Toshio Yasumi from a story by Ryunosuke Akuta-
gawa. (W).

2327   PORTRAIT OF JASON. (Film-Makers' Distribution Center-
1967-Shirley Clarke). A documentary interview, no screenplay. (NYTFR, W).

2328   PORTRAIT OF LENIN. (Artkino-1967-Serge Yutkevich). An
original screenplay by Evgeny Gabrilovich and Serge Yutkevich. (W).

2329   PORTRAITS OF WOMEN. (Allied Artists-1972-Jorn Donner).
An original screenplay by Jorn Donner. (FF).

2330   THE POSEIDON ADVENTURE. (20th Century-Fox-1972-
Ronald Neame). Stirling Silliphant and Wendell Mayes au-
thored this screenplay, based upon a novel by Paul Gallico;
Coward, 1969, 347p. (FF, LACOPL, Q).

2331   THE POSSESSION OF JOEL DELANEY. (Paramount-1972-
Waris Hussein). A screenplay by Matt Robinson and Grimes
Grice, based on the novel by Ramona Stewart; Little, Brown
& Co., 1970, 246p. (W, LACOPL, Q).

2332   THE POSTGRADUATE. (Kariofilms-1970-Harold Kovner).
A screenplay by Harold Kovner and Jay Campbell. (W).

2333   THE POWER. (MGM-1968-Byron Haskin). A screenplay by
John Gay, based on the novel by Frank M. Robinson; Lippin-
cott, 1956. (Q, FF, FM, NYTFR, W, LC, AMPAS,
LACOPL).

2334   PREHISTORIC WOMEN. (20th Century-Fox-1967-Michael
Carreras). Henry Younger wrote this original screenplay.
(FF, W, LC, AMPAS).

2335   PREMONITION. (Transvue-1972-Alan Rudolph). A screenplay by Alan Rudolph. (W).

2336   THE PRESIDENT'S ANALYST. (Paramount-1967-Theodore
J. Flicker). An original screenplay by Theodore J. Flicker.
(FF, FM, NYTFR, W, LC, AMPAS, Q).

2337   PRETTY MAIDS ALL IN A ROW. (MGM-1971-Roger Vadim).
A screenplay by Gene Roddenberry, based on a novel by
Francis Pollini; Dell, 1969. (W, LACOPL, Q).

2338   PRETTY POISON. (20th Century-Fox-1968-Noel Black). A
        screenplay by Lorenzo Semple, Jr., based on the novel She
        Let Him Continue by Stephen Geller; Dutton, 1966. (Q, FF,
        NYTFR, FM, W, LC, AMPAS, LACOPL).

2339   THE PRIEST AND THE GIRL. (New Yorker-1973-Joaquim
        Pedro de Andrade). An original screenplay by Joaquim Pedro
        de Andrade. (W).

2340   THE PRIEST'S WIFE. (Warner Bros.-1971-Dino Risi). An
        original screenplay by Ruggero Maccari and Bernardino Zap-
        poni. (W, Q).

2341   PRIME CUT. (National General-1972-Michael Ritchie). Rob-
        ert Dillon wrote this original screenplay. (FF, Q).

2342   THE PRIME OF MISS JEAN BRODIE. (20th Century-Fox-
        1969-Ronald Neame). A screenplay by Jay Presson Allen,
        based on his play published by Samuel French, 1969, 94p.;
        and adapted from the novel by Muriel Spark; Lippincott,
        1961. (FF, W, LC, AMPAS, LACOPL, Q).

        THE PRINCESS see A TIME IN THE SUN

2343   PRISM. (Corn King-1971-Anitra Pivnick). An original
        screenplay by Anitra Pivnick. (W).

2344   PRISON GIRLS. (American International-1973-Thomas De-
        Burton). Burton Gershfeld wrote this original screenplay.
        (W, FF).

2345   PRISON GUARD. (Filmaco-1973-Ivan Renc). This original
        screenplay was authored by Ivan Renc. (W).

2346   THE PRISONER OF SECOND AVENUE. (Warner Bros.-
        1974-Melvin Frank). Neil Simon wrote this screenplay based
        on his own stage play; Random House, 1972, 87p. (V,
        LACOPL).

2347   LA PRISONNIERE. (AVCO Embassy-1969-Henri-Georges
        Clouzot). Screenplay written directly for the screen by
        Monique Lange, Marcel Moussy, and Henri-Georges Clouzot.
        (FF, W).

2348   PRIVATE DUTY NURSES. (New World-1972-George Armitage).
        This original screenplay is credited to George Armitage.
        (FF).

2349   THE PRIVATE LIFE OF SHERLOCK HOLMES. (United Artists
        -1970-Billy Wilder). I. A. L. Diamond and Billy Wilder
        wrote this original screenplay. (W, Q).

2350   THE PRIVATE NAVY OF SGT. O'FARRELL. (United Artists-

1968-Frank Tashlin).   A screenplay by Frank Tashlin which
was based on a story by John L. Greene and Robert M.
Fresco. (FF, NYTFR, FM, W, LC, Q, AMPAS).

2351   PRIVATE PARTS. (MGM-1972-Paul Bartel). An original
       screenplay co-authored by Philip Kearney and Les Rendel-
       stein. (W).

2352   PRIVILEGE. (Universal-1967-Peter Watkins). Norman Bog-
       ner wrote the screenplay for this film which was based on
       a story by Johnny Speight. A novelization based on the origi-
       nal screenplay was written by John Burke; Avon Books,
       1967, 160p. (FF, NYTFR, FM, W, LACOPL, AMPAS, Q).

2352a THE PRIZE. (MGM-1964-Mark Robson). An Ernest Leh-
       man screenplay based on the novel by Irving Wallace; Simon
       & Schuster, 1962, 768p. (LACOPL, AMPAS, Q, NYTFR,
       W, LC, FF).

2353   THE PRODUCERS. (Embassy-1968-Mel Brooks). An origi-
       nal screenplay written by Mel Brooks. (FF, NYTFR,
       AMPAS, Q).

2354   THE PROFESSIONALS. (Columbia-1966-Richard Brooks).
       A screenplay by Richard Brooks, based on the novel A Mule
       for the Marquessa by Frank O'Rourke; Morrow, 1966. (FF,
       NYTFR, LC, W, AMPAS, LACOPL, Q).

2355   THE PROFITEER. (Belial-1974-Sergio Nasca). Sergio Nas-
       ca wrote this original screenplay. (V).

2356   PROJECT X. (Paramount-1968-William Castle). A screen-
       play by Edmund Morris, based on the novels by Leslie P.
       Davies. (FF, W, LC, AMPAS, Q).

2357   THE PROJECTED MAN. (Universal-1967-Ian Curteis). A
       screenplay by John C. Cooper and Peter Bryan, based on an
       original story by Frank Quattrocchi. (FF, W, Q).

2358   THE PROJECTIONIST. (Maron-1971-Harry Hurwitz). An
       original work for the screen written by Harry Hurwitz. (W,
       Q).

2359   PROLOGUE. (Vaudeo-1970-Robin Spry). A screenplay by
       Sherwood Forest, from a story by Sherwood Forest and Rob-
       in Spry. (W).

2360   PROMISE AT DAWN. (AVCO Embassy-1970-Jules Dassin).
       A screenplay by Jules Dassin, adapted from a novel by Ro-
       main Gary; Harper, 1961, 337p. (W, LACOPL, Q).

2361   PROMISE HER ANYTHING. (Paramount-1966-Arthur Hiller).
       William Peter Blatty wrote the screenplay based on a story

by Arne Sultan and Marvin Worth.   (FF, NYTFR, LC, W, AMPAS, Q).

2361a PROMISES, PROMISES.   (NTD, INC.-1964-King Donovan). A screenplay by William Welch and Tommy Noonan, based on a play by Edna Sheklow.   (FF).

2362   PROSTITUTION.   (Stratford-1965-).   An original screenplay by Maurice Boutel.   (W).

2363   THE PROUD AND THE DAMNED.   (Prestige-1972-Ferde Grofe, Jr.).   An original screenplay written by Ferde Grofe, Jr.   (W).

2364   PRUDENCE AND THE PILL.   (20th Century-Fox-1968- Fielder Cook).   Hugh Mills wrote the screenplay taken from his novel; Lippincott, 1965.   (Q, FF, NYTFR, FM, W, LC, AMPAS, LACOPL).

2365   PSYCHE 59.   (Columbia-1964-Alexander Singer).   A screen- play by Julian Halevy, based on the novel by Françoise Des Ligneris.   (FF, NYTFR, Q).

2366   PSYCHO-CIRCUS.   (American International-1967-John Moxey). Peter Welbeck wrote this screenplay.   (FF, W, AMPAS, Q).

2367   THE PSYCHOPATH.   (Paramount-1966-Freddie Francis). This original screenplay was written by Robert Bloch.   (FF, NYTFR, LC, W, AMPAS, Q).

2368   PSYCH-OUT.   (American International-1968-Richard Rush). A screenplay by E. Hunter Willett and Betty Ulius, based on a story by Betty Tusher.   (FF, NYTFR, FM, W, LC, AMPAS, Q).

2368a PSYCHOUT FOR MURDER.   (Times-1971-Edward Ross & Ted Kneeland).   No author credit available for screenplay.   (W, Q).

2369   THE PUBLIC EYE.   (Universal-1972-Carol Reed).   Peter Shaffer wrote this screenplay based on his one-act play of the same title; Stein, 1964, 120p.   (FF, LACOPL, Q).

2370   PUFNSTUF.   (Universal-1970-Hollingsworth Morse).   An original screenplay written by John Fenton Murray and Si Rose.   (Q, W).

2371   PULP.   (United Artists-1972-Michael Hodges).   This original screenplay is attributed to Michael Hodges.   (W, Q, FF).

2371a THE PUMPKIN EATER.   (Royal-1964-Jack Clayton).   A screenplay by Harold Pinter, based on the novel by Penelope Mortimer; McGraw Hill, 1962.   (FF, LACOPL, NYTFR, W, Q).

2372 PUNISHMENT PARK. (Sherpix-1971-Peter Watkins). No
      screenplay credits available. (W).

2373 PUPPET ON A CHAIN. (Cinerama-1972-Geoffrey Reeve).
      Alistair MacLean wrote this screenplay based on his novel;
      Doubleday, 1969, 281p. (FF, LACOPL, Q).

2374 THE PURSUIT OF HAPPINESS. (Columbia-1971-Robert Mull-
      igan). Jon Boothe and George L. Sherman wrote the screen-
      play, based on a novel by Thomas Rogers; New American
      Library, 1968, 237p. (W, Q, LACOPL).

2375 PUSS AND KRAM. (1967-Jonas Cornell). An original screen-
      play by Jonas Cornell. (NYTFR).

2376 PUSSYCAT, PUSSYCAT, I LOVE YOU. (United Artists-
      1970-Rod Amateau). An original screenplay authored by Rod
      Amateau. (Q, W).

2377 PUTNEY SWOPE. (Cinema V-1969-Robert Downey). An
      original screenplay by Robert Downey. (FF, Q, W).

2378 PUZZLE OF A DOWNFALL CHILD. (Universal-1970-Jerry
      Schatzberg). A screenplay by Adrian Joyce, from a story by
      Jerry Schatzberg and Adrian Joyce. (W, Q).

2378a PYRO. (American International-1964-Julio Coll). A screen-
      play by Louis De Los Arcos and Sidney W. Pink, based on
      an original story by Sidney W. Pink. (FF, W, Q).

2379 THE PYX. (Cinerama-1973-Harvey Hart). Robert Schlitt
      wrote the screenplay based on a novel by John Buell; Farrar,
      1959. (W, LACOPL).

2380 QUACKSER FORTUNE HAS A COUSIN IN THE BRONX.
      (UMC-1970-Waris Hussein). An original screenplay by Gab-
      riel Walsh. (W, Q).

2381 QUADROON. (Presidio-1972-Jack Weis). An original screen-
      play written by Sarah Riggs. (W).

2382 QUE HACER. (Impact-1973-Saul Landau, Nina Serrano, &
      Raul Ruiz). An original screenplay by Saul Landau, Nina
      Serrano, and Raul Ruiz. (W).

2383 THE QUEEN. (Grove Press-1968-Frank Simon). No screen-
      play credit since this a documentary. (FF, NYTFR, Q).

2384 QUEEN OF BLOOD. (American International-1966-Curtis
      Harrington). An original screenplay by Curtis Harrington.
      (FF, W, LC, AMPAS, Q).

2385 THE QUEENS. (Royal Films International-1968-Luciano

Salce, Mario Monicelli, Mauro Bolognini, Antonio Pietrangeli). A film in four parts. "Queen Sabina" written by Ruggero Maccari, Luigi Magni and Luciano Salce, based on a
story by Franco Indovina. "Queen Armenia" written by Suso
Cecchi D'Amico, Tonino Guerra, and Giorgio Salvioni.
"Queen Elena" written by Rodolfo Sonego, who also wrote
"Queen Marta." (FF, NYTFR, FM, W, Q).

2386   QUEST FOR LOVE. (Rank-1971-Ralph Thomas). An original screenplay by Terence Feely, adapted from the short
story "Random Quest" by John Wyndham. (W).

2387   QUICK, BEFORE IT MELTS. (MGM-1965-Delbert Mann).
Dale Wasserman wrote the screenplay based on the novel by
Philip Benjamin; Random House, 1964. (FF, LC, W,
AMPAS, LACOPL, Q).

2387a THE QUICK GUN. (Columbia-1964-Sidney Salkow). A screenplay by Robert E. Kent, based on a story by Steve Fisher.
(LC, FF, AMPAS, W, Q).

2388   QUIET DAYS IN CLICHY. (Grove-1970-Jens-Joergen Thorsen). A screenplay by Jen-Joergen Thorsen, based on Henry
Miller's novel; Grove Press, 1965. (W, LACOPL).

2389   A QUIET PLACE IN THE COUNTRY. (Lopert-1970-Elio
Petri). A screenplay by Luciano Vincenzoni and Elio Petri,
from a story by Tonino Guera and Elio Petri. (W, Q).

2390   THE QUILLER MEMORANDUM. (20th Century-Fox-1966-
Michael Anderson). A screenplay by Harold Pinter, based
on the novel The Berlin Memorandum by Adam Hall aka
Elleston Trevor; Simon & Schuster, 1965. (FF, NYTFR, LC,
W, AMPAS, LACOPL, Q).

2391   A QUIXOTE WITHOUT LA MANCHA. (Columbia-1970-Miguel
M. Delgado). An original screenplay by Mario Moreno Reyes
and Jaimie Salvador. (W).

2392   R. P. M. (Columbia-1970-Stanley Kramer). An original
screenplay written by Erich Segal. (W, Q).

2393   RABBIT, RUN. (Warner Bros.-1970-Jack Smight). A
screenplay by Howard B. Kreitsek, based on the novel by
John Updike; Knopf, 1960. (W, LACOPL, Q).

2394   THE RABBLE. (Frank Lee International-1968-Hiroshi Inagaki). A screenplay by Shintaro Mimyura, Misato Ide and
Hiroshi Inagaki. (FF, NYTFR, W).

2395   RACHEL, RACHEL. (Warner Bros.-7 Arts-1968-Paul New-
man). A screenplay by Stewart Stern, based on the novel
A Jest of God by Margaret Laurence; Knopf, 1966, 213p. (Q,
FF, NYTFR, FM, W, LC, AMPAS, LACOPL).

2396   RACING FEVER. (Allied Artists-1965-William Grefe).   An
       original screenplay by William Grefe. (W, AMPAS, Q).

2397   RAGE. (Columbia-1967-Gilberto Gazcon).   Teddi Sherman
       and Gilberto Gazcon authored this original screenplay.   (FF,
       LC, W, AMPAS, Q).

2398   RAGE. (Warner Bros.-1972-George C. Scott).   An original
       screenplay written by Philip Friedman and Dan Kleinman. A
       novel based on the screenplay was written by Philip Fried-
       man; Warner Paperback Library, 1972.   (W, FF, LACOPL,
       Q).

2399   A RAGE TO LIVE.   (United Artists-1965-Walter Grauman).
       A screenplay written by John T. Kelley, from the novel by
       John O'Hara; Random House, 1949.   (NYTFR, LC, W,
       AMPAS, LACOPL, Q).

2400   THE RAGMAN'S DAUGHTER.   (Penelope Films-1974-Harold
       Becker).   Alan Sillitoe wrote this original screenplay.   (HR).

2401   RAID ON ROMMEL. (Universal-1971-Henry Hathaway).   An
       original screenplay written by Richard Bluel. (W, Q).

2402   RAIDERS FROM BENEATH THE SEA. (20th Century-Fox-
       1965-Maury Dexter).   A screenplay by Harry Spalding, based
       on a story by F. Paul Hall.   (FF, LC, W, AMPAS, Q).

2403   THE RAILROAD MAN. (Continental-1965-Pietro Germi).   An
       original screenplay by Pietro Germi, Alfredo Giannetti and
       Luciano Vincenzoni.   (NYTFR, W, AMPAS, Q).

2404   THE RAILWAY CHILDREN. (Universal-1971-Lionel Jeffries).
       A screenplay by Lionel Jeffries, from a novel by E. Nesbit;
       Dutton, 1974.   (W, LACOPL, Q).

2405   THE RAIN PEOPLE. (Warner Bros.-7 Arts-1969-Francis
       Ford Coppola).   An original screenplay by Francis Ford Cop-
       pola.   (FF, W, AMPAS, Q).

2406   RAMPAGE AT APACHE WELLS.   (Columbia-1966-Harald
       Philipp).   No screenplay credit given.   Based on a novel by
       Karl May.   (W).

2407   RAMPARTS OF CLAY.   (Cinema V-1971-Jean-Louis Bertu-
       celli).   A screenplay by Jean Duvignaud, based on his book
       Change at Shebika, adapted by Jean-Louis Bertucelli; Panthe-
       on, 1970, 303p.   (W, LACOPL, Q).

2408   RAPTURE.   (International Classics-1965-John Guillermin).
       Stanley Mann wrote the screenplay based on a novel by Phyl-
       lis Hastings, Rapture in My Rags.   (NYTFR, LC, W,
       AMPAS, Q).

2409   THE RARE BREED. (Universal-1966-Andrew V. McLaglen).
        A screenplay by Ric Hardman. (FF, NYTFR, LC, W,
        AMPAS, Q).

2410   RASCAL. (Buena Vista-1969-Norman Tokar). A screenplay
        by Harold Swanton, based on the book by Sterling North;
        Dutton, 1963, 189p. (W, LC, AMPAS, LACOPL, Q).

2411   RASPUTIN--THE MAD MONK. (20th Century-Fox-1966-Don
        Sharp). An original screenplay by John Elder. (FF, LC,
        W, AMPAS, Q).

2412   RAT PFINK AND BOO BOO. (Craddock-1966-Ray Dennis
        Steckler). An original screenplay by Ronald Haydock, from
        a story by Ray Dennis Steckler. (W, AMPAS).

2413   THE RATS ARE COMING! THE WEREWOLVES ARE HERE!
        (Mishkin-1972-Andy Milligan). An original screenplay by
        Andy Milligan. (FF).

        RAVAGED see THE JESUS TRIP

2414   THE RAVAGERS. (Hemisphere-1965-Eddie Romero). An
        original story and screenplay written by Cesar J. Amigo and
        Eddie Romero. (W, AMPAS, Q).

2415   RAVEN'S END. (New Yorker-1970-Bo Widerberg). An origi-
        nal screenplay written by Bo Widerberg. (W, Q).

2416   RAW MEAT. (American International-1973-Gary Sherman).
        An original screenplay by Ceri Jones, from a story by Gary
        Sherman. (W).

2416a   READY FOR THE PEOPLE. (Warner Bros.-1964-Buzz Kulik).
        A work written by E. M. Parsons and Sy Salkowitz, from a
        magazine story by Eleazar Lipsky. (FF).

2417   A REASON TO LIVE, A REASON TO DIE! (K-Tel Interna-
        tional-1974-Tonino Valerii). An original screenplay by Ton-
        ino Valerii and Ernesto Gastaldi. (HR).

2418   REBEL ROUSERS. (Four Star Excelsior-1970-Martin B.
        Cohen). An original screenplay by Abe Polsky and Michael
        Kars, and Martin B. Cohen. (W).

2419   REBELLION. (Toho-1968-Masaki Kobayashi). Shinobu
        Hashimoto wrote the screenplay based on the novel by Yasu-
        hiko Takiguchi. (FF, NYTFR, W, Q).

2420   THE RECKONING. (Columbia-1969-Jack Gold). A screen-
        play by John McGrath, based on a novel The Harp That Once
        by Patrick Hall. (W, Q).

2421   THE RED ANGEL. (Daiei-1971-Yasuzo Masumura). An
       original screenplay by Ryozo Kasahara. (W).

2422   RED BEARD. (Frank Lee International-1968-Akira Kurosa-
       wa). A screenplay by Masato Ide, Hideo Iguni, Ryuzo Kiku-
       shima and Akira Kurosawa, based on the novel by Shugoro
       Yamamoto. (FF, NYTFR, W, Q).

2423   RED DESERT. (Rizzoli-1965-Michelangelo Antonioni). A
       screenplay by Michelangelo Antonioni and Tonino Guerra.
       (FF, W, AMPAS, Q).

2424   RED DRAGON. (Woolner Bros.-1967-Ernst Hofbauer). A
       screenplay by Hans Karl Kubiak and W. P. Zibaso, based on
       the novel River of the Three Junks by Georges Godefrot.
       (FF, W).

2425   RED LANTERNS. (Times-1965-Vasilis Georgiadis). Alecos
       Galanos wrote the screenplay based on his play. (FF, W,
       AMPAS, Q).

2426   RED LINE 7000. (Paramount-1965-Howard Hawks). A
       screenplay written by George Kirgo, based on a story by
       Howard Hawks. (LC, NYTFR, W, AMPAS, Q).

2427   RED LION. (Toho-1971-Kihachi Okamoto). A screenplay by
       Kihachi Okamoto and Sakae Hirosawa. (W).

2427a RED LIPS. (Royal-1964-Giuseppe Bennati). A screenplay
       written by Paolo Levi and Federico Zardi, based on a story
       by Giuseppe Bennati and Paolo Levi. (NYTFR, FF).

       THE RED MANTLE see HAGBARD AND SIGNE

2428   RED PSALM. (Macmillan Audio Brandon-1973-Miklos Jans-
       co). An original screenplay by Gyula Hernadi. (W).

2429   RED SKY AT MORNING. (Universal-1971-James Goldstone).
       A screenplay by Marguerite Roberts, based on a novel by
       Richard Bradford; Lippincott, 1968. (W, LACOPL, Q).

2430   RED SUN. (National General-1972-Terence Young). A
       screenplay by Laird Koenig, Denne Bart Petitclerc, William
       Roberts, and Lawrence Roman, based on a story by Laird
       Koenig. (FF, Q).

2431   THE RED TENT. (Paramount-1971-Mickail K. Kalatozov).
       An original screenplay by Ennio de Concini and Richard
       Adams. (W, Q).

2432   RED TOMAHAWK. (Paramount-1967-R. G. Springsteen). A
       screenplay by Steve Fisher, based on a story by Steve Fisher
       and Andrew Craddock. (FF, W, LC, AMPAS, Q).

2433   THE REDEEMER. (Empire-1966-Joseph Breen). A screen-
        play by Tom Blackburn, Robert Hugh O'Sullivan, John T.
        Kelly, and James O'Hanlon. (W, Q).

2434   REFINEMENTS IN LOVE. (Hollywood International-1971-
        Carlos Tobalina). An original work for the screen by Carlos
        Tobalina. (W).

2435   A REFLECTION OF FEAR. (Columbia-1973-William A.
        Fraker). A screenplay by Edward Hume, based on the novel
        Go to Thy Deathbed by Stanton Forbes; Doubleday, 1968, 192p.
        (W, LACOPL, FF).

2436   REFLECTIONS IN A GOLDEN EYE. (Warner Bros. -7 Arts
        -John Huston). A screenplay by Chapman Mortimer and
        Gladys Hill, based on the novel by Carson McCullers; Hough-
        ton, 1941.   (Q, FF, NYTFR, FM, W, LC, AMPAS,
        LACOPL).

2437   THE REIVERS. (Cinema Center Film-1969-Mark Rydell). A
        screenplay by Irving Ravetch and Harriet Frank, Jr., based
        on the novel by William Faulkner; Random House, 1962. (W,
        Q, LACOPL, AMPAS).

2438   RELATIONS. (Cambist-1971-Hans Abramson). An original
        screenplay by Hans Abramson. (W).

2439   THE RELUCTANT ASTRONAUT. (Universal-1967-Edward J.
        Montagne). A screenplay by Jim Fritzell and Everett Green-
        baum, based on an idea by Don Knotts. (FF, W, LC,
        AMPAS, Q).

2440   A REPORT ON THE PARTY AND THE GUESTS. (Sigma III-
        1968-Jan Nemec). A screenplay by Ester Krumbachova and
        Jan Nemec, based on a short story by Ester Krumbachova.
        (FF, NYTFR).

2441   THE REPTILE. (20th Century-Fox-1966-John Gilling). An
        original screenplay by John Elder. (FF, LC, W, AMPAS).

2442   REPULSION. (Royal Films International-1965-Roman Polan-
        ski). A screenplay by Roman Polanski. (FF, NYTFR, W).

2443   REQUIEM FOR A GUNFIGHTER. (Embassy-1965-Spencer G.
        Bennet). A screenplay by R. Alexander, from a story by
        Evens W. Cornell and Guy J. Tedesco. (W, AMPAS).

2444   REQUIEM FOR MOZART. (Artkino-1967-V. Gorikker). A
        screenplay that was uncredited, but is based on the story by
        Alexander Pushkin, "Mozart and Salieri, " in Complete Prose
        Tales, Norton, 1966. (W, LACOPL).

2445   THE RESTLESS NIGHT. (Casino-1965-Falk Harnack). An original screenplay by Horst Budjuhn. (W, Q).

2446   RESURRECTION. (Artkino-1966). An uncredited screenplay
        based on the novel by Leo Tolstoy; Heritage Press, 1963.
        (W, LACOPL).

2447   RESURRECTION OF EVE. (Mitchell Bros.-1973-Artie Mitch-
        ell & Jon Fontana). An original screenplay by Artie Mitch-
        ell and Jon Fontana. (W).

2448   THE RESURRECTION OF ZACHARY WHEELER. (Vidtronics-
        1971-Robert Wynn). An original screenplay by Jay Sims &
        Tom Rolf. (W).

2449   LE RETOUR D'AFRIQUE. (New Yorker-1973-Alain Tanner).
        An original screenplay by Alain Tanner. (W).

2450   RETURN FROM THE ASHES. (United Artists-1965-J. Lee
        Thompson). A screenplay by Julius Epstein, based on the
        novel by Hubert Monteilhet; Simon & Schuster, 1963.
        (NYTFR, LC, W, AMPAS, LACOPL, Q).

2451   THE RETURN OF COUNT YORGA. (American International
        -1972-Bob Kelljan). A screenplay by Bob Kelljan and Yvonne
        Wilder, based on characters created by Bob Kelljan. (FF,
        Q).

2452   THE RETURN OF MR. MOTO. (20th Century-Fox-1965-
        Ernest Morris). A screenplay by Fred Eggers, based on a
        character created by John P. Marquand. (NYTFR, LC,
        AMPAS, Q).

2453   RETURN OF SABATA. (United Artists-1972-Frank Kramer).
        A screenplay and story by Renato Izzo and Gianfranco Paro-
        lini. (FF).

2454   RETURN OF THE DRAGON. (Bryanston-1974-Bruce Lee).
        An original screenplay by Bruce Lee. (V, W).

2455   RETURN OF THE SEVEN. (United Artists-1966-Burt Ken-
        nedy). A screenplay by Larry Cohen. (FF, NYTFR, LC,
        W, AMPAS, Q).

2456   REVENGE. (Rank-1971-Sidney Hayers). An original screen-
        play by John Kruse. (W).

2457   REVENGE OF THE GLADIATORS. (Paramount-1965-Michel
        Lupo). An original screenplay written by Lionello de Felice
        and Ernesto Guida. (W, Q).

2458   THE REVENGERS. (National General-1972-Ray Kellogg). A
        screenplay by Wendell Mayes, based on a story by Steven W.
        Carabatsos. (W, Q).

2459 THE REVOLUTIONARY. (United Artists-1970-Paul Williams). A screenplay by Hans Koningsberger, from his novel; Farrar, 1967. (W, LACOPL, Q).

REVOLUTIONS PER MINUTE see R. P. M.

2460 THE REWARD. (20th Century-Fox-1965-Serge Bourguignon). A screenplay by Serge Bourguignon, based on a book by Michael Barrett; Farrar, 1956. (NYTFR, LC, W, AMPAS, LACOPL, Q).

2460a RHINO! (MGM-1964-Ivan Tors). A screenplay by Art Arthur and Arthur Weiss, from a story by Art Arthur. (FF, NYTFR, W, Q, LC).

2461 THE RIBALD TALES OF ROBIN HOOD. (Adam-1969-Richard Kanter). An original screenplay by Richard Kanter, based on a story by Lawrence Morse. (W).

2462 RICHARD. (Billings Associates-1972-Lorees Yerby & Harry Hurwitz). A screenplay written by Lorees Yerby and Harry Hurwitz, based on an idea by Bertrand Castelli. (W, FF).

2463 RIDE BEYOND VENGEANCE. (Columbia-1966-Bernard McEveety). A screenplay by Andrew J. Fenady, based on the novel The Night of the Tiger by Al Dewlen. (FF, NYTFR, LC, W, AMPAS, Q).

2464 RIDE THE HIGH WIND. (Feature Film Corporation of America-1968-David Millin). No screenplay credit; based on the novel North of Bushman's Rock by George Harding. (FF).

2464a RIDE THE WILD SURF. (Columbia-1964-Don Taylor). An original screenplay by Jo and Art Napoleon. (AMPAS, LC, FF, NYTFR, W, Q).

2465 THE RIDE TO HANGMAN'S TREE. (Universal-1967-Al Rafkin). A screenplay by Luci Ward, Jack Natteford and William Bowers, based on a story by Luci Ward and Jack Natteford. (FF, W, LC, AMPAS, Q).

2466 RIDER ON THE RAIN. (AVCO Embassy-1970-Rene Clement). A story and original screenplay by Sebastien Japrisot. (W, Q).

2467 RIGHT ON! (Concept East-1971-Herbert Danska). A screenplay by The Original Last Poets. (W).

2468 RING OF BRIGHT WATER. (Cinerama-1969-Jack Couffer). A screenplay by Jack Couffer and Bill Travers, based on the autobiographical novel by Gavin Maxwell; Longmans, 1960, 211p. (FF, W, AMPAS, LACOPL, Q).

2468a RING OF TREASON. (Paramount-1964-Robert Tronson).
This original screenplay was written by Frank Launder and
Peter Barnes. (FF, NYTFR).

2469 RINGS AROUND THE WORLD. (Columbia-1967-Gil Cates).
Script by Victor Wolfson. (FF, LC, W, AMPAS, Q).

2469a RIO CONCHOS. (20th Century-Fox-1964-Gordon Douglas).
Joseph Landon and Clair Huffaker based their screenplay on
the novel Guns of Rio Conchos by Clair Huffaker. (W, Q,
AMPAS, LC, FF, NYTFR).

2470 RIO LOBO. (National General-1970-Howard Hawks). A
screenplay by Leigh Brackett and Burton Wohl, from a story
by Burton Wohl. (W, Q).

2471 RIOT. (Paramount-1969-Buzz Kulik). A screenplay by James
Poe, based on the novel by Frank Elli; Coward, 1966, 255p.
(FF, W, LC, AMPAS, LACOPL, Q).

2472 RIOT ON SUNSET STRIP. (American International-1967-
Arthur Dreifus). A screenplay by Orville Hampton. (FF,
W, LC, AMPAS, Q).

2473 RIP-OFF. (Alliance-1972-Donald Shebib). An original
screenplay written by William Fruet. (W, Q).

2474 THE RISE AND FALL OF THE WORLD AS SEEN FROM A
SEXUAL POSITION. (Meyer-1972-Arthur Meyer). Script
written by Arthur Meyer. (W).

2475 THE RISE OF LOUIS XIV. (Brandon-1970-Roberto Rossellini). An original screenplay by Philippe Erlanger. (W,
NYTFR, V).

2476 RIVALS. (AVCO Embassy-1972-Krishna Shah). A screenplay
written by Krishna Shah. (FF, Q).

2477 RIVERRUN. (Columbia-1970-John Korty). An original
screenplay by John Korty. (W).

2478 THE ROAD HUSTLERS. (American International-1968-Larry
E. Jackson). An original screenplay by Robert Barron. (FF,
AMPAS).

2479 ROAD TO SALINA. (AVCO Embassy-1971-George Lautner).
A screenplay by George Lautner, Pascal Jardin, and Jack
Miller, based on the novel Sur la Route de Salina by Maurice
Cury. (W, Q).

2480 ROBBERY. (Embassy-1967-Peter Yates). A screenplay by
Edward Boyd, Peter Yates, and George Markstein. (FF,
FM, NYTFR, W, AMPAS, Q).

2481   ROBBY. (Bluewood-1968-Ralph C. Bluemke). An original
        screenplay by Ralph C. Bluemke. (FF, NYTFR, W).

2481a   ROBIN AND THE 7 HOODS. (Warner Bros.-1964-Gordon
        Douglas). An original screenplay by David R. Schwartz.
        (AMPAS, LC, FF, NYTFR, W, Q).

2482   ROBIN HOOD. (Buena Vista-1973-Wolfgang Reitherman). A
        story and screenplay by Larry Clemmons, based on charac-
        ters and story conceptions by Ken Anderson. (W).

2482a   ROBINSON CRUSOE ON MARS. (Paramount-1964-Byron
        Haskin). Ib Melchior and John C. Higgins, based their
        screenplay on the novel Robinson Crusoe by Daniel Defoe;
        Dodd, Mead & Co., 1946, 425p. (FF, NYTFR, Q).

2483   ROMANCE OF A HORSETHIEF. (Allied Artists-1971-Abra-
        ham Polonsky). An original screenplay by David Opatoshu.
        (W, Q).

2484   ROME WANTS ANOTHER CAESAR. (1974-Miklos Jancso).
        An original screenplay by Miklos Jancso and Giovanni Gagliar-
        do. (HR, V, NYT).

2485   ROMEO AND JULIET. (Embassy-1966-Paul Czinner). A
        documentary of a ballet performance. No script. (W, Q).

2486   ROMEO AND JULIET. (Paramount-1968-Franco Zeffirelli).
        This screenplay was written by Franco Brusati, Masolino
        D'Amico, and Franco Zeffirelli, based on the play by William
        Shakespeare. (Q, FF, NYTFR, FM, W, LC, AMPAS,
        LACOPL).

2487   ROOMMATES. (Pantages-1971-Jack Baran). An original
        screenplay by Jack Baran. (W).

2488   THE ROOMMATES. (GFC-1973-Arthur Marks). An original
        work for the screen by Arthur Marks and John Durren. (W,
        FF).

2489   ROPE OF FLESH. (Eve-1965-Russ Meyer). A screenplay
        by Raymond Friday Locke and William E. Sprague, based on
        the novel Streets Paved with Gold by Friday Locke. (W,
        LC, AMPAS).

2490   A ROSE FOR EVERYONE. (Royal International-1967-Franco
        Rossi, and Nino Manfredi, based on the play Procura Se una
        Rosa by Glaucio Gil. (FF, NYTFR, FM, W, Q).

2491   ROSELAND. (Boxoffice International-1973-C. Fredric Hobbs).
        An original screenplay by C. Fredric Hobbs. (W).

2492   ROSEMARY'S BABY. (Paramount-1968-Roman Polanski). A

screenplay by Roman Polanski, based on the novel by Ira
Levin; Random House, 1967.   (Q, FF, NYTFR, FM, W,
LC, AMPAS, LACOPL).

2493   ROSIE! (Universal-1968-David Lowell Rich).   A screenplay
by Samuel Taylor, based on the play A Very Rich Woman
adapted by Ruth Gordon from the play Les Joies de Famille
by Philippe Heriat.   (FF, NYTFR, FM, W, AMPAS, Q).

2494   ROTTEN TO THE CORE.   (Cinema V-1965-John Boulting).
An original story and screenplay by Jeffrey Dell, John Warren, and Roy Boulting.   (NYTFR, W, AMPAS, Q).

2495   ROUGH MAGIC.   (New Yorker-1972-Timothy Knox).   No
screenplay credits available.   (W).

2496   ROUGH NIGHT IN JERICHO.   (Universal-1967-Arnold Laven).
A screenplay by Sydney Boehm and Marvin H. Albert, based
on the novel The Man in Black by Marvin H. Albert.   (FF,
NYTFR, FM, W, AMPAS).

2497   ROUND TRIP.   (Continental-1967-Pierre Dominique Gaisseau).
An original screenplay by William Duffy.   (NYTFR, W, Q).

2498   THE ROUND UP.   (Altura-1969-Miklos Jancso).   An original
screenplay by Gyula Heradi.   (FF, W, Q).

2499   THE ROUNDERS.   (MGM-1965-Burt Kennedy).   A screenplay
by Burt Kennedy, based on a novel by Max Evans; Macmillan,
1960.   (Q, FF, LC, W, AMPAS, LACOPL, NYTFR).

2499a ROUSTABOUT.   (Paramount-1964-John Rich).   A screenplay
by Anthony Lawrence and Allan Weiss, from a story by Allan
Weiss.   (FF, NYTFR, AMPAS, LC, W, Q).

2500   THE ROWDYMAN.   (Crowley-1973-Peter Carter).   An original screenplay by Gordon Pinsent.   (W).

2501   THE ROYAL HUNT OF THE SUN.   (National General-1969-
Irving Lerner).   Philip Yordan wrote the screenplay based up-
on a play by Peter Shaffer; Stein & Day, 1965, 84p.   (W,
AMPAS, LACOPL, Q).

2502   RUBY.   (Bartlett-1971-Dick Bartlett).   An original screenplay
by Ray Loring and Dick Bartlett.   (W).

2503   THE RULING CLASS.   (AVCO Embassy-1972-Peter Medak).
A screenplay by Peter Barnes, based on his play; Grove
Press, 1969, 114p.   (FF, LACOPL, Q).

2504   RUN, ANGEL, RUN.   (Fanfare-1969-Jack Starrett).   A
screenplay by Jerome Wish and V. A. Furlong aka Valerie
Starrett.   (FF, W, AMPAS, Q).

2505 RUN, APPALOOSA, RUN. (Buena Vista-1966-Larry Lansburgh). A screenplay by Janet Lansburgh, based on a story
by Larry Lansburgh. (W, LC, AMPAS).

2506 RUN FOR YOUR WIFE. (Allied Artists-1967-Gian Luigi Polidoro). A screenplay by Rudolfo Sonego, Rafael Azcona, Ennio Flaiano and Gian Luigi Polidoro. (FF, W, AMPAS, Q).

2507 RUN LIKE A THIEF. (Feature Film Corporation of America-
1968-Harry Spalding). An original screenplay by Myron J.
Gold. (FF, AMPAS).

2508 RUN, RUN, JOE. (Pacific Theatres-1974-Giuseppe Colizzi).
An original screenplay by Giuseppe Colizzi. (HR).

RUN, STRANGER, RUN see HAPPY MOTHER'S DAY ...
LOVE, GEORGE

2509 RUN WILD, RUN FREE. (Columbia-1969-Richard C. Sarafi-
an). A screenplay written by David Rook, based on the novel
The White Colt, by David Rook; Dutton, 1967. (FF, W, LC,
AMPAS, LACOPL, Q).

2510 RUNAWAY GIRL. (Laurel Films and United Screen Arts-
1966-Hamil Petroff). An original story and screenplay by
Stewart Cohn. (FF).

2511 RUSH TO JUDGMENT. (Impact-1967-Emile de Antonio). A
series of interviews based on the book Rush to Judgment by
Mark Lane; Holt, 1966, 478p. (NYTFR, W, AMPAS, Q).

2512 RUSS MEYER'S VIXEN. (Eve-1969-Russ Meyer). A screenplay by Robert Rudelson, based on a story by Russ Meyer
and Anthony James Ryan. (FF, W, Q).

2513 THE RUSSIANS ARE COMING! THE RUSSIANS ARE COM-
ING! (United Artists-1966-Norman Jewison). A screenplay by
William Rose, based on the novel The Off-Islanders by Na-
thaniel Benchley; McGraw-Hill, 1961. (Q, FF, NYTFR, LC,
W, AMPAS, LACOPL).

2514 RYAN'S DAUGHTER. (MGM-1970-David Lean). An original
screenplay by Robert Bolt. (W, Q).

2515 SABATA. (United Artists-1970-Frank Kramer). A screenplay
written directly for the screen by Renato Izzo and Gianfranco
Parolini. A novel based on the screenplay was written by
Brian Fox, 1970, Award Books. (W, Q, LACOPL).

2516 THE SABOTEUR: CODE NAME--MORITURI. (20th Century-
Fox-1965-Bernhard Wicki). A screenplay by Daniel Taradash,
based on the novel Morituri by Werner Joerg Luddecke.
(NYTFR, W, AMPAS).

2517   SACCO AND VANZETTI. (UMC-1971-Giuliano Montaldo). An
        original screenplay by Favrizio Onofri and Giuliano Montaldo.
        (W, Q).

2518   A SAFE PLACE. (Columbia-1971-Henry Jaglom). An origi-
        nal screenplay written by Henry Jaglom. (W, Q).

2519   THE SAILOR FROM GIBRALTAR. (Lopert-1967-Tony Rich-
        ardson). This screenplay was written by Christopher Isher-
        wood, Don Magner, and Tony Richardson, based on the novel
        by Marguerite Duras; Grove Press, 1966, 318p. (FF,
        NYTFR, W, LC, AMPAS, LACOPL, Q).

2520   THE ST. VALENTINE'S DAY MASSACRE. (20th Century-
        Fox-1967-Roger Corman). An original screenplay by Howard
        Browne. (FF, NYTFR, FM, LC, AMPAS).

2521   LA SALAMANDRE. (New Yorker-1972-Alain Tanner). A
        screenplay by Alain Tanner and John Berger. (FF).

2522   SALESMAN. (Maysles Film-1969-). A documentary film by
        Albert and David Maysles and Charlotte Zwerin. The script
        was published by New American Library, 1969, 128p. (FF,
        W, MCC, Q, SCH).

2523   SALLAH. (Palisades International-1965-Ephraim Kishon).
        An original story and screenplay by Ephraim Kishon. (W,
        AMPAS).

2524   SALT AND PEPPER. (United Artists-1968-Richard Donner).
        An original screenplay by Michael Pertwee. (FF, NYTFR,
        W, LC, AMPAS, Q).

2525   SALT OF THE EARTH. (Independent Productions Corp. -
        1965-Herbert Biberman). An original screenplay by Michael
        Wilson, in Salt of the Earth: The Making of a Film; Beacon
        Press, 1965, 373p. (LACOPL, Q, FF).

2526   SALTO. (Kanawha-1966-Tadeusz Konwicki). An original
        screenplay by Tadeusz Konwicki. (NYTFR, W, Q).

2526a   SALVATORE GIULIANO. (Royal-1964-Francesco Rosi). A
        screenplay written by Francesco Rosi, Suso Cecchi d'Amico,
        Enzo Provenzale, and Franco Solinas. (NYTFR, FF).

2527   THE SALZBURG CONNECTION. (20th Century-Fox-1972-Lee
        H. Katzin). A screenplay by Oscar Millard, based on a
        novel by Helen MacInnes; Harcourt, 1968. (FF, LACOPL).

2528   SAM WHISKEY. (United Artists-1969-Arnold Laven). An
        original story and screenplay by William W. Norton. (FF,
        LC, AMPAS, Q).

2529 SAMBIZANGA. (New Yorker-1973-Sarah Maldoror). A screenplay by Mario de Andrade, Maurice Pons, and Sarah Maldoror, from the novel La Vraie Vie de Domingos Xavier by Luandino Vieira. (W).

2529a SAMSON AND THE SLAVE QUEEN. (American International-1964-Umberto Lanzi). An original screenplay by Guido Malatesta and Umberto Lenzi. (FF, NYTFR, Q, W).

2530 SAMURAI (part 2). (Toho-1967-Kiroshi Inagaki). An original screenplay by Tokuhei Wakao and Hiroshi Inagaki. (W, AMPAS).

2531 SAMURAI (part 3). (Toho-1967-Kiroshi Inagaki). Tokuhei Wakao and Hiroshi Inagaki wrote this original screenplay. (W, AMPAS).

2532 SAMURAI ASSASSIN. (Tojo-Mifune-1965-Kihachi Okamoto). A screen play by Shinobu Hashimoto, based on the novel Samurai Nippon by Jiromasa Gunji. (FF, W, Q).

2533 THE SAND PEBBLES. (20th Century-Fox-1966-Robert Wise). A screenplay by Robert Anderson, based on the novel by Richard McKenna; Harper, 1962. (FF, NYTFR, LC, W, AMPAS, LACOPL, Q).

2534 THE SANDPIPER. (MGM-1965-Vincente Minelli). A screenplay by Dalton Trumbo and Michael Wilson, from an original story by Martin Ransohoff. (NYTFR, LC, W, AMPAS, Q).

THE SANDPIT GENERALS see THE WILD PACK

2535 SANDRA. (Royal-1966-Luchino Visconti). An original screenplay by Luchino Visconti, Suso Cecchi d'Amico, and Enrico Medioli. (FF, W, Q).

2536 SANDRA, THE MAKING OF A WOMAN. (Mini-1970-Gary Graver). An original screenplay written by Gary Graver and Robert Aiken. (W).

2537 SANDS OF BEERSHEBA. (Landau-Unger-1966-Alexander Ramati). This screenplay is attributed to Alexander Ramati, based on his book. (FF, NYTFR, W, Q.

2538 SANDS OF THE KALAHARI. (Paramount-1965-Cy Endfield). A screenplay by Cy Endfield, based on the novel by William Mulvihill; Putnam, 1960. (NYTFR, LC, W, AMPAS, LACOPL, Q).

SANTA CLAUS HAS BLUE EYES see BAD COMPANY

2539 SANTEE. (Crown International-1973-Gary Nelson). This screenplay written by Tom Blackburn was based on an original story written by Brand Bell. (W).

2540   THE SARAGOSSA MANUSCRIPT. (Amerpole Enterprise-1972
       -Wojciech J. Has). A screenplay by Tadeusz Kwiatkowski,
       based on the novel The Saragossa Manuscript by Jan Potocki;
       Orion Press, 1960. (FF, LACOPL).

2541   SASUKE AGAINST THE WIND. (Bijou-1973-Masahiro Shin-
       oda). A screenplay by Yoshiyuki Fukuda, based on a novel
       by Koji Nakada. (W).

2542   THE SATAN BUG. (United Artists-1965-John Sturges). A
       screenplay by James Clavell and Edward Anhalt, based on
       the novel by Ian Stuart aka Alistair MacLean; Scribner, 1962.
       (FF, LC, W, AMPAS, Q).

2543   SATAN'S SADISTS. (Independent-International-1970-Al Adam-
       son). An original screenplay by Dennis Wayne. (W).

2544   SATURDAY NIGHT IN APPLE VALLEY. (Emerson-1965-
       John Myhers). An original screenplay by John Myhers. (W,
       AMPAS).

2545   SAUL AND DAVID. (Rizzoli Films & World Entertainment
       Corporation-1968-Marcello Baldi). An original screenplay
       by Ottavio Jemma, Flavio Nicolini, Tonino Guerra, Emilio
       Cordero, and Marcello Baldi. (FF).

2546   SAVAGE! (New World-1973-Cirio H. Santiago). An original
       screenplay written by Ed Medard. (W, Q).

2547   THE SAVAGE IS LOOSE. (Campbell Devon Productions-1974
       -George C. Scott). Max Ehrlich and Frank De Felitta wrote
       this original screenplay. (HR).

2548   SAVAGE MESSIAH. (MGM-1972-Ken Russell). A screenplay
       by Christopher Logue, based on the book by H. S. Ede;
       Outerbridge, 1971, 160p. (W, FF, LACOPL, Q).

2549   SAVAGE PAMPAS. (Comet-1967-Hugo Fregonese). A screen-
       play by Hugo Fregonese and John Melson, based on the novel
       Pampa Barbara by Homero Manzi and Ulises Petit De Murat.
       (FF, AMPAS).

2550   THE SAVAGE SEVEN. (American International-1968-Richard
       Rush). A screenplay by Michael Fisher, based on a story
       by Rosalind Ross. (FF, NYTFR, W, LC, AMPAS, Q).

2551   THE SAVAGE WILD. (American International-1970-Gordon
       Eastman). An original screenplay written by Gordon East-
       man. (W, Q).

2552   SAVAGES. (Angelika-1972-James Ivory). A screenplay by

James Ivory, George Swift Trow, and Michael O'Donoghue.
The screenplay was published by Grove Press, 1973, 152p.
(W, LACOPL).

2553   SAVE THE CHILDREN. (Paramount-1973-Stan Lathan).
Narration written by Matt Robinson; a documentary. (W).

2554   SAVE THE TIGER. (Paramount-1973-John G. Avildsen). A
screenplay by Steve Shagan, based on the novel of the same
name; Dial Press, 1972, 311p. (W, LACOPL, Q, FF).

2555   SAY HELLO TO YESTERDAY. (Cinerama-1971-Alvin Rakoff). A screenplay by Alvin Rakoff and Peter King written
directly for the screen. (W, Q).

2556   SAY IT WITH FLOWERS. (1974-Pierre Grimblat). A screenplay by Tonino Guerra, Lucile Laks, and Pierre Grimblat,
from the book by Christine Charrière. (V).

2557   SCALAWAG. (Paramount-1973-Kirk Douglas). A screenplay
by Albert Maltz, Sid Fleishman, from a story by Robert
Louis Stevenson. (W).

2558   THE SCALPHUNTERS. (United Artists-1968-Sydney Pollack).
A screenplay by William Norton, from an original story.
(FF, NYTFR, FM, W AMPAS, Q).

2559   SCANDALOUS JOHN. (Buena Vista-1971-Robert Butler). A
screenplay by Bill Walsh and Don Da Gradi, based on a book
by Richard Gardner; Doubleday, 1963. (W, LACOPL, Q).

2560   SCARECROW. (Warner Bros.-1973-Jerry Schatzberg). An
original screenplay by Garry Michael White. (W, Q).

2561   SCARECROW IN A GARDEN OF CUCUMBERS. (New Line
Cinema-1972-Robert J. Kaplan). An original screenplay written by Sandra Scoppettone. (W, FF).

2562   SCARLET CAMELLIA. (Shiro Kido-1973-Yoshitaro Nomura).
A screenplay by Masato Moida, based on a novel by Shugoro
Yamamoto. (W).

2563   SCARS OF DRACULA. (American Continental-1971-Roy Ward
Baker). An original screenplay by John Elder, based on
character created by Bram Stoker. (W).

2564   THE SCAVENGERS. (Aquarius-1971-R. L. Frost). An original screenplay by R. W. Cresse. (W).

2565   SCENES FROM A MARRIAGE. (Cinema V-1974-Ingmar Bergman). An original screenplay by Ingmar Bergman. Screenplay published by Pantheon Books, 1974, 199p. (V, NYT,
LACOPL).

SCHIZOID see LIZARD IN A WOMAN'S SKIN

2566   SCHLOCK. (Jack H. Harris-1973-John Landis). An original
       screenplay by John Landis. (W).

2567   SCHOOL FOR SEX. (Toho-1967-Ryo Kinoshita). A screen-
       play by Toshiro Ide, based on a story by Yukio Mishima.
       (FF, NYTFR).

       SCHOOL OF LOVE see SCHOOL FOR SEX

2568   SCORE. (Audubon-1973-Radley Metzger). A screenplay by
       Jerry Douglas, based on his play. (W).

2569   SCORPIO. (United Artists-1973-Michael Winner). A screen-
       play by David W. Rintels and Gerald Wilson, from a story by
       David W. Rintels. (W, Q, FF).

2570   SCORPIO 70. (Lake-1970-Ronald Sullivan). An original
       screenplay by Dario Finelli. (W).

       SCRATCH HARRY see THE EROTIC THREE

2571   SCREAM AND SCREAM AGAIN. (American International-
       1970-Gordon Hessler). A screenplay by Christopher Wicking,
       from a novel by Peter Saxon. (W, Q).

2572   SCREAM BLACULA SCREAM. (American International-1973-
       Bob Kelljan). Joan Torres, Raymond Koenig, and Maurice
       Jules wrote the screenplay which was based on a story by
       Joan Torres and Raymond Koenig. (Q, W).

2573   A SCREAM IN THE STREETS. (Boxoffice-1972-Carl Monson).
       An original screenplay written by Erick Norden. (FF, W).

2574   SCREAM OF THE DEMON LOVER. (New World-1971-J. L.
       Merino). An original story and screenplay by E. Colombo.
       (W).

2575   SCROOGE. (National General-1970-Ronald Neame). A screen-
       play by Leslie Bricusse, based on Charles Dickens' A Christ-
       mas Carol; World Publishing Co., 1961. (W, LACOPL, Q).

2576   THE SEA GULL. (Warner Bros.-7 Arts-1968-Sidney Lumet).
       A filmed version of Moura Budberg's translation of the play
       by Anton Chekhov, in John Gassner's Twenty Best European
       Plays on the American Stage; Crown, 1957, 733p. (FF,
       NYTFR, Q, W, LC, AMPAS, LACOPL).

2577   THE SEA PIRATE. (Paramount-1967-Sergio Bergonzelli). A
       screenplay by Georges de la Grandière, adapted by J. Sever-
       ac. (Q, FF, LC, AMPAS).

2577a SEANCE ON A WET AFTERNOON. (Artixo-1964-Bryan Forbes). An original screenplay by Bryan Forbes. (AMPAS, Q, W, FF, NYTFR).

2578 SEASIDE SWINGERS. (Embassy-1965-James Hill). A screenplay by Anthony Marriot, Jeri Matos, and James Hill, from a story by Anthony Marriot. (W, AMPAS).

2579 SEBASTIAN. (Paramount-1968-David Greene). A screenplay by Gerald Vaughan-Hughes, based on an original screenstory by Leo Marks. (FF, NYTFR, W, Q, LC, AMPAS).

2580 THE SECOND BEST SECRET AGENT IN THE WHOLE WIDE WORLD. (Embassy-1966-Lindsay Shonteff). A screenplay by Howard Griffiths and Lindsay Shonteff. (FF, NYTFR, W, AMPAS).

2581 THE SECOND COMING OF SUZANNE. (Barry Film-1974-Michael Barry). An original script by Michael Barry. (V).

2582 SECONDS. (Paramount-1966-John Frankenheimer). A screenplay by Lewis John Carlino, based on the novel by David Ely; Pantheon, 1963. (FF, NYTFR, LC, W, AMPAS, LACOPL).

2583 LE SECRET. (Valoria-1974-Robert Enrico). A screenplay by Pascal Jardin and Robert Enrico, from a novel by Francis Rick. (V).

2584 SECRET AGENT FIREBALL. (American International-1966-Mario Donen aka Martin Donan). An original screenplay by Sergio Martino aka Julian Barry. (FF, LC, W, AMPAS, Q).

2585 SECRET AGENT SUPER DRAGON. (United Screen Arts-1966-Calvin Jackson Padget). A screenplay by Bill Coleman, Mike Mitchell, Remigio Del Grosso and Roberto Ambroso, from an original story by Calvin Jackson Padget. (FF, W, AMPAS, Q).

2586 SECRET CEREMONY. (Universal-1968-Joseph Losey). A screenplay by George Tabori, based on a short story by Marco Denevi. (Q, FF, NYTFR, FM, W, LC, AMPAS).

2586a THE SECRET DOOR. (Allied Artists-1964-Gilbert L. Kay). A screenplay by Charles Martin, based on the story "Paper Door" by Stephen Longstreet. (FF, NYTFR, LC, AMPAS, W, Q).

2587 THE SECRET INVASION. (United Artists-1964-Roger Corman). An original screenplay by R. Wright Campbell. (AMPAS, LC, FF, NYTFR, W, Q).

2587a THE SECRET LIFE OF AN AMERICAN WIFE. (20th Century-Fox-1968-George Axelrod). An original screenplay by George

Axelrod.   (FF, NYTFR, FM, LC, AMPAS, Q).

2588   THE SECRET OF BLOOD ISLAND.   (Universal-1965-Quentin
       Lawrence).   An original screenplay by John Gilling.   (W,
       LC, AMPAS).

2589   THE SECRET OF MAGIC ISLAND.   (Embassy-1965-Jean
       Tourane).   An original screenplay by Louis de Vilmorin.   (W,
       Q).

2590   THE SECRET OF MY SUCCESS.   (MGM-1965-Andrew L.
       Stone).   An original work for the screen by Andrew L. Stone.
       (NYTFR, LC, W, AMPAS, Q).

2591   THE SECRET OF SANTA VITTORIA.   (United Artists-1969-
       Stanley Kramer).   A screenplay by William Rose and Ben
       Maddow, from a novel by Robert Crichton; Simon & Schuster,
       1966.   (Q, W, AMPAS, LACOPL).

2592   SECRET SCROLLS.   (Toho-1968-Hiroshi Inagaki).   A screen-
       play by Hiroshi Inagaki and Takeshi Kimura, based on the
       novel Yagya Bugeicho by Kosuke Gomi.   (W, FF, NYTFR).

2593   THE SECRET SEVEN.   (MGM-1966-Alberto De Martino).   A
       screenplay by Alberto De Martino and Sandro Continenza.
       (FF, LC, W, AMPAS, Q).

2594   THE SECRET WAR OF HARRY FRIGG.   (Universal-1968-
       Jack Smight).   A screenplay by Peter Stone and Frank Tarl-
       off, based on a story by Frank Tarloff.   (Q, FF, NYTFR,
       FM, W, AMPAS).

2595   SECRET WORLD.   (20th Century-Fox-1969-Robert Freeman).
       A screenplay by Gerard Brach and Jackie Glass.   (FF, Q).

2595a SEDUCED AND ABANDONED.   (Continental-1964-Pietro Ger-
       mi).   A screenplay by Pietro Germi, Luciano Vincenzoni,
       Agenore Incrocci, Furio Scarpelli, and based on an original
       idea by Pietro Germi and Luciano Vincenzoni.   (FF, NYTFR,
       W, Q, AMPAS).

2596   THE SEDUCERS.   (Cinemation-1970-Ottavio Lorenzo Ricci-
       ardi).   An original screenplay by Lorenzo Ricciardi.   (W).

2597   THE SEDUCTION OF INGA.   (Cinemation-1972-Joseph W.
       Sarno).   This original screenplay was written by Joseph W.
       Sarno.   (W).

2598   SEE NO EVIL.   (Columbia-1971-Richard Fleischer).   A
       screenplay by Brian Clemens.   A novel based on the original
       screenplay was written by William Hughes; Award Books,
       1971.   (W, Q, LACOPL).

2599   THE SEED OF MAN. (SRL-1970-Marco Ferreri). An origi-
        nal work for the screen written by Marco Ferreri and Sergio
        Bazzini. (W).

2600   SEIZURE. (American International-1974-Oliver Stone). A
        screenplay written by Edward Mann and Oliver Stone, from
        an original screen story by Oliver Stone. (V).

2600a   SEND ME NO FLOWERS. (Universal-1964-Norman Jewison).
        A screenplay by Julius Epstein, based on the play by Norman
        Barasch and Carroll Moore; Samuel French, 1961, 77p. (FF,
        LACOPL, NYTFR, W, Q, LC, AMPAS).

2601   SENSO. (Fleetwood-1968-Luchino Visconti). A screenplay by
        Luchino Visconti and Suso Cecchi d'Amico, with the collabor-
        ation of Giorgio Prosperi, Carlo Alianello and Giorgio Bas-
        sani, based on a novella by Camillo Boito. Screenplay of
        Senso may be found in Two Screenplays by Luchino Visconti,
        Orion Press, 1970, pp. 103-186. (LACOPL, FF).

2602   A SEPARATE PEACE. (Paramount-1972-Larry Peerce). A
        screenplay by Fred Segal, based on the novel by John Knowles;
        Macmillan, 1959, 186p. (FF, LACOPL, Q).

2603   SEPARATION. (Continental-1968-Jack Bond). A screenplay
        by Jane Arden, based on her own story. (FF, W).

2604   SERAFINO. (Royal-1970-Pietro Germi). A screenplay by
        Leo Benvenuti, Piero de Bernardi, Tullio Pinelli, Pietro
        Germi, based on a story by Alfredo Giannetti. (Q, W).

2605   THE SERGEANT. (Warner Bros.-7 Arts-1968-John Flynn).
        A screenplay by Dennis Murphy, based on his novel; Viking,
        1958. (Q, FF, NYTFR, FM, W, LC, AMPAS, LACOPL).

2606   SERGEANT DEADHEAD. (American International-1965-Nor-
        man Taurog). An original screenplay by Louis M. Heyward.
        (NYTFR, LC, W, Q, AMPAS).

2607   SERGEANT RYKER. (Universal-1968-Buzz Kulik). A screen-
        play by Seeleg Lester and William D. Gordon, based on a
        story by Seeleg Lester. (FF, NYTFR, Q, W, AMPAS).

2608   THE SERPENT. (AVCO Embassy-1973-Henri Verneuil). A
        screenplay by Henri Verneuil and Gilles Perrault, based on a
        novel by Pierre Nord. (W, HR).

2609   SERPICO. (Paramount-1973-Sidney Lumet). A screenplay
        written by Waldo Salt and Norman Wexler, based on the book
        by Peter Maas; Viking, 1973, 311p. (W, LACOPL).

2609a   THE SERVANT. (The Landau Releasing Organization-1964-
        Joseph Losey). Harold Pinter wrote the screenplay based on

the novel by Robin Maugham; Harcourt, 1949. (LACOPL, FF, NYTFR, W, Q).

2610   A SESSION WITH THE COMMITTEE. (Commonwealth United-1969-Del Jack). No screenplay credit. (FF, W).

2610a   SEVEN DAYS IN MAY. (Paramount-1964-John Frankenheimer). A screenplay by Rod Serling, based on the novel by Fletcher Knebel and Charles W. Bailey II; Harper, 1962. (Q, W, NYTFR, FF, LACOPL, AMPAS, LC).

2611   SEVEN DWARFS TO THE RESCUE. (Childhood-1965-P. W. Tamburella). An original screenplay by P. W. Tamburella. (W, Q).

2611a   SEVEN FACES OF DR. LAO. (MGM-1964-George Pal). A screenplay by Charles Beaumont, based on the novel The Circus of Dr. Lao by Charles G. Finney; Avon, 1935, 119p. (FF, LACOPL, W, LC, AMPAS, Q).

2612   SEVEN GOLDEN MEN. (Warner Bros.-7 Arts-1969-Marco Vicario). An original screenplay written by Marco Vicario and Mariano Ozores. (FF, Q, W).

2613   SEVEN GUNS FOR THE MacGREGORS. (Columbia-1968-Frank Garfield). A screenplay by Enzo dell'Aquila, Fernando di Leo, David Moreno, and Duccio Tessari, based on a story by David Moreno. (FF, W).

2614   THE SEVEN MINUTES. (20th Century-Fox-1971-Russ Meyer). A screenplay written by Richard Warren Lewis, based on the novel by Irving Wallace; Simon & Schuster, 1969, 607p. (W, LACOPL, Q).

2615   THE SEVEN UPS. (20th Century-Fox-1973-Philip D'Antoni). A screenplay by Albert Ruben, Alexander Jacobs, from a story by Sonny Grosso. (W).

2616   SEVEN WOMEN. (MGM-1966-John Ford). A screenplay by Janet Green and John McCormick, based on the short story Chinese Finale by Norah Lofts. (FF, NYTFR, LC, W, AMPAS, Q).

2617   1776. (Columbia-1972-Peter H. Hunt). A screenplay by Peter Stone, based on a musical play with a book by Peter Stone, and music and lyrics by Sherman Edwards; Viking. 1970. 171p. (W, FF, LACOPL, Q).

2618   THE SEVENTH CONTINENT. (U-M-1968-Dusan Vukotic). A screenplay by Dusan Vukotic and Andro Lusicic, based on an original story by Ruzena Fischerova. (FF, NYTFR, W).

2618a   THE SEVENTH DAWN. (United Artists-1964-Lewis Gilbert). A screenplay by Karl Tunberg, based on the novel The Durian

Tree by Michael Keon; Simon & Schuster, 1960, 309p. (W,
FF, Q, LACOPL, AMPAS, NYTFR).

2619   THE SEVENTH JUROR. (Trans-Lux-1964-George Lautner).
A screenplay by Jacques Robert, based on a novel by Francis
Didelot, with dialogue by Pierre Laroche. (FF, NYTFR, Q,
W).

2619a A SEVERED HEAD. (Columbia-1971-Dick Clement). A
screenplay by Frederic Raphael, based on the novel by Iris
Murdoch and J. B. Priestley; Chatto, 1964, 107p. (W,
LACOPL, Q).

2620   SEX AND THE SINGLE GAY. (Bizarre-1970-Pat Rocco). A
script written by Pat Rocco. (W).

SEX AND THE TEENAGER see TO FIND A MAN

2621   SEX FREAKS. (Rainbow Distributors-1974-M. C. Von Hellen).
A film written by M. C. Von Hellen. (V).

2622   LE SEX SHOP. (Peppercorn-Wormser-1973-Claude Berri).
An original screenplay by Claude Berri. (W).

2623   THE SEX THIEF. (International Amusement-1974-Martin
Campbell). An original screenplay by Edward Hyde. (V).

2624   SHADOW HUNTERS. (Toho-1973-Toshio Masuda). An original screenplay by Takao Saito and Kanao Ikegami. (W).

2625   SHADOW OF EVIL. (7 Arts-1966-André Hunebelle). A
screenplay by Pierre Foucaud, Raymond Borel, André Hunebelle, Michel Lebrun, Richard Caron, and Patrice Rondard,
based on the novel Lila de Calcutta by Jean Bruce. (FF).

2626   SHADOWS OF FORGOTTEN ANCESTORS. (Artkino-1967-
Sergei Paradjhanov). An original screenplay by Ivan Chendey
and Sergei Paradghanov. (W).

2627   SHAFT. (MGM-1971-Gordon Parks). A screenplay by Ernest
Tidyman and John D. F. Black, based on the novel by Ernest
Tidyman; Macmillan, 1970, 188p. (W, LACOPL, Q).

2628   SHAFT IN AFRICA. (MGM-1973-John Guillermin). An original screenplay by Stirling Silliphant, based on characters created by Ernest Tidyman. (W, Q).

2629   SHAFT'S BIG SCORE! (MGM-1972-Gordon Parks). A screenplay written for the screen by Ernest Tidyman, based on his
characters created for SHAFT. (FF, Q).

2630   SHAKESPEARE WALLAH. (Walter Reade-Sterling-1966-
James Ivory). A story and screenplay by R. Prawer Jhabvala

and James Ivory. The screenplay was published by Grove
Press, 1973, 152p. (FF, NYTFR, W, Q).

2631   THE SHAKIEST GUN IN THE WEST. (Universal-1968-Alan
       Rafkin). A screenplay by Jim Fritzell and Everett Green-
       baum, based on the screenplay by Edmund Hartmann and
       Frank Tashlin, The Paleface. (FF, NYTFR, FM, W,
       AMPAS, Q).

2632   SHALAKO. (Cinerama-1968-Edward Dmytryk). A screenplay
       by J. J. Griffith, Hal Hopper and Scot Finch, based on the
       novel by Louis L'Amour. (FF, NYTFR, AMPAS, Q).

2633   SHAME. (Lopert-1968-Ingmar Bergman). A screenplay by
       Ingmar Bergman; Grossman Publisher, 1972, 191p. (FF,
       NYTFR, W, AMPAS, LACOPL, Q).

2634   SHAME, SHAME, EVERYBODY KNOWS HER NAME. (J.E.R.
       -1970-Joseph Jacoby). An original story and screenplay by
       William Dorsey Blake. (W).

2635   THE SHAMELESS OLD LADY. (Continental-1966-Rene Allio).
       A screenplay by Rene Allio, based on a story by Bertolt
       Brecht. (FF, NYTFR, W, Q).

2636   SHAMUS. (Columbia-1973-Buzz Kulik). An original screen-
       play by Barry Beckerman. (W, Q, FF).

2637   SHANKS. (Paramount-1974-William Castle). An original
       screenplay by Ranald Graham. (V, HR).

2638   SHARK. (Excelsior-1970-Samuel Fuller). An original screen-
       play by Samuel Fuller and John Kingsbridge. (W).

2639   SHATTERHAND. (Goldstone Film Enterprises-1968-Hugo
       Fregonese). A screenplay by Ladislas Fodor and Robert A.
       Stemmle, based on a story by Karl May. (FF, NYTFR, W,
       AMPAS).

2640   SHE. (MGM-1965-Robert Day). A screenplay by David Chan-
       tier, based on the novel by H. Rider Haggard; Harper, 1886.
       (NYTFR, LC, W, AMPAS, Q, LACOPL).

2641   SHE AND HE. (Brandon-1967-Susumu Hani). An original
       screenplay by Susumu Hani. (W).

2642   THE SHE BEAST. (Europix Consolidated-1966-Mike Reeves).
       An original work for the screen written by Michael Byron.
       (FF).

2643   SHE FREAK. (Sonney Amusement Enterprises-1967-Byron
       Mabe). David F. Friedman wrote this original screenplay.
       (FF, AMPAS).

2644   SHENANDOAH. (Universal-1965-Andrew V. McLaglen). An
        original screenplay written by James Lee Barrett. (NYTFR,
        LC, W, AMPAS, Q).

2645   THE SHEPHERD GIRL. (Frank Lee-1965-Lo Chen). No
        screenplay credit available. (NYTFR).

2646   SHINBONE ALLEY. (Allied Artists-1971-). A screenplay
        by Joe Darion, based on the "Archy and Mehitabel" stories
        by Don Marquis; Doubleday, 1930, 264p., and on the musical
        "Shinbone Alley" by Joe Darion and Mel Brooks. (W, Q).

2647   SHIP OF FOOLS. (Columbia-1965-Stanley Kramer). A
        screenplay by Abby Mann, based on the novel by Katherine
        Anne Porter; Little, Brown & Co., 1962. (NYTFR, LC, W,
        AMPAS, LACOPL, Q).

2647a   SHOCK TREATMENT. (20th Century-Fox-1964-Denis Sand-
        ers). Sydney Boehm wrote the screenplay which was taken
        from the novel by Winifred Van Atta. (FF, NYTFR, W, LC,
        AMPAS, Q).

2648   SHOCK TROOPS. (United Artists-1969-Costa-Gavras). A
        screenplay by Costa-Gavras, based on a novel by Jean-Pierre
        Chabrol. (FF, W, Q).

2649   THE SHOES OF THE FISHERMAN. (MGM-1968-Michael
        Anderson). A screenplay written by John Patrick and James
        Kennaway, based on the novel by Morris L. West; Morrow,
        1963. (Q, FF, NYTFR, FM, W, LC, AMPAS, LACOPL).

2650   SHOOT IT: BLACK, SHOOT IT: BLUE. (Levitt-Pickman-
        1974-Dennis McGuire). An original screenplay by Dennis
        McGuire, from the novel Shoot It by Paul Tyner; Atlantic-
        Little, Brown, 1968, 212p. (V, LACOPL).

2651   SHOOT LOUD, LOUDER ... I DON'T UNDERSTAND. (Em-
        bassy-1967-Eduardo de Filippo). A screenplay by Eduardo
        de Filippo and Suso Cecchi d'Amico, based on the play Le
        Voci de Dentro (The Voices from Within) by Eduardo de
        Filippo. (FF, NYTFR, FM, W).

2652   SHOOT OUT. (Universal-1971-Henry Hathaway). A screen-
        play by Marguerite Roberts, based on the novel, The Lone
        Cowboy by Will James, 1930. (W, LACOPL, Q).

2653   THE SHOP ON MAIN STREET. (Prominent Films-1966-Jan
        Kadar and Elmar Klos). A screenplay by Ladislav Grossman,
        Jan Kadar, and Elmar Klos, based on a story by Ladislav
        Grossman. (FF, NYTFR, LC, W, AMPAS, Q).

2653a   A SHOT IN THE DARK. (United Artists-1964-Blake Edwards).
        This screenplay was written by Blake Edwards and William

Peter Blatty, based upon the plays by Harry Kurnitz and Marcel Achard; Random House, 1962. (FF, LACOPL, NYTFR, LC, AMPAS, Q, W).

2654   SHOWDOWN. (Universal-1973-George Seaton). An original screenplay by Theodore Taylor, based on a story by Hank Fine. (W, Q).

2655   SHOWDOWN FOR ZATOICHI. (Daiei-1968-Kenji Misumi). A screenplay by Daisuke Ito, based on an original story by Kan Shimozawa. (FF, NYTFR).

2656   THE SHUTTERED ROOM. (Warner Bros.-7 Arts-1968-David Greene). A screenplay written by D. B. Ledrov and Nathaniel Tanchuck, based on the novel by H. P. Lovecraft and August Derleth; Arkham House, 1959, 313p. (FF, NYTFR, FM, W, AMPAS, LACOPL, Q).

2657   THE SICILIAN CLAN. (20th Century-Fox-1970-Henri Verneuil). A screenplay by Henri Verneuil, Jose Giovanni, and Pierre Pellegri, from a novel by Auguste le Breton. (W, Q).

2658   SIDDHARTHA. (Columbia-1973-Conrad Rooks). Screenplay adapted by Conrad Rooks, based on a novel by Hermann Hesse; New Directions, 1951. (W, LACOPL, Q).

SIDELONG GLANCES OF A PIGEON KICKER see PIGEONS

2659   SIGN OF THE VIRGIN. (Brandon-1969-Zbynek Brynych). A screenplay by Milan Uhde and Zbynek Brynych, based on a story by Milan Uhde. (W).

2660   SIGNPOST TO MURDER. (MGM-1965-George Englund). A screenplay by Sally Benson, based on a play by Monte Doyle. (W, LC, Q).

2660a THE SILENCE. (Janus-1964-Ingmar Bergman). An original screenplay by Ingmar Bergman, published in Film Trilogy; Orion Press, 1967, 143p. (LACOPL, FF, NYTFR, W, Q).

2661   SILENCE. (Cinema Financial of America-1974-John Korty). A screenplay by Mary Mackey and Ellen Geer. (V, W).

2662   THE SILENCERS. (Columbia-1966-Phil Karlson). A screenplay by Oscar Saul, based on the novels The Silencers and Death of a Citizen by Donald Hamilton. (Q, FF, NYTFR, LC, W, AMPAS).

2663   SILENT RUNNING. (Universal-1972-Douglas Trumbull). A screenplay by Deric Washburn, Mike Cimino and Steve Bochco. (FF, W, Q).

2665   SIMON OF THE DESERT.   (Altura Films-1969-Luis Buñuel).
       A screenplay by Luis Buñuel and Julio Alejandro, based on a
       story by Luis Buñuel; in Three Screenplays, Orion Press,
       1969, pp. 197-245.   (Q, FF, W, LACOPL, MCC, SCH).

2666   SINDERELLA AND THE GOLDEN BRA.   (Manson-1965-Loel
       Minnardi).   A screenplay by Frank Squires from a story by
       Loel Minnardi, Frank Squires, and Les Szarvas.   (W).

2667   SINFUL DAVEY.   (United Artists-1969-John Huston).   A
       screenplay by James R. Webb, based on the book The Life of
       David Haggart by David Haggart.   (FF, W, LC, AMPAS, Q).

2668   THE SINFUL DWARF.   (Boxoffice International-1973-Vidal
       Raski).   An original screenplay by William Mayo.   (W).

2668a SING AND SWING.   (Universal-1964-Lance Comfort).   A
       screenplay by Lyn Fairhurst, based on an idea by Harold
       Shampan.   (FF, Q, W, LC, AMPAS).

2669   THE SINGING NUN.   (MGM-1966-Henry Koster).   A screen-
       play by Sally Benson and John Furia, Jr., from a story by
       John Furia, Jr.   (Q, FF, NYTFR, LC, W, AMPAS).

2670   SISTERS.   (American International-1973-Brian de Palma).   A
       screenplay by Brian de Palma, and Louisa Rose, from a
       story by Brian de Palma.   (W, Q).

2671   SITTING TARGET.   (MGM-1972-Douglas Hickox).   A screen-
       play written by Alexander Jacobs, based on the novel by
       Laurence Henderson; St. Martin's, 1970, 238p.   (FF,
       LACOPL, Q).

2672   SITUATION HOPELESS--BUT NOT SERIOUS.   (Paramount-
       1965-Gottfried Reinhardt).   A screenplay by Silvia Reinhardt,
       adapted by Jan Lustig from The Hiding Place by Robert Shaw;
       World, 1959.   (NYTFR, LC, W, AMPAS, LACOPL, Q).

2673   SIX IN PARIS.   (New Yorker-1969-Jean Douchet, Jean
       Rouche, Jean Daniel Pollet, Eric Rohmer, Jean-Luc Godard,
       Claude Chabrol).   A film in six episodes each written by a
       different writer, including Jean Douchet and Georges Keller,
       Jean Rouche, Jean Daniel Pollet, Eric Rohmer, Jean-Luc
       Godard, and Claude Chabrol.   (FF, AMPAS).

2674   SKEZAG.   (Soho Cinema-1971-Joe Freedman and Philip F.
       Messina).   A documentary interview.   No screenplay credit.
       (W).

2675   THE SKI BUM.   (AVCO Embassy-1971-Bruce Clark).   A
       screenplay by Marc Siegler and Bruce Clark, based on the
       novel by Romain Gary; Harper, 1965.   (W, LACOPL, Q).

2676   SKI FEVER. (Allied Artists-1969-Curt Siodmak). A screenplay by Curt Siodmak and Robert Joseph, based on a story
by Frank Agrama and Edward Zatlyn. (W, AMPAS, Q).

2677   SKI PARTY. (American International-1965-Alan Rafkin).
A screenplay by Robert Kaufman. (NYTFR, LC, W,
AMPAS, Q).

2678   SKIDOO. (Paramount-1969-Otto Preminger). A screenplay
by Doran William Cannon. (FF, W, LC, AMPAS, Q).

2679   THE SKIN GAME. (William Mishkin-1966-Arnold L. Miller).
A screenplay written directly for the screen by Bob Kesten.
(FF).

2680   SKIN GAME. (Warner Bros.-1971-Paul Bogart). A screenplay by Pierre Marton aka Peter Stone, from a story by
Richard Alan Simmons. (W, Q).

2681   THE SKULL. (Paramount-1965-Freddie Francis). An original screenplay by Milton Subotsky. (W, LC, AMPAS, Q).

2682   SKULLDUGGERY. (Universal-1970-Gordon Douglas). Nelson
Gidding wrote this original screenplay. (W, Q).

2683   THE SKY PIRATE. (FilmMakers-1970-Andrew Meyer). An
original screenplay written by Andrew Meyer. (W).

2684   SKYJACKED. (MGM-1972-John Guillermin). A screenplay
by Stanley R. Greenberg, based on a novel by David Harper,
Hijacked; Dodd, 1970, 211p. (W, LACOPL).

2685   THE SLAMS. (MGM-1973-Jonathan Kaplan). Richard L.
Adams wrote this original screenplay. (W).

2686   SLAUGHTER. (American International-1972-Jack Starrett).
An original screenplay written by Mark Hanna and Don Williams. (W, FF, Q).

2687   SLAUGHTERHOUSE-FIVE. (Universal-1972-George Roy Hill).
A screenplay by Stephen Geller, based on a novel by Kurt
Vonnegut, Jr.; Delacorte Press, 1969, 186p. (W, LACOPL,
Q).

2688   SLAUGHTER'S BIG RIPOFF. (American International-1973-
Gordon Douglas). An original screenplay by Charles Johnson,
based on characters created by Don Williams. (W, Q).

2689   SLAVES. (Continental-1969-Herbert J. Biberman). An original screenplay by Herbert J. Biberman, John O. Killens, and
Alida Sherman. (FF, W, AMPAS, Q).

2690   SLEEPER. (United Artists-1973-Woody Allen). An original screenplay written by Woody Allen. (W).

2691   THE SLEEPING BEAUTY. (Royal-1966-Apollinariy Dudko &
       Konstantin Sergeyev). A screenplay by Apollinariy Dudko,
       Konstantin Sergeyev, and Joseph Shapiro, based on the story
       by Charles Perrault. (FF, W).

2692   THE SLEEPING CAR MURDER. (7 Arts-1966-Costa Gavras).
       A screenplay by Costa Gavras and Sebastien Japrisot, based
       on a novel by Sebastien Japrisot. (FF, NYTFR, W, AMPAS,
       Q).

2693   THE SLENDER THREAD. (Paramount-1965-Sydney Pollack).
       A screenplay by Stirling Silliphant, suggested by a story in
       Life magazine by Shana Alexander. (NYTFR, LC, W,
       AMPAS, Q).

2694   SLEUTH. (20th Century-Fox-1972-Joseph L. Mankiewicz).
       A screenplay by Anthony Shaffer, based on his play; Dodd,
       1970, 125p. (FF, LACOPL, Q).

2695   SLIPSTREAM. (Pacific Rim-1974-David Acomba). A screen-
       play by William Fruet, from an original story by David
       Acomba. (V).

2696   SLITHER. (MGM-1973-Howard Zieff). An original screen-
       play by W. D. Richter. (W, Q).

2697   SLOGAN. (Royal-1970-Pierre Grimblat). A screenplay by
       Pierre Grimblat. (W, Q).

2698   SLOW RUN. (Film-Makers' Distribution Center-1968-Larry
       Kardish). An original screenplay by Larry Kardish. (FF,
       NYTFR, W).

2699   SMASHING TIME. (Paramount-1967-Desmond Davis). An
       original screenplay written by George Melly. (FF, NYTFR,
       FM, W, LC, AMPAS).

2700   SMIC, SMAC, SMOC. (GSF-1971-Claude Lelouch). An origi-
       nal work for the screen by Claude Lelouch. (FF, W, Q).

2701   SMITH! (Buena Vista-1969-Michael O'Herlihy). A screen-
       play by Louis Pelletier, based on a book by Paul St. Pierre,
       Breaking Smith's Quarter Horse. (W, LC, AMPAS, Q).

2702   SMOKY. (20th Century-Fox-1966-George Sherman). A
       screenplay by Harold Medford, based on a screenplay by
       Lillie Hayward, Dwight Cummins, and Dorothy Yost. Taken
       from the novel Smoky, by Will James; Scribner, 1929. (FF,
       LC, W, AMPAS, LACOPL, Q).

2703   THE SMUGGLERS. (New Yorker-1969-Luc Moullet). An

original screenplay by Luc Moullet. (FF).

2704   SNOW JOB. (Warner Bros.-1972-George Englund). A screen-
       play by Ken Kolby and Jeffrey Bloom, based on a story by
       Richard Gallagher. (W, Q).

2705   SNOWBALL EXPRESS. (Buena Vista-1972-Norman Tokar).
       A screenplay by Don Tait, Jim Parker, Arnold Margolin,
       based on Chateau Bon Vivant by Frankie and John O'Rear;
       Macmillan, 1967, 240p. (Q, W, LACOPL).

2706   SO LONG, BLUE BOY. (Maryon-1973-Gerald Gordon). An
       original screenplay by David Long and Chris Long. (W).

2707   LE SOCRATE. (New Yorker-1969-Robert Lapoujade). An
       original screenplay by Robert Lapoujade. (W).

2708   SOCRATES. (New Yorker-1971-Roberto Rossellini). An orig-
       inal screenplay by Roberto Rossellini and Marcella Mariani.
       (W).

2709   SOFI. (Golden Bear-1968-Robert Carlisle). A screenplay by
       Don Eitner and Tom Troupe, based on the short story Diary
       of a Madman by Nicolai Gogol; New American Library, 1960.
       (FF, NYTFR, W, AMPAS, LACOPL).

2709a THE SOFT SKIN. (Cinema V-1964-François Truffaut). An
       original screenplay by François Truffaut and Jean-Louis
       Richard. (FF, W).

2710   SOL MADRID. (MGM-1968-Brian G. Hutton). A screenplay
       by David Karp, based on the novel Fruit of the Poppy by Ro-
       bert Wilder; Putnam, 1965. (Q, FF, NYTFR, FM, W, LC,
       AMPAS, LACOPL).

2711   SOLDIER BLUE. (AVCO Embassy-1970-Ralph Nelson). A
       screenplay by John Gay, from the novel Arrow in the Sun by
       Theodore V. Olsen; Doubleday, 1969, 187p. (W, LACOPL,
       Q).

2712   SOLEIL-O. (New Yorker-1973-Med Hondo). An original
       screenplay by Med Hondo. (W).

2713   SOLOMON KING. (Sal-Wa-1974-Sal Watts & Jack Bomay). A
       screenplay written by Sal Watts, from a story by Jim Alston.
       (V).

2714   SOME CALL IT LOVING. (CineGlobe-1973-James B. Harris).
       James B. Harris wrote this original screenplay. (W).

2715   SOME GIRLS DO. (United Artists-1971-Ralph Thomas). An
       original screenplay written by David Osborne and Liz Charles-
       Williams. (W).

2716   SOME KIND OF A NUT. (United Artists-1969-Garson Kanin).
        An original screenplay by Garson Kanin). (FF, W, AMPAS,
        Q).

2717   SOME OF MY BEST FRIENDS ARE ... (American Interna-
        tional-1971-Mervyn Nelson). An original screenplay written
        by Mervyn Nelson. (W).

2718   SOMEONE BEHIND THE DOOR. (GSF-1971-Nicholas Gess-
        ner). A screenplay written by Jacques Robert, Mac Behm,
        Nicolas Gessner, and Lorenzo Ventavoli, based on a novel
        by Jacques Robert. (W, Q).

2719   SOMETHING BIG. (National General-1971-Andrew V. Mac-
        Laglen). An original story and screenplay by James Lee
        Barrett. (W, Q).

2720   SOMETHING FOR EVERYONE. (National General-1970-Har-
        old Prince). A screenplay by Hugh Wheeler, based on the
        novel The Cook, by Harry Kressing; Random House, 1965.
        (W, Q, LACOPL).

2721   SOMETIME SWEET SUSAN. (Variety-1974-Fred Donaldson).
        No screen play credits available. (V).

2722   SOMETIMES A GREAT NOTION. (Universal-1971-Paul New-
        man). A screenplay by John Gay, from the novel by Ken
        Kesey; Viking, 1964. (W, LACOPL, Q).

2723   SON OF A GUNFIGHTER. (MGM-1966-Paul Landres). An
        original screenplay by Clarke Reynolds. (FF, LC, W,
        AMPAS, Q).

        SON OF BLOB see BEWARE THE BLOB

2723a   THE SON OF CAPTAIN BLOOD. (Paramount-1964-Tullio De-
        Michelli). Story and screenplay by Casey Robinson, from
        characters created by Rafael Sabatini. (LC, AMPAS, W, Q,
        FF).

2724   THE SONG AND THE SILENCE. (Cloverhouse-1969-Nathan
        Cohen). An original screenplay by Nathan Cohen. (FF, W,
        Q).

2725   SONG OF NORWAY. (Cinerama-1970-Andrew L. Stone). A
        screen story and screenplay by Andrew L. Stone, suggested
        from the musical Song of Norway by Milton Lazarus, Robert
        Wright, and George Forrest. (Q, W).

2726   SONNY & JED. (K-Tel-1974-Sergio Corbucci). A screenplay
        by Sabatino Ciuffini, Mario Amendola, Adriano Bolzoni, Jose
        Maria Forque and Sergio Corbucci, based on an original
        story by Sergio Corbucci. (HR, V).

2727   SONS AND MOTHERS.   (Artkino-1967-Mark Donskoi).   A
       screenplay written by Z. Voskresenskala and I. Donskoia.
       (NYTFR, W).

2728   SONS OF GOOD EARTH.   (Frank Lee International-1967-Hu
       King-chuan).   An original screenplay by Hu King-chuan.
       (NYTFR).

2729   THE SONS OF KATIE ELDER.   (Paramount-1965-Henry Hath-
       away).   A screenplay by William H. Wright, Allan Weiss and
       Harry Essex, based on a story by Talbot Jennings.   (NYTFR,
       LC, W, AMPAS, Q).

2730   THE SORCERERS.   (Allied Artists-1968-Michael Reeves).   A
       screenplay by Michael Reeves and Tom Baker, based on an
       original idea by John Burke.   (FF, W, Q).

2731   THE SOUL OF NIGGER CHARLEY.   (Paramount-1973-Larry
       G. Spangler).   A screenplay by Harold Stone, from a story
       by Larry G. Spangler.   (W, Q).

2732   SOUL SOLDIER.   (Fanfare-1972-John Cardos).   An original
       screenplay by Marlene Weed.   (FF).

2733   SOUND OF HORROR.   (Europix Consolidated 1967-Jose An-
       tonio Nives-Conde).   An original screenplay by San-X-Abar
       Banel.   (FF).

2734   THE SOUND OF MUSIC.   (20th Century-Fox-1965-Robert
       Wise).   A screenplay by Ernest Lehman, based on the musi-
       cal play by Howard Lindsay and Russel Crouse; Random
       House, 1960, 141p.   (FF, LC, Q, W, AMPAS, LACOPL).

2735   SOUNDER.   (20th Century-Fox-1972-Martin Ritt).   A screen-
       play by Lonne Elder III, based on the novel by William H.
       Armstrong; Harper & Row, 1969, 116p.   (FF, W, Q,
       LACOPL).

2736   THE SOUTHERN STAR.   (Columbia-1969-Sidney Hayers).   A
       screenplay by David Pursall, Jack Seddon, based on a novel
       by Jules Verne.   (W, AMPAS, Q).

2737   SOYLENT GREEN.   (MGM-1973-Richard Fleischer).   A
       screenplay by Stanley R. Greenberg, based on the novel Make
       Room, Make Room by Harry Harrison; Berkeley, 1973, 208p.
       (W, FF, Q, LACOPL).

2738   THE SPECTRE OF EDGAR ALLAN POE.   (Cinerama-1974-
       Mohy Quandour).   An original screenplay by Mohy Quandour.
       (V).

       SPEED LIMIT: 65   see   THE LIMIT

2739   SPEEDWAY.   (MGM-1968-Norman Taurog).   An original
       screenplay by Phillip Shuken.   (FF, NYTFR, FM, W, LC,
       AMPAS, Q).

2740   THE SPIDER'S STRATAGEM.   (New Yorker-1973-Bernardo
       Bertolucci).   A screenplay by Bernardo Bertolucci, Edoardo
       de Gregoria, Marilu Pavolini, after the Jorge Luis Borges
       story.   (W).

2741   THE SPIKES GANG.   (United Artists-1974-Richard Fleischer).
       A screenplay by Irving Ravetch and Harriet Frank, Jr.   (HR,
       V).

2742   SPINOUT.   (MGM-1966-Norman Taurog).   A screenplay by
       Daniel L. Fapp.   (FF, NYTFR, LC, W, AMPAS, Q).

2743   THE SPIRIT IS WILLING.   (Paramount-1968-William Castle).
       A screenplay by Ben Starr, based on the novel The Visitors
       by Nathaniel Benchley; McGraw-Hill, 1965.   (FF, W, LC,
       AMPAS, LACOPL, Q).

2744   SPIRITS OF THE DEAD.   (American International-1969-Roger
       Vadim, Louis Malle, Federico Fellini).   A film made up of
       three episodes.   "Metzengerstein" was written by Roger Vad-
       im and Pascal Cousin.   "William Wilson" was written by
       Louis Malle, with dialogue by Daniel Boulanger.   The screen-
       play by Federico Fellini and Bernardino Zapponi was called
       "Never Bet the Devil Your Head, or Toby Dammit."   All
       three stories were based on works by Edgar Allan Poe that
       can be found in Complete Stories and Poems; Doubleday, 1966.
       (FF, W, LC, Q, LACOPL).

2745   THE SPLIT.   (MGM-1968-Gordon Flemyng).   A screenplay by
       Robert Sabaroff, based on the novel The Seventh by Richard
       Stark.   (FF, NYTFR, FM, W, LC, AMPAS, Q).

2746   SPOILS OF THE NIGHT.   (William Mishkin-1969-Shinji Mura-
       yama).   An original screenplay by Masashige Narusawa.   (FF,
       W).

2747   THE SPOOK WHO SAT BY THE DOOR.   (United Artists-
       1973-Ivan Dixon).   A screenplay by Sam Greenlee, Melvin
       Clay, based on the novel by Sam Greenlee; Baron, 1969,
       248p.   (W, LACOPL).

2748   THE SPORTING CLUB.   (AVCO Embassy-1971-Larry Peerce).
       A screenplay by Lorenzo Semple, Jr., based on a novel by
       Thomas McGuane; Simon & Schuster, 1968, 220p.   (W,
       LACOPL, Q).

2749   THE SPOTS ON MY LEOPARD.   (Falcon American-1974-Tim
       Spring).   An original screenplay by Beyer Boshoff.   (V).

2750 SPREE. (United Producers-1967-Mitchell Leisen and Walon Green). An original screenplay by Sydney Field. (W, LC, AMPAS).

2751 SPY IN YOUR EYE. (American International-1966-Vittorio Sala). A screenplay by Romano Ferraro, Adriano Baracco and Adriano Bolzoni. (FF, LC, W, Q).

2752 THE SPY WHO CAME IN FROM THE COLD. (Paramount-1965-Martin Ritt). A screenplay by Paul Dehn and Guy Trosper, from the novel by John Le Carré; Coward, 1963. (NYTFR, LC, W, AMPAS, LACOPL, Q).

2753 THE SPY WITH A COLD NOSE. (Embassy-1966-Daniel Petrie). An original story and screenplay by Ray Galton and Alan Simpson. (FF, NYTFR, W, AMPAS, Q).

2754 THE SPY WITH MY FACE. (MGM-1966-John Newland). A screenplay by Clyde Ware and Joseph Calvelli, from a story by Clyde Ware. (FF, W, Q).

2755 SPYS. (20th Century-Fox-1974-Irvin Kershner). A screenplay by Malcolm Marmorstein, Lawrence J. Cohen, and Fred Freeman. An original novel based on the screenplay was written by T. Robert Joyce; Pocket Books, 1974, 128p. (V, LACOPL).

2756 SQUARES. (Plateau International-1972-Patrick J. Murphy). An original screenplay by Mary Ann Saxon. (W).

2757 SSSSSSSS. (Universal-1973-Bernard L. Kowalski). A screenplay by Hal Dresner, from a story by Dan Striepeke. (W, Q).

2758 STACEY! (New World-1973-Andy Sidaris). A screenplay by William Edgar, from a story by Andy Sidaris and Leon Mirell. (W).

2758a STAGE TO THUNDER ROCK. (Paramount-1964-William F. Claxton). An original screenplay by Charles Wallace. (FF).

2759 STAGECOACH. (20th Century-Fox-1966-Gordon Douglas). A screenplay by Joseph Landon, based on a screenplay by Dudley Nichols; Simon & Schuster, 1971, 152p.; and the short story "Stage to Lordsburg" by Ernest Haycox. (FF, LC, W, AMPAS, Q).

2760 STAIRCASE. (20th Century-Fox-1969-Stanley Donen). A screenplay by Charles Dyer, based on his play; Grove Press, 1966, 88p. A novelization written by Charles Dyer based on the play was published by Doubleday, 1969, 284p. (FF, W, AMPAS, LACOPL, Q).

2761   THE STALKING MOON. (National General-1969-Robert Mulligan). Alvin Sargent wrote the screenplay based on the novel by Theodore V. Olsen; Doubleday, 1965. (FF, W, AMPAS, LACOPL, Q).

2762   STAND UP AND BE COUNTED. (Columbia-1972-Jackie Cooper). An original screenplay by Bernard Slade. (FF, Q).

2763   STANLEY. (Crown International-1972-William Grefe). A screenplay written by Gary Crutcher, based on an original story by William Grefe. (FF, Q, W).

2764   STAR! (20th Century-Fox-1968-Robert Wise). A screenplay by William Fairchild. (FF, NYTFR, W, LC, AMPAS, Q).

2765   STAR SPANGLED GIRL. (Paramount-1971-Jerry Paris). A screenplay by Arnold Margolin & Jim Parker, based on the play by Neil Simon; Random House, 1969, 120p. (W, LACOPL, Q).

2766   STARDUST. (Columbia-1974-Michael Apted). An original story and screenplay written by Ray Connolly. (V, W).

2767   START THE REVOLUTION WITHOUT ME. (Warner Bros.-1970-Bud Yorkin). A screenplay by Fred Freeman and Lawrence J. Cohen. (W, Q).

2768   STATE OF SIEGE. (Cinema 5-1973-Constantine Costa-Gavras). A screenplay written directly for the screen by Franco Solinas and Constantine Costa-Gavras. (W, Q).

2768a STATION SIX-SAHARA. (Allied Artists-1964-Seth Holt). An original screenplay by Bryan Forbes and Brian Clemens. (FF, NYTFR, W, Q, LC, AMPAS).

2769   THE STATUE. (Cinerama-1971-Rod Amateau). A screenplay by Alec Coppel and Denis Norden, based on a story by Alec Coppel. (W, Q).

2770   STAVISKY. (Cinemation-1974-Alain Resnais). An original screenplay by Jorge Semprun. (NYT, V, W).

2771   STAY AWAY, JOE. (MGM-1968-Peter Tewksbury). A screenplay by Burt Kennedy and Michael A. Hoey, based on the novel by Dan Cushman; 1953. (FF, W, LC, AMPAS, LACOPL, Q).

2772   THE STEAGLE. (AVCO Embassy-1971-Paul Sylbert). A screenplay by Paul Sylbert, based on the novel by Irvin Faust; Random House, 1966. (W, LACOPL, Q).

2773   STEEL ARENA. (L-T-1973-Mark L. Lester). An original screenplay by Mark L. Lester. (W).

2774   STEELYARD BLUES.   (Warner Bros.-1973-Alan Myerson).
An original screenplay by David S. Ward.   (W, Q).

2775   STEFANIA.   (Chancellor-1968-Yiannis Dalianidis).   A screenplay by Nelly Theodorou, based on her novel Stephania Sto
Anamorfotirio.   (FF, NYTFR, W).

2776   THE STEPMOTHER.   (Crown International-1972-Hikmet Avedis).   A screenplay by Hikmet Avedis.   (FF, W).

2777   STEPPENWOLF.   (Peter J. Sprague-1974-Fred Haines).   A
screenplay by Fred Haines, from the novel by Herman Hesse;
Holt, 1966.   (V, LACOPL, W).

2778   THE STERILE CUCKOO.   (Paramount-1969-Alan J. Pakula).
A screenplay by Alvin Sargent, based on the novel by John
Nichols; McKay, 1965.   (FF, W, LC, AMPAS, LACOPL, Q).

2779   THE STEWARDESSES.   (Sherpix-1970-Alf Silliman, Jr.).   An
original screenplay by Alf Silliman, Jr.   (W, Q).

THE STEWARDESSES [1972] see THE SWINGIN' STEWARD-
ESSES

2780   STICKS AND STONES.   (Filmteam-1970-Stan Lo Presto).   A
screenplay by Tom O'Keefe.   (W).

2781   STIGMA.   (Cinerama-1972-David E. Durston).   A screenplay
by David E. Durston.   (FF, Q).

2782   STILETTO.   (AVCO Embassy-1969-Bernard Kowalski).   A
screenplay by A. J. Russell, based on the novel by Harold
Robbins.   (FF, W, AMPAS, Q).

2783   THE STING.   (Universal-1973-George Roy Hill).   A screenplay by David S. Ward.   A novelization based on the screenplay was written by Robert Weverka; Bantam Books, 1973,
154p.   (W, LACOPL, Q).

2784   STING OF DEATH.   (Thunderbird International Pictures-1967-
William Grefe).   An original screenplay by Al Dempsey.   (FF,
LC).

2785   STOLEN KISSES.   (Lopert-1969-François Truffaut).   A screenplay by François Truffaut, Bernard Revon and Claude de Givray.   The screenplay is published and appears in The Adventures of Antoine Doinel; Simon & Schuster, 1971, 320p.   (FF,
W, AMPAS, Q, LACOPL).

2786   THE STONE KILLER.   (Columbia-1973-Michael Winner).   A
screenplay by Gerald Wilson, from A Complete State of Death
by John Gardner; Viking, 1969, 255p.   (W, LACOPL).

2787   THE STOOLIE. (Jama-1972-John G. Avildsen). An original
        screenplay by Eugene Price, Larry Alexander, and Marc B.
        Ray. (W).

2788   STOP THE WORLD--I WANT TO GET OFF. (Warner Bros.-
        1966-Philip Saville & Michael Lindsay-Hogg). A screenplay
        by Anthony Newley and Leslie Bricusse, based on their musi-
        cal play; Ludlow Music Co., 1961, 24 p. (FF, LC, W,
        AMPAS, LACOPL, Q).

2788a   STOP TRAIN 349. (Allied Artists-1964-Rolf Haedrich). Vic-
        tor Vicas scripted the film, from a story by Will Tremper
        with collaboration by Jim Henaghan and dialogue by Norman
        Borisoff. (FF, NYTFR, W, Q).

2789   STORK TALK. (Parade-1964-Michael Forlong). A screen-
        play by Donald Ford, based on a play by Gloria Russell, with
        additional dialogue by Peter Rosser and William Hepper.
        (FF).

2789a   THE STORY OF A THREE DAY PASS. (Sigma III-1968-Mel-
        vin Van Peebles). A screenplay by Melvin Van Peebles,
        based on his novel. (FF, NYTFR, W).

2790   STORY OF A WOMAN. (Universal-1970-Leonardo Bercovici).
        A screen play written by Leonardo Bercovici. (W, AMPAS,
        Q).

2790a   STRAIT-JACKET. (Columbia-1964-William Castle). An orig-
        inal screenplay by Robert Bloch. (LC, AMPAS, W, Q, FF,
        NYTFR).

2791   STRANDED. (Compton-1965-Juleen Compton). An original
        screenplay by Juleen Compton. (W).

2792   THE STRANGE AFFAIR. (Paramount-1968-David Greene).
        A screenplay by Stanley Mann, based on the novel by Bernard
        Toms. (FF, FM, NYTFR, W, LC, AMPAS, Q).

2793   STRANGE BEDFELLOWS. (Universal-1965-Melvin Frank).
        A screenplay by Melvin Frank and Michael Pertwee, based on
        a story by Norman Panama and Melvin Frank. (FF, LC, W,
        AMPAS, Q).

2794   THE STRANGE EXORCISM OF LYNN HART. (Classic Films-
        1974-Marc Lawrence). An original screenplay by F. A. Foss.
        (HR).

2795   THE STRANGE VENGEANCE OF ROSALIE. (20th Century-
        Fox-1972-Jack Starrett). An original screenplay by Anthony
        Greville-Bell and John Kohn. (FF).

2796   THE STRANGER. (Paramount-1967-Luchino Visconti). A

screenplay by Suso Cecchi d'Amico, George Conchon, and
Emmanuel Robles, based on the novel by Albert Camus;
Knopf, 1946. (FF, NYTFR, FM, W, AMPAS, LACOPL, Q).

STRANGER IN THE HOUSE see COP-OUT

2797   A STRANGER IN TOWN. (MGM-1968-Vance Lewis aka Luigi
Vanzi). A screenplay by Warren Garfield and John Mangione.
(FF, NYTFR, W, LC, AMPAS, Q).

2798   A STRANGER KNOCKS. (Trans-Lux-1965-Johan Jacobsen).
An original screenplay by Finn Methling. (FF, W, Q).

2799   THE STRANGER RETURNS. (MGM-1968-Vance Lewis aka
Luigi Vanzi). A screenplay by Bob Ensescalle, Jr., and
Jone Mang aka Giuseppe Mangione, based on a story by Tony
Anthony. (FF, NYTFR, FM, W, Q).

2800   STRANGERS. (Aquarius-1972-Larry Spelvin). A screenplay
written by Larry Spelvin. (W).

2800a   THE STRANGLER. (Allied Artists-1964-Burt Topper). Bill
S. Ballinger was responsible for writing this screenplay. (FF,
NYTFR, LC).

2801   STRATEGY OF TERROR. (Universal-1969-Jack Smight). A
screenplay by Robert L. Joseph. (FF).

2802   STRAW DOGS. (Cinerama-1972-Sam Peckinpah). A screenplay by David Zelag Goodman and Sam Peckinpah, based on
the novel The Siege of Trencher's Farm by Gordon M. Williams; Morrow, 1969, 222p. (FF, LACOPL, Q, W).

2803   THE STRAWBERRY STATEMENT. (MGM-1970-Stuart Hag-
mann). A screenplay by Israel Horovitz, based on The
Strawberry Statement: Notes of a College Revolutionary by
James Simon Kunen; Random House; 1969, 150p. (W,
LACOPL, Q).

2803a   STRAY DOG. (Toho-1964-Akira Kurosawa). An original
screenplay by Akira Kurosawa and Ryuzo Kikushima. (FF,
NYTFR).

2804   STREET GANGS OF HONG KONG. (Cinerama-1974-Chang
Cheh and Kuei Chih-hung). No screenplay credits available.
(V, W).

2805   THE STREET IS MY BEAT. (Emerson-1966-Irvin Berwick).
A screenplay by Harold Livingston and Irvin Berwick. (FF,
W, AMPAS).

2806   THE STUD FARM. (McAbee-1969-Jac Zacha). An original
screenplay by Ian Ogilvie and M. J. Margolis. (W).

2807   THE STUDENT TEACHERS. (New World-1973-Jonathan Kap-
        lan). An original screenplay by Danny Opatoshu. (W).

2808   A STUDY IN TERROR. (Columbia-1966-James Hill). A
        screenplay by Donald and Derek Ford, based on characters
        created by Sir Arthur Conan Doyle. (FF, NYTFR, LC, W,
        AMPAS, Q).

2809   SUB ROSA RISING. (Sherpix-1971-Jerry Abrams). A docu-
        mentary; no screenplay credits available. (W).

2810   THE SUBJECT WAS ROSES. (MGM-1968-Ulu Grosbard). A
        screenplay by Frank D. Gilroy, based on his play; Random
        House, 1965, 210p. (FF, NYTFR, W, LC, AMPAS, LACOPL,
        Q).

2811   SUBMARINE X-1. (United Artists-1969-William Graham). A
        screen play by Donald S. Sanford and Guy Elmes, based on
        a story by John C. Champion and Edmund North. (FF, W,
        LC, AMPAS, Q).

2812   SUBTERFUGE. (Commonwealth United-1969-Peter Graham
        Scott). An original screenplay by David Whitaker. (W).

2813   SUBURBAN ROULETTE. (Argent-1968-Herschell Gordon Lew-
        is). A screenplay written directly for the screen by James
        Thomas. (FF, W).

2814   SUBURBAN WIVES. (Scotia International-1973-Derek Ford).
        An original screenplay by Derek Ford. (W).

2815   SUBURBIA CONFIDENTIAL. (Cambist-1966-A. C. Stephen).
        Jason Underwood wrote this original screenplay. (FF).

2816   IL SUCCESSO. (Embassy-1965-Mauro Morassi). An original
        work for the screen by Ettore Scola and Ruggero Maccari.
        (FF, W, Q).

2817   SUCCUBUS. (Trans American-1969-Jess (Jesus) Franco).
        An original screenplay by Pier A. Caminneci. (FF, Q).

2818   SUCH A GORGEOUS KID LIKE ME. (Columbia-1973-François
        Truffaut). An original screenplay by Jean-Loup Dabadie, and
        François Truffaut, based on a novel by Henry Farrell; Dela-
        corte Press, 1967. (W, LACOPL, Q).

2819   SUCH GOOD FRIENDS. (Paramount-1971-Otto Preminger).
        A screenplay written by Esther Dale aka Elaine May, based
        on a novel by Lois Gould; Random House, 1970, 277p. (W,
        LACOPL, Q).

2820   THE SUCKER. (Royal-1967-Gerard Oury). A screenplay by
        Gerard Oury, Marcel Jullian and Georges-Andre Tabet, based

on an original story by Gerard Oury. (FF, NYTFR, W, Q).

2821   SUDDEN TERROR. (National General-1971-John Hough). A
       screenplay by Ronald Harwood, from the novel Eyewitness
       by Mark Hebden; Harcourt, 1966. (W, LACOPL, Q).

2822   SUDDENLY, A WOMAN! (PMK-1968-Anker). Anker wrote
       the screenplay, based on the novel Gudrun by John V. Jen-
       sen. (FF).

2823   SUGAR COOKIES. (General Film-1973-Theodore Gershuny).
       A screenplay by Lloyd Kaufman and Theodore Gershuny.
       (W).

2824   SUGAR HILL. (American International-1974-Paul Maslansky).
       An original screenplay by Tim Kelly. (HR).

2825   THE SUGARLAND EXPRESS. (Universal-1974-Steven Spiel-
       berg). An original screenplay by Hal Barwood and Matthew
       Robbins, from a story by Steven Spielberg, Hal Barwood,
       and Matthew Robbins. (HR, V, W).

2826   SULLIVAN'S EMPIRE. (Universal-1967-Harvey Hart and
       Thomas Carr). An original screenplay by Frank Chase.
       (FF, W, AMPAS, Q).

2827   SUMMER OF '42. (Warner Bros.-1971-Robert Mulligan). A
       screenplay written by Herman Raucher, based on his novel
       of the same name; Putnam, 1971, 251p. (W, LACOPL, Q).

2828   SUMMER RUN. (Lighthouse-1974-Leon Capetanos). An
       original screenplay by Leon Capetanos. (V).

2829   SUMMER WISHES, WINTER DREAMS. (Columbia-1973-Gil-
       bert Cates). An original screenplay by Stewart Stern. (W,
       Q).

2830   SUMMERTIME KILLER. (AVCO Embassy-1973-Antonio Is-
       asi). A screenplay by R. Buckley and B. Degas. (W).

2831   SUMMERTREE. (Columbia-1971-Anthony Newley). A
       screenplay by Edward Hume and Stephen Yafa, based on a
       play by Ron Cowen; Random House, 1968, 106p. (W,
       LACOPL, Q).

2832   SUNDAY BLOODY SUNDAY. (United Artists-1971-John
       Schlesinger). A screenplay by Penelope Gilliatt; published
       by Viking Press; 1971, 135p. (W, LACOPL, Q).

2832a SUNDAY IN NEW YORK. (MGM-1964-Peter Tewksbury).
       Norman Krasna wrote the screenplay which was taken from
       his play; Random House, 1962. (AMPAS, FF, W, Q, LC,
       LACOPL, NYTFR).

2833   SUNFLOWER.   (AVCO Embassy-1970-Vittorio De Sica).   An
        original story and screenplay by Antonio Guerra and Cesare
        Zavattini.   (W, Q).

2834   SUNSCORCHED.   (Feature Film Corporation of America-
        1968-Mark Stevens).   A screenplay by Irving Dennis and
        Mark Stevens, based on an original story by Mark Stevens.
        (FF).

2835   THE SUPER COPS.   (United Artists-1974-Gordon Parks).   A
        screenplay by Lorenzo Semple, Jr. , based on the book by L.
        H. Whittemore; Stein, 1973, 359p.   (HR, LACOPL, W).

2836   SUPER FLY.   (Warner Bros.-1972-Gordon Parks).   An origi-
        nal screenplay by Phillip Fenty.   (FF, Q).

2837   SUPER FLY T. N. T.   (Paramount-1973-Ron O'Neal).   A
        screenplay by Alex Haley, from a story by Ron O'Neal and
        Sig Shore.   (W, Q).

2838   SUPERBEAST. (United Artists-1972-George Schenck).   A
        screenplay written by George Schenck.   (W, FF, Q).

2839   SUPERCHICK.   (Crown International-1973-Ed Forsyth).   No
        screen play credits available.   (W, Q).

2840   SUPERDAD.   (Buena Vista-1974-Vincent McEveety).   A
        screenplay by Joseph L. McEveety, based on a story by Har-
        lan Ware.   (V, W).

2841   SUPPORT YOUR LOCAL GUNFIGHTER.   (United Artists-
        1971-Burt Kennedy).   A screenplay by James Edward Grant.
        (W, Q).

2842   SUPPORT YOUR LOCAL SHERIFF.   (United Artists-1969-
        Burt Kennedy).   A screenplay written by William Bowers.
        (FF, LC, AMPAS, Q).

2843   SUPPOSE THEY GAVE A WAR AND NOBODY CAME.   (Cine-
        rama-1970-Hy Averback).   A screenplay by Don McGuire and
        Hal Captain, from a story by Hal Captain.   (W, AMPAS, Q).

2843a   SURF PARTY.   (20th Century-Fox-1964-Maury Dexter).   An
        original work written for the screen by Harry Spalding.
        (FF, NYTFR, W, Q, LC).

2844   THE SWAPPERS.   (Trans American-1970-Derek Ford).   An
        original screenplay by Stanley Long and Derek Ford.   (W).

        SWEDISH FLY GIRLS see CHRISTA

2845   SWEDISH WEDDING NIGHT.   (Royal-1965-Ake Falck).   An
        original screenplay written by Lars Widding.   (NYTFR, W, Q).

2846   THE SWEET BODY OF DEBORAH. (Warner Bros.-7 Arts-
        1969-Romolo Guerrieri). A screenplay by Ernesto Gastaldi,
        based on a story by Ernesto Gastaldi and Luciano Martino.
        (FF, W, LC, Q).

2847   SWEET CHARITY. (Universal-1969-Bob Fosse). A screen-
        play by Peter Stone, based on the musical play by Neil Simon,
        Cy Coleman (music), and Dorothy Fields (lyrics); Random
        House, 1966, 113p., and the screenplay for Nights of Cabiria
        by Federico Fellini, Tullio Pinelli and Ennio Flaiano. (FF,
        W, AMPAS, LACOPL, Q).

2848   SWEET GEORGIA. (Box Office International-1972-Edward
        Boles). No screenplay credit available. (FF).

2849   SWEET JESUS, PREACHER MAN. (MGM-1973-Henning
        Schellerup). A screenplay by John Cerullo, M. Stuart Mad-
        den, and Abbey Leitch. (W, Q).

        SWEET KILL see THE AROUSERS

2850   SWEET LIGHT IN A DARK ROOM. (Promenade-1966-Jiri
        Weiss). A screenplay by Jiri Weiss and Jan Otcenasek,
        based on a story by Jan Otcenasek. (FF, NYTFR, W, Q).

2851   SWEET LOVE, BITTER. (Film 2 Associates-1967-Herbert
        Danska). A screenplay by Herbert Danska and Lewis Jacobs,
        based on the novel Night Song by John Williams; Farrar,
        1961. (Q, FF, NYTFR, FM, W, AMPAS, LACOPL).

2852   SWEET NOVEMBER. (Warner Bros.-7 Arts-1968-Robert El-
        lis Miller). An original screenplay by Herman Raucher.
        (FF, W, LC, AMPAS, Q).

2853   THE SWEET RIDE. (20th Century-Fox-1968-Harvey Hart).
        A screenplay by Tom Mankiewicz, based on a novel by Willi-
        am Murray; New American Library, 1967. (Q, FF, NYTFR,
        FM, LC, AMPAS, LACOPL).

2854   SWEET SAVIOUR. (Trans World-1971-Bob Roberts). Matt
        Cavanaugh wrote this original screenplay. (W).

2855   SWEET SKIN. (Times Film Corporation-1966-Jacques Poit-
        renaud). A screenplay by Jacques Sigurd and Jacques Poit-
        renaud, based on a story by Alain Maury. (FF).

2856   SWEET SUGAR. (Dimension-1973-Michel Levesque). An
        original screenplay by Don Spencer. (W, FF).

2857   SWEET SUZY. (Signal 166-1973-Russ Meyer). A screenplay
        by Russ Meyer, Len.Neubauer, from a story by Russ Meyer
        and A. James Ryan. (W).

2858   SWEET SWEETBACK'S BAADASSSSS SONG. (Cinemation-
        1971-Melvin Van Peebles). An original screenplay by Mel-
        vin Van Peebles. (W, Q).

2859   THE SWIMMER. (Columbia-1968-Frank Perry). A screen-
        play by Eleanor Perry, based on a short story by John
        Cheever (The New Yorker, July 18, 1964). Screenplay pub-
        plished by Stein & Day, 1967, 127p. (Q, FF, NYTFR, FM,
        MCC, W, LC, AMPAS, LACOPL).

2860   THE SWIMMING POOL. (AVCO Embassy-1970-Jacques De-
        ray). A screenplay by Jean-Emmanuel Conil and Jean-
        Claude Carrière and Jacques Deray. (W, Q).

2861   THE SWINGER. (Paramount-1966-George Sidney). A screen-
        play by Lawrence Roman. (FF, NYTFR, LC, W, AMPAS,
        Q).

2862   SWINGERS' PARADISE. (American International-1965-Sidney
        J. Furie). An original story and screenplay by Peter Myers
        and Ronald Cass. (W, LC, AMPAS, Q).

2862a   THE SWINGIN' MAIDEN. (Columbia-1964-Gerald Thomas).
        Vivian Cox and Leslie Bricusse, based their screenplay on
        an original story by Harold Brooke and Kay Bannerman.
        (FF, NYTFR, W, Q).

2863   THE SWINGIN' STEWARDESSES. (Hemisphere-1972-Michael
        Thomas). An original screenplay by Manfred Gregor. (FF).

2864   A SWINGIN' SUMMER. (United Screen Arts-1965-). An
        original script attributed to Robert Sparr. (W, AMPAS, Q).

2865   THE SWINGING CHEERLEADERS. (Centaur-1974-Jack Hill).
        Jane Witherspoon and Betty Conklin wrote this original screen-
        play. (V, W).

2866   SWORD OF ALI BABA. (Universal-1965-Virgil Vogel). A
        screenplay by Edmund Morrison and Oscar Brodney. (FF,
        LC, W, AMPAS, Q).

2867   THE SWORD OF DOOM. (Toho-1967-Kihachi Okamoto). A
        screenplay by Shinobu Hashimoto, based on a novel by Kaizan
        Nakazato. (FF, NYTFR, FM, W, Q).

2868   THE SWORD OF EL CID. (Eldorado-1965-M. Iglesias). No
        screenplay credits given. (W, Q).

2869   SWORD OF VENGEANCE. (Toho-1973-Kenji Misumi). A
        screenplay written by Kazuo Koike, from a story by Gozeki
        Kojima and Jazuo Koike. (W).

2870   SWORDS OF DEATH. (Toho-1971-Tomu Uchida). An original screenplay written by Daisuke Ito. (W).

2871   SYLVIA. (Paramount-1965-Gordon Douglas). A screenplay
       by Sydney Boehm, based on the novel by E. V. Cunningham.
       (FF, LC, W, AMPAS, Q).

2872   SYMPATHY FOR THE DEVIL. (New Line Cinema-1970-
       Jean-Luc Godard). An original screenplay by Jean-Luc God-
       ard. (W).

2873   SYMPHONY FOR A MASSACRE. (7 Arts-1965-Jacques De-
       ray). A screenplay adapted by Jose Giovanni, Claude Sautat
       and Jacques Deray, based on the novel Les Mystifiés by A.
       Reynaud Fourton. (NYTFR, Q).

2874   SYNANON. (Columbia-1965-Richard Quine). A screenplay
       by Ian Bernard and S. Lee Pogostin, based on a story by
       Barry Oringer and S. Lee Pogostin. (FF, LC, W, AMPAS,
       NYTFR, Q).

2874a THX 1138. Warner Bros.-1971-George Lucas). A screen-
       play by George Lucas and Walter Murch, from a story by
       George Lucas. (W, Q).

2875   T. R. BASKIN. (Paramount-1971-Herbert Ross). Peter
       Hyams wrote this original screenplay. (W, Q).

2876   TAFFY AND THE JUNGLE HUNTER. (Allied Artists-1965-
       Terry O. Morse). A screenplay by Arthur Hoerl, from a
       story by Donald Zimbalist. (W, AMPAS, Q).

2877   THE TAKE. (Columbia-1974-Robert Hartford-Davis). A
       screenplay by Del Reisman and Franklin Coen from a novel
       Sir, You Bastard by G. F. Newman; Simon & Schuster, 1970,
       287p. (V, LACOPL, W).

2878   TAKE A GIRL LIKE YOU. (Columbia-1970-Jonathan Miller).
       A screenplay by George Melly from the novel by Kingsley
       Amis; Harcourt, 1960. (W, LACOPL, Q).

2879   TAKE IT ALL. (Lopert-1966-Claude Jutra). A screenplay
       by Claude Jutra. (Q, FF, NYTFR, W).

2880   TAKE THE MONEY AND RUN. (Cinerama-1969-Woody Al-
       len). An original screenplay by Woody Allen and Mickey
       Rose. (FF, W, AMPAS, Q).

2881   THE TAKING OF PELHAM ONE TWO THREE. (United
       Artists-1974-Joseph Sargent). A screenplay by Peter Stone,
       from the novel by John Godey; Putnam, 1973, 316p. (V,
       LACOPL, W).

2882   TAKING OFF. (Universal-1971-Milos Forman). A screenplay by Milos Forman, John Guare, Jean-Claude Carrière, and John Klein. (W, Q).

2883   TALES FROM THE CRYPT. (Cinerama-1972-Freddie Francis). A screenplay by Milton Subotsky, based on stories in comics Tales from the Crypt and The Vault of Horror by Al Feldstein, Johnny Craig, and William Gaines. (Q, FF).

2884   TALES THAT WITNESS MADNESS. (Paramount-1973-Freddie Francis). Jay Fairbank wrote this original screenplay. (W).

2885   THE TALL BLOND MAN WITH ONE BLACK SHOE. (Cinema V-1973-Yves Robert). An original screenplay by Yves Robert and Francis Veber. (W).

2886   THE TALL WOMEN. (Allied Artists-1967-Cechet Grooper). A screenplay by Mino Roli, based on a script by Mike Ashley. (FF, W, Q).

TAM LIN see THE DEVIL'S WIDOW

2886a   TAMAHINE. (MGM-7 Arts-1964-Philip Leacock). A screenplay by Denis Cannan, based on the novel by Thelma Nicklaus. (Q, FF, W, NYTFR).

2887   THE TAMARIND SEED. (AVCO Embassy-1974-Blake Edwards). A screenplay by Blake Edwards, based on the novel by Evelyn Anthony; Coward, 1971, 246p. (V, LACOPL, W).

2888   THE TAMING. (Times Film Corporation-1968-Robert Arkless). A screenplay by Robert Arkless. (FF).

2889   THE TAMING OF THE SHREW. (Columbia-1967-Franco Zeffirelli). A screenplay by Paul Dehn, Suso Cecchi d'Amico and Franco Zeffirelli, based on the play by William Shakespeare. (AMPAS, FF, FM, LACOPL, LC, NYTFR, Q, V, W).

2890   TAMMY AND THE MILLIONAIRE. (Universal-1967-Sidney Miller, Ezra Stone & Leslie Goodwins). A screenplay by George Tibbles, based on Tammy Out of Time, Bobbs-Merrill, 1948; and Tammy Tell Me True, Bobbs-Merrill, 1959, two novels by Cid Ricketts Sumner. (AMPAS, FF, LACOPL, Q, W).

2890a   LOS TARANTOS. (Sigma III-1964-Roviera-Beleta). An original screenplay by Alfredo Manas and Roviera Beleta. (NYTFR, FF).

2891   TARGETS. (Paramount-1968-Peter Bogdanovich). A screenplay by Peter Bogdanovich, based on a story by Polly Platt and Peter Bogdanovich. (AMPAS, FF, LC, NYTFR, Q, W).

2892   TARZAN AND THE GREAT RIVER. (Paramount-1967-Robert
        Day). A screenplay by Bob Barbash, based on a story by
        Bob Barbash and Lewis Reed and the characters created by
        Edgar Rice Burroughs. (AMPAS, FF, LC, Q, W).

2893   TARZAN AND THE JUNGLE BOY. (Paramount-1968-Robert
        Gordon). A screenplay by Stephen Lord, based on characters
        created by Edgar Rice Burroughs. (AMPAS, FF, LC, Q,
        W).

2894   TARZAN AND THE VALLEY OF GOLD. (American Interna-
        tional-1967-Robert Day). A screenplay by Clair Huffaker,
        based on the characters created by Edgar Rice Burroughs.
        (AMPAS, FF, LC, W).

2895   TARZANA, THE WILD GIRL. (Ellman Enterprises-1973-
        James Reed). Philip Shaw wrote this original screenplay.
        (w).

2896   TARZAN'S DEADLY SILENCE. (National General-1970-Robert
        L. Friend). A screenplay by Lee Erwin, Jack A. Robinson,
        John Considine, and Tim Considine, based on stories by Ed-
        gar Rice Burroughs. (W, Q).

2897   A TASTE OF HELL. (Boxoffice International-1973-Neil Ya-
        rema & Basil Bradbury). An original screenplay written by
        Neil Yarema. (W).

2898   TASTE THE BLOOD OF DRACULA. (Warner Bros.-1970-
        Peter Sasdy). A screenplay written by John Elder. (W, Q).

2899   TAXI FOR TOBRUK. (7 Arts-1965-Denys de la Patelliere).
        A screenplay by Michel Audiard, Rene Havard, and Denys
        de la Patellière. (FF, Q).

2900   A TEAR IN THE OCEAN. (Levitt-Pickman-1973-Henri Glaes-
        er). A screenplay by Henri Glaeser and A. P. Quince, from
        a novel by Manes Sperber. (W).

2901   TEARS OF HAPPINESS. (Mutual Film Enterprises-1974-Sarky
        Mouradian). An original screenplay by Sarky Mouradian.
        (HR).

2902   TEENAGE COWGIRLS. (Kairio-1973-Ted Denver). No screen-
        play credits. (W).

2903   TEENAGE MOTHER. (Cinemation-1968-Jerry Gross). A
        screenplay by Jerry Gross, based on an original story by
        Nicholas Demetroules. (FF, NYTFR, W).

2904   THE TELEPHONE BOOK. (Rosebud-1971-Nelson Lyon). An
        original screenplay by Nelson Lyon. (W).

2905   TELL ME IN THE SUNLIGHT. (Movie-Rama-1967-Steve
        Cochran). A screenplay by Jo Heims, based on an original
        story by Robert Stevens. (FF, W, Q).

2906   TELL ME LIES. (Continental-1968-Peter Brook). Screen-
        play based on the stage production with original text by Denis
        Cannan, Peter Brook, Albert Hunt, Sally Jacobs, Michael
        Kustow, Adrian Mitchell, Richard Peaslee; Bobbs-Merrill
        Co., 1968, 214p. (FF, FM, W, LACOPL, AMPAS, SCH).

2907   TELL ME THAT YOU LOVE ME, JUNIE MOON. (Para-
        mount-1970-Otto Preminger). A screenplay by Marjorie Kel-
        logg, based on her novel; Farrar, 1968. (W, LACOPL, Q).

2908   TELL THEM WILLIE BOY IS HERE. (Universal-1969-Abra-
        ham Polonsky). A screenplay by Abraham Polonsky, from
        the novel Willie Boy, A Desert Manhunt by Henry Lawton;
        Paisano Press, 1960, 224p. (W, AMPAS, LACOPL, Q).

2909   TEN DAYS' WONDER. (Levitt-Pickman-1972-Claude Chab-
        rol). A screenplay by Paul Gardner and Eugene Archer,
        based on the novel Ten Days' Wonder by Ellery Queen aka
        Frederic Damay and Manfred Lee; Little, Brown & Co.,
        1948. (FF, LACOPL, Q).

2910   TEN FROM YOUR SHOW OF SHOWS. (Continental-1973-Max
        Liebman). Written by Mel Tolkin, Lucille Kallen, Mel
        Brooks, Tony Webster, Sid Caesar, and Max Liebman. (W, FF).

2911   TEN LITTLE INDIANS. (7 Arts-1966-George Pollock). A
        screenplay by Peter Yeldman and Peter Welbeck, based on
        the novel and play by Agatha Christie; French, 1946, 95p.
        (FF, NYTFR, W, AMPAS, LACOPL).

2912   10 RILLINGTON PLACE. (Columbia-1971-Richard Fleischer).
        A screenplay by Clive Exton, based on a novel by Ludovic
        Kennedy; Simon & Schuster, 1961, 288p. (W, LACOPL).

2913   TENCHU. (Japanese Film Exchange-1972-Hideo Gosha). A
        screenplay by Shinobu Hashimoto. (W).

2914   THE TENDER MOMENT. (Maron-1971-Michel Boisrond).
        A screenplay by Claude Brule, Annette Wademant, and Mi-
        chel Boisrond. (W).

2915   TENDER SCOUNDREL. (Embassy-1967-Jean Becker). A
        screenplay by Albert Simonin, Jean Becker, and Daniel Boul-
        anger. (FF, NYTFR, W).

2916   THE TENDER WARRIOR. (Safari-1971-Stewart Raffill). An
        original screenplay by Stewart Raffill and David Dalie. (W).

2917   THE 10TH VICTIM. (Embassy-1965-Elio Petri). A screenplay by Elio Petri, Ennio Flaiano, Tonino Guerra and Giorgio Salvione, based on a novel by Robert Sheckley. (NYTFR, W, AMPAS).

2918   10:30 P. M. SUMMER. (Lopert-1966-Jules Dassin). A screenplay by Jules Dassin and Marguerite Duras, based on the novel by Marguerite Duras, Ten-Thirty on a Summer Night; Grove Press, 1962, 108p. (FF, NYTFR, LC, W, AMPAS, LACOPL).

2919   TEOREMA. (Continental-1969-Pier Paolo Pasolini). A screenplay by Pier Paolo Pasolini, based on his novel. (FF, AMPAS).

2920   THE TERMINAL MAN. (Warner Bros.-1974-Mike Hodges). A screenplay written by Mike Hodges, based on a novel by Michael Crichton; Knopf, 1972, 247p. (W, V. LACOPL).

2921   THE TERRACE. (Royal-1964-Leopoldo Torre Nilsson). A screenplay by Beatriz Guido. (FF, NYTFR).

2922   TERROR IN THE CITY. (Allied Artists-1966-Allen Baron). An original screenplay by Allen Baron. (FF, NYTFR, LC, AMPAS).

2922a   TERROR IN THE WAX MUSEUM. (Cinerama-1973-Georg Fenady). An original screenplay by Jameson Brewer. (W).

2923   TERROR-CREATURES FROM THE GRAVE. (Pacemaker Pictures-1967-Ralph Zuker). A screenplay by Roberto Natale and Romano Migliorini. (FF).

2924   THE TERRORNAUTS. (Embassy-1967-Montgomery Tully). John Brunner wrote the screenplay, based on the novel The Wailing Asteroid by Murray Leinster. (FF, W).

2925   TERRY WHITMORE, FOR EXAMPLE. (Grove-1969-Bill Brodie). An original screenplay by Bill Brodie. (W).

2926   TEXAS ACROSS THE RIVER. (Universal-1966-Michael Gordon). A screenplay by Wells Root, Harold Greene, and Ben Starr. (FF, NYTFR, LC, W, AMPAS).

2927   THE TEXAS CHAIN SAW MASSACRE. (Bryanston-1974-Tobe Hooper). A screenplay written directly for the screen by Kim Henkel and Tobe Hooper. (V).

2828   THE TEXICAN. (Columbia-1966-Lesley Selander). An original screenplay by John C. Champion. (FF, LC, W, AMPAS).

2929   THANK HEAVEN FOR SMALL FAVORS. (International Classics-1965-Jean-Pierre Mocky). A screenplay by Michel Servin, Alain Moury, and Jean-Pierre Mocky, based on a novel by Michel Servin. (FF, W).

2930   THANK YOU ALL VERY MUCH. (Columbia-1969-Waris Hussein). A screenplay by Margaret Drabble, based on her novel The Millstone; Morrow, 1965. (FF, W, LACOPL).

2931   THANOS AND DESPINA. (Grove-1970-Nico Papatakis). An original screenplay by Nico Papatakis. (W).

2932   THAT DARN CAT. (Buena Vista-1965-Robert Stevenson). A screenplay by Mildred and Gordon Gordon and Bill Walsh, based on the book Undercover Cat by the Gordons; Doubleday, 1973, 180p. (NYTFR, LC, AMPAS, LACOPL).

2933   THAT FUNNY FEELING. (Universal-1965-Richard Thorpe). An original screenplay by David R. Schwartz. (NYTFR, LC, W, AMPAS).

2934   THAT MAN BOLT. (Universal-1973-Henry Levin and David Lowell Rich). An original screenplay by Quentin Werty [aka Ranald MacDougall] and Charles Johnson. (W).

2935   THAT MAN FLINTSTONE. (Columbia-1966-Joseph Barbera and William Hanna). Harvey Bullock and Ray Allen wrote this original screenplay. (W, LC).

2935a   THAT MAN FROM RIO. (Lopert-1964-Philippe de Broca). Screenplay and adaptation by J. P. Rappeneau, Ariane Mnouchkine, Daniel Boulanger, and Philippe de Broca, with additional dialogue by Daniel Boulanger. (FF, NYTFR, Q, W).

2936   THAT MAN GEORGE. (Allied Artists-1968-Jacques Deray). Henri Lanoi, Jose Giovanni, Suzanne Arduini and Jacques Deray wrote this screenplay, from a novel Les Pilleurs de Dimanche by Robert Page-Jones. (FF, W).

2937   THAT MAN IN ISTANBUL. (Columbia-1966-Anthony Isasi). A screenplay by George Simonelli and Nat Wachsberger. (FF, NYTFR, LC, W).

2938   THAT TENDER TOUCH. (World Premiere-1969-Russel Vincent). An original screenplay by Russel Vincent. (W).

2939   THAT TENNESSEE BEAT. (20th Century-Fox-1966-Richard Brill). An original screenplay by Paul Schneider. (FF, W, AMPAS).

2940   THAT WOMAN. (Globe-1968-Will Tremper). A screenplay written by Will Tremper. (FF, NYTFR).

2941   THAT'LL BE THE DAY. (Walter Reade-1974-Claude Whatham). A work written directly for the screen by Ray Connolly. (HR, V).

2942   THAT'S ENTERTAINMENT. (United Artists-1974-Jack Haley,

Jr.). A documentary written by Jack Haley, Jr. (V, W).

2943   THEATRE OF BLOOD. (United Artists-1973-Douglas Hickox).
       A screenplay by Anthony Greville-Bell. (W, FF).

       THEATRE OF DEATH see BLOOD FIEND

2944   THERE IS NO 13. (Unset-1974-William Sachs). An original
       screenplay by William Sachs. (V).

2945   THERE WAS A CROOKED MAN. (Warner Bros.-1970-Joseph
       L. Mankiewicz). An original screenplay by David Newman
       and Robert Benton. (W, AMPAS).

2946   THERE WAS AN OLD COUPLE. (Artkino-1967-Grigory
       Choukhrai). A screenplay by Yuli Dounsky and Vleri Fried.
       (NYTFR, W).

2947   THERE'S A GIRL IN MY SOUP. (Columbia-1970-Roy Boult-
       ing). A screenplay by Terence Frisby, from his play of the
       same name. (W).

2948   THERE'S ALWAYS VANILLA. (Cambist-1972-George Ro-
       mero). An original story and screenplay by Rudolph J. Ric-
       ci. (W, FF).

2949   THERESE AND ISABELLE. (Audubon-1968-Radley Metzger).
       A screenplay by Jesse Vogel, based on his novel La Bâtarde
       by Violette Leduc; Farrar, 1965, 488p. (FF, NYTFR, FM,
       W, LACOPL).

2950   THESE ARE THE DAMNED. (Columbia-1965-Joseph Losey).
       A screenplay by Evan Jones, based on the novel The Chil-
       dren of Light by H. L. Lawrence. (NYTFR, W, AMPAS).

2950a THEY ALL DIED LAUGHING. (Continental-1964-Don Chaffey).
       A screenplay by Robert Hamer and Donald Taylor, based on
       the novel Don Among the Dead Men by C. E. Vulliamy.
       (NYTFR, FF, Q).

2951   THEY CALL HER ONE EYE. (American International-1974-
       Alex Fridolinski). A screenplay by Alex Fridolinski and Bo
       Vibenius. (V).

2952   THEY CALL ME MR. TIBBS. (United Artists-1970-Gordon
       Douglas). A screenplay by Alan R. Trustman and James R.
       Webb, based on a story by Alan R. Trustman, based on
       characters created by John Ball. (W).

2953   THEY CALL ME TRINITY. (AVCO Embassy-1972-E. B.
       Clucher). A work written directly for the screen by E. B.
       Clucher aka Enzo Barboni. (FF).

2954   THEY CAME FROM BEYOND SPACE. (Embassy-1967-Freddie Francis). A screenplay by Milton Subotsky, based on the novel The Gods Hate Kansas by Joseph Millard. (FF, W, AMPAS).

2955   THEY CAME TO ROB LAS VEGAS. (Warner Bros.-7 Arts-1969-Antonio Isasi). A screenplay by Antonio Isasi, Jo Eisinger, Luis Comeron, and Jorge Illa, based on a novel by Andre Lay. (FF, W, AMPAS).

2956   THEY MIGHT BE GIANTS. (Universal-1971-Anthony Harvey). A screenplay by James Goldman, based on his play. (W).

2957   THEY ONLY KILL THEIR MASTERS. (MGM-1972-James Goldstone). A screenplay by Lane Slate. (FF).

2958   THEY SHOOT HORSES, DON'T THEY? (Cinerama-1969-Sydney Pollack). A screenplay by James Poe and Robert E. Thompson, based on the novel by Horace McCoy; Avon, 1969, 319p. (FF, W, AMPAS, LACOPL, SCH, MCC).

2959   THE THIEF OF PARIS. (Lopert-1967-Louis Malle). A screenplay by Louis Malle, Jean-Claude Carrière and Daniel Boulanger, based on the novel Le Voleur by Georges Darien. (FF, NYTFR, W, LC, AMPAS).

2960   THE THIEF WHO CAME TO DINNER. (Warner Bros.-1973-Bud Yorkin). A screenplay by Walter Hill, based on the novel by Terrence L. Smith; Doubleday, 1971, 176p. (W, LACOPL).

2961   THIEVES LIKE US. (United Artists-1974-Robert Altman). A screenplay by Calder Willingham, Joan Tewkesbury, and Robert Altman, based on the novel by Edward Anderson. (HR).

2961a   THE THIN RED LINE. (Allied Artists-1964-Andrew Marton). A screenplay by Bernard Gordon, based on the novel by James Jones; Scribner, 1962. (NYTFR, FF, LACOPL, Q, W).

2962   THE THING WITH TWO HEADS. (American International-1972-Lee Frost). A screenplay by Lee Frost, Wes Bishop, and James Gordon White. (W).

2963   THE THINGS OF LIFE. (Columbia-1970-Claude Sautet). A screenplay by Jean-Loup Dabadie, based on a novel by Paul Guimard. (W).

2963a   THE THIRD SECRET. (20th Century-Fox-1964-Charles Crichton). Robert L. Joseph wrote this original screenplay. (LC, AMPAS, FF, NYTFR, Q, W).

2964   30 IS A DANGEROUS AGE, CYNTHIA. (Columbia-1968-

Joseph McGrath). A screenplay by Dudley Moore, Joseph
McGrath and John Wells. (FF, NYTFR, FM, W, LC,
AMPAS).

2965   36 HOURS. (MGM-1965-George Seaton). A screenplay by
George Seaton, based on the novel by Roald Dahl, Beware of
the Dog, and a story by Carl K. Hittleman and Luis H.
Vance. (FF, LC, W, AMPAS).

2966   THIS IS A HIJACK. (Fanfare-1973-Barry Pollack). No
screenplay credits available. (W).

2967   THIS MAN MUST DIE. (Allied Artists-1970-Claude Chabrol).
A screenplay by Claude Chabrol and Paul Gegauff, based on
a novel by Nicholas Blake. (W).

2968   THIS PROPERTY IS CONDEMNED. (Paramount-1966-Sydney
Pollack). A screenplay by Francis Ford Coppola and Fred
Coe and Edith Sommer, suggested by a one-act play by Ten-
nessee Williams. (FF, NYTFR, LC, W, AMPAS).

2969   THIS SAVAGE LAND. (Universal-1969-). No screen writing
credits available. (W).

2970   THIS SPECIAL FRIENDSHIP. (Pathe Contemporary-1967-
Jean Delannoy). A screenplay by Jean Aurenche, based on
the novel by Roger Peyrefitte; Vanguard, 1950. (FF,
NYTFR, W, AMPAS, LACOPL).

2971   THE THOMAS CROWN AFFAIR. (United Artists-1968-Nor-
man Jewison). An original screenplay written by Alan R.
Trustman. (FF, NYTFR, W, LC, AMPAS).

2972   THOMASINE AND BUSHROD. (Columbia-1974-Gordon Parks,
Jr.). Max Julien wrote this original screenplay. (V, W).

2973   THOROUGHLY MODERN MILLIE. (Universal-1967-George
Roy Hill). An original screenplay by Richard Morris. (FF,
NYTFR, FM, W, LC, AMPAS).

2974   THOSE CALLAWAYS. (Buena Vista-1965-Norman Tokar). A
screenplay by Louis Pelletier, based on the book Swiftwater
by Paul Annixter; Wyn, 1950. (FF, LC, W, AMPAS,
LACOPL).

2975   THOSE DARING YOUNG MEN IN THEIR JAUNTY JALOPIES.
(Paramount-1969-Ken Annakin). A screenplay by Jack Davies
and Ken Annakin; Putnam, 1969, 80p. (FF, W, LC, AMPAS,
LACOPL).

2976   THOSE DIRTY DOGS. (Cinema Financial of America-1974-
Giuseppe Rosati). Carl Veo, Giuseppe Rosati and Henry
Lovet wrote this original screenplay. (V).

2977 THOSE FANTASTIC FLYING FOOLS. (American International-1967-Don Sharp). A screenplay by Dave Freeman, based on a story by Peter Welbeck, inspired by the writing of Jules Verne. (FF, W, LC, NYTFR, FM, AMPAS).

2978 THOSE MAGNIFICENT MEN IN THEIR FLYING MACHINES ... (HOW I FLEW FROM LONDON TO PARIS IN 25 HOURS AND 11 MINUTES). (20th Century Fox-1965-Ken Annakin). A screenplay by Jack Davies and Ken Annakin, based on a book by Ronald Searle; W. W. Norton, 1965. (FF, LC, W, AMPAS, LACOPL).

2979 A THOUSAND CLOWNS. (United Artists-1965-Fred Coe). A screenplay by Herb Gardner, based on his play; Random House, 1962, 126p. (NYTFR, LC, W, AMPAS, LACOPL).

2980 THE THOUSAND PLANE RAID. (United Artists-1969-Boris Sagal). A screenplay by Donald S. Sanford, from a story by Robert Vincent Wright, and based on a book by Ralph Barker, The Thousand Plan; Chatto, 1965, 260p. (W, LACOPL).

2981 THREE. (Impact-1967-Aleksander Petrovic). A screenplay by Antonije Isakovic and Aleksandar Petrovic. (NYTFR, AMPAS).

2982 THREE. (United Artists-1969-James Salter). A screenplay by James Salter, from a story by Irwin Shaw, "Then There Were Three," in Selected Short Stories of Irwin Shaw; Random House, 1961, pp. 391-426. (W).

2983 THREE BITES OF THE APPLE. (MGM-1967-Alvin Ganzer). A screenplay by George Wells. (FF, NYTFR, FM, LC, AMPAS).

2984 THREE GUNS FOR TEXAS. (Universal-1968-David Lowell Rich, Paul Stanley, and Earl Bellamy). A screenplay by John D. F. Black. (FF, W, AMPAS).

2985 THREE HUNDRED YEAR WEEKEND. (Cinerama-1971-Victor Stoloff). A screenplay by Victor Stoloff, with additional dialogue by William Devane and Jerome Alden. (W).

2986 THREE IN THE ATTIC. (American International-1969-Richard Wilson). A screenplay by Stephen Yafa, based on his novel Paxton Quigley's Had the Course; Lippincott, 1967. (FF, W, LC, AMPAS, LACOPL).

2987 3 INTO 2 WON'T GO. (Universal-1969-Peter Hall). A screenplay by Edna O'Brien, based on the novel by Andrea Newman; Doubleday, 1967, 214p. (FF, W, AMPAS, LACOPL).

2988   THREE LIVES. (Impact-1971-Louva Irvine, Susan Kleckner, & Robin Mide). A documentary with no screen writing credits. (W).

2988a   THE THREE LIVES OF THOMASINA. (Buena Vista-1964-Don Chaffey). A screenplay by Robert Westerby, based on the book by Paul Gallico, Thomasina, the Cat Who Thought She Was God; Doubleday, 1957, 288p. (LC, AMPAS, W, Q, FF, LACOPL).

2989   THE THREE MUSKETEERS. (20th Century-Fox-1974-Richard Lester). A screenplay by George MacDonald Fraser, based on the novel by Alexandre Dumas; Washington Square Press, 1967, 629p. (MFB, V, LACOPL, W).

2989a   3 NUTS IN SEARCH OF A BOLT. (Harlequin International-1964-Tommy Noonan). An original screenplay by Tommy Noonan and Ian McGlashan. (FF).

2990   3 ON A COUCH. (Columbia-1966-Jerry Lewis). A screenplay by Bob Ross and Samuel A. Taylor, based on a story by Arne Sultan and Marvin Worth. (FF, NYTFR, LC, W, AMPAS).

2991   THE THREE SISTERS. (Brandon-1969-Samson Samsonov). A screenplay by Samson Samsonov, based on the play by Anton Chekhov; Macmillan, 1969, 160p. (FF, W, LACOPL).

2992   THREE THE HARD WAY. (Allied Artists-1974-Gordon Parks, Jr.). A screenplay by Eric Bercovici and Jerry Ludwig. (V).

2993   THREE TOUGH GUYS. (Paramount-1974-Duccio Tessari). A screenplay and story by Luciano Vincenzoni and Nicola Badalucco. (HR, V, W).

2994   THREESOME. (Howard Mahler-1970-Lee Beale). An original screenplay by Kenneth Pressman. (W).

2995   THE THRILL KILLERS. (Hollywood Star-1965-Ray Dennis Steckler). An original screenplay by Ray Dennis Steckler and Gene Pollock. (W).

2996   THUMB TRIPPING. (AVCO Embassy-1972-Quentin Masters). A screenplay by Don Mitchell, from his novel; Little, Brown & Co., 1970, 182p. (W, FF, LACOPL).

2997   THUNDER ALLEY. (American International-1967-Richard Rush). A screenplay by Sy Salkowitz. (FF, NYTFR, LC, AMPAS).

2998   THUNDERBALL. (United Artists-1965-Terence Young). A screenplay by Richard Maibaum and John Hopkins, from an original story by Kevin McClory and Jack Whittingham, based on the Ian Fleming novel; Viking, 1961. (NYTFR, LC, W, AMPAS, LACOPL).

2999   THUNDERBOLT AND LIGHTFOOT. (United Artists-1974-Michael Cimino). An original screenplay by Michael Cimino. (V, W).

3000   A TIA TULA. (United International-1965-Miguel Picazo). A screenplay by Luis Enciso, based on the novel by Miguel de Unamuno. (NYTFR).

3001   ... TICK ... TICK ... TICK ... (MGM-1970-Ralph Nelson). An original screenplay by James Lee Barrett. (W, LC, Q).

3002   TICKLE ME. (Allied Artists-1965-Norman Taurog). Elwood Ullman and Edward Bernds wrote this original screenplay. (NYTFR, LC, W, Q, AMPAS).

3003   LA TIERRA PROMETIDA. (Tricontinental-1974-Miguel Littin). An original screenplay written by Miguel Littin. (V, W).

3004   THE TIGER AND THE PUSSYCAT. (Embassy-1967-Dino Risi). An original screenplay by Age and Scarpelli (Agenore Incrocci and Furio Scarpelli) and Dino Risi. (FF, NYTFR, W, AMPAS, Q).

3005   THE TIGER MAKES OUT. (Columbia-1967-Arthur Hiller). Murray Schisgal wrote the screenplay based on his play The Tiger; Coward, 1963, 120p. (Q, FF, NYTFR, FM, W, LC, AMPAS, LACOPL).

3006   A TIGER TALKS. (Buena Vista-1964-Norman Tokar). Lowell S. Hawley based his screenplay on the novel by Ian Niall; William Morrow, 1960, 250p. (FF, LACOPL, NYTFR, Q, W).

3007   TIKO AND THE SHARK. (MGM-1966-Folco Quilici). A screenplay by Folco Quilici, Ottavio Alessi, Augusto Frassineti, and Giorgio Prosperi, based on the novel Ti-Coyo and His Shark by Clement Richer, and an adaptation by Italo Calvino; Knopf, 1951. (Q, FF, LC, W, LACOPL).

TILL DEATH US DO PART see ALF 'N' FAMILY

3008   TILL SEX DO US PART. (Astro-1974-Vilgot Sjoman). A screenplay by Vilgot Sjoman in collaboration with the cast. (HR, W).

3009   A TIME FOR DYING. (Etoile-1971-Budd Boetticher). An original screenplay by Budd Boetticher. (W).

3010   A TIME FOR KILLING.   (Columbia-1967-Phil Karlson).
       Halsted Welles wrote the screenplay which was based on a
       novel by Nelson and Shirley Wolford.   (FF, W, LC, AMPAS,
       Q).

3011   A TIME IN THE SUN.   (Universal-1970-Ake Falck).   A
       screenplay by Ake Falck and Lars Widding, from the novel
       The Princess by Gunnar Mattsson; Dutton, 1966, 160p.   (W,
       LACOPL).

3012   TIME LOST AND TIME REMEMBERED.   (Continental-1966-
       Desmond Davis).   An original screenplay by Edna O'Brien.
       (FF, NYTFR, W, AMPAS, Q).

3013   TIME OF INDIFFERENCE.   (Continental-1966-Francesco Ma-
       selli).   A screenplay by Suso Cecchi d'Amico, based on a
       novel by Alberto Moravia; New American Library, 1962.   (FF,
       NYTFR, W, LACOPL, Q).

3014   TIME OF ROSES.   (Cinema Dimensions-1970-Risto Jarva).
       A work written by Risto Jarva and Peter von Bagh, Jaakko
       Pakkazvirta.   (W).

3015   A TIME TO SING.   (MGM-1968-Arthur Dreifuss).   Robert E.
       Kent and Orville H. Hampton co-authored this original screen-
       play.   (Q, FF, W, LC, AMPAS).

3016   'TIS PITY SHE'S A WHORE.   (Euro International-1973-Giu-
       seppe Patroni Griffi).   A screenplay by Giuseppe Patroni
       Griffi, Alfio Valdarnini, and Carlo Carunchio, based on a
       play by John Ford; Hill, 1968, 97p.   (W, HR, LACOPL).

3017   TO BE A CROOK.   (Comet-1967-Claude Lelouch).   An origi-
       nal screenplay written by Claude Lelouch.   (NYTFR, W, Q).

3018   TO BE FREE.   (Magarac-1972-Ned Bosnick).   An original
       work for the screen by Ned Bosnick.   (W).

3019   TO COMMIT A MURDER.   (Cinerama-1970-Edouard Molinaro).
       A screenplay by Edouard Molinaro and Jacques Robert, based
       on a novel by Jacques Robert.   (W, Q).

3020   TO DIE OF LOVE.   (MGM-1972-Andre Cayatte).   An original
       screenplay by Andre Cayatte and Albert Naud.   (W, FF, Q).

3021   TO FIND A MAN.   (Columbia-1972-Buzz Kulik).   A screen-
       play written by Arnold Schulman, based on the novel by S. J.
       Wilson.   (W, Q).

3022   TO INGRID MY LOVE, LISA.   (Cannon-1969-Joseph Sarno).
       No screenplay credits available.   (W).

3023   TO KILL A CLOWN.   (20th Century-Fox-1972-George Bloomfield). A screenplay by George Bloomfield and I. C. Rapoport, based on Master of the Hounds by Algis Budrys. (W, Q).

3024 TO LOVE OPHELIA. (Cineriz-1974-Flavio Mogherini). An original screenplay by Flavio Mogherini and Giorgio Salvioni. (V).

TO LOVE SOMEBODY see MELODY

3025 TO SIR, WITH LOVE. (Columbia-1967-James Clavell). A screenplay written by James Clavell, based on the novel by E. R. Braithwaite; Prentice-Hall, 1959, 216p. (W, Q, FF, NYTFR, FM, LC, AMPAS, LACOPL).

3026 TO TRAP A SPY. (MGM-1966-Don Medford). An original screenplay by Sam Rolfe. (FF, W, AMPAS, Q).

3027 TOBRUK. (Universal-1967-Arthur Hiller). An original screenplay by Leo V. Gordon. (Q, FF, NYTFR, FM, W, LC, AMPAS).

3028 TODAY WE KILL ... TOMORROW WE DIE! (Cinerama-1971-Tonino Cervi). An original screenplay written by Dario Argento. (W).

3029 THE TODD KILLINGS. (National General-1971-Barry Shear). A screenplay by Dennis Murphy and Joel Oliansky, from a story by Mann Rubin. (W, Q).

3030 TOGETHER BROTHERS. (20th Century-Fox-1974-William A. Graham). A screenplay written by Jack De Witt and Joe Greene, from a story by Jack De Witt. (V, W).

3031 TOGETHER FOR DAYS. (Olas-1973-Michael Shultz). A screenplay by William B. Branch, from a story by Lindsay Smith. (W).

3032 TOKOLOSHE. (Artist International-1973-Peter Prowse). This original screenplay was written by Peter Prowse. (W).

3033 TOKYO STORY. (New Yorker-1972-Yasujiro Ozu). An original screenplay by Kogo Noda and Yasujiro Ozu. (FF).

3034 TOM. (Four Star International-1973-Greydon Clark). An original screenplay by Greydon Clark and Alvin L. Fast. (W).

3035 TOM SAWYER. (United Artists-1973-Don Taylor). A screenplay by Robert B. and Richard M. Sherman; based on The Adventures of Tom Sawyer by Mark Twain; Watts, 314p. (W, LACOPL).

3036 TOMB OF LIGEIA. (American International-1965-Roger

Corman). A screenplay by Robert Towne, based on the story
by Edgar Allan Poe; in Complete Stories and Poems, Doubleday, 1966. (NYTFR, LC, AMPAS, LACOPL).

3037   TOMB OF TORTURE. (Trans-Lux-1966-William Grace). A
screenplay by Anthony Kristye and Johnny Seemonell. (FF).

3038   TOMORROW. (Filmgroup-1972-Joseph Anthony). A screenplay by Horton Foote, based on a short story in the collection Knight's Gambit by William Faulkner; Random House,
1949. (FF, W, LACOPL).

3039   TONIO KROGER. (Pathe Contemporary-1968-Rolf Thiele).
A screenplay by Erika Mann and Ennio Flaiano, based on the
novel by Thomas Mann; in Thomas Mann Reader, Knopf,
1950. (FF, NYTFR, W, LACOPL).

3040   TONY ROME. (20th Century-Fox-1967-Gordon Douglas). A
screenplay by Richard L. Breen, based on the novel Miami
Mayhem by Marvin H. Albert. (FF, Q, NYTFR, FM, W,
LC, AMPAS).

3041   TOO LATE THE HERO. (Cinerama-1970-Robert Aldrich). A
screenplay by Robert Aldrich and Lukas Heller, from a story
by Robert Aldrich and Robert Sherman. (W).

3042   TOP OF THE HEAP. (Fanfare-1972-Christopher St. John).
An original screenplay by Christopher St. John. (FF).

3043   TOPAZ. (Universal-1969-Alfred Hitchcock). A screenplay
by Samuel Taylor, based on the novel by Leon Uris; McGraw-
Hill, 1967. (W, LACOPL).

3043a   TOPKAPI. (United Artists-1964-Jules Dassin). A screenplay by Monja Danischewsky, based upon The Light of Day
by Eric Ambler; Alfred Knopf, 1962, 243p. (LACOPL, FF,
NYTFR, W, Q, AMPAS).

3044   TORA! TORA! TORA! (20th Century-Fox-1970-Richard
Fleischer). A screenplay by Larry Forrester, Hideo Oguni,
Ryuzo Kikushima, based on the books by Gordon W. Prange
and Ladislas Farago; Broken Seal, Random House, 1967,
439p. (W, LACOPL, Q).

3045   TORN CURTAIN. (Universal-1966-Alfred Hitchcock). A
screenplay and original story by Brian Moore. (FF,
NYTFR, LC, W, Q, AMPAS).

3046   TORSO. (Joseph Brenner-1974-Sergio Martino). An original
screenplay by E. Gastaldi and E. Martino. (V, W).

3047   TORTURE GARDEN. (Columbia-1968-Freddie Francis). A
screenplay by Robert Bloch, based on his short stories.
(FF, FM, NYTFR, W, AMPAS, Q).

3048 THE TOUCH. (Cinerama-1971-Ingmar Bergman). An original work for the screen written by Ingmar Bergman. (W, Q).

3049 A TOUCH OF CLASS. (AVCO Embassy-1973-Melvin Frank). An original screenplay by Melvin Frank and Jack Rose. (W, Q).

3050 THE TOUCHABLES. (20th Century-Fox-1968-Robert Freeman). A screenplay by Ian La Frenais, based on a script by David and Donald Cammell and an Original Idea by Robert Freeman. (FF, NYTFR, W, LC, Q).

3051 TOUGH. (Dimension-1974-Horace Jackson). An original screenplay written by Horace Jackson. (HR, W).

3052 TOUT VA BIEN. (New Yorker-1973-Jean-Luc Godard and Jean-Pierre Gorin). An original screenplay by Jean-Luc Godard and Jean-Pierre Gorin. (W).

3053 TOWER OF SCREAMING VIRGINS. (Maron-1972-François Legrand aka Franz Antel). A screenplay by Kurt Nachmann, based on the novel The Tower of Nesle by Alexandre Dumas, and a story by Fritz Umgelter. (FF).

3054 THE TOWERING INFERNO. (20th Century-Fox-1974-John Guillermin and Irwin Allen). A screenplay by Stirling Silliphant, based on The Tower by Richard Martin Stern; McKay, 1973, 343p., and The Glass Inferno by Thomas N. Scortia & Frank M. Robinson; Doubleday, 1974, 435p. (V, W, HR, LACOPL, MFB).

3055 A TOWN CALLED HELL. (Scotia International-1971-Robert Parrish). An original screenplay by Richard Aubrey. (W).

3056 TOWN TAMER. (Paramount-1965-Leslie Selander). A screenplay by Frank Gruber, based on his novel; Rinehart, 1957, 221p. (W, LC, AMPAS, LACOPL, Q).

3057 THE TOY BOX. (Boxoffice International-1972-Ron Garcia). An original screenplay by Ron Garcia. (FF).

3058 TOYS ARE NOT FOR CHILDREN. (Maron-1972-Stanley H. Brasloff). A screenplay by Macs McAree, from a story by Stanley H. Brasloff. (W, FF).

3059 TRACK OF THUNDER. (United Artists-1968-Joseph Kane). An original screenplay by Maurice J. Hill. (FF, NYTFR, FM, W, AMPAS, Q).

3060 TRADER HORN. (MGM-1973-Reza S. Badiyi). An original screenplay written by William Norton and Edward Harper, from an original story by Edward Harper. (W, Q).

3061   TRADER HORNEE.   (Entertainment Ventures-1970-Tsanusdi).
David F. Friedman is credited with this original story and
screenplay. (W).

3062   TRAFFIC.   (Columbia-1972-Jacques Tati and Jacques La-
Grange). No screenplay credits available. (W, FF, Q).

3063   THE TRAIN. (United Artists-1965-John Frankenheimer). A
screen play by Franklin Coen and Frank Davis, based on Le
Front de l'Art by Rose Valland. (FF, LC, W, AMPAS, Q).

3064   THE TRAIN ROBBERS. (Warner Bros.-1973-Burt Kennedy).
Burt Kennedy wrote this original screenplay. (Q, W, FF).

3065   TRAITOR'S GATE. (Columbia-1966-Freddie Francis). A
screenplay by John Samson, based on the novel by Edgar
Wallace. (FF, LC, Q).

3066   THE TRAMPLERS. (Embassy-1966-Albert Band). A screen-
play by Ugo Liberatore and Albert Band, based on the novel
Guns of North Texas by Will Cook. (FF, Q, NYTFR, W,
AMPAS).

3067   TRANS-EUROPE-EXPRESS. (Trans American-1968-Alain
Robbe-Grillet). A screenplay written by Alain Robbe-Grillet.
(FF, NYTFR, W).

3068   TRANSPORT FROM PARADISE. (Impact-1967-Zbynek
Brynych). Arnost Lustig and Zbynek Brynych wrote the
original screenplay, from an original story by Arnost Lustig.
(NYTFR).

3069   THE TRAP. (Continental-1968-Sidney Hayers). A screenplay by David Osborn, from an original story. (FF).

3070   TRASH. (Andy Warhol-1970-Paul Morrissey). An original
screenplay by Paul Morrissey. (W).

3071   THE TRAVELING EXECUTIONER. (MGM-1970-Jack Smight).
An original screenplay authored by Garrie Bateson. (W).

3072   TRAVELS WITH MY AUNT. (MGM-1972-George Cukor). A
screenplay written by Jay Presson Allen and Hugh Wheeler,
based on a novel by Graham Greene; Viking, 1969, 244p.
(W, Q, FF, V, LACOPL).

3073   TREASURE ISLAND. (National General-1972-John Hough).
A screenplay by Wolf Mankowitz and Orson Welles, from the
novel by Robert Louis Stevenson; Scribner, 1905. (W,
LACOPL, Q).

3074   THE TREASURE OF MAKUBA. (Producers Releasing Organi-
zation-1967-Joe Lacy aka Jose Maria Elorrieta). A screen-

play by Manuel M. Remis and Jose Maria Elorrieta. (FF, W).

3075   TREASURE OF SAN GENNARO. (Paramount-1968-Dino Risi). A screenplay by Adriano Baracco, Ennio de Concini, Dino Risi, and Nino Manfredi, based on a story by Ennio de Concini and Dino Risi. (FF, NYTFR, W, Q).

3076   TREASURE OF SILVER LAKE. (Columbia-1965-Harald Reinl). A screenplay by H. G. Petersen, based on a novel by Karl May. (W, Q, AMPAS).

3077   THE TREE. (Robert Guenette-1969-Robert Guenette). An original screenplay by Robert Guenette. (FF, W).

3078   THE TRIAL OF BILLY JACK. (Taylor-Laughlin-1974-Frank Laughlin). An original screenplay by Frank and Teresa Christina. An original paperback novel based on the screenplay was written by Howard Liebling, and published by Billy Jack Enterprises, 1974, 189p. (V, LACOPL, W).

3079   TRIAL OF JOAN OF ARC. (Pathe Contemporary-1965-Robert Bresson). A screenplay by Brobert Bresson, based on the minutes of Joan of Arc's trial. (FF, W, Q).

3080   THE TRIAL OF THE CATONSVILLE NINE. (Cinema V-1972-Gordon Davidson). A screenplay by Daniel Berrigan and Saul Levitt, based on a play by Daniel Berrigan; Bantam Books, 1971, 109p. (W, LACOPL).

3081   TRICK BABY. (Universal-1973-Larry Yust). A screenplay by T. Raewyn, A. Neuberg, and Larry Yust, based on a novel by Iceberg Slim. (W).

3082   TRILOGY. (Allied Artists-1969-Frank Perry). A screenplay by Truman Capote and Eleanor Perry, based on stories by Truman Capote; Macmillan, 1969, 276p. (W, AMPAS, LACOPL, MCC, SCH).

3083   TRINITY IS STILL MY NAME. (AVCO Embassy-1973-E. B. Clucher). An original screenplay by E. B. Clucher. (W, FF, V).

3084   THE TRIP. (American International-1967-Roger Corman). A screenplay by Jack Nicholson. (FF, NYTFR, W, LC, AMPAS).

3085   THE TRIP. (1974-Vittorio De Sica). A screenplay by Diego Fabbri, Massimo Franciosa, and Luisa Montagnana, from a novel by Luigi Pirandello. (V).

3086   TRIPLE CROSS. (Warner Bros.-7 Arts-1967-Terence Young). A screenplay by Rene Hardy, based on the book The Eddie

Chapman Story by Frank Owen. (FF, NYTFR, LC, AMPAS, Q).

3087   TRIPLE ECHO. (Altura-1973-Michael Apted). A screenplay by Robin Chapman, from a novel by H. E. Bates. (W).

3088   TRIPLE IRONS. (National General-1973-Chang Cheh). An original screenplay by I Kuang. (W).

3089   TRISTANA. (Maron-1970-Luis Buñuel). A screenplay by Luis Buñuel and Julio Alejandro, based on the novel by Benito Pérez Galdós; Simon & Schuster, 1971, 144p. (W, LACOPL, Q).

3090   TROG. (Warner Bros.-1970-Freddie Francis). A screenplay by Aben Kandel, from a story by Peter Bryan and John Gilling. (W).

3091   TROIKA. (Emerson-1969-Fredric Hobbs). An original screenplay by Fredric Hobbs. (W).

3092   THE TROJAN WOMEN. (Cinerama-1971-Michael Cacoyannis). A screenplay by Michael Cacoyannis, adapted from the Edith Hamilton translation of the play by Euripides; play and screenplay published by Bantam Books; 1971, 116p. (W, LACOPL).

3093   TROPIC OF CANCER. (Paramount-1970-Joseph Strick). A screenplay by Joseph Strick and Betty Botley, based on the novel by Henry Miller; Grove Press, 1961. (W, LACOPL, Q).

3094   TROPICAL ECSTACY. (Haven-1970-Armando Bo). A screenplay by Armando Bo. (W).

3095   TROPICS. (New Yorker-1969-Gianni Amico). A screenplay by Gianni Amico and Francesco Tullio Altan. (FF, NYTFR, W).

3096   TROUBLE MAN. (20th Century-Fox-1972-Ivan Dixon). An original screenplay by John D. F. Black. (FF).

3097   THE TROUBLE WITH ANGELS. (Columbia-1966-Ida Lupino). A screenplay by Blanche Hanalis, based on the novel by Jane Trahey, Life with Mother Superior; 1963. (FF, Q, NYTFR, LC, W, AMPAS, LACOPL).

3098   THE TROUBLE WITH GIRLS. (MGM-1969-Peter Tewksbury). A screenplay by Arnold and Lois Peyser, from a story by Mauri Grashin, and a novel by Day Keene and Dwight Babcock. (W, LC, AMPAS, Q).

3098a   THE TROUBLEMAKER. (Janus-1964-Theodore J. Flicker). An original screenplay by Buck Henry and Theodore J. Flicker. (FF, NYTFR).

3099   TRUCK STOP WOMEN. (LT-1974-Mark L. Lester). A
        screenplay by Mark L. Lester, Paul Deason, from a story
        by Paul Deason. (V, W).

3100   TRUCK TURNER. (American International-1974-Jonathan
        Kaplan). A screenplay by Leigh Chapman and Oscar Willi-
        ams, and Michael Allin. (V).

3101   TRUE GRIT. (Paramount-1969-Henry Hathaway). A screen-
        play by Marguerite Roberts, based on the novel by Charles
        Portis; Simon & Schuster, 1968, 215p. (FF, W, LC,
        AMPAS, LACOPL).

3102   TRUNK TO CAIRO. (American International-1966-Manaheim
        Golan). A screenplay by Marc Behm and Alexander Ramati.
        (FF, W, LC, AMPAS, Q).

3103   THE TRUTH ABOUT SPRING. (Universal-1965-Richard
        Thorpe). A screenplay by James Lee Barrett, based on a
        story by Henry De Vere Stacpoole. (NYTFR, LC, W,
        AMPAS, Q).

3104   THE TRYGON FACTOR. (Warner Bros.-7 Arts-1969-Cyril
        Frankel). A screenplay by Derry Quinn and Stanley Munro,
        based on an original story by Derry Quinn. (FF, W, Q).

3105   THE TSAR'S BRIDE. (Artkino-1966-Vladimir Gorikker). A
        screenplay by A. Donatov and V. Gorikker, based on the
        opera by Rimsky-Korsakov. (FF, NYTFR, W).

3106   TSCHAIKOVSKY. (Artkino-1972-Dimitri Tiomkin). No
        screenplay credits available. (W).

3107   TURKISH DELIGHT. (Cinemation-1974-Paul Verhoeven). A
        screenplay authored by Gerard Soeteman; original novel based
        on screenplay by Jan Wolkeas; Dell, 1974, 178p. (HR,
        LACOPL, W).

3108   TURN ON TO LOVE. (Haven International-1969-John G.
        Avildsen). A screenplay by Atlas Geodesic, based on a story
        by Herman Worth. (W).

3109   THE TWELVE CHAIRS. (UMC-1970-Mel Brooks). A screen-
        play by Mel Brooks, based on a novel by Ilf and Petrov, The
        Complete Adventures of Ostap Bender; Random House, 1962,
        395p. (W, LACOPL, Q).

3110   THE 25TH HOUR. (MGM-1967-Henri Verneuil). A screen-
        play by Henri Verneuil, Françoise Boyer, and Wolf Manko-
        witz, based on the novel by C. Virgil Gheorghiu; Knopf, 1950.
        (FF, NYTFR, FM, W, LC, AMPAS, LACOPL, Q).

3111   TWILIGHT PEOPLE. (Dimension-1972-Eddie Romero). A

screenplay by Jerome Small and Eddie Romero. (FF).

3112   TWINS OF EVIL. (Universal-1972-John Hough). A screen-
play by Tudor Gates, based on characters created by Joseph
Sheridan Le Fanu (Carmilla, a novel), in Maurice Lane
Richardson's Novels of Mystery from the Victorian Age,
Duell, 1946. (FF, LACOPL).

3113   A TWIST OF SAND. (United Artists-1969-Don Chaffey). A
screenplay by Marvin H. Albert, based on the novel by Geof-
frey Jenkins. (FF, LC, AMPAS, Q).

3114   TWISTED NERVE. (National General-1969-Roy Boulting). A
screenplay by Leo Marks and Roy Boulting, based on a story
by Roger Marshall, adapted from an idea by Roger Marshall
and Jeremy Scott. (FF, W, Q).

3115   TWITCH OF THE DEATH NERVE. (Hallmark-1973-Mario
Bava). An original screenplay by Mario Bava. (W).

3116   "2". (Chevron-1969-Mac Ahlberg). A screenplay by Peer
Guldbrandsen, based on the novel Jeg--En Kvinde II by Siv
Holm. (See also I, A WOMAN.) (FF, W).

3117   TWO. (Colmar Ltd.-1974-Charles Trieschmann). An original screenplay by Charles Trieschmann. (V, W).

3117a TWO ARE GUILTY. (MGM-1964-Andre Cayatte). Andre
Cayatte, Charles Spaak, and Henri Jeanson wrote this original screenplay. (FF, NYTFR).

3118   TWO ENGLISH GIRLS. (Janus-1972-François Truffaut). A
screenplay by François Truffaut and Jean Gruault, based on
the novel Les Deux Anglaises et le Continent by Henri-Pierre
Roche. (FF).

3119   TWO FOR THE ROAD. (20th Century-Fox-1967-Frederic
Raphael). An original screenplay by Frederic Raphael, pub-
lished by Holt, Rinehart, and Winston; 1967, 142p. (MCC,
SCH, FF, NYTFR, FM, W, LC, AMPAS, Q, V. LACOPL).

3120   TWO GENTLEMEN SHARING. (American International-1969-
Ted Kotcheff). A screenplay by Evan Jones, based on the
novel by David Stuart Leslie. (FF, Q).

3121   TWO HUNDRED MOTELS. (United Artists-1971-Frank Zappa
and Tony Palmer). A screenplay by Frank Zappa and Tony
Palmer. (W, Q).

3122   TWO-LANE BLACKTOP. (Universal-1971-Monte Hellman).
A screenplay by Rudolph Wurlitzer and Will Corry, from a
story by Will Corry. (W).

3123   TWO MULES FOR SISTER SARA. (Universal-1970-Don Siegel). A screenplay by Albert Maltz, from a story by Bud
Boetticher. (W, Q).

3124   THE TWO OF US. (Cinema V-1968-Claude Berri). A screenplay by Claude Berri; novelization by Claude Berri published
by Morrow, 1968, 156p. (FF, NYTFR, W, AMPAS,
LACOPL, Q).

3125   TWO ON A GUILLOTINE. (Warner Bros.-1965-William Conrad). A screenplay by Henry Slesar and John Kneubuhl,
from a story by Henry Slesar. (FF, LC, W, AMPAS, Q).

3126   TWO OR THREE THINGS I KNOW ABOUT HER. (New York-
er-1970-Jean-Luc Godard). An original screenplay by Jean-
Luc Godard. (W, NYTFR).

3127   TWO PEOPLE. (Universal-1973-Robert Wise). An original
screenplay by Richard DeRoy. (W, Q).

3128   2000 YEARS LATER. (Warner Bros.-7 Arts-1969-Burt
Tenzer). An original screenplay by Bert Tenzer. (FF, W,
AMPAS, Q).

3129   2001: A SPACE ODYSSEY. (MGM-1968-Stanley Kubrick).
A screenplay by Stanley Kubrick and Arthur C. Clarke, based
on the short story "The Sentinel" by Arthur C. Clarke and on
his novel; New American Library, 1968. (MCC, FM, FF,
NYTFR, W, LC, AMPAS, LACOPL, Q).

3130   TWO WEEKS IN SEPTEMBER. (Paramount-1968-Serge Bourguignon). A screenplay by Vahe Katcha, Pascal Jardin, and
Serge Bourguignon. (FF, Q, W).

3131   THE UGLY DACHSHUND. (Buena Vista-1966-Norman Tokar).
A screenplay by Albert Aley, based on the book by G. B.
Stern; Macmillan, 1938. (FF, NYTFR, LC, W, AMPAS,
LACOPL, Q).

3132   THE UGLY ONES. (United Artists-1968-Eugenio Martin). A
screenplay by Don Prindle, Eugenio Martin, and Jose Maesso,
based on the novel The Bounty Killer by Marvin H. Albert.
(FF, NYTFR, LC, Q).

3133   ULYSSES. (Continental-1967-Joseph Strick). A screenplay by
Joseph Strick and Fred Haines, based on the novel by James
Joyce; Random House, 1961, 783p. (FF, NYTFR, FM,
W, AMPAS, LACOPL, Q).

3134   ULZANA'S RAID. (Universal-1972-Robert Aldrich). An original screenplay by Alan Sharp. (W, FF).

3134a   THE UMBRELLAS OF CHERBOURG. (Landau Releasing

Organization-1964-Jacques Demy). An original screenplay by
Jacques Demy. (FF, Q, W, AMPAS, NYTFR).

3135   THE UNCLE. (Lenart-1966-Desmond Davis). A screenplay
        by Desmond Davis and Margaret Abrams, based on the book
        by Margaret Abrams; Houghton, 1962. (FF, NYTFR, W,
        LACOPL, Q).

3136   UNCLE VANYA. (Artkino-1972-Andre Mikhalkov-Konchalov-
        sky). An uncredited screenplay, based upon a play by Anton
        Chekhov; University of Minnesota Press, 1969, 86p. (W,
        FF, LACOPL).

3137   AN UNCOMMON THIEF. (Artkino-1967-Eldar Ryazanov). An
        original screenplay by Emil Braginsky and Eldar Ryazanov.
        (W).

3138   UNDER MILK WOOD. (Altura-1973-Andrew Sinclair). A
        screenplay written by Andrew Sinclair, published by Simon &
        Schuster, 1972, 95p., which was based on a play by Dylan
        Thomas; New Directions, 1954, 107p. (W, LACOPL, Q).

3139   UNDERGROUND. (United Artists-1970-Arthur H. Nadel). A
        screenplay by Ron Bishop and Andy Lewis, from a story by
        Marc L. Roberts and Ron Bishop. (W, Q).

3140   THE UNDERTAKER AND HIS PALS. (Howco-1967-David C.
        Graham). A screenplay written by T. L. P. Twicegood.
        (W).

3141   UNDERWORLD INFORMERS. (Continental-1965-Ken Annakin).
        A screenplay by Alun Falconer, based on a novel by Douglas
        Warner. (NYTFR, W, Q).

3142   UNHOLY ROLLERS. (American International-1972-Vernon
        Zimmerman). A screenplay by Howard R. Cohen, based on
        a story by Vernon Zimmerman and Howard R. Cohen. (W,
        FF, Q).

3143   THE UNINHIBITED. (Peppercorn-Wormser-1968-Juan-Antonio
        Bardem). A screenplay by Henri-François Rey, based on his
        novel Mechanical Piano; Farrar, 1965. (FF, NYTFR, W,
        LACOPL).

3144   UNMAN, WITTERING AND ZIGO. (Paramount-1971-John
        Mackenzie). A screenplay by Simon Raven, based on the play
        by Giles Cooper, in Six Plays for Radio; British Broadcasting
        Co., 1966, 296p. (W, LACOPL, Q).

3144a   THE UNSINKABLE MOLLY BROWN. (MGM-1964-Charles
        Walters). A screenplay by Helen Deutsch, based on the mus-
        ical play with a book by Richard Morris; Putnam, 1961, 181p.
        (FF, LACOPL, Q, W, NYTFR).

3145 UNSTRAP ME. (Hawk Serpent-1968-George Kuchar). A
screenplay by George Kuchar, based on the story "The Trip
to Chicago" by Walter Gutman. (FF, NYTFR).

3146 UP FROM THE BEACH. (20th Century-Fox-1965-Robert
Parris). A screenplay by Stanley Mann and Claude Brule,
based on Epitaph for an Enemy by George Barr, adapted by
Howard Clewes; Harper, 1959. (NYTFR, LC, W, AMPAS,
LACOPL, Q).

3147 UP IN THE CELLAR. (American International-1970-Theo-
dore J. Flicker). A screenplay by Theodore J. Flicker,
based on The Late Wonder Boy by Angus Hall. (W).

3148 UP THE DOWN STAIRCASE. (Warner Bros.-7 Arts-1967-
Robert Mulligan). A screenplay by Tad Mosel, based on the
novel by Bel Kaufman; Prentice-Hall, 1964. (FF, NYTFR,
FM, W, LC, AMPAS, LACOPL, Q).

3149 UP THE JUNCTION. (Paramount-1968-Peter Collinson). A
screenplay by Roger Smith, based on the book by Nell Dunn;
Lippincott, 1966. (FF, NYTFR, FM, W, LC, AMPAS,
LACOPL, Q).

3150 UP THE MacGREGORS. (Columbia-1968-Frank Garfield). A
screenplay by Fernando di Leo, Enzo dell'Aquila, Paolo Levi,
Jose Maria Rodriguez, and Franco Giraldi, based on a story
by Fernando di Leo and Enzo dell'Aquila. (FF, Q, FM, W,
LC).

3151 UP THE SANDBOX. (National General-1972-Irvin Kershner).
A screenplay by Paul Zindel, from a novel by Anne Richardson Roiphe; Simon & Schuster, 1970, 155p. (W, FF, Q).

3152 UP TO HIS EARS. (Lopert-1966-Philippe de Broca). A work
for the screen written by Daniel Boulanger and Philippe de
Broca, based on a novel by Jules Verne. (FF, NYTFR, LC,
W).

3153 THE UPPER HAND. (Paramount-1967-Denys de la Patel-
lière). A screenplay by Alphonse Boudard and Denys de la
Patellière, based on a novel by Auguste le Breton. (FF, W,
Q).

3154 UPTIGHT. (Paramount-1968-Jules Dassin). A screenplay by
Jules Dassin, Ruby Dee and Julian Mayfield, based on the
novel The Informer by Liam O'Flaherty; Grosset, 1925. (FF,
NYTFR, FM, W, LC, AMPAS, Q).

3155 UPTOWN SATURDAY NIGHT. (Warner Bros.-1974-Sidney
Poitier). An original screenplay by Richard Koenakamp.
(W, V).

3156   UTAMARO AND HIS FIVE WOMEN. (New Yorker-1972-Kenji
       Mizoguchi). A screenplay by Yoshikata Yoda, from a novel
       by Kanil Kunieda. (W).

3157   THE VALACHI PAPERS. (Columbia-1972-Terence Young).
       A screenplay by Stephen Geller, adapted from the book by
       Peter Maas; Putnam, 1968, 285p. (W, FF, LACOPL, Q).

3158   VALDEZ IS COMING. (United Artists-1971-Edwin Sherin).
       A screenplay by Roland Kibbee and David Rayfiel, based on
       a novel by Elmore Leonard. (Q, W).

3159   VALI. (Film-Makers-1967-Sheldon Rochlin). A script writ-
       ten by Vali Myers and Rudi Rappold. (W).

3160   VALLEY OF BLOOD. (Mica-1973-Dean Turner). An origi-
       nal screenplay by Wayne Forsythe. (W).

3161   THE VALLEY OF GWANGI. (Warner Bros.-7 Arts-1969-
       James O'Connolly). An original screenplay written by Willi-
       am E. Bast. (FF, W, AMPAS, Q).

3162   VALLEY OF MYSTERY. (Universal-1967-Joseph Leytes).
       A screenplay by Richard Neal and Lowell Barrington, based
       on a story by Richard Neal and Larry Marcus. (FF, W,
       LC, AMPAS, Q).

3163   VALLEY OF THE DOLLS. (20th Century-Fox-1967-Mark
       Robson). A screenplay by Helen Deutsch and Dorothy Kings-
       ley, based on the novel by Jacqueline Susann; Geis, 1966,
       442p. (FF, NYTFR, FM, W, LC, AMPAS, LACOPL, Q).

3164   VAMPIRE CIRCUS. (20th Century-Fox-1972-Robert Young).
       A screenplay by Judson Kinberg, based on a story by George
       Baxt and Wilbur Stark. (FF, Q).

3165   THE VAMPIRE DOLL. (Toho-1972-Michio Yamamoto). No
       screenplay credits available. (W).

3166   THE VAMPIRE LOVERS. (American International-1970-Roy
       Ward Baker). An original screenplay by Tudor Gates. (W).

3167   VANISHING POINT. (20th Century-Fox-1971-Richard C. Sara-
       fian). A screenplay by Guillermo Cain, based on a story by
       Malcolm Hart. (W, Q).

3168   VARIETY LIGHTS. (Pathe Contemporary-1965-Alberto Lat-
       tuada and Federico Fellini). A screenplay by Federico Fel-
       lini, Ennio Flaiano, Alberto Lattuada, Tullio Pinelli, from a
       story by Federico Fellini. Screenplay published in Early
       Screenplays by Federico Fellini; Grossman, 1971, 198p. (W,
       AMPAS, LACOPL, Q).

3169 THE VAULT OF HORROR. (Cinerama-1973-Roy Ward Baker).
      An original screenplay by Milton Subotsky. (W, Q).

3170 THE VELVET VAMPIRE. (New World-1971-Stephanie Roth-
      man). A screenplay by Maurice Jules, Charles S. Swartz,
      and Stephanie Rothman. (W).

3171 THE VENETIAN AFFAIR. (MGM-1967-Jerry Thorpe). A
      screenplay by E. Jack Neuman, based on the novel by Helen
      MacInnes; Harcourt, 1963. (FF, NYTFR, W, LC, LACOPL,
      Q, AMPAS).

3172 THE VENGEANCE OF FU MANCHU. (Warner Bros.-7 Arts-
      1968-Jeremy Summers). A screenplay by Peter Welbeck,
      based on characters created by Sax Rohmer. (FF, NYTFR,
      FM, W, AMPAS).

3173 THE VENGEANCE OF SHE. (20th Century-Fox-1968-Cliff
      Owen). A screenplay by Peter O'Donnell, based on charac-
      ters created by Sir H. Rider Haggard. (FF, FM, NYTFR,
      W, LC, AMPAS, Q).

3174 VENOM. (Peppercorn-Wormser-1968-Knud Lief Thomsen).
      An original screenplay by Knud Lief Thomsen. (FF, NYTFR,
      W).

3175 VENUS IN FURS. (American International-1970-Jess Franco).
      A screenplay by Jess Franco and Marvin Wald, from a story
      by Jess Franco. (Q, W).

3176 THE VERDICT. (1974-Andre Cayatte). An original screen-
      play by Andre Cayatte, Henri Coupon, Pierre Dumayet, and
      Paul Andreota. (V).

3177 A VERY CURIOUS GIRL. (Regional-1970-Nelly Kaplan). A
      script and dialogue written by Nelly Kaplan, Claude Makovski,
      adapted by Nelly Kaplan, Claude Makovski, J. Berguine, and
      M. Fabre. (W, Q).

3178 A VERY HANDY MAN. (Rizzoli-1966-Alessandro Blasetti).
      A screenplay by Sergio Amidei and Alessandro Blasetti,
      based on the play Liola by Luigi Pirandello. (FF, Q, NYTFR,
      W, AMPAS).

      VERY HAPPY ALEXANDER see ALEXANDER

3179 A VERY NATURAL THING. (New Line-1974-Christopher
      Larkin). A screenplay by Christopher Larkin and Joseph Co-
      encas. (V, W).

3180 A VERY SPECIAL FAVOR. (Universal-1965-Michael Gordon).
      A screenplay by Stanley Shapiro and Nate Monaster. (Q,
      NYTFR, LC, W, AMPAS).

IL VIAGGIO see THE TRIP

3181   VICE AND VIRTUE. (MGM-1965-Roger Vadim). A screenplay by Roger Vadim and Roger Vailland, based on the novels
Justine, Putnam, 1966, 291p., and Juliette, Grove Press,
1968, 1205p., by the Marquis de Sade. (FF, LC, W,
LACOPL, Q).

3182   LA VIE DE CHATEAU. (Royal-1967-Jean-Paul Reppeneau).
A screenplay by Alain Cavalier, Claude Sautet, Daniel Boulanger, and Jean-Paul Rappeneau. (FF, NYTFR, W).

3183   THE VIKING QUEEN. (20th Century-Fox-1967-Don Chaffey).
A screenplay by Clarke Reynolds, based on an original story
by John Temple-Smith. (FF, W, LC, AMPAS, Q).

3184   VILLA RIDES. (Paramount-1968-Buzz Kulik). A screenplay
by Robert Towne and Sam Peckinpah, based on the book
Pancho Villa by William Douglas Lansford; Sherbourne Press,
1965, 283p. (FF, NYTFR, FM, Q, W, LC, AMPAS,
LACOPL).

3185   VILLAGE OF THE GIANTS. (Embassy-1965-Bert I. Gordon).
A screenplay by Alan Caillou, based on the novel The Food
of the Gods by H. G. Wells; Scribner, 1924. (W, AMPAS,
LACOPL, Q).

3186   VILLAIN. (MGM-1971-Michael Tuchner). A screenplay by
Dick Clement, Ian La Frenais, adapted by Al Lettieri, from
the novel The Burden of Proof by James Barlow; Simon &
Schuster, 1968, 254p. (W, Q, LACOPL).

3187   VINCENT, FRANÇOIS, PAUL ... AND THE OTHERS. (1974-
Claude Sautet). A screenplay by Jean-Loup Dabadie, Claude
Neron, Claude Sautet, and based on a book by Claude Neron.
(V).

3188   LE VIOL. (Freena Films-1968-Jacques Doniol-Valcroze).
A work for the screen written by Jacques Doniol-Valcroze.
(FF, NYTFR).

3189   THE VIOLENT FOUR. (Paramount-1968-Carlo Lizzani). A
screenplay by Dino Mauri, Massimo de Rita and Carlo Lizzani. (FF, NYTFR, W, Q).

VIOLENT JOURNEY see THE FOOL KILLER

3190   THE VIOLENT ONES. (Feature Film Corporation of Amer-
ica-1967-Fernando Lamas). A screenplay by Doug Wilson
and Charles Davis, based on a story by Fred Freiberger
and Herman Niller. (FF, W, AMPAS).

3191   THE VIRGIN AND THE GYPSY. (Chevron-1970-Christopher

Miles). A screenplay by Alan Plater, based on the novella
by D. H. Lawrence, in Short Novels, vol. 2; William Heine-
mann Ltd., 1956. (W, LACOPL, Q).

3192 THE VIRGIN SOLDIERS. (Columbia-1970-John Dexter). A
screenplay by John Hopkins, based on a novel by Leslie
Thomas; Little, Brown & Co., 1966. (W, LACOPL, Q).

3193 THE VIRGIN WITCH. (Joseph Brenner-1973-Ray Austin).
An original screenplay by Klaus Vogel. (W).

3194 THE VISCOUNT. (Warner Bros.-1967-Maurice Cloche). A
screenplay written by Clark Reynolds, based on the novel
Bonne Mesure by Jean Bruce. (FF, NYTFR, W, LC,
AMPAS, Q).

3194a THE VISIT. (20th Century-Fox-1964-Bernhard Wicki). Ben
Barzman based his screenplay on the play by Friedrich
Duerrenmatt; Random House, 1958, 115p. (FF, LACOPL,
NYTFR, W).

3195 VISIT TO A CHIEF'S SON. (United Artists-1974-Lamont
Johnson). An original screenplay by Albert Ruben. (HR,
W).

3196 THE VISITORS. (United Artists-1972-Elia Kazan). An original screenplay by Chris Kazan. (FF, Q).

3197 LA VISTA. (Promenade-1966-Antonio Pietrangeli). A screenplay by Ettore Scola, Ruggero Maccari, and Antonio Pietrangeli. (FF, NYTFR, W).

3198 VIVA LA MUERTE. (Raab-1971-Fernando Arrabal). An
original screenplay by Fernando Arrabal. (W).

3198a VIVA LAS VEGAS. (MGM-1964-George Sidney). An original
screenplay by Sally Benson. (FF, AMPAS, LC, NYTFR, Q,
W).

3199 VIVA MARIA. (United Artists-1965-Louis Malle). A screenplay written by Louis Malle and Jean-Claude Carrière.
(NYTFR, LC, W, AMPAS, Q).

VIXEN see RUSS MEYER'S VIXEN

3200 THE VIXENS. (Stratford-1969-Harvey Cort). A screenplay
by Al Rosati and Harvey Cort. (FF, W).

3201 VON RYAN'S EXPRESS. (20th Century-Fox-1965-Mark Robson). A screenplay by Wendell Mayes and Joseph Landon,
based on the novel by David Westheimer; Doubleday, 1964.
(NYTFR, LC, W, AMPAS, LACOPL, Q).

3202   THE VULTURE. (Paramount-1967-Lawrence Huntington). A
        screenplay by Lawrence Huntington. (FF, NYTFR, FM, W,
        LC, AMPAS, Q).

3203   W. (Cinerama-1974-Richard Quine). A screenplay by Gerald
        Di Pego and James Kelly, from a story "Chance for a Kill-
        ing" by James Kelly and Ronald Shusett. (V, W).

        W. I. A. see WOUNDED IN ACTION

3203a   WR--MYSTERIES OF THE ORGANISM. (Cinema V-1971-
        Dusan Makavejev). This original screenplay was written by
        Dusan Makavejev. (W).

3204   WACO. (Paramount-1966-R. G. Springsteen). A screenplay
        by Steve Fisher, based on the novel Emporia by Harry San-
        ford and Max Lamb. (FF, FM, LC, W, AMPAS, Q).

3205   WAIT UNTIL DARK. (Warner Bros.-7 Arts-1967-Terence
        Young). A screenplay by Robert and Jane-Howard Carring-
        ton, based on the play by Frederick Knott; Dramatists Play
        Service, 1967, 89p. (FF, NYTFR, W, LC, AMPAS,
        LACOPL, Q).

3206   WAITING FOR CAROLINE. (Lopert-1969-Ron Kelly). A
        screenplay by George C. Robertson and Ron Kelly. (W, LC,
        Q).

        WAKE IN FRIGHT see OUTBACK

3207   WAKE UP AND DIE. (Rizzoli-1968-Carlo Lizzani). A
        screenplay by Ugo Pirro and Carlo Lizzani. (FF).

3208   WALK, DON'T RUN. (Columbia-1966-Charles Walters). A
        screenplay by Sol Saks, based on a story by Robert Russell
        and Frank Ross. (FF, NYTFR, LC, W, AMPAS, Q).

3209   WALK IN THE SHADOW. (Continental-1966-Basil Dearden).
        A work written for the screen by Janet Green and John Mc-
        Cormick. (FF, NYTFR, W, AMPAS, Q).

3210   A WALK IN THE SPRING RAIN. (Columbia-1970-Guy Green).
        A screenplay by Stirling Silliphant, based on a novel by Ra-
        chel Maddux; Doubleday, 1966. (W, LACOPL).

3211   A WALK WITH LOVE AND DEATH. (20th Century-Fox-
        1969-John Huston). A screenplay by Dale Wasserman, adapt-
        ed by Hans Koningsberger from his novel; Simon & Schuster,
        1961. (W, AMPAS, LACOPL, Q).

3212   WALKABOUT. (20th Century-Fox-1971-Nicolas Roeg). A
        screenplay by Edward Bond, from a novel by James Vance
        Marshall; Doubleday, 1959. (W, LACOPL, Q).

3213 THE WALKING STICK. (MGM-1970-Eric Till). A screenplay by George Bluestone, based on the novel by Winston
Graham; Doubleday, 1967. (W, LACOPL, Q).

3214 WALKING TALL. (Cinerama-1973-Phil Karlson). An original story and screenplay by Mort Briskin. (W).

3215 WALL OF FLESH. (Provocative-1969-Joe Sarno). An original work for the screen by Joe Sarno. (W).

3216 THE WALLS OF HELL. (Hemisphere Pictures-1965-Gerardo
De Leon and Eddie Romero). A screenplay by Ferde Grofe,
Jr., Cesar Amigo, and Eddie Romero. (NYTFR, LC,
AMPAS).

3217 WANDA. (Bardene International-1971-Barbara Loden). A
screenplay written directly for the screen by Barbara Loden.
(W).

3218 THE WANDERER. (Leacock Pennebaker-1969-Jean-Gabriel
Albicocco). A screenplay by Isabelle Riviere and Jean-Gab-
riel Albicocco, based on the 1912 novel Le Grand Meaulnes
by Henri Alain-Fournier. (W, FF).

3219 WAR AND PEACE. (Continental-1968-Sergei Bondarchuk).
A screenplay by Sergei Bondarchuk and Vasily Solovyov,
based on the novel by Leo Tolstoy; Norton, 1966. (FF,
NYTFR, FM, W, AMPAS, Q, LACOPL).

3220 THE WAR BETWEEN MEN AND WOMEN. (National General-
1972-Melville Shavelson). A screenplay by Melville Shavelson and Danny Arnold. (W, Q).

3221 WAR GODS OF THE DEEP. (American International-1965-
Jacques Tourneur). A screenplay by Charles Bennett and
Louis M. Heyward. (NYTFR, LC, W, AMPAS, Q).

3221a WAR IS HELL. (Allied Artists-1964-Burt Topper). An original screenplay by Burt Topper. (FF, W, Q).

THE WAR IS OVER see LA GUERRE EST FINIE

3222 WAR ITALIAN STYLE. (American International-1967-Luigi
Scattini). A screenplay by Franco Castellano and Pipolo
(Giuseppe Moccia), based on an idea by Fulvio Lucisano. (FF,
W, LC, Q).

3223 THE WAR LORD. (Universal-1965-Franklin Schaffner). A
screenplay by John Collier, Millard Kaufman, based on the
play The Lovers by Leslie Stevens. (W, LC, AMPAS, Q).

3224 THE WAR OF THE ZOMBIES. (American International-1966-
Giuseppe Vari). No screenplay credits available. (W, LC, Q).

3225   WAR PARTY. (20th Century-Fox-1965-Lesley Selander). A
       screenplay by George Williams and William Marks. (FF,
       LC, W, AMPAS).

3226   THE WAR WAGON. (Universal-1967-Burt Kennedy). A
       screenplay by Clair Huffaker, based on his novel Badman.
       (FF, NYTFR, FM, W, LC, AMPAS, Q).

3227   WARKILL. (Universal-1968-Ferde Grofe, Jr.). A screen-
       play by Ferde Grofe, Jr. (FF, W, AMPAS, Q).

3228   A WARM DECEMBER. (National General-1973-Sidney Poit-
       ier). A work written for the screen by Lawrence Roman.
       (W, Q).

3229   WARM IN THE BUD. (FilmMakers-1970-Rudolph Caringi).
       A screenplay by Rudolph Caringi, adapted from Spring's
       Awakening by Frank Wedekind. (W).

3230   WARNING SHOT. (Paramount-1967-Buzz Kulik). A screen-
       play by Mann Rubin, based on the novel 711--Officer Needs
       Help by Whit Masterson; Dodd, 1965. (FF, NYTFR, FM,
       W, LC, AMPAS, LACOPL, Q).

3231   WATCHED. (Penthouse-1974-John Parsons). A screenplay
       by John Parsons. (V, W).

3232   WATERHOLE NO. 3. (Paramount-1967-William Graham).
       A screenplay by Joseph Steck and Robert R. Young. (FF,
       NYTFR, FM, W, LC, Q, AMPAS).

3233   WATERLOO. (Paramount-1971-Sergei Bondarchuk). A
       screenplay by H. A. L. Craig and Sergei Bondarchuk. (W).

3234   WATERMELON MAN. (Columbia-1970-Melvin Van Peebles).
       An original screenplay by Herman Raucher. (W, Q).

3235   WATTSTAX. (Columbia-1973-Mel Stuart). No script credits
       available; a documentary. (W, Q).

3236   WAY OUT. (Premier Presentations-1967-Irvin S. Yeaworth,
       Jr.). A screenplay by Jean Yeaworth, Rudy and Shirley Nel-
       son, based on the play The Addicts by John Gimenez. (FF,
       NYTFR, W AMPAS).

3237   WAY ... WAY OUT. (20th Century-Fox-1966-Gordon Doug-
       las). A screenplay by William Bowers and Laslo Vadnay.
       (FF, NYTFR, LC, W, AMPAS, Q).

3238   THE WAY WE LIVE NOW. (United Artists-1970-Barry
       Brown). A screenplay by Daniel Tamkus and Barry Brown,
       based on a novel by Warren Miller; Little, Brown, & Co.,
       1958. (W, LACOPL, Q).

3239   THE WAY WE WERE.   (Columbia-1973-Sydney Pollack).   A
screenplay by Arthur Laurents, from his novel; Harper, 1972,
264p.   (W, V. LACOPL, Q).

3240   THE WAY WEST.   (United Artists-1967-Andrew V. McLaglen).   A screenplay by Ben Maddow and Mitch Lindemann,
based on the novel by A. B. Guthrie, Jr.; Sloane, 1949.
(FF, NYTFR, FM, W, LC, AMPAS, Q, LACOPL).

3241   WE ARE ALL NAKED.   (Citel-USA-1970-Claude Pierson).
An original screenplay by Huguette Boisvert.   (W).

3242   WE STILL KILL THE OLD WAY.   (Lopert-1968-Elio Petri).
A screenplay by Elio Petri and Ugo Pirro, adapted from the
novel A Ciascuno il Suo (To Each His Own) by Leonardo
Sciascia.   (FF, NYTFR, W, Q).

3243   WEB OF FEAR.   (Comet-1967-François Villiers).   A screenplay by Jacques Sigurd and Jean-Pierre Ferrière, based on
a novel by Jean-Pierre Ferrièrre.   (FF).

3244   WEDDING IN BLOOD.   (New Line Cinema-1974-Claude Chabrol).   An original screenplay by Claude Chabrol.   (HR, W).

3245   WEDDING IN WHITE.   (AVCO Embassy-1973-William Fruet).
An original screenplay written by William Fruet.   (W, Q).

3246   WEDDING NIGHT.   (American International-1970-Piers Haggard).   A screenplay by Robert I. Holt and Lee Dunne, from
a story by Robert I. Holt.   (W, Q).

3247   THE WEDDING PARTY.   (Ajay-1969-Cynthia Munroe, Brian
De Palma, and Wilford Leach).   Writeen by Cynthia Munroe,
Brian De Palma, and Wilford Leach.   (Q, FF, W).

3248   THE WEDNESDAY CHILDREN.   (Venture-1973-Robert D.
West).   An original screenplay by Robert D. West.   (W).

3249   WEDNESDAY'S CHILD.   (Cinema V-1972-Ken Loach).   A
screenplay by David Mercer, from his TV play "In Two
Minds."   (W, FF, Q).

3249a WEEKEND.   (Cinema-Video International-1964-Palle Kjaerulff-
Schmidt).   Klaus Rifbjerg authored this original screenplay.
(FF, NYTFR).

3250   WEEKEND.   (Grove Press-1968-Jean-Luc Godard).   A
screenplay by Jean-Luc Godard; Simon & Schuster, 1972,
188p.   (FF, NYTFR, W, Q, LACOPL).

3251   WEEKEND AT DUNKIRK.   (20th Century-Fox-1966-Henri
Verneuil).   A screenplay by François Boyer, based on a
novel by Robert Merle; Knopf, 1951.   (FF, NYTFR, LC, W,
LACOPL).

3252   WEEKEND, ITALIAN STYLE.   (Marvin-1968-Dino Risi).   A
        screenplay by Dino Risi, based on a story by Ennio de Con-
        cini and Dino Risi.   (FF, NYTFR, W).

3253   WEEKEND MURDERS.   (MGM-1972-Michele Lupo).   A
        screenplay by Fabio Pittorru, Massimo Felisatti, and Sergio
        Donati, with additional dialogue by Sergio Donati.   (FF).

3254   WEEKEND OF FEAR.   (JD-1966-Joe Danford).   An original
        screenplay by Joe Danford.   (W).

        WEEKEND WIVES see WEEKEND, ITALIAN STYLE

3255   WELCOME HOME, SOLDIER BOYS.   (20th Century-Fox-
        1972-Richard Compton).   An original screenplay by Guerdon
        Trueblood.   (FF, Q).

3256   WELCOME KOSTYA!   (Artkino-1965-Ilya Klimov).   An origi-
        nal work for the screen by S. Lingin and I. Nusinov.
        (NYTFR).

3257   WELCOME TO ARROW BEACH.   (Warner Bros.-1974-Laur-
        ence Harvey).   A screenplay by Wallace C. Bennett, adapted
        by Jack Gross, Jr., from an original story by Wallace C.
        Bennett.   (V, W).

3258   WELCOME TO HARD TIMES.   (MGM-1967-Burt Kennedy).
        A screenplay by Burt Kennedy, based on the novel by E. L.
        Doctorow; Simon & Schuster, 1960.   (FF, NYTFR, FM, W,
        LC, Q, AMPAS, LACOPL).

3259   WELCOME TO THE CLUB.   (Columbia-1971-Walten Shenson).
        A screenplay by Clement Biddle Wood, from his novel of the
        same name; McGraw-Hill, 1966.   (W, FF, LACOPL, Q).

3260   WEREWOLF OF WASHINGTON.   (Diplomat-1973-Milton
        Moses Ginsberg).   An original screenplay by Milton Moses
        Ginsberg.   (W).

3261   WEREWOLVES ON WHEELS.   (Fanfare-1971-Michel Levesque).
        A screenplay by David M. Kaufman and Michel Levesque.
        (W).

3262   WESTWORLD.   (MGM-1973-Michael Crichton).   An original
        screenplay written by Michael Crichton.   (W, Q, V).

3262a   WHAT A WAY TO GO!   (20th Century-Fox-1964-J. Lee
        Thompson).   Betty Comden and Adolph Green wrote the
        screenplay which was based on a story by Gwen Davis.
        (NYTFR, AMPAS, LC, W, Q, FF).

3263   WHAT ABOUT JANE?   Sherpix-1972-Tom Hanley).   A script
        written by Tom Hanley.   (W, FF).

3264   WHAT AM I BID? (Emerson-1967-Gene Nash). A screenplay by Gene Nash. (FF, W, AMPAS).

3265   WHAT BECAME OF JACK AND JILL? (20th Century-Fox-
1972-Bill Bain). A screenplay by Roger Marshall, based on
the novel The Ruthless Ones by Laurence Moody. (FF, Q).

3266   WHAT DID YOU DO IN THE WAR, DADDY? (United Artists-
1966-Blake Edwards). A screenplay by William Peter Blatty,
from a story by Blake Edwards and Maurice Richlin. (FF,
NYTFR, LC, W, AMPAS, Q).

3267   WHAT DO I TELL THE BOYS AT THE STATION? (August-
1972-Simon Nuchtern). A screenplay by William C. Reilly
and Simon Nuchtern. (W).

3268   WHAT DO YOU SAY TO A NAKED LADY? (United Artists-
1970-Allen Funt). A screenplay by Allen Funt. (W).

3269   WHAT EVER HAPPENED TO AUNT ALICE? (Cinerama-
1969-Lee H. Katzin). A screenplay by Theodore Apstein,
based on the novel The Forbidden Garden by Ursula Curtiss;
Dodd, 1962. (FF, W, AMPAS, LACOPL, Q).

3270   WHATEVER HAPPENED TO MISS SEPTEMBER? (808 Pic-
tures-1973-Jerry Denby). An original screenplay by Adam
Baum. (W).

3271   WHAT'S GOOD FOR THE GOOSE. (National Showmanship-
1969-Menahem Golan). An original screenplay by Menahem
Golan. (W).

3272   WHAT'S NEW PUSSYCAT? (United Artists-1965-Clive Donner).
An original screenplay written by Woody Allen. (NYTFR, Q,
LC, W, AMPAS).

3273   WHAT'S SO BAD ABOUT FEELING GOOD? (Universal-1968-
George Seaton). A screenplay by George Seaton and Robert
Pirosh, based on an incident in the novel I Am Thinking of
My Darling by Vincent McHugh; Simon & Schuster, 1943.
FF, FM, NYTFR, Q, W, AMPAS, LACOPL).

3274   WHAT'S THE MATTER WITH HELEN? (United Artists-1971-
Curtis Harrington). An original screenplay by Henry Farrell.
(W).

3275   WHAT'S UP DOC? (Warner Bros.-1972-Peter Bogdanovich).
A screenplay by Buck Henry, David Newman, and Robert Ben-
ton, based on a story by Peter Bogdanovich. (W, FF, Q).

3276   WHAT'S UP, TIGER LILY? (American International-1966-
Senkichi Tanigzuchi). Script in English by Woody Allen,
Frank Buxton, Len Maxwell, Louise Lasser, Mickey Rose,

from a story by Julie Bennett and Bryna Wilson. (FF,
NYTFR, W, AMPAS, Q).

3277 WHEN DINOSAURS RULED THE EARTH. (Warner Bros.-
1971-Val Guest). An original screenplay by Val Guest. (W).

3278 WHEN EIGHT BELLS TOLL. (Cinerama-1971-Etienne Per-
ier). A screenplay by Alistair MacLean, based on his novel;
Doubleday, 1966. (W, Q, LACOPL).

3279 WHEN THE BOYS MEET THE GIRLS. (MGM-1966-Alvin
Ganzer). A screenplay by Robert E. Kent, based on the
musical play Girl Crazy by Guy Bolton with music and lyrics
by George and Ira Gershwin; New World Music Co., 1954.
(FF, LC, W, AMPAS, LACOPL, Q).

3280 WHEN THE LEGENDS DIE. (20th Century-Fox-1972-Stuart
Millar). A screenplay by Robert Dozier, based on the novel
by Hal Borland; Bantam Books, 1963, 216p. (FF, LACOPL,
Q).

3281 WHEN WOMEN HAD TAILS. (Film Ventures International-
1973-Pasquale Festa Campanile). No screenplay credit available. (W).

3282 WHERE ANGELS GO--TROUBLE FOLLOWS. (Columbia-1968
-James Neilson). A screenplay by Blanche Hanalis, based
on characters created by Jane Trahey. (FF, NYTFR, FM,
W, LC, AMPAS, Q).

3283 WHERE DOES IT HURT? (Cinerama-1972-Rod Amateau). A
screenplay by Rod Amateau and Budd Robinson, from their
novel The Operator. (W, FF, Q).

3284 WHERE EAGLES DARE. (MGM-1969-Brian G. Hutton). A
screenplay by Alistair MacLean, based on his novel; Doubleday, 1967. (FF, Q, W, LC, AMPAS, LACOPL).

3285 WHERE IT'S AT. (United Artists-1969-Garson Kanin). An
original screenplay by Garson Kanin. (FF, W, LC, Q,
AMPAS).

3285a WHERE LOVE HAS GONE. (Paramount-1964-Edward Dmytryk). John Michael Hayes based his screenplay on the novel
by Harold Robbins; Simon & Schuster; 1962, 350p. (FF,
LACOPL, NYTFR, LC, AMPAS, Q, W).

3286 WHERE THE BULLETS FLY. (Embassy-1967-John Gilling).
An original screenplay by Michael Pittcock. (NYTFR, W,
AMPAS, Q).

3287 WHERE THE RED FERN GROWS. (Doty-Dayton-1974-Nor-
man Tokar). A screenplay by Douglas Stewart, Eleanor

Lamb from a novel by Wilson Rawls; Doubleday, 1961. (V, W, LACOPL).

3288   WHERE THE SPIES ARE. (MGM-1966-Val Guest). A screenplay by Val Guest and Wolf Mankowitz, based on the novel Passport to Oblivion by James Leasor; Lippincott, 1964. (FF, Q, NYTFR, LC, W, AMPAS, LACOPL).

3289   WHERE WERE YOU WHEN THE LIGHTS WENT OUT? (MGM-1968-Hy Averback). A screenplay by Everett Freeman and Karl Tunberg, based on the play Monsieur Masu.e by Claude Magnier. (FF, NYTFR, FM, W, LC, AMPAS, Q).

3290   WHERE'S JACK? (Paramount-1969-James Clavell). An original screenplay by Rafe and David Newhouse. (W, LC, Q).

3291   WHERE'S POPPA? (United Artists-1970-Carl Reiner). An original screenplay by Robert Klane. (W).

3292   WHICH WAY TO THE FRONT? (Warner Bros.-1970-Jerry Lewis). A screenplay by Gerald Gardner, Dee Caruso, from a story by Gerald Gardner, Dee Caruso, and Richard Miller. (W, Q).

3293   WHIRLPOOL. (Cinemation-1970-J. R. Larrath). An original work for the screen by J. R. Larrath. (W).

3294   WHIRLWIND. (Toho-1968-Hiroshi Inagaki). An original screenplay by Hiroshi Inagaki. (FF, NYTFR, W, V).

3295   THE WHISPERERS. (Lopert-1967-Bryan Forbes). A screenplay written by Bryan Forbes, based on the novel by Robert Nicolson; Knopf, 1961. (FF, NYTFR, Q, FM, W, AMPAS, LACOPL).

3296   THE WHITE DAWN. (Paramount-1974-Philip Kaufman). A screenplay by James Houston and Tom Rickman, based on the book by James Houston; Harcourt, 1971, 275p. (V, LACOPL, W).

3297   WHITE LIGHTNING. (United Artists-1973-Joseph Sargent). An original screenplay by William Norton. (W, V, Q).

3298   WHITE SISTER. (Columbia-1973-Alberto Lattuada). An original screenplay by Iaia Fiastri, Alberto Lattuada, Tonino Guerra, and Ruggero Maccari, from a story by Tonino Guerra and Ruggero Maccari. (W).

3299   WHITE VOICES. (Rizzoli-1965-Pasquale Festa Campanile and Massimo Franciosa). An original screenplay by Pasquale Festa Campanile, Massimo Franciosa, and Luigi Magni. (FF, W, Q).

3300   WHO IS HARRY KELLERMAN AND WHY IS HE SAYING
        THOSE TERRIBLE THINGS ABOUT ME? (National General-
        1971-Ulu Grosbard). An original screenplay by Herb Gard-
        ner. (W, Q).

3301   WHO KILLED MARY WHAT'S'ERNAME? (Cannon-1971-Ernie
        Pintoff). An original screenplay by John O'Toole. (W, Q).

3302   WHO KILLED TEDDY BEAR? (Magna-1965-Joseph Cates).
        An original screenplay by Leon Tokatyan, Arnold Drake,
        from a story by Arnold Drake. (W, AMPAS, Q).

3303   WHO SAYS I CAN'T RIDE A RAINBOW! (Transvue-1971-
        Edward Mann). An original screenplay by Edward Mann and
        Daniel Hauer. (W).

3304   WHO SLEW AUNTIE ROO? (American International-1972-
        Curtis Harrington). A screenplay by Robert Blees and James
        Sangster, with additional dialogue by Gavin Lambert. Based
        on an original story by David Osborn. (W).

3305   WHO'S AFRAID OF VIRGINIA WOOLF? (Warner Bros.-1966
        -Mike Nichols). A screenplay by Ernest Lehman, based on
        the play by Edward Albee; Atheneum, 1962, 242p. (FF,
        NYTFR, Q, LC, W, AMPAS, LACOPL, V).

3306   WHO'S MINDING THE MINT? (Columbia-1967-Howard Mor-
        ris). An original screenplay by R. S. Allen and Harvey Bul-
        lock. (FF, Q, NYTFR, FM, W, LC, AMPAS).

3307   WHO'S THAT KNOCKING AT MY DOOR? (Joseph Brenner
        Associates-1969-Martin Scorsese). An original screenplay
        written by Martin Scorsese. (FF, W).

3308   WHY. (Hallmark Releasing Corporation-1972-Nanni Loy). A
        screenplay by Sergio Amidei and Amilio Sanna, based on an
        idea by Rodolfo Sonego. (FF).

3309   WHY BOTHER TO KNOCK. (7 Arts-1965-Cyril Frankel). A
        screenplay by Denis Cannan, Frederick Gotfurt, and Freder-
        ick Raphael, from the novel by Clifford Hanley. (FF, W,
        AMPAS, Q).

3310   WHY ROCK THE BOAT? (Columbia-1974-John Howe). A
        screenplay by William Weintraub, based on his novel. (V).

3311   THE WICKED DREAMS OF PAULA SCHULTZ. (United Art-
        ists-1968-George Marshall). A screenplay by Burt Styler,
        Albert E. Lewin and Nat Perrin, based on a story by Ken
        Englund. (FF, NYTFR, FM, W, LC, Q, AMPAS).

3312   WICKED, WICKED. (MGM-1973-Richard L. Bare). A
        screenplay by Richard L. Bare. (W).

3313   THE WICKER MAN. (Warner Bros.-1974-Robin Hardy). An
        original screenplay by Anthony Shaffer. (V).

3314   THE WIFE SWAPPERS. (Eagle-1970-Derek Ford). An origi-
        nal screenplay by Stanley Long and Derek Ford. (W).

3315   THE WILD AFFAIR. (Goldstone Film Enterprises-1966-John
        Krish). A screenplay by John Krish, based on the novel The
        Last Hours of Sandra Lee by William Sansom; Little, Brown
        & Co., 1961. (FF, AMPAS, LACOPL).

3315a   WILD AND WONDERFUL. (Universal-1964-Michael Ander-
        son). Larry Markes and Michael Morris and Waldo Salt
        were responsible for this screenplay, which was taken from
        a screen story by Richard M. Powell and Phillip Rapp, and
        in turn was based on a story by Dorothy Crider. (FF,
        NYTFR, W, Q).

3316   THE WILD ANGELS. (American International-1966-Roger
        Corman). An original screenplay by Charles B. Griffith.
        (FF, NYTFR, LC, W, AMPAS, Q).

3317   THE WILD BUNCH. (Warner Bros.-7 Arts-1969-Sam Peck-
        inpah). A screenplay by Walon Green and Sam Peckinpah,
        based on a story by Walon Green and Roy N. Sickner. (FF,
        W, AMPAS).

3318   THE WILD CHILD. (United Artists-1970-François Truffaut).
        A screenplay by François Truffaut, Jean Gruault, adapted
        from the novel by Jean Itard. Screenplay published by Wash-
        ington Square Press, 1973, 189p. (W, LACOPL, Q).

3319   THE WILD COUNTRY. (Buena Vista-1971-). A screenplay
        by Calvin Clements, Jr., and Paul Savage, based on Little
        Bitches by Ralph Moody; Norton, 1950, 260p. (W, LACOPL,
        Q).

3320   THE WILD EYE. (American International-1968-Paolo Ca-
        vara). A screenplay by Paolo Cavara and Tonino Guerra, in
        collaboration by Alberto Moravia, based on a story by Paolo
        Cavara, Fabio Carpi, and Ugo Pirro. (FF, NYTFR, LC).

        WILD IN THE SKY see BLACK JACK

3321   WILD IN THE STREETS. (American International-1968-Barry
        Shear). A screenplay by Robert Thom, based on his story
        "The Day It All Happened, Baby" (Esquire, 1966). (FF, W,
        Q, NYTFR, FM, LC, AMPAS, V).

3322   WILD 90. (Supreme Mix-1968-Norman Mailer). An impro-
        vised screenplay. (FF, NYTFR, W).

3323   WILD ON THE BEACH. (20th Century-Fox-1965-Maury

Dexter). A screenplay by Harry Spaulding, from a story by
Hank Tani. (Q, W, LC, AMPAS).

3324   THE WILD PACK. (American International-1972-Hall Bart-
       lett). Screenplay written by Hall Bartlett, based on a collec-
       tion of stories, Capitães da Areia by Jorge Amado. (FF).

3325   THE WILD RACERS. (American International-1968-Daniel
       Haller). An original screenplay by Max House. (FF, W,
       LC, AMPAS, Q).

3326   THE WILD REBELS. (Crown International-1967-William
       Grefe). An original screenplay by William Grefe. (FF, W,
       AMPAS).

3327   WILD ROVERS. (MGM-1971-Blake Edwards). An original
       screenplay written by Blake Edwards. (W, Q).

3328   THE WILD SCENE. (Four Star Excelsior-1970-William Row-
       land). An original screenplay by Michael Kraike and William
       Keys. (W).

3329   WILD SEED. (Universal-1965-Brian G. Hutton). An original
       screenplay by Les Pine, from a story by Les Pine and Ike
       Jones. (W, LC, AMPAS).

3330   WILD, WILD PLANET. (MGM-1967-Anthony Dawson aka An-
       tonio Margheriti). A screenplay by Ivan Reiner. (FF, W,
       LC, Q).

3331   WILD WILD WINTER. (Universal-1966-Lennie Weinrib). An
       original screenplay by David Malcolm. (FF, LC, W, AMPAS,
       Q).

3332   WILL PENNY. (Paramount-1968-Tom Gries). An original
       screenplay by Tom Gries. (FF, FM, NYTFR, W, LC,
       AMPAS, Q).

3333   WILLARD. (Cinerama-1971-Daniel Mann). A screenplay by
       Gilbert A. Ralston, based on Ratman's Notebooks, a novel by
       Stephen Gilbert; Viking, 1968, 184p. (W, LACOPL, Q).

3334   WILLY McBEAN AND HIS MAGIC MACHINE. (Magna-1965-
       Arthur Rankin, Jr.). An original screenplay by Arthur Ran-
       kin, Jr. (W, AMPAS).

3335   WILLY WONKA AND THE CHOCOLATE FACTORY. (Par-
       amount-1971-Mel Stuart). A screenplay by Roald Dahl, based
       on his novel, Charlie and the Chocolate Factory; Knopf, 1964.
       (W. LACOPL, Q).

3336   WINDFLOWERS. (Film-Makers' Distribution Center-1968-
       Adolfas Mekas). An original screenplay by Adolfas Mekas.
       (FF, NYTFR, W).

3337   THE WINDSPLITTER. (POP-1971-Julius D. Feigelson). An
       original screenplay by Julius D. Feigelson. (W).

3338   THE WINNER. (Gillmore-Kingsley-1966-François Reichen-
       bach). No author credits available. (W).

3339   WINNING. (Universal-1969-James Goldstone). An original
       work for the screen by Howard Rodman. (FF, AMPAS).

3340   WINTER A-GO-GO. (Columbia-1965-Richard Benedict). A
       screenplay by Bob Kanter, from a story by Reno Carell.
       (W, LC, AMPAS, Q).

3341   WINTER KEPT US WARM. (Film-Makers' Distribution Cen-
       ter-1968-David Secter). A screenplay by David Secter, John
       Porter, and John Clute. (FF, NYTFR, W).

3342   WINTER WIND. (Grove-1970-Miklos Jancso). An original
       screen play by Gyula Hernadi and Miklow Jancso. (W).

3343   WISE GUYS. (Universal-1969-). A screenplay by Robert
       Enrico and Jose Giovanni, from the novel Le Haut-Fer. (W).

3344   A WITCH WITHOUT A BROOM. (Producers Releasing Or-
       ganization-1967-Joe Lacy). An original screenplay by Howard
       Berk. (FF, W, Q).

3345   WITCHCRAFT. (20th Century-Fox-1965-Don Sharp). An
       original screenplay by Harry Spalding. (FF, Q, LC,
       AMPAS).

3346   THE WITCHES. (Lopert-1969-Luchino Visconti, Mauro Bo-
       lognini, Pier Paolo Pasolini, Franco Rossi, and Vittorio De
       Sica). An episodic drama with segments written by Giuseppe
       Patroni Griffi, Age and Scarpelli, Bernardino Zapponi, Pier
       Paolo Pasolini, Franco Rossi, Luigi Magni, Cesare Zavattini,
       Fabio Carpi, and Enzio Muzii. (W).

3347   THE WITCHMAKER. (Excelsior-1969-William O. Brown).
       William O. Brown wrote this original screenplay. (W).

3348   WITH SIX YOU GET EGGROLL. (National General-1968-
       Howard Morris). A screenplay by Gwen Bagni, Paul Dubov,
       Harvey Bullock, and R. S. Allen, based on an original story
       by Gwen Bagni and Paul Dubov. (FF, NYTFR, AMPAS, Q).

3349   WITHOUT A STITCH. (VIP-Sherpix-1970-Annelise Meineche).
       A screenplay by Annelise Meineche and John Hilbard, based
       on a novel by Jean Bjorneboe. (W, Q).

3350   WITHOUT APPARENT MOTIVE. (20th Century-Fox-1972-
       Philippe Labro). A screenplay by Philippe Labro and Jacques
       Lanzmann, based on the novel Ten Plus One by Ed McBain;

Simon & Schuster, 1963.   (W, LACOPL, Q).

3351   WOMAN AND TEMPTATION.   (Prentoulis-1969-Armando Bo).
Armando Bo is credited with this original screenplay.   (FF).

3351a   WOMAN IN THE DUNES.   (Pathe Contemporary-1964-Hiroshi
Teshigahara).   Kobo Abe wrote the original screenplay.   (FF).

3352   WOMAN OF STRAW.   (United Artists-1964-Basil Dearden).
A screenplay by Robert Muller, Stanley Mann, and Michael
Relph, based on the novel by Catherine Arley; Random House,
1958.   (FF, LC, AMPAS, LACOPL, NYTFR, Q, W).

3352a   A WOMAN ON FIRE.   (Commonwealth United-1970-Fernando
di Leo).   An original screenplay by Fernando di Leo and
Antonio Racioppi.   (W).

3353   WOMAN TIMES SEVEN.   (Embassy-1967-Vittorio De Sica).
An original screenplay attributed to Cesare Zavattini.   (FF,
W, AMPAS, Q).

3354   A WOMAN UNDER THE INFLUENCE.   (Faces International-
1974-John Cassavetes).   An original screenplay by John
Cassavetes.   (V, W).

3355   THE WOMAN WHO WOULDN'T DIE.   (Warner Bros.-1965-
Gordon Hessler).   A screenplay by Dan Mainwaring, based
on a novel by Jay Bennett.   (NYTFR, LC, W, AMPAS, Q).

3356   WOMEN IN CAGES.   (New World-1972-Jerry de Leon).   An
original screenplay by David Osterhout and Jim Watkins.
(W).

3357   WOMEN IN CELL BLOCK 7.   (Aquarius-1974-Rino di Silvestro).   A screenplay by Rino di Silvestro.   (V, W).

WOMEN IN LIMBO see LIMBO

3358   WOMEN IN LOVE.   (United Artists-1970-Ken Russell).   A
screenplay by Larry Kramer, based on the novel by D. H.
Lawrence; Viking, 1950, 473p.   (W, LACOPL, V, Q).

3359   WOMEN IN REVOLT.   (Andy Warhol-1972-Andy Warhol).
No screenplay credits available.   (FF).

WOMEN IN THE SUN see FEMMES AU SOLEIL

3360   WOMEN OF THE PREHISTORIC PLANET.   (Realart-1966-
Arthur Pierce).   An original screenplay by Arthur Pierce.
(FF, LC, W, AMPAS, Q).

3361   WONDER WOMEN.   (General-1973-Robert O'Neil).   A screenplay by Lou Whitehill, adaptation by Robert O'Neil.   (W).

3362 WOODSTOCK. (Warner Bros.-1969-Michael Wadleigh). A documentary; no screenplay credits. (W, Q).

3363 THE WORLD IS JUST A "B" MOVIE. (Robinson-1971-R. D. Robinson). An original screenplay by R. D. Robinson. (W).

3364 THE WORLD OF HANS CHRISTIAN ANDERSEN. (United Artists-1971-). An animated feature, based on the works of Hans Christian Andersen. (W).

3364a THE WORLD OF HENRY ORIENT. (United Artists-1964-George Roy Hill). A screenplay by Nora Johnson and Nunnally Johnson, based on a novel by Nora Johnson; Little, Brown & Co., 1958. (FF, LACOPL, LC, AMPAS, NYTFR, W, Q).

3365 THE WORLD OF SPORT FISHING. (Allied Artists-1972-Bud Morgan). An original script by Pat Smith. (FF).

3366 WORLD WITHOUT SUN. (Columbia-1964-Jacques-Yves Cousteau). Commentary written by James Dugan, Al Ramrus, and Jim Schmerer. (FF, NYTFR, LC, W, Q).

3367 THE WORLD'S GREATEST ATHLETE. (Buena Vista-1973-Robert Scheerer). An original screenplay by Gerald Gardner and Dee Caruso. (W, Q).

3368 WOUNDED IN ACTION. (Myriad-1966-Irving Sunasky). A screenplay written by Irving Sunasky. (W).

3369 THE WRATH OF GOD. (MGM-1972-Ralph Nelson). A screenplay by Ralph Nelson, based on a novel by James Graham; Doubleday, 1971, 277p. (Q, FF, W, LACOPL).

3370 THE WRECKING CREW. (Columbia-1969-Phil Karlson). A screenplay by William McGivern, based on the novel by Donald Hamilton. (FF, W, LC, AMPAS, Q).

3371 THE WRESTLER. (Entertainment Ventures-1974-Jim Westman). An original screenplay by Eugene Gump. (V, W).

3372 THE WRONG BOX. (Columbia-1966-Bryan Forbes). A screenplay by Larry Gelbart and Burt Shevelove, based on the novel by Robert Louis Stevenson and Lloyd Osbourne; Scribner, 1905. (FF, NYTFR, LC, W, AMPAS, LACOPL, Q).

3373 WUSA. (Paramount-1970-Stuart Rosenberg). A screenplay by Robert Stone, from his novel A Hall of Mirrors; Houghton, 1966. (W, LACOPL, Q).

3374 WUTHERING HEIGHTS. (American International-1971-Robert Fuest). A screenplay by Patrick Tilley, from the novel by

Emily Brontë; Norton, 1963. (W, LACOPL, Q).

3375 X Y & ZEE. (Columbia-1972-Brian G. Hutton). An original work for the screen by Edna O'Brien. (FF, Q).

3375a YANCO. (Jay K. Hoffman-1964-Servando Gonzalez). An original screenplay by Servando Gonzalez. (FF, NYTFR, W, Q).

3376 A YANK IN VIET-NAM. (Allied Artists-1964-Marshall Thompson). A screenplay by Jane Wardell and Jack Lewis, from an original story by Jack Lewis. (FF).

3376a THE YEAR OF THE CANNIBALS. (American International-1970-Liliana Cavani). A screenplay by Liliana Cavani and Italo Moscati, based on the play Antigone by Sophocles. (FF).

3377 YEAR OF THE HORSE. (Dienstag-Orkin-1966-Irving Sunasky). A screenplay by Irving Sunasky. (W, AMPAS).

3378 YEAR OF THE WOMAN. (1973-Sandra Hochman). A film written by Sandra Hochman; documentary. (W).

3379 YEAR ONE. (Italnoleggio-1974-Roberto Rossellini). A screenplay by Roberto Rossellini, Luciano Scaffa and Marcello Mariani. (V).

3380 THE YELLOW ROLLS-ROYCE. (MGM-1965-Anthony Asquith). A screenplay by Terence Rattigan. (NYTFR, LC, W, AMPAS, Q).

3381 YELLOW SUBMARINE. (United Artists-1968-George Dunning). A screenplay by Lee Minoff, Al Brodax, Jack Mendelsohn, and Erich Segal, from an original story by Lee Minoff, based on the song "Yellow Submarine" by John Lennon and Paul McCartney. The book based on the film was written by Max Wilk, and published by New American Library, 1968, 128p. (FF, NYTFR, W, LC, AMPAS, LACOPL, Q).

3382 YESTERDAY GIRL. (1967-Alexander Kluge). A screenplay by Alexander Kluge, based on his story "Anita G." (NYTFR).

3382a YESTERDAY, TODAY AND TOMORROW. (Embassy-1964-Vittorio De Sica). "Adelina" by Eduardo de Filippo, with the collaboration of Isabella Quarantotti; "Anna" by Cesare Zavattini and Billa Billa, based on a short story by Alberto Moravia; "Mara" by Cesare Zavattini. (FF, W, NYTFR, LC, AMPAS, Q).

3383 YO YO. (Magna-1967-Pierre Etaix). A screenplay by Pierre Etaix and Jean-Claude Carrière. (NYTFR).

3384   YOG--MONSTER FROM SPACE. (American International-1971-Ishiro Honda). A screenplay by El Ogawa. (W).

3385   YOLANTA. (Artkino-1966-Vladimir Gorikker). An opera conducted by B. Khaikin. (W).

3386   YOU CAN'T WIN 'EM ALL. (Columbia-1970-Peter Collinson). A screenplay by Leo Gordon. (W, Q).

3387   YOU ONLY LIVE TWICE. (United Artists-1967-Lewis Gilbert). A screenplay by Roald Dahl, based on the novel by Ian Fleming; New American Library, 1964, 240p. (FF, NYTFR, FM, W, Q, LC, AMPAS, LACOPL).

3388   YOU ONLY LOVE ONCE. (Sigma III-1969-Dirk Sanders). Dirk Sanders wrote this original screenplay. (W, Q).

3389   YOU'LL LIKE MY MOTHER. (Universal-1972-Lamont Johnson). A screenplay by Jo Heims, based on the novel by Naomi A. Hintze; Putnam, 1969, 191p. (FF, LACOPL).

3390   YOUNG AMERICANS. (Columbia-1967-Alex Grasshoff). A documentary written by Alex Grasshoff. (W, LC).

3390a   YOUNG AND WILLING. (Universal-1964-Ralph Thomas). Nicholas Phipps and Mordecai Richler's screenplay is based on the play The Tinker by Laurence Dobie and Robert Simon. (FF, NYTFR, Q, W).

        THE YOUNG ANIMALS see BORN WILD

3391   YOUNG APHRODITES. (Janus-1967-Nikos Koundouros). A screenplay by Vassilis Vassilikos and Costas Sphikas, based on Daphnis and Chloe by Longus and the Pastoral Idylls of Theocritus. (FF, W).

3392   YOUNG BILLY YOUNG. (United Artists-1969-Burt Kennedy). A screenplay by Burt Kennedy, based on the novel Who Rides with Wyatt? by Will Henry; Random House, 1955. (FF, LC, AMPAS, LACOPL).

3393   YOUNG CASSIDY. (MGM-1965-Jack Cardiff). A screenplay by John Whiting, based on Mirror in My House by Sean O'-Casey; Macmillan, 1956, 2 vols. (FF, LC, W, AMPAS, LACOPL, Q).

3394   A YOUNG COUPLE. (Trans World-1971-Rene Gainville). An original screenplay by Jean-Louis Curtis. (W).

3395   YOUNG DILLINGER. (Allied Artists-1965-Terry O. Morse). An original screenplay by Don Zimbalist and Arthur Hoerl. (NYTFR, LC, W, AMPAS, Q).

3396   YOUNG FRANKENSTEIN. (20th Century-Fox-1974-Mel
        Brooks). A screenplay by Gene Wilder, Mel Brooks, based
        on characters by Mary Shelley. Novelization based on
        screenplay written by Gilbert Pearlman; Ballantine Books,
        1974, 152p. (V, LACOPL, W).

3397   YOUNG FURY. (20th Century-Fox-1965-Chris Nyby). A
        screenplay by Steve Fisher, from a story by Steve Fisher
        and A. C. Lyles. (W, LC, AMPAS, Q).

3398   THE YOUNG GIRLS OF ROCHEFORT. (Warner Bros. -7
        Arts-1968-Jacques Demy). An original screenplay by Jacques
        Demy. (FF, NYTFR, FM, W, LC, AMPAS, Q).

3399   THE YOUNG LORD. (Beta-1970-Gustav Rudolf Sellner). A
        screenplay and story by Wilhelm Hauff. (W).

3400   THE YOUNG LOVERS. (MGM-1965-Samuel Goldwyn, Jr.).
        A screenplay by George Garrett, based on the novel by Julian
        Halevy; Simon & Schuster, 1955. (FF, LC, AMPAS,
        LACOPL).

3401   THE YOUNG NURSES. (New World-1973-Clinton Kimbro).
        An original screenplay by Howard R. Cohen. (W).

3402   THE YOUNG RUNAWAYS. (MGM-1968-Arthur Dreifuss). A
        screenplay by Orville H. Hampton. (FF, NYTFR, W, LC,
        AMPAS, Q).

3403   THE YOUNG SINNER. (United Screen Arts-1965-Tom Laugh-
        lin). A screenplay by Tom Laughlin. (W, AMPAS, Q).

3404   THE YOUNG, THE EVIL AND THE SAVAGE. (American In-
        ternational-1968-Anthony Dawson aka Antonio Margheriti). A
        screenplay by Anthony Dawson and Frank Bottar, based on a
        story by John Simonelli. (FF, NYTFR, FM, LC, AMPAS,
        Q).

3405   YOUNG TORLESS. (Kanawha-1968-Volker Schlondorff). A
        screenplay by Volker Schlondorff, based on the novel by Ro-
        bert Musil; Pantheon, 1955. (FF, NYTFR, FM, W,
        LACOPL, Q).

3406   THE YOUNG WARRIORS. (Universal-1967-John Peyser). A
        screenplay by Richard Matheson, based on his novel The
        Beardless Warriors; Little, Brown & Co., 1960. (FF,
        NYTFR, W, LC, AMPAS, Q, LACOPL).

3407   YOUNG WINSTON. (Columbia-1972-Richard Attenborough).
        A screenplay by Carl Foreman, based on A Roving Commis-
        sion: My Early Life by Sir Winston Churchill. The screen-
        play was published by Ballantine, 1972, 157p. (LACOPL,
        Q, W, FF).

3408   A YOUNG WORLD. (Lopert-1966-Vittorio De Sica). A screenplay and dialogue by Cesare Zavattini. (FF, NYTFR, W).

3408a   YOUNGBLOOD HAWKE. (Warner Bros.-1964-Delmer Daves). A screenplay by Delmer Daves, based on the novel by Herman Wouk; Doubleday, 1962, 783p. (FF, LACOPL, NYTFR, W, Q, LC, AMPAS).

3409   YOUR CHEATING HEART. (MGM-1965-Gene Nelson). A screenplay by Stanford Whitmore. (NYTFR, Q, LC, AMPAS, W).

3410   YOUR THREE MINUTES ARE UP. (Cinerama-1973-Douglas N. Schwartz). An original screenplay by James Dixon. (W, V).

3411   YOU'RE A BIG BOY NOW. (7 Arts-1967-Francis Ford Coppola). A screenplay by Francis Ford Coppola, based on a novel by David Benedictus. (FF, Q, NYTFR, FM, W, AMPAS).

3412   YOU'RE LYING. (Grove Press, 1973-Vilgot Sjoman). No screenplay credits available. (W).

3413   YOURS, MINE AND OURS. (United Artists-1968-Melville Shavelson). A screenplay by Melville Shavelson and Mort Lachman, from a story by Madelyn Davis and Bob Carroll, Jr. (FF, NYTFR, FM, W, Q, LC, AMPAS).

3414   YOU'VE GOT TO BE SMART. (Producers Releasing Organization-1967-Ellis Kadison). An original screenplay by Ellis Kadison. (FF, W).

3415   YOU'VE GOT TO WALK IT LIKE YOU TALK IT OR YOU'LL LOSE THAT BEAT. (JER-1971-Peter Locke). An original screenplay by Peter Locke. (W).

3416   Z. (Cinema V-1969-Costa-Gavras). A screenplay by Jorge Semprun and Costa-Gavras, based on the novel by Vassili Vassilikos; Ballantine Books, 1968, 376p. (FF, W, AMPAS, LACOPL).

3417   Z.P.G. (Paramount-1972-Michael Campus). A screenplay by Max Ehrlich and Frank De Felitta. (FF, Q, W).

3418   ZABRISKIE POINT. (MGM-1970-Michelangelo Antonioni). A screenplay by Michelangelo Antonioni, Fred Gardner, Sam Shepard, Tonino Guerra, and Clare Peplo. (W, AMPAS, Q).

3419   ZANDY'S BRIDE. (Warner Bros.-1974-Jan Troell). A screenplay by Marc Norman, based on the novel The Stranger by Lillian Bos Ross; Morrow, 1942. (V, LACOPL, W).

3420   ZARDOZ.   (20th Century-Fox-1974-John Boorman).   A
       screenplay by John Boorman, a paperback original by John
       Boorman with Bill Stair was published by Signet, 1974. (HR,
       V, LACOPL, W).

3421   ZATOICHI.   (Daiei-1968-Kimoyoshi Yasuda).   No screenplay
       credits available.   (FF, NYTFR, W).

3422   ZATOICHI AT LARGE.   (Toho-1973-Kazuo Mori).   An origi-
       nal screenplay by Kinya Naoi, from a story by Kan Shimo-
       zawa.   (W).

3423   ZATOICHI MEETS YOJIMBO.   (Bijou-1971-Kihachi Okamoto).
       An original screenplay by Tetsuo Yoshida.   (W).

3424   ZATOICHI'S CANE SWORD.   (Daiei-1971-Kimiyoshi Yasuda).
       An original screenplay by Ryozo Kasahari.   (W).

3425   ZEBRA IN THE KITCHEN.   (MGM-1965-Ivan Tors).   A
       screenplay by Art Arthur, from a story by Elgin Ciampi.
       (W, LC, AMPAS).

3426   ZERO IN THE UNIVERSE.   (Film-Makers' Distribution Cen-
       ter-1966-George Moorse).   A screenplay by Jock Livingston
       and George Moorse.   (FF, NYTFR).

       ZERO POPULATION GROWTH   see   Z. P. G.

3427   ZIGZAG.   (MGM-1970-Richard A. Colla).   A screenplay by
       John T. Kelley, from a story by Robert Enders.   (W, Q).

3428   ZITA.   (Regional-1968-Robert Enrico).   A screenplay by
       Lucienne Hamon, Pierre Pelegri and Robert Enrico, based
       on a story by Lucienne Hamon.   (FF, NYTFR, AMPAS, Q).

3429   ZULU.   (Embassy-1964-Cy Endfield).   A screenplay by John
       Prebble and Cy Endfield, from an original story by John
       Prebble.   (FF, NYTFR, W, Q, LC, AMPAS).

INDEX

Chabrol, Jean-Pierre 2648
Chamberlain, William 21a
Champion, John C. 132, 380,
    1664, 2811, 2928
Champreux, Jacques 1361, 1582
Chandler, Len 926a
Chandler, Raymond 1752, 1897
Chaney, Will 1368
Chanslor, Roy 470
Chantier, David 2640
Chaplin, Charles 618, 1616
Chaplin, Geraldine 1365
Chapman, Graham 73
Chapman, Leigh 785, 3100
Chapman, Robin 3087
Charles, Ernest A. 2316
Charles-Williams, Liz 696,
    2186, 2715
Charriere, Christine 2556
Charriere, Henri 2230
Chase, Borden 150, 1239,
    1866
Chase, Frank 2826
Chase, James Hadley 905,
    1223, 2095
Chase, Patricia 1239
Chayefsky, Paddy 67, 1379,
    2223
Cheever, John 2859
Chekhov, Anton 212, 282a, 909,
    2576, 2991, 3136
Chendey, Ivan 2626
Cherry, Stanley Z. 399, 1512
Chesnoff, Richard Z. 138
Chetwynd, Lionel 105
Chiara, Piero 573, 1362, 1878
Chien, Chang 1941
Chih-po, Wang 1844
Chorelle, Valentin 476
Christian, H. R. 10, 278
Christian, Tina Chad 142
Christie, Agatha 57, 2018a,
    2023, 2024, 2911
Christina, Frank 253, 3078
Christina, Teresa 253, 3078
Christophe, Jean 2165
Christopher, John 2115
Chulyukin, Yuri 157
Churchill, Sir Winston 982a,
    3407
Chytilova, Vera 657
Ciampi, Elgin 3425
Ciampi, Yves 1920

Cimino, Michael 1847, 2663,
    2999
Cistheri, Raymond 1933
Ciuffini, Sabatino 1176a, 2726
Clair, Richard 223
Clark, Benjamin 517
Clark, Bruce 2049, 2675
Clark, Chris 1653
Clark, Greydon 3034
Clark, Matt 1360
Clarke, Arthur C. 3128
Clarke, Shirley 599a
Clarke, T. E. B. 1869
Clavell, James 1622, 1680, 2542,
    3025
Clay, Melvin 2747
Cleary, Jon 1336
Cleese, John 73
Cleland, John 939, 940
Clemens, Brian 77, 441, 606,
    802, 1178, 2598, 2768a
Clemens, Harold 1644
Clement, Dick 1262, 1570, 2202,
    3186
Clement, Henry 772
Clement, Rene 677a, 1579
Clements, Calvin 989, 1596, 3319
Clements, Harold 615
Clemins, Harold 1601
Clemmons, Larry 2482
Clewes, Howard 3146
Clifford, Francis 2056
Clouse, Robert 841, 1274
Clouzot, Henri-Georges 2347
Clucher, E. B. see Barboni, E.
Clute, John 3341
Coe, Fred 2968
Coen, Franklin 59, 275, 2877,
    3063
Coen, Guido 142, 2162
Coencas, Joseph 3179
Coghill, Nevill 798
Cohen, Albert J. 2051
Cohen, Herman 219, 625
Cohen, Howard R. 3142, 3401
Cohen, Larry 268, 585, 655,
    1308, 1452, 1536, 2455, 2755,
    2767
Cohen, Martin B. 2418
Cohen, Nathan 2724
Cohen, Ronald M. 309, 1182
Cohn, Stewart 2510
Colbert, Stanley 1371

Marks, Louis 1881
Marks, Ted 1874
Marks, William 178, 1608,
  3225
Markson, David 779
Markstein, George 2137, 2480
Marlowe, Christopher 798
Marlowe, Derek 661
Marmorstein, Malcolm 2755
Marquand, John P. 2452
Marquis, Don 2646
Marriott, Anthony 698, 2578
Marshall, Garry 1202, 1412
Marshall, James Vance 3212
Marshall, Peter 1748, 1906a
Marshall, Roger 75, 300,
  1315, 3114, 3265
Marshall, Wendy 2162
Martin, A. Z. 1826
Martin, Charles 1418, 1472,
  2586a
Martin, Douglas D. 1395
Martin, Eugenio 3132
Martin, Jim 269
Martin, Louis 2089a
Martin, Mardik 1927
Martin, Troy Kennedy 1533,
  1548, 1600
Martino, E. 3046
Martino, Luciano 2846
Martino, Sergio see Barry,
  Julian
Martinson, Rita 926a
Marton, George 2304
Marton, Pierre see Stone,
  Peter
Marx, Arthur 429, 867, 1161a,
  1476, 1488
Maselli, Francesco 982
Massie, Robert K. 2085
Masteroff, Joe 417
Masterson, Whit 3230
Mather, Berkely 1120, 1753a
Matheson, Richard 567, 576a,
  690, 750, 769, 1667, 1694,
  2151, 3406
Matos, Jeri 2578
Matsumoto, Toshio 1090
Matsura, Kendo 164, 1632
Matsuyama, Zenzo 610
Matter, Alex 842, 897
Matthieu, Martial 2192
Mattson, Arne 161, 2004

Mattsson, Gunnar 3011
Maugham, Robin 2609a
Maugham, W. Somerset 20a,
  2138
Maule, Hamilton 172
Maurer, Norman 2212
Mauri, Dino 3189
Maury, Alain 2855
Maxfield, Henry S. 829
Maxwell, Gavin 2468
Maxwell, Robert 406
May, Elaine 2077, 2819
May, Karl 1012, 2406, 2639,
  3076
Mayes, Wendell 171, 714, 1392,
  1491, 2330, 2458, 3201
Mayfield, Julian 3154
Mayo, James 1258
Mayo, William 2668
Maysles, Albert 2522
Maysles, David 2522
Mazin, Charles E. 51
Mazursky, Paul 39, 320, 322,
  1286, 1458
Mead, Shepherd 1421
Medard, Ed 2546
Medford, Harold 948a, 2702
Medioli, Enrico 660, 1724, 1804,
  2535
Medvedkine, Alexandre 1266
Meineche, Annelise 3349
Mekas, Adolfas 3336
Melchior, Ib 63, 2299, 2482a
Melendez, Jeronimo M. 1331
Melfi, Leonard 1650
Melly, George 2699, 2878
Melson, John 190, 477, 2549
Meltcher, Ira 1525
Melville, Herman 181
Melville, Jean-Pierre 831a, 1169
Mendelsohn, Jack 3381
Menger, W. H. 293
Menken, Robin 926a
Menzel, Jiri 439, 556
Mercer, David 811, 2003, 2112,
  3249
Mercer, Suzanne 1446
Mercer, William 777
Merimee, Prosper 450
Merle, Robert 682, 3251
Merrill, Bob 1092
Metcalfe, Kenneth 159
Methling, Finn 2798

Wolford, Nelson 3010
Wolford, Shirley 3010
Wolfson, Victor 982a, 2469
Wolkeas, Jan 3107
Wolman, Dan 840
Wood, Charles 204, 495, 1321,
    1408, 1630a, 1750
Wood, Christopher 587
Wood, Clement Biddle 174, 3259
Wood, William 1739a
Woodburn, Bob 1729
Woodhouse, Hugh 1129
Woods, Jack 223
Woodward, Derek 2730
Woolrich, Cornell 351, 366,
    1966
Wooten, Rosemary 2260
Worth, Herman 3108
Worth, Marvin 2361, 2990
Wouk, Herman 3408a
Wren, Percival C. 201
Wright, Gilbert 1923
Wright, Norman 1621
Wright, Ralph 1589
Wright, Robert 2725, 2980
Wright, Tom 1263
Wright, William H. 2729
Wurlitzer, Rudolph 1161, 2241,
    3122
Wyndham, John 2386
Wynn, Tracy Keenan 1754

Yablonsky, Yabo 139
Yafa, Stephen 2831, 2986
Yahiro, Fuji 392, 1214
Yamamoto, Shugoro 1505, 1607,
    2422, 2562
Yamatoya, Jiku 584
Yang, Chiang 1004
Yanne, Jean 520
Yarema, Neil 2897
Yasumi, Toshio 1478, 2326
Yates, Peter 2480
Yates, Richard 368
Yeaworth, Jean 3236
Yehoshua, A. B. 2123
Yeldham, Peter 31, 169, 565,
    1723, 1751, 2014, 2911
Yensid, Retlaw 1709
Yerby, Lorees 2462
Yergin, Irving 2021

Yoda, Yoshikota 641, 3156
Yordan, Philip 190, 440, 540a,
    933, 2501
York, Susannah 1481
Yoshida, Tetsuo 1854
Yost, Dorothy 2702
Young, Clarence Upson 1238
Young, John Sacret 490
Young, Robert 3232
Young, Terence 531, 1923a
Younger, Henry 649, 2334
Youngson, Robert 1050, 1095,
    1809a
Yueh-ting, Wang 883
Yust, Larry 1358, 3081
Yutkevich, Serge 2328

Zacharias, Steven 1285
Zachary, Richard 980
Zagor, Michael 1873
Zappa, Frank 3121
Zapponi, Bernardino 558, 956,
    957, 2340, 2744, 3346
Zardi, Federico 2427a
Zatlyn, Edward 2676
Zavattini, Cesare 29, 1114,
    2294, 2833, 3346, 3353,
    3382a, 3408
Zefferelli, Franco 382, 2486,
    2889
Zetterling, Mai 799, 1152, 1801,
    2091
Zhgeidze, Suliko 950
Zibaso, W. P. 2424
Zila, John Jr. 1311
Zilahy, Lajos 21
Zilber, Jacob 1497
Zimbalist, Donald 2876, 3395
Zimmerman, Vernon 1332, 3142
Zindel, Paul 866, 1860, 3151
Zohar, Uri 910, 2123
Zola, Emile 1104
Zucherro, Joseph 159
Zugsmith, Albert 2012, 2153
Zukrowski, Wojciech 730, 1770
Zurlini, Valerio 277
Zweiback, A. Martin 419, 1926
Zwerin, Charlotte 2522